BY FLOWING WATERS

Christ Jesus, High Priest of the new and eternal covenant, taking human nature, introduced into this earthly exile the hymn that is sung throughout all ages in the halls of heaven. He joins the entire human community to himself, associating it with his own singing of this canticle of divine praise.

For he continues his priestly work through the agency of his Church, which is unceasingly engaged in praising the Lord and interceding for the salvation of the whole world.

Constitution on the Sacred Liturgy, §83

BY FLOWING WATERS
CHANT FOR THE LITURGY

A Collection of Unaccompanied Song
for Assemblies, Cantors, and Choirs

by

PAUL F. FORD

THE LITURGICAL PRESS

Collegeville   *Minnesota*

1   2   3   4   5   6   7   8   9   10

CONTENTS

I. THE ANTIPHONARY

PROPER OF THE SEASONS

THE PROPER OF SAINTS

COMMONS

RITUAL MASSES, MASSES FOR VARIOUS NEEDS, AND VOTIVE MASSES

LITURGY FOR THE DEAD

II. CHANTS FOR THE ORDER OF THE MASS

III. CHANTS FOR THE ORDINARY OF THE MASS

COMMON TONES

APPENDIX

INDEXES

A Musical Foreword

By Flowing Waters attempts to make it possible for an American congregation to sing English words which fit easily into the old chant melodies. A graceful ecumenical translation has been fitted to an adaptation of the traditional chant historically associated with it. To a large extent it succeeds admirably, with clear and simple phrases for responses, and well-marked verses for the cantor. It is a pleasure to see chant so sympathetically handled. I have always believed that the flexibility of chant is no other than the flexibility of language being sung, and that past difficulties have arisen from English words being fitted to the music meant for Latin text. Surely the chant melodies can and will survive being adapted for a natural flow of the vernacular, and will add immeasurably to our worship in so doing. I agree totally with Paul F. Ford's statement that "modal music in free rhythm wears well." Surely the use of this volume would enrich our lives in many ways.

Alice Parker

A Liturgical Foreword

In the fall of 1965, the Catholic bishops of the world assembled in council took part in daily eucharistic celebrations. At the time one element of those Masses seemed innovative as well as highly successful: The sacred song consisted of simple chant melodies, as settings for antiphons and verses from the biblical Book of Psalms. Today the present collection, *By Flowing Waters: Chant for the Liturgy,* is in direct succession to those great liturgical moments.

With near unanimity the assembled bishops had already decreed that the critical editions of the Gregorian chant for Latin liturgies should be augmented: "It is desirable also that an edition be prepared containing the simpler melodies, for use in small churches." Saint Peter's Basilica in Rome with its Sistine and Julian choirs was hardly a "small church," but the fruit of the conciliar decision was first experienced there. What was achieved was not some radical innovation but the sound recovery of a sound tradition: song integrated into the liturgy, song not beyond the capacity of an ordinary gathering of Christian believers, song following both the Hebrew and the Christian legacy of the psalms of David.

By 1965 the liturgical use of the language of the people instead of Latin had become almost universal. Nevertheless the Latin *Graduale Simplex* of 1967 and 1974—which was the next stage of simple psalm chants for the eucharist—demonstrated several influential principles. First was the commitment to a restoration of psalmody as the song of the Church in the eucharist—and not merely in the liturgy of the hours, which unhappily remains largely limited to the ordained and to religious. Next was the norm of noble simplicity, which permits the whole assembly of worshipers to sing psalms and antiphons to simpler melodies and especially melodies (and texts) that could be employed on repeated occasions throughout a season—instead of the impossible rule, rarely observed, of a fresh and complex chant for each Sunday celebration. This was not only a norm of simplicity but also one of diversity and openness.

Our experience for more than three decades has allowed the broadest and healthiest freedom in the choice of sung texts for Mass. But the pride of place for the psalms has not yet been truly achieved despite official encouragement. As an example, the National Conference of Catholic Bishops, in a fundamental 1967 decree that was promptly confirmed by the Apostolic See, regularly preferred psalmody even as it opened the way to a freer choice of diverse responsorial songs and hymns at Mass. Carefully and correctly, however, it limited the many alternatives for the chants between the readings to "other collections of psalms and antiphons in English, as supplements to the Simple Gradual, including psalms in responsorial form, metrical and similar versions of psalms . . ."

In turn, the admirable openness to diversity that is coupled with priority for psalmody demands the kind of sung resources that Dr. Paul Ford has prepared for the present book. On the one hand are the best traditions of simple and unaccompanied chant that meet the expectations of esthetic quality and musical scholarship, well supported by Dr. Ford's rationale and exposition. On the other hand and more important, this is a collection for congregations of praying Christians. It is not beyond the singing capacity of ordinary assemblies, cantors, and choirs, but is always faithful to the psalms of holy Scripture. As the conciliar fathers declared: "To achieve the reform, progress, and adaptation of the liturgy, it is essential to promote that warm and living love for Scripture to which the venerable tradition of both Eastern and Western rites give testimony."

Neither the Hebrew nor the Greek Scriptures can be completely or perfectly reflected in any single English dress. This is particularly true of the song of the Hebrew psalms and the antiphons as well. The version of the psalms in the present collection is from the approved Catholic edition of the New Revised Standard Version. The translation has been chosen for the very high quality of its language—based upon a traditional style, but successfully contemporary and singable. It has the additional advantage of its ecumenical acceptance, which is particularly important in the light of the dogmatic constitution *Dei Verbum*. The latter demanded fidelity to the best critical text of the Scriptures and opened the door to ecumenical collaboration in biblical translation.

All in all, this makes *By Flowing Waters* an invaluable contribution, for which the English speaking churches will long remain in Paul Ford's debt. He has combined liturgical and musical scholarship with an intense pastoral commitment and purpose. The door was opened by the Second Vatican Council, with its dedication to liturgical reform, progress, and adaptation. Today the door needs not only to be kept open but to be opened still more widely. Dr. Ford's undertaking is in the fullest harmony with the conciliar spirit, a spirit that today must be supported anew.

Frederick R. McManus

DEDICATORY ACKNOWLEDGEMENTS

I wish to hereby acknowledge the people I kept in mind in the five years I have spent in the preparation of this book, principally my dad and Fr. St. Sure:

• my dad, **BERNARD FORD**, with whom I sang in the chant choir at St. Anne's, Ridgecrest, California, and Gerard Pottebaum, who was the choir director

• the people and priests of the dioceses of Fresno and Monterey, who prayed and paid for my seminary formation, especially St. Anne's, Ridgecrest, on the occasion of their golden jubilee as a parish

• Dimitri Kostiw, music director at St. John's Cathedral, Fresno, California, who introduced me to de Victoria, Britten, and Langlais

• Philip Abinante, who introduced me to Poulenc, Peeters, and Bach

• **DONALD ST. SURE**, S.J., who taught me chant, John Brady, S.J., who first explained the rites of the Church to me, George Crain, S.J., who taught me Latin, and (the late) Joseph Geary, S.J., who taught me Greek

• Esther Frankian, my organ teacher

• Msgr. Peter Nugent, who introduced me to the *Graduale Simplex*

• Fathers Charles Miller, C.M., and (the late) Theodore Wiesner, C.M., Vicentian liturgists in the tradition of Archbishop Annibale Bugnini, C.M.

• Fr. John Schiavone (co-founder and collaborator), Fr. Al Burnham, Fr. Ray Dreiling, Msgr. Joe Greeley, Fr. John Griesbach, Tom Griesbach, Fr. Larry Herrera, Fr. Arthur Holquin, Fr. Mike Jennett, Fr. Luigi Lazzari, Fr. Perry Leiker, Msgr. Dick Loomis, Fr. Pat McCormick, Brook Muller, Chuck Muller, Fr. Joe Shea, and the rest of the members of the Renaissance Chorale 1967–1973

• Abbot Francis Benedict, Fr. Luke Dysinger, Fr. Paul Pluth, and the Benedictine monks of Saint Andrew's Abbey, California, with whom I have made years of music

• (the late) Luke Eberle and Augustine de Noble, priest-monks of Mount Angel Abbey, Oregon, who taught me how to English the chant, and Paschal Cheline and Jeremy Driscoll, who encouraged me

• Owen Alstott, Frank Brownstead, Fr. Cyprian Consiglio, Bob Hurd, Paul Inwood and Catherine Christmas, Dominic and Kathleen MacAller, Jackson Schoos, and J. Michael Thompson, all dear to me for music and so much more

• the people, deacons, and priests in these California parishes who asked me to be cantor, choir director, catechist, and liturgist: St. Luke's, Temple City; Mother of Good Counsel, Los Angeles; Visitation, Los Angeles; and Blessed Junipero Serra, Camarillo

• my students at St. John's Seminary, and my faculty colleagues there, and Cardinal Mahony and the Board of Directors for their generous sabbatical provision which enabled me to finish this book

• my friends at Oregon Catholic Press, especially Bill Schuster, for his chant expertise, his attention to detail, and his never-failing sense of humor—without Bill this book would not exist

• Msgr. Craig Cox, judicial vicar for the Archdiocese of Los Angeles, for introducing me to Msgr. Frederick R. McManus without whose help this book would never have come to be; and Bishop Sylvester Ryan

• my new friends at The Liturgical Press—Fr. Michael Naughton, Mark Twomey, Peter Dwyer, Kay Weiss, Colleen Stiller, and Ann Blattner

• my colleagues in the Society for Catholic Liturgy and in the Consultation on Popular Chant at the New Camaldoli Hermitage, Big Sur, California

• Michael Downey and Gabe Huck, encouragers

• my wife, Janice Daurio, the love of my life

• in memory of Bishop Aloysius J. Willinger, C.Ss.R. *("Trahe nos, Virgo, Curremus")*, Cardinal Timothy Manning ("Mary the Dawn, Christ the Perfect Day"), Paul King Jewett ("My Lord, What a Morning"), Fr. Wilfrid Weitz, O.S.B. ("Peace be with you"), Fr. Gaetan Loriers, O.S.B. *("Montes Gelboe"),* and Dom Joseph Warrilow, O.S.B. *("Iam non dicam")*

• in gratitude to the monks of Solesmes whose lives and work have kept and restored the treasury of chant in the Church, especially Dom Jean Claire, O.S.B., and (the late) Dom Raymond Le Roux, O.S.B.

INTRODUCTION

There is a New Testament text to which, for centuries, the Church has turned whenever she wishes to discuss liturgical music, dedicate musical instruments, and encourage church musicians.

> Let the word of Christ dwell in you richly; teach and admonish one another in all wisdom; and with gratitude in your hearts sing psalms, hymns, and spiritual songs to God (Colossians 3:16 NRSV).

The movement is first from the Word outside to the Word inside, from ears to heart. The meaning of the phrase "dwell in you" is "make a home in your heart." Only after the Word has begun to make its home in our hearts does it rise to the surface and overflow in spoken wisdom and sung gratefulness.

But music does not come only at the end of this process. Music, especially song, also has the gift to open the heart to receive the Word and to allow the Word to be ruminated upon so that the full home-making, life-changing power of the Word may work its effect. But in all this the Word of God has priority.

The music in *By Flowing Waters: Chant for the Liturgy* has ancient sources but only one Source, the Word. Anyone familiar with the history of chant knows that the original Greek and Latin words themselves "created" the music that was meant to convey them to the heart and then to express the heart's fullness. This volume has two objectives and one goal. With respect to the antiphons, acclamations, hymns, and songs its whole aim is to allow the music which expressed the meaning of the original words to try to convey the same meaning to those who speak English. With respect to the psalmody (the ways to sing psalms, canticles, and other long texts) its whole aim is to let these ancient tones become the tunes to carry the Hebrew and Greek poetry (the 102 psalms, and 19 canticles of the Bible used in this book) which is freshly translated into English in the New Revised Standard Version.

By Flowing Waters contains nearly 700 authentic chants and songs based on authentic chants for use by assemblies, cantors, and choirs. This treasury is intended to be an example of the best and most accessible of the Roman Catholic plainsong tradition. It is also intended to be ecumenical in its use of the NRSV, its design for eucharistic worship in liturgical churches, and its adaptability by free churches who wish to add chant to the sung prayer styles of their congregations. Everywhere the goal of this book is to let the text be primary and the music its servant.

By Flowing Waters includes the entire repertory of the *Graduale Simplex,* as well as a ninth suite of psalms and antiphons for the last weeks of the Church year. It also includes the entire repertory of *Jubilate Deo* (the universal chant collection authorized by Pope Paul VI in 1974) with fresh English lyrics as well as the original Latin and Greek. It also provides settings for singing the readings based on the models provided in the 1973 *Ordo Cantus Missae.* Thus this volume is complete for those who want to chant the entire renewed liturgy according to the model envisioned by Vatican II, incorporating new adaptations in English of ancient Greek and Latin chants for the Order of the Mass and for the Ordinary of the Mass.

This volume attempts to reintroduce the singing of the psalms in the eucharistic service. It employs psalm verses with great variety and freedom of choice. It reestablishes the antiphon as a refrain and the response or alleluia as a true response.[1] It presumes an orientation of the people toward psalms, which includes an understanding of the imagery and the historical and cultural background of the psalms. Preparation for the use of *By Flowing Waters* should not be merely musical but requires a study of the religious values of the psalms or psalm verses. In addition, those who sing the texts must appreciate that the words of different speakers are placed on their lips—now the words of the Lord, now the words of the psalmist, etc. For this reason this book incorporates the division between cantor and choir put forward by Richard S. Hanson in his three-volume edition, *The Psalms in Modern Speech*

---

[1] The substance of these three sentences is taken from pp. 10–11 of the Introduction to *THE SIMPLE GRADUAL: An English translation of the antiphons and responsories of the* Graduale Simplex *for use in English-speaking countries,* prepared and published by the International Committee on English in the Liturgy, Inc. (Washington, DC: ICEL, 1968). This edition also contains "Norms for Translation" which, among other things, states: "The texts of antiphons, even those taken from the psalter, sometimes need modification: to achieve fully the meaning appropriate to a liturgical season or particular feast; to ensure the people's understanding of the text; to match the rhythmical and vocal requirements of chant in the vernacular (see Instruction *Musicam Sacram* no. 54)." On 23 January 1968 the Consilium for the Implemention of the Constitution on the Liturgy produced the norms for translation of the *Graduale Simplex* which were confirmed by Pope Paul VI on the same day and published in *Notitiæ* 4 (1968), p. 10, now found in *Documents of the Liturgy, 1963–1979: Conciliar, Papal, and Curial Texts* (Collegeville, MN: The Liturgical Press, 1982), hereafter abbreviated "DOL"—in this case DOL 120.

(Philadelphia: Fortress, 1968) mentioned throughout the Performance Notes (pp. 417–428).

By Flowing Waters is intended to appeal to those cantors looking for resources for unaccompanied song for eucharistic liturgy and to restore to cantors a version of their own proper book (as the sacramentary belongs to presiders, the lectionary to readers, and the gospel book to deacons). It hopes to contribute to the revitalization of the ministries of psalmist, cantor, schola cantorum, and choir. Designed to be especially useful at times and in settings where and when there are limited resources (that is, one trained cantor), this collection also aspires to find a home in university chapels, convents, monasteries, cathedrals, and other settings with great choral and instrumental resources.

By reintroducing musicians, composers, and liturgists to the *responsoria brevia* style of the responsorial psalms and alleluia psalms (that is, where the response is one or two or even three "alleluias") and the other litanic ("call and response") forms in this collection, it hopes to illustrate and underscore the work of worship on the part of all worshipers, thus giving new meaning to the word 'liturgy' and to the keynote of the liturgical renewal, "full, active, conscious participation." The litanic/responsorial style of the entire collection tosses the work of worship back and forth between the cantor and the assembly.

This volume wishes to attract those who are intrigued by the idea of using chant. It is familiar to those who grew up with chant while at the same time accessible to those who are unfamiliar with chant. Musicians and liturgists who know plainsong know that modal music in free rhythm "wears longer" and "delivers" the text unobtrusively. The songs in *By Flowing Waters* allow the melodies which arose from the singing of the texts in their original Latin and Greek to live again through harmonious weddings to English translations of these texts. At one time the product of ancient European Christian cultures, the authentic chants and the songs based on authentic chants in *By Flowing Waters* can serve as a common meeting ground for today's diverse and sometimes antagonistic musical cultures—in this sense it aims to be "transcultural."

How and Why This Book Came to Be

From childhood I have loved to sing in church. In former days I have loved to lead the singing of my schoolmates from desert grade school through farming community minor and major seminary, the singing of my fellow monks at a desert monastery, and the singing of my co-worshippers at Evangelical graduate school and Roman Catholic parish. For the most part, this song was supported by wonderfully resonant buildings, so that even and perhaps especially when it was unaccompanied, its simplicity conveyed the words right down into the heart. There remains nothing more lovable (and often lovelier) to me than the sound of my fellow human beings joined in song to celebrate God in all the moods and seasons of life. I suspect that most pastoral musicians have similar feelings.

It is sometimes said that Catholics can't sing. Thomas Day explains this "inability" by pointing out that Catholics missed their musical apprenticeship:

> The Roman Catholic Church, back in the 1960s, tried to launch the musical equivalent of the Great Leap Forward. One week there was silence at Mass; the next week the congregation was supposed to sing four hymns which took Protestants four centuries to develop. Congregations in the United States . . . never struggled through a stage of musical apprenticeship or even infancy. With very little preparation, they went immediately into the "advanced class."

What was Day's prescription to parishes?

> Most parishes should go back, as it were, return to the primitive state they never really knew, and try to go through a stage of development that they missed. They need to lower their expectations . . . *a greater use of unaccompanied chantlike singing would make sense. The most homely church music ever written, the most folklike of all music for congregation is any kind of chanted dialogue (preferably unaccompanied) involving priest, cantor, and people.*[2]

The last sentence is emphasized here because it has become the principal reason for the book you have in your hands. ***By Flowing Waters*** is a primer of liturgical music designed to tutor assemblies and their ministers in the homely ways of singing the Mass, not just singing at Mass.[3]

---

[2] *Why Catholics Can't Sing* (New York, Doubleday, 1990), pp. 119–120 (emphasis added).

[3] In the memorable Italian expression of the editors of *Notitiæ*, the journal of the now Congregation for Divine Worship and the Discipline of the Sacraments: "Cantare *la* Messa,

By Flowing Waters is an unofficial version of the second of two official song books of the Roman liturgy, the *Graduale Romanum* (the Roman Gradual) and the *Graduale Simplex* (the Simple Gradual). As the sacramentary is the presider's book, the book of the gospels the deacon's and the lectionary the reader's, the "gradual" is the liturgical book belonging to schola cantorum, the school of cantors, the professional liturgical singers (but such collections almost always include songs for people). As John Ainslie said in his Introduction to *The Simple Gradual for Sundays and Holydays:*

> The *Simple Gradual* is for the singing of the Proper of the Mass in English. But it is more than that. *It is a properly integrated part of the liturgical renewal.* The chants of the *Simple Gradual* offer a musically and textually simpler way to celebrate the Eucharist—first, through the sacred song which is a reflective response and welcome to God's word (the chants between the biblical readings) and, second, through the singing of the Entrance, Offertory, and Communion Songs, which accompany the processional entrance, the preparation of the gifts of bread and wine, and the period of the Communion. And since it is the entire assembled congregation who celebrate the Eucharist, "it is desirable that the assembly of the faithful should participate in the songs of the 'Proper' as much as possible, especially through simple responses and other suitable settings" (*Instruction on Music in the Liturgy,* no. 33).[4]

The implication of the emphasized sentence is: "Without knowledge of the Simple Gradual, especially its forms, one does not yet understand the liturgical renewal." It is almost like a Rosetta Stone, a missing link or even the golden key which unlocks the mysteries of the intentions of liturgical musical renewal of the Second Vatican Council.

The four principle characteristics of the Simple Gradual guided the preparation of *By Flowing Waters.* First, the chants are interchangeable within a particular period of the Church year or in relation to a particular occasion. Second, it attempts to reintroduce the singing of the psalms in

---

dunque, e non solo cantare *durante* la Messa" (1969, p. 406, as found in R4 in *Documents of the Liturgy, 1963-1979: Conciliar, Papal, and Curial Texts* [Collegeville, MN: The Liturgical Press, 1982], DOL 4154).

  [4] (London: Geoffrey Chapman, 1970), emphasis added.

the eucharistic service. Its third characteristic is its purpose: It affords a greater opportunity for community participation in song—especially through congregational singing of brief refrains and responses to the longer verses sung by a cantor, schola, or choir. Fourth and finally, it enlarges the options and increases the flexibility of the sung parts of the eucharistic liturgy.

The style of the songs of the Simple Gradual is what could be called litanic or responsorial, the call of the cantor and/or choir and the response of the assembly. The music of these songs is drawn from the treasury of what is commonly called Gregorian chant but might more accurately be called plainsong. In fact the Simple Gradual contains Mozarabic (Old Spanish) and Ambrosian (Milanese) chants as well as Gregorian chants. All of these melodies are hundreds of years old and some may have their origins in the music sung by women and men at worship in the first half-millenium of the Christian experience.

The Simple Gradual is also innovative in its brief, almost litanic responses to the first reading, in the litanic alleluia psalms, and the antiphons of acclamation during Lent. By restricting its palette of melodic colors to nine patterns for the psalm responses and to six for the alleluia psalms, the Simple Gradual achieves the goal of all good ritual music: familiarity with variety. By recovering the eight so-called ecclesiastical modes, the Simple Gradual expands the range of human emotion capable of being expressed by music. And the music wears well.

The litanic style of the Simple Gradual is its greatest virtue. The call and response way of singing makes the assembly work and it makes cantors and choirs work at making the assembly work (the chief vocation of the pastoral musician). This is important for several reasons: liturgy is everyone's work and not just the achievement of experts witnessed by an appreciative audience; the litanic style is not, however, too much work —its familiarity and variety contribute to a lively exchange between the assembly and its ministers; finally, this work drives home the meaning of the text of the Word of God.

Thus song and music chosen for liturgy have a *"ministerial function because sacred song, closely bound to the text . . . forms a necessary or integral part of the solemn liturgy. [It] will be the more holy the more closely it is joined to the liturgical rite, whether by adding delight to prayer, fostering oneness of spirit, or investing the rites with greater solemnity.*[5] In light of what Colossians 3:16 says, liturgical music enhances the movement of the Word into the heart, draws the hearts of all participants into unity, and educes from these hearts wisdom and prayer.

How and Why the Simple Gradual Came About

The Simple Gradual began to be collected in the early 1960s and was used experimentally at the daily Masses during the final period of the Second Vatican Council in 1965. Archbishop Bugnini tells the complex story of its origins in his indispensable history, *Reform of the Liturgy.*[6]

The *General Instruction of the Roman Missal* (as well as the Appendix by the U.S. Bishops) refers to the *Simple Gradual* at three critical points, when it discusses what can be sung at the entrance (26), between the readings (36), and at communion (56). *Music in Catholic Worship* similarly refers to it (60 and 63). In order of official preference, the Simple Gradual would seem to rank after texts assigned in the Lectionary and Sacramentary and after the Roman Gradual but before any other collection of psalms and antiphons or supplementary and substitute songs and hymns.

Two printings of the first edition (1967) and two printings of the second typical (or normative) edition (1975) were made.[7] The second edition incorporates the *Kyriale Simplex* (a collection of simpler but authentic chant ordinaries) and some elements of the *Ordo Cantus Missæ* (the music for the dialogues, acclamations, and other texts of the Mass) as well as all the changes consequent upon the revision of the General Roman Calendar, the psalter, the Roman Missal, and the Lectionary. The International Committee (now Commission) on English in the Liturgy prepared an official translation of the first edition in 1968; ICEL added a fine, freeing essay, "Introductory Information for Composers and Publishers."

---

[5] The foregoing passage in italic is a pastiche of quotations from Vatican II, the Constitution on the Sacred Liturgy, *Sacrosanctum Concilium,* 4 December 1963, §112 (DOL 1 no. 112).

[6] Annibale Bugnini's *Reform of the Liturgy. 1948–1975* (Collegeville, MN: The Liturgical Press, 1990) mentions the Graduale Simplex on the following pages: 120–122, 144, 149, 150, 151, 168, 170, 236, 349, 362, 363, 387, 404, 405, 888, 891–897, and 907.

[7] Bugnini explains in n. 23 on p. 896 why only the second edition is typical.

We yet await an official, complete edition of the Simple Gradual. What you now hold in your hands is a humble effort to join an ecumenical, inclusive language English translation of each text to an authentic chant melody adapted to convey the sense of the text.

Celebrating eucharist with this wedding of new texts to old tunes calls for a surrender of culture and sub-culture on behalf of all who use *By Flowing Waters* for worship. It is claiming too much to say that chant is transcultural. What little we can say with certainty about chant is that it represents a melange of eastern and western European musics from perhaps before the fourth century to the thirteenth, musics which seem to show the influence of Judaism and Islam. It is enough to say that this chant speaks for no one's precise culture now and therefore it is transcultural to everyone now and yet it preserves the memory of the matrix cultures through which Christianity passed on its way to the world church at the end of the twentieth century.

It could be argued that chant is too culturally specific. I argue that the simple chants of *By Flowing Waters* represent one transcultural point of departure for the second phase of the liturgical renewal which we are just beginning. As Chupungco reminds us, the first phase is the recovery of the Roman Rite and the second phase will be its reinculturation.[8]

CONCLUSION

Why U.S. Catholics Didn't, Don't, Won't, Can't, and Could-be-taught-to Sing are secondary questions. Why Sing is also a secondary question. Why Worship At All is the primary question.

Right-brain, intuitive answers to that primary question can be found in Poulenc's "The Dialogues of the Carmelites" or in the more recent story of the Franciscan who stepped forward from the ranks of prisoners in Auschwitz and volunteered to take the place of the young husband and father in the hunger bunker. What happened next is well known and yet still amazing: From the place where captors and captives had expected the hellish howls of men whose parched and famished bodies began to consume their own protein came the sound of hymns and songs. Fr. Kolbe had gotten his fellow condemned to sing until day by

---

[8] Ansgar J. Chupungco, O.S.B., *Liturgies of the Future: The Process and Methods of Inculturation* (New York: Paulist, 1989).

day, one by one, the song diminished. Finally Maximilian's solitary voice was stilled by an injection of carbolic acid.

Left-brain, discursive reasons for worship can be found in much of the original and subsequent documentation of the liturgical renewal. Here is a passage which may serve to represent them all:

> Christ Jesus, High Priest of the new and eternal covenant, taking human nature, introduced into this earthly exile the hymn that is sung throughout all ages in the halls of heaven. He joins the entire human community to himself, associating it with his own singing of this canticle of divine praise.
>
> For he continues his priestly work through the agency of his Church, which is unceasingly engaged in praising the Lord and interceding for the salvation of the whole world.[9]

Christians sing because they have something to sing about (the goodness of God) and to sing for (the salvation of the world) and someone to sing with (the Son of God). Without an experience of God, without a sense of what God is up to in the universe, without a fellow singer and animator, we are and should be mute. As Thomas Merton reminds us, Christ sings and dances with us even in the fiery furnace (or the hunger bunker).

May this effort at Englishing the Simple Gradual and other chant resources contribute to that song.

Paul F. Ford, Ph.D.
Professor of Theology and Liturgy
St. John's Seminary
Camarillo, California

The Epiphany, 1999

---

[9] DOL 1 no. 83.

How to Use This Book

This section is devoted to help you to get the most out of *By Flowing Waters*. The first pages of this "how to" section concern the heart of this book, the music for seasons and the saints; these pages will also give you the key to using the commons, the ritual and votive masses, the masses for various needs, and the liturgy of the dead. **The most important directions are printed in semibold type.**

For the signs used in the actual music, see "Signs" at the end of this explanation, p. xxxiii.

Abbreviations

Whenever the following explanation directly cites the official Introduction to the *Graduale Simplex*,[10] you will see "GS" and the paragraph number, in parenthesis. "LMI" indicates the 1981 Introduction to the Lectionary and "GIRM" indicates the Introduction to the Sacramentary. Any chant marked *"Jubilate Deo"* means that this chant is found both in the *Graduale Simplex* and the resource called *Jubilate Deo*[11]; such chants are presented in English and the original Greek or Latin in order to keep alive among Catholics of the Roman Rite a minimum shared repertory.

A Word about Pitch

The pitch in authentic chant is not fixed. When my editors and I decided to make the chants of this book available in modern notation, we decided to limit our range to C–d and to use key signatures with no more than two sharps or flats. Because the music offered here is in the movable Do system, performers should feel free to transpose any chant into keys which will invite the greatest participation for the particular assembly to which they are ministering.

---

[10] The 22 November 1974 Introduction of the Sacred Congregation of Divine Worship to the *editio typica altera* of the *Graduale Simplex*, reprinted in DOL. It is a collation of DOL 533 and 537.

[11] Pope Paul VI asked that this brief anthology be prepared in order to keep the tradition of people from various nations singing the simpler melodies when they gather to worship together. Extracts for this edition are drawn from the first edition (1974) and not the second (1986) because the second collects many more elaborate chants and, in my opinion, unwittingly works against the pope's intention.

MUSICIANS

Next a word about the persons needed for the singing of the chants of *By Flowing Waters*. The minimum number is one cantor and an assembly. But provisions are made throughout the book (**indicated by score expressions and/or underlined verse numbers**) for one or two psalmists, a schola (a small group of psalmists or cantors, usually four) or scholas, two or more cantors, a choir or choirs, and choirs and even the assembly divided into women and men or children and adults, depending on the level of solemnity (see p. xxxiii). Whether these music ministers are vested and move in procession will also depend on the level of solemnity and the practice of your parish. The need for and kind of accompaniment will depend on the acoustic of your worship space as well as the level of solemnity.

The *Graduale Simplex* gives special prominence to the psalmist, a role defined by the 1981 Lectionary for Mass: Introduction as follows:

The psalmist, that is the cantor of the psalm, is responsible for singing . . . the chants between the readings—the psalm or other biblical canticle, the gradual and *Alleluia,* or other chant. The psalmist may, as occasion requires, intone the *Alleluia* and verse (LMI 56).

As you will read below, the chants between the readings in the *Graduale Simplex* consist of one or even two responsorial psalms, the *Alleluia* and verse, the *Alleluia* psalm, the tract (a psalm without response, sung during Lent), and the acclamation antiphon (a Lenten acclamation sung after at least one verse of the psalm). Depending on the level of solemnity, there is often work for more than one psalmist!

When any verse of a chant between the readings is meant to be sung by more than one psalmist (**indicated by the underlined verse number**), these psalmists may form a schola to sing such verses from the ambo (if it can accommodate them), or from near the ambo, or from some other suitable place (LMI 33 and 34; GIRM 36).

Psalms sometimes need to be sung by different solo and ensemble voices so that all may understand who it is who is speaking in the psalm (God, an individual, a man, a woman, men, women, two different choirs, pilgrims, residents, and the like). **Such nuances are discussed in the Performance Notes** section on pp. 417–428 under the name of the season or feast.

The Antiphonary

The Antiphonary is the heart of the *Graduale Simplex:* It contains two kinds of chants for seasons, feasts, commons, and rituals: processional chants and chants between the readings. Instructions about matters specific to seasons are found at Advent Season I, Ash Wednesday and the First Sunday of Lent, Easter Season I, and Ordinary Time I. Some individual celebrations have instructions peculiar to them, which are spelled out at each celebration.

For the great solemnities of the church year, as well as for feasts which, when they fall on Sundays in Ordinary Time, take the place of such Sundays, the *Graduale Simplex* offers a suite of processional chants and chants between the readings especially chosen for the day: "In the Proper of Saints there are proper chants for the celebrations that have precedence when they coincide with a Sunday" (GS 16).

GS 15 says, "In the Proper of Seasons not every Sunday has its own proper chants; instead there are one or more formularies for each liturgical season that may be used on the Sundays throughout that season. Each feast of the Lord does have proper chants." A later paragraph in the same document gives permission to "mix and match" antiphons/psalms and responses/psalms within a season: "When more than one formulary is given for the same season, the choice of one of them is optional, according to what seems best for the occasion. Some parts may even be chosen from one formulary and some from another" (GS 21). Such choices would depend on what the assembly knows already or can be taught easily.

But these choices also depend primarily on the Liturgy of the Word proclaimed that day, particularly the communion song, which in the tradition has always tried to show the reception of the eucharist as the fulfillment of the readings, especially the gospel.[12] The overarching rule guiding the selection of songs to be sung at any liturgy is the following:

> "The power of a liturgical celebration to share faith will frequently depend upon its unity—a unity drawn from the liturgical feast and season or from the readings appointed in the lectionary as well as the artistic unity flowing form the skillful selection of options,

---

[12] DOL 4276.

music, and related arts. *The scriptures ought to be the source and inspiration of sound planning* for it is of the very nature of celebration the people hear the saving words and works of the Lord and then respond in meaningful signs and symbols. Where the readings of the lectionary possess a thematic unity, the other elements ought to be so arranged as to constitute a setting for and response to the message of the Word" (*Music in Catholic Worship,* §20, emphasis added).

A similar freedom to choose also applies to the commons of the various kinds of saints: "The arrangement of the Commons of Saints corresponds to the commons in the Roman Missal, in such a way, however, that only one formulary is given for each class of saints. But this formulary has several chants for the different parts of the Mass, thus providing the option to use whichever chant is best suited to a particular saint" (GS 17).

There are two basic kinds of chants in the *Graduale Simplex,* processional chants and responsorial chants. Each kind has its own guidelines.

The Processional Chants

Not counting the chant for the gospel procession for the moment, there are three processional chants in the *Graduale Simplex:* "the entrance, offertory, and communion chants . . . made up of an antiphon, verse, and reprise of the antiphon" (GS 13). **At least one verse must be sung** and all the verses provided may be sung, plus the doxology *(Glory to the Father,* etc.) which is found on pp. 375–378. **If the antiphon is well-known to the assembly or if it is well-rehearsed, the cantor sings up to the asterisk and then the assembly continues to the end. If the antiphon is being introduced to the assembly, the cantor sings the entire antiphon through and then the assembly repeats the antiphon. The assembly repeats the antiphon after each verse and after the doxology,** as the official introduction says:

The entrance, offertory, and communion antiphons are sung with one verse or with several as the circumstances suggest. An antiphon is repeated after the verses of a psalm. But there is an option regarding versicles, even including omission of some of them, provided the versicles retained express a complete thought.

The verses for the entrance and communion antiphon may conclude with the Doxology (GS 19).

Roman Catholic congregations are not accustomed to singing the doxology at the end of the procession during Preparation of the Gifts and the typical edition does not mention it specifically. Congregations in other communions always sing the doxology at this time. Singing the doxology would depend on the level of solemnity.

People familiar with chant will notice that **each verse of these processional chants is intoned,** that is, there are preparation tones (a note or group of notes for each of the italicized syllables) which lead up to the recitation tone (the pitch at which most of the words of the psalm verse are sung).

Suggestions for abbreviating the number of verses to be sung are found in the Performance Notes. But why would you want to sing many verses? In order to accomplish the four goals of the entrance song and the three goals of the communion song! About each of these songs the *General Instruction of the Roman Missal* tells us:

> The purpose of [the entrance] song is to open the celebration, intensify the unity of the gathered people, lead their thoughts to the mystery of the season or feast, and accompany the procession of priest and ministers (GIRM 26).

> The function [of the communion song] is to express outwardly the communicants' union in spirit by means of the unity of their voices, to give evidence of joy of heart, and to make the procession to receive Christ's body [and blood] more fully an act of the community (GIRM 56i).

Every minister knows instinctively when unity and prayerfulness have arrived in the assembly; every liturgist knows that there is more to gathering and communing than the mere cessation of ritual movement. Here presider and cantor have a special need to communicate well with each other so that, when unity and prayerfulness are evident, the one may indicate to the other that is is time to sing the last verse of the psalm or to begin the doxology.

If one had to say what is the most important processional chant to be sung, it would be the communion song. For this reason GS 21 says:

At communion the singing of Ps. 33 *I will bless the Lord,* with the response *Alleluia* or *Taste and see,* is always permitted.

But, as is indicated at the end of this volume, p. 386, other suitable chants may be chosen at will.

The Mozarabic setting of Psalm 34 (33V), **645,** is one of the most exciting songs in this entire volume and would be most appropriate during the Easter Season.

The Chants between the Readings

These chants are perhaps the greatest "innovation" of the *Graduale Simplex.* They are based on the simple responsories, the *responsoria brevia,* of the ancient Liturgy of the Hours in both monasteries and cathedrals.

There is a critical difference between the customary way responsorial psalms and alleluia psalms (that is, where the response is one or two or even three "alleluias") are sung today and the way they are sung in the *responsoria brevia* style. We are used to the psalmist singing the entire responsorial antiphon which is then repeated by the assembly; then the psalmist usually sings two (or even more) verses of the psalm or canticle and then the assembly repeats the antiphon. In the *responsoria brevia* style, the psalmist begins to sing the psalm and **the response emerges from within the text.** If the assembly knows the response well or if it is well-rehearsed, they can sing the response immediately; if they do not, the psalmist sings the response as it emerges from the text and then the assembly repeats it. **The assembly repeats the response after each verse of the psalm.**

To illustrate this difference, see the responsorial psalm **3**, Psalm 80 with the response, "Come and set us free, Lord mighty God." The psalmist begins by singing: "Give ear, O Shepherd of Israel, you who lead Joseph like a flock!" If the assembly knows the response well, they can sing it immediately; if they do not, the psalmist sings it as it emerges from the text and then the assembly repeats it.

This is even clearer in the responsorial psalm **12**, Psalm 122 with the response, "Let us go to the house of the Lord!" The psalmists (notice that the verse number is underlined) no sooner sing, "I was glad when they said to me," than the assembly (if they know it) replies, "Let us go to the house of the LORD!" (If the assembly do not know it, the psalmists sing "Let us go to the house of the LORD!" as it emerges from the text and then the assembly repeats it.) In fact the Performance Note for this psalm says that it is best performed by two scholas alternating on the verses (e.g., schola one sings verse 1, schola two sings verse 2, etc.), in imitation of the way the crowds of pilgrims, schola two, sang this song as they entered Jerusalem, to the encouragement of the residents of the city, schola one.

As another example, see the alleluia psalm **5**. The psalmist sings, "LORD, you were favorable to your land; you restored the fortunes of Jacob"; and, if the assembly knows to sing the alleluia at this point, they can sing it immediately; if they do not, the psalmist sings the alleluia as it emerges from the text and then the assembly repeats it.

As a final example, see the alleluia psalm **23**. This is a double alleluia psalm, of which there are seven kinds in this book. (For the most successful participation, these double psalms ought to be rehearsed before the liturgy.) The psalmist sings, "O sing to the LORD a new song"; and, if the assembly knows to sing the first alleluia (or set of alleluias, as applicable) at this point, they can sing it immediately; if they do not, the schola or choir may sing the alleluia. The psalmist then sings, "for he has done marvelous things"; to which the assembly responds with the second alleluia (or set of alleluias, as applicable).

Thus, there are the five kinds of chants between the readings:

The chants between the readings, depending on the season of the liturgical year, are made up of:
a. [1] a responsorial psalm, with psalm verse or [2] *Alleluia* as the response;
b. [3] a psalm without a response, traditionally called a "tract";
c. [4] an *Alleluia* with psalm verses for the seasons when the *Alleluia* is sung or [5] another gospel acclamation without *Alleluia* for the period from Ash Wednesday to Easter (GS 14).

When you look at the models—Advent Season I, First Sunday of Lent, Easter Season I, and Ordinary Time I, you will see that the *Graduale Simplex* makes it possible to respond to the second reading with a second responsorial psalm (in Lent, Responsorial Psalm II and, throughout the rest of the year, the Alleluia Psalm—Easter provides two Alleluia Psalms!).

And during Lent there is a special Gospel Acclamation Antiphon for each Sunday; it is meant to be sung by the assembly with at least one verse of one of the responsorial psalms, sung to the processional psalm tone in the same mode as the antiphon (to assist you in remembering that tone, consult the doxology in that psalm tone, found on pp. 375–378).

And how are these options arranged and used?

When there are two readings before the gospel:

a. Outside Lent and the Easter season, the responsorial psalm is sung after the first reading; after the second reading, the psalm with *Alleluia* as the verse or the antiphon *Alleluia* with its own verses.

b. During Lent, after the first reading, the first responsorial psalm is sung; after the second, either the second responsorial psalm or an antiphon of acclamation or a tract.

c. During the Easter season, after the first reading the first or second psalm with *Alleluia* as the verse is sung; after the second reading, either the second psalm with *Alleluia* as the verse or the antiphon *Alleluia* with its verses.

Whenever there is only a single reading before the gospel, a single chant may be chosen at will from those appropriate to the reading.

At least five verses of a psalm, chosen at will, are always sung, whenever more than five are given (GS 21).

There is no doxology sung at the end of any of the chants between the readings.

Chants for the Order of the Mass

Any special directions for the use of this section is found in the rubrics throughout the section. Your use of these chants will depend on the level of solemnity of the day in question as well as how your parish wishes to celebrate such days.

Chants for the Ordinary of the Mass

The Mass parts provided are numbered sequentially in order to make it easier, as desired, to have an Ordinary made up of selections from the different settings. Rather than singing the entire *Agnus Dei/Lamb of God,* the congregation may simply respond with the *miserere nobis/have mercy on us* and *dona nobis pacem/grant us peace.*

LEVELS OF SOLEMNITY

Throughout this explanation I have used the term "levels of solemnity" (or synonyms) to remind church musicians of an essential principle: Every use of the ceremonial, environmental, and musical options found in our liturgical books must clearly show that solemnities are more important than feasts, and that feasts are more important than memorials and ordinary days. The "Table of Liturgical Days according to Their Order of Precedence" is printed in every sacramentary and lectionary but few see it as what it is: a topographical map of the Church's annual liturgical journey. In light of this principle of graduated or progressive solemnity, local liturgists must reassess their local "traditions" concerning the use of incense, the book of the gospel, candles, processional cross, number and vesture of ministers, processions, vesture, flowers and branches, and banners. Of course, "pulling out all the stops" is not necessarily the best way to increase solemnity; it can often be oppressive; sometimes "less is more." In many communities the music is made to bear the full weight of implementing the progressive solemnity —an unfair burden. Nevertheless musicians must reexamine not only what gets sung, but who sings it, and how it is sung.

TEMPI AND ACCIDENTALS

There are no tempi marked in this book. The flow of the words themselves and their intelligibility in your worship space should dictate the rate of singing. Each phrase should retain its natural word accents with the unaccented syllables sung in a style more legato rather than less.

The only one accidental in chant is Ti-flat, usually indicated by the flat sign but in Mode IV by the natural sign. The accidental "remains in effect only throughout the word in which it occurs or up to the nearest solid bar line (i.e., Quarter Bar, Half Bar, Full Bar, or Double Bar)."[13]

SIGNS

In the body of the book the following signs have the following meanings:

---

[13] *Gregorian Chant Practicum* (based on *Music Fourth Year—Gregorian Chant* by Justine Bayard Ward), prepared by Theodore Marier et al. (Washington, DC: Catholic University of America Press, 1990), p. 85.

Psalm numbers are printed in their Hebrew and Vulgate numbers whenever these two numbers differ; "V" means the psalm number of the Vulgate edition. Any reference after the colon indicates the verse of the psalm or other text (usually biblical) from which the antiphon or response is taken. In responsorial psalms the citation in parenthesis indicates the source of the antiphon; if this citation is only a number, it indicates that the antiphon is from a verse of the same psalm as the responsorial psalm.

Information printed above the staff in the right corner indicates biblical source for the responsorial psalm, tract, or alleluia psalm, as well as the cultural family of the particular chant when it differs from Gregorian chant, usually Mozarabic (Old Spanish) or Ambrosian (Milanese).

℟ indicates the assembly's response. ℣ indicates the verse sung by the psalmist(s), cantor(s), schola(s), or choir(s).

Underscoring of a verse number means this verse may sung by the choir or by schola rather than by the cantor.

Underscoring of any syllable indicates that this syllable in sung to two or more notes as indicated by the psalm tone, usually by a solid slur but sometimes by a dashed slur.

Slurs which occur *above* two or three notes at the same pitch indicate distrophas or tristrophas (respectively), and they are performed by a slight pulse on each note. Slurs which occur *above* two notes within a group of three or more notes over one syllable indicate a pressus, and they are performed by an emphatic intensification, rather than a pulsation, of the two notes tied together.

Italics at the beginning of a verse indicate the intonation of the psalm tone; one, two, and even three syllables may form this intonation; *italics* toward the end of the first or second line of verse indicate syllables which precede the musical accent(s).

Bold indicates the syllable(s) on which the musical accent(s) fall(s). **Bold** at or near the beginning of a verse indicate the musical accent(s) in the intonation of the special double responsorial psalm tones. In several modes and responsorial tones the bracket above bold syllables in the final cadences indicates that the musical accent is distributed evenly over these syllables.

Acute accents (´) indicate the syllable on which (or, in the case of an underlined syllable, during which) the pitch rises at the beginning of the middle or final cadence of the particular psalm tone.

Grave accents (`) indicate the syllable on which (or, in the case of an underlined syllable, during which) the pitch falls at the beginning of the middle or final cadence of the particular psalm tone.

The asterisk (*) in an antiphon indicates an option; at this point in the antiphon the choir or even the assembly may join the cantor, either in the repetition of the antiphon after each verse or even at the very first intonation of the antiphon. The asterisk in a psalm tone or text indicates the middle or mediant cadence, "the temporary stopping place in the middle of the psalm verse which divides the verse into two parallel phrases, thus accommodating the parallel structure of the Hebrew psalmodic poetry."[14]

The dagger (†) is the sign of the Flex, the "momentary drop in the melody in the event of a very long line of text prior to the mediant cadence."[15] The use of the dagger with the abbreviation "E.S." indicates alternate endings which add the word "alleluia" for use during the Easter Season.

The superscript comma (') in a responsorial psalm, tract, or alleluia psalm indicates the place where a pause for breath may be taken.

The following note shapes are defined thus:

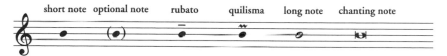

The filled-in notehead indicates the basic unit of pitch duration. When it is enclosed in parentheses, the note is optional. When it is modified by a horizontal line (episema), you slightly emphasize the syllable by prolonging the tone. When it is modified by a jagged line, you "lengthen the note or notes preceeding it"; the quilisma note itself "is sung lightly, leading to the following note."[16] The open notehead

[14] *Gregorian Chant Practicum*, p. 47.
[15] Ibid., p. 86.
[16] Mary Berry, *Plainchant for Everyone: An Introduction to Plainsong* (Croydon: Royal School of Church Music, 1979), p. 14.

doubles the basic unit of pitch duration. The stemless double whole notehead indicates the reciting tone in a psalm tone.

The bar lines are defined thus:

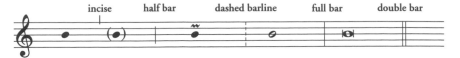

The incise or quarter barline "shows the smallest phrase unit; avoid taking a breath at this point." The half barline indicates the completion of a larger segment; "normally a breath may be taken here." The dashed barlines (used only in the psalmody) indicates that the note(s) which follow the dashed barlines indicate either of the two ways to sing the mediant cadence, depending on the pointing (the marking) of the psalm; in other words, everything up to the dashed barline is common and only what follows the dashed barline is different. The full barline indicates the termination of a complete musical phrase; "this should be followed by one or two rests."[17] The double barline indicates the end of the piece or the place where, when two different groups are singing, they alternate.

A NOTE TO SCHOLARS

In your perusal of this volume you will notice that, in the psalmody, I have disaggregated neumes and abbreviated intonations, when setting some psalm verses using processional psalm tones I, III, IV, VI, and VII, as well as the responsorial psalm tones C 2, C 3, D *, E 1, E 2, E 5, E 5 *, and E *. (It was easier to keep the rules in processional psalm tones II, V, and VIII and in responsorial tones C 1, C 4, C *, D 1, E 3, and E 4). In the antiphons, acclamations, hymns, and songs I have treated many phrases more syllabically than you might have preferred. I had two rules in mind: When the text in question was to be sung by the assembly, the tune needed to be straightforward, singable, and unfussy; when the text was to be sung by the cantor, choir, or psalmist, the psalm tone needed to convey the sense of the psalm easily to the assembly, in natural sounding English.

In the context of Gregorian melodies, my sense is that English syllables are stressed in two ways: a) by lengthening them, and b) by singing

---

[17] All the citations in this paragraph are from Berry, p. 16.

them on the first note which moves above or below the tenor or domi-
nant of the mode. Thus, these syllables must be naturally stressed English
syllables. English also prefers strong endings (or, to use Hiley's terminol-
ogy, English prefers accentual cadences rather than cursive cadences[18]),
so I paid special attention to the use of the tones in their mediant and
final cadences. Let me explain what my reasoning was systematically by
speaking of intonations and cadences in the psalmody and of modal and
melodic integrity of the antiphons, acclamations, hymns, and songs.

Intonations in the Psalmody

When we are speaking about intonations, we are talking about how
to handle the singing of unstressed syllables which precede the first
stressed syllable. Here I have been guided by the exemplary piece of
Mozarabic chant in the *Graduale Simplex,* pp. 454–459, **654** of this
volume. There you can see intonations that are accentual rather than
cursive. The fullest form of the intonation (podatus-clivis, similar to
psalm tone VII) is reserved for anapestic words like *benedícam* and
exquisívi and for the paeonic word *magnificáte.* The modified intonation
form (punctum-porrectus) is reserved for iambic words like *gustáte* and
vallábit and for anacrusistic syllable(s) as in the phrase *in Dómino* or in
the word *respícite.* The abbreviated intonation form (podatus) is reserved
for trocaic words or phrases like *ípse* and *quis es* and for dactylic words
like *dívites.* In my marrying of the NRSV translation of Psalm 34 to this
tune, I used the fullest form for phrases like "I will bless" (v. 1), the
modified form for phrases like "my soul" (v. 2), and the abbreviated
form for phrases like "Come, O" (v. 11).

Performing this marriage ceremony taught me greater sensitivity to
English stresses and ways to achieve them using plainsong psalm tones,
a sensitivity and methods which I have applied to the intonations of the
processional psalm tones I, III, IV, VI, and VII. I added an extra preliminary punctum to tones I, III, IV, and VI so that I could accommodate
anapestic words and phrases in these ones; I also removed the standard
preliminary punctum when the verse began with trocaic or dactylic
words or phrases. In tone VII I disaggregated the podatus and clivis in
intonations which begin with anapestic words or phrases.

---

[18] David Hiley, *Western Plainchant: A Handbook* (Oxford: Clarendon, 1993), p. 62.

Cadences in the Psalmody

Abrupt mediation   On July 8 and December 12, 1912, the Sacred Congregation for Rites gave permission, in the case of verses which terminate on monosyllables, for abrupt mediations in psalm tones with mediants of one accent (tones II, IV, VI, and VIII). Psalms in English has many more such verses than psalms in Latin, so I used this permission extensively.

Disaggregation of neumes   In explaining the responsorial psalm tones of the *Graduale Simplex* (pp. 440–445), the editors point out that when the psalm verse ends with a dactyl, an extra note may be inserted or the podatus or clivis may be disaggregated into its components, that is, into two notes (pp. 440, 442, 443, and 444). One can see in these directives a preference for cadences that are more accentual than cursive. I regularly used these flexibilities throughout this book, not just in responsorial psalmody but also in processional psalmody, whenever I could not apply the standard rules. I was particularly concerned about wedding any psalm verse which ends with a trochee or a trocaic phrase or a dactyl or a dactylic phrase with any processional psalm tones which ends with a dotted podatus (I a 2, VII c, VII d), a dotted clivis (I f, III a, VII c 2, VII a), or a torculus (I g 2). I also worked painstakingly with any processional psalm tone whose final cadence consists of one accent with preparatory syllables meant to be sung on two-note neumes. Because my rule has been that the psalm tone needed to convey the sense of the psalm easily to the assembly, in natural sounding English, I carefully disaggregated any neume which tended to lend musical stress to an unstressed English syllable.

Modal and Melodic Integrity
of the Antiphons, Acclamations, Hymns, and Songs

As I said above, my sense about singing English to Gregorian melodies and modes is that lengthening of any syllables (singing them longer or on two or more notes) stresses these syllables and that these syllables need to be naturally stressed English syllables. I wanted to enable assemblies to sing these melodies somewhat easily. Since the original melodies are in many cases centonized, I looked not only at melodies in the same mode but the same melody applied to different sets of words to discern the melodic scheme common to all. Frequently enough this scheme is very syllabic and thus more suited to an English text.

I take full responsibility for the errors and decisions made in this book and beg those who use it to write me about any corrections and improvements they would suggest (paulfford@sjs-sc.org). Corrections will be available over the World Wide Web at (http://www.litpress.org/byflowingwaters) and will be incorporated in future printings.

Paul F. Ford

Advent Season I

Entrance Antiphon

Psalm 25 (24V):1–2a

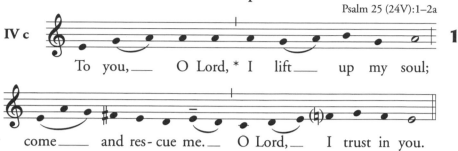

IV c

To you, ___ O Lord, * I lift ___ up my soul;

come ___ and res - cue me. ___ O Lord, ___ I trust in you.

Psalm 25 (24V)

2c, 3a, 4, 5, 7bc, 8, 9
or

℣ 1 *Do* _not_ ___ let my en - e - mies ex - ult *o - ver* **me;** *

do not let those who wait for you be **put** to shame.

Flex: and teach me, †

2 _Make_ me to know your *wàys,* O **LORD;** *
  teach me **your** pàths.

3 _Lead_ me in your truth, and teach mè, †
    for you are the God of *mỳ salva*tion; *
  for you I wait **all** dày long.

4 _accord_ing to your steadfast *lòve re*member me, *
  for your goodness' **sake,** Ò LORD!

5 _Good_ and upright *ìs the* **LORD;** *
  therefore he instructs sinners in **the** wày.

6 He _leads_ the humble in *whàt is* **right,** *
  and teaches the humble **his** wày.

The following is the arrangement of the chants between the readings:

When there are two readings before the gospel, the chants are arranged as follows: The responsorial psalm is sung after the first reading; after the second reading, either the Alleluia psalm or the antiphon *Alleluia* with its own verses is sung.

Whenever there is only one reading before the gospel, a single chant from among the following may be chosen at will.

Responsorial Psalm E 1   **Psalm 80 (79V)**
(5) 2c, 1ab, 2bc, 7–11, 14

℣ 1 Give ear, O Shep - herd of **Is** - ra - el, *

you who lead *Jo - seph* **like** a flock!

℟ Come and set us free, Lord, might - y God. ___

℣2 and *come to* **save** us! ℣3 *and* **plant- ed** it.

2   Stir **úp** your might, *
       and *cóme to* **save** us!

3   You brought a vine out of **É**gypt; *
       you drove out the nations *ánd* **planted** it.

4   You cleared the **gróund** for it; *
       it took deep root and *fílled* **the** land.

5   The mountains were covered **with íts** shade, *
       the mighty cedars *wíth its* **branch**es;

6   it sent out its branches **to thé** sea, *
       and its shoots *tó the* **Riv**er.

7   Turn again, O **Gód** of hosts; *
       look down from heaven, and see; have re*gárd* **for this** vine.

2

Alleluia　　　　　　　　　　　　　　　　　　Psalm 85 (84V)
1,7

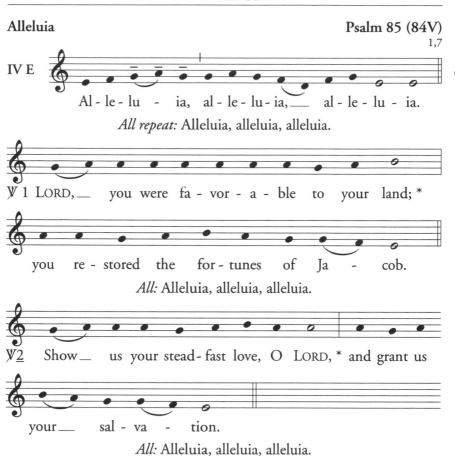

IV E

Al - le - lu - ia, al - le - lu - ia,— al - le - lu - ia.

All repeat: Alleluia, alleluia, alleluia.

℣ 1 LORD,— you were fa - vor - a - ble to your land; *

you re - stored the for - tunes of Ja - cob.

All: Alleluia, alleluia, alleluia.

℣2 Show— us your stead - fast love, O LORD, * and grant us

your— sal - va - tion.

All: Alleluia, alleluia, alleluia.

4

or **Alleluia Psalm** E *　　　　　　　　　　Psalm 85 (84V)
1–7 (See Performance Notes)

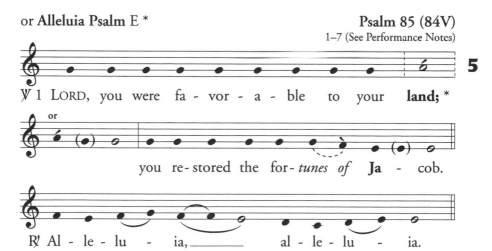

℣ 1 LORD, you were fa - vor - a - ble to your **land;** *

or

you re - stored the for - *tunes of* **Ja** - cob.

℟ Al - le - lu - ia,——— al - le - lu - ia.

5

3

2 You forgave the iniquity of your **péo**ple; *
  you *pardòned* **all** their sin.

3 You withdrew all your **wráth;** *
  you turned from your <u>*hòt*</u> **an**ger.

<u>4</u> Restore us again, O God of our salvá**tion,** *
  and put away your indig*natìon* **toward** us.

<u>5</u> Will you be angry with us forév**er?** *
  Will you prolong your anger to all *genèr*ations?

<u>6</u> Will you not revive us a**gáin,** *
  so that your people may re*joice ìn* **you?**

<u>7</u> Show us your steadfast **lóve,** O LORD, *
  and grant us your <u>*sàl*</u>**va**tion.

Preparation of the Gifts Antiphon

Psalm 25 (24V):3

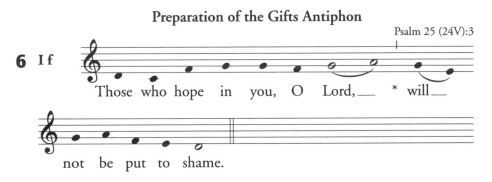

6 I f

Those who hope in you, O Lord,___ * will___

not be put to shame.

Psalm 25 (24V)

1–2b, 6, 10, 20, 22

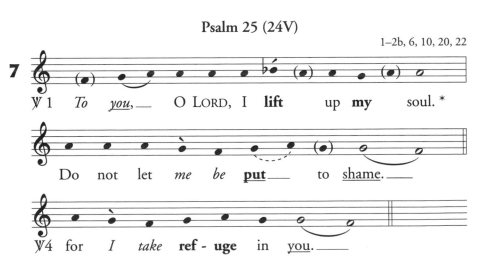

7

℣ 1 *To you,*___ O LORD, I **lift** up **my** soul. *

Do not let *me be* **put**___ to <u>shame.</u>___

℣ 4 for *I take* **ref - uge** in <u>you.</u>___

2   *Be mindful of your mercy, O LORD, and **óf** your **stead**fast love, * *
for they hàve been **from** of old.

3   *All* the paths of the LORD are steadfast **lóve** and **faith**fulness, * *
for those who keep his covenànt and **his** decrees.

4   *O guard* my **lífe**, and deliver me; * *
do not let me be put to shame, for *I take* **refuge** in you.

5   *Redeem* **Ís**rael, O God, * *
out of àll its **trou**bles.

Communion Antiphon

Psalm 85 (84V):12

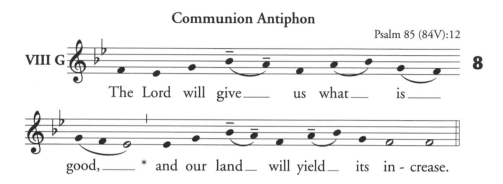

The Lord will give____ us what____ is____

good,____ * and our land__ will yield__ its in - crease.

Psalm 85 (84V)

8–13 (followed by 1–7; see Performance Notes)

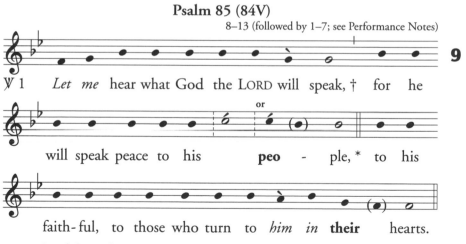

℣ 1   *Let me* hear what God the LORD will speak, † for he

will speak peace to his **peo** - ple, * to his

faith-ful, to those who turn to *him in* **their** hearts.

2   *Surely* his salvation is at hand for those who **féar** him, * *
that his glory may *dwèll in* **our** land.

3   *Steadfast* love and faithfulness will **méet;** * *
righteousness and peace will *kìss each* **oth**er.

4   *Faithful*ness will spring up from the **gróund,** * *
and righteousness will look *dòwn from* **the** sky.

5

5   *The LORD* will give what is **góod,** *
     and our land will *yìeld its* **in**crease.

6   *Righteous*ness will go be**fóre** him, *
     and will make a *pàth for* **his** steps.

7   *LORD, you* were favorable to your **lánd;** *
     you restored the for*tùnes of* **Ja**cob.

8   *You for*gave the iniquity of your **péo**ple; *
     you *pàrdoned* **all** their sin.

9   *You with*drew all your **wráth;** *
     you turned from *yòur hot* **an**ger.

10   *Restore* us again, O God of our sal**vá**tion, *
     and put away your indig*nàtion* **toward** us.

11   *Will you* be angry with us for**é**ver? *
     Will you prolong your anger to all *gèner*ations?

12   *Will you* not revive us a**gáin,** *
     so that your people *mày re*joice in you?

13   *Show us* your steadfast **lóve,** O LORD, *
     and grant us *yòur sal*vation.

Advent Season II

Entrance Antiphon

Isaiah 45:8

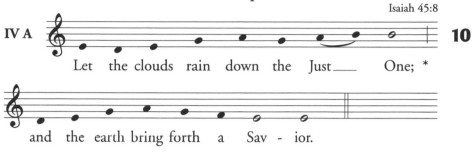

IV A

Let the clouds rain down the Just___ One; *

and the earth bring forth a Sav - ior.

Psalm 19 (18V)

1–6

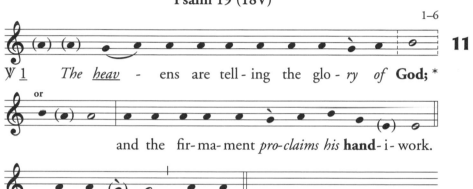

℣ 1   *The* <u>*heav*</u> - ens are tell - ing the glo - *ry of* **God;** *

or

and the fir-ma-ment *pro-claims his* **hand**-i- work.

Flex: for the sun, †

2   <u>*Day*</u> to day *pòurs forth* **speech,** *
    and night to *nìght declares* **know**ledge.

3   *There is* <u>*no*</u> speech, nor *àre there* **words;** *
    thèir voice is **not** heard;

4   <u>*yet*</u> their voice goes out through *àll the* **earth,** *
    and their words to *thè end of* **the** world.

5   *In the* <u>*heav*</u>ens he has set a tent for the sùn, †
    which comes out like a bridegroom from his *wèdding* **can**opy, *
    and like a strong *màn runs its* **course** with joy.

6   *Its* <u>*ris*</u>ing is from the end of the heavèns, †
    and its circuit *tò the* **end** of them; *
    and nothing *ìs hid from* **its** heat.

Responsorial Psalm D 1 e **Psalm 122 (121V)**
(1b) 1–9 (See Performance Notes)

12

℣1 I was glad *when they* **said** to me, * ℟ "Let us go

up re - joic - ing to the house of the LORD!"

or

℣2 Our feet are **stand** - ing * with-in your gates, *O Je-* **ru**- sa-lem.

℟ "Let us go up re-joic - ing to the house of the LORD!"

3 Jerusalem—built as a **cí**ty *
  that is bound firm*ly* to**geth**er.

4 To it the tribes go up, the tribes of the **LÓRD,** *
  as was decreed for Israel, to give thanks to the *nàme of* **the** LORD.

5 For there the thrones for judgment were set **úp,** *
  the thrones of the *hòuse of* **Da**vid.

6 Pray for the peace of Jerúsalem: *
  "May they pros**pèr** *who* **love** you.

7 Peace be within your **wálls,** *
  and security with*ìn your* **tow**ers."

8 For the sake of my relatives and **fríends** *
  I will say, "Peace *bè with***in** you."

9 For the sake of the house of the LORD our **Gód,** *
  Ì will **seek** your good.

Alleluia **Psalm 80 (79V)**
1ab, 14

13 II D

Al- le- lu - ia, al - le-lu - ia,__ al - le - lu - ia.

All repeat: Alleluia, alleluia, alleluia.

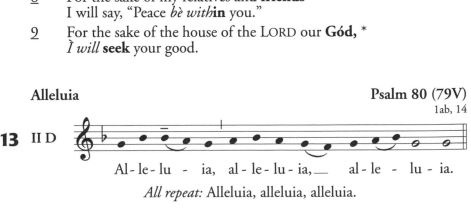

℣ 1 *Give ear,* O Shep-herd of **Is** - ra-el, *

you who lead Jo - *seph* **like** a flock!

All: Alleluia, alleluia, alleluia.

2   *Turn again,* O **Gód** of hosts; *
look down from heaven, and see; have regard *for* **this** vine.

All: Alleluia, alleluia, alleluia.

or **Alleluia Psalm** C 1   **Psalm 80 (79V)**
1ab, 8, 14–19

14

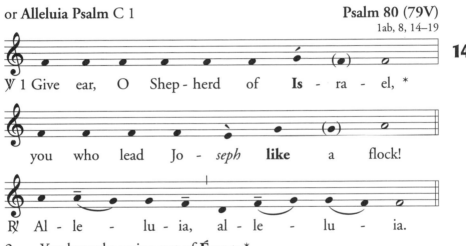

℣ 1 Give ear, O Shep-herd of **Is** - ra - el, *

you who lead Jo - *seph* **like** a flock!

℟ Al - le - lu - ia, al - le - lu - ia.

2   You brought a vine out of **É**gypt; *
you drove out the nations *ànd* **plant**ed it.

3   Turn again, O **Gód** of hosts; *
look down from heav*èn,* **and** see;

4   have regard for this **víne,** *
the stock that your right *hànd* **plant**ed.

5   They have burned it with fire, they have **cút** it down; *
may they perish at the rebuke of *yòur* **coun**tenance.

6   But let your hand be upon the one at your **ríght** hand, *
the one whom you made strong *fòr* **your**self.

7   Then we will never turn **báck** from you; *
give us life, and we will call *òn* **your** name.

8   Restore us, O LORD **Gód** of hosts; *
let your face shine, that we *mày* **be** saved.

9

Preparation of the Gifts Antiphon

Luke 1:28, 42

15 I g

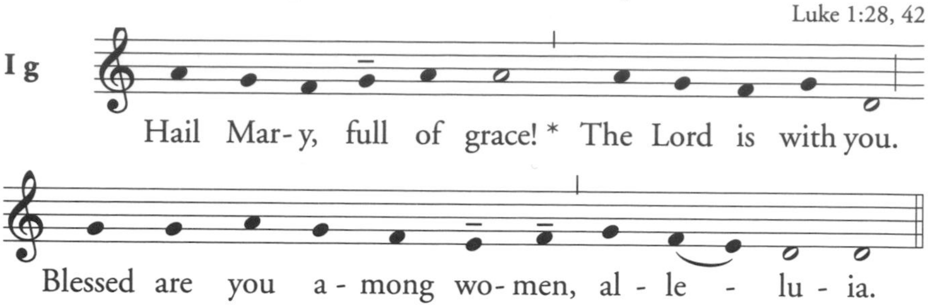

Hail Mar-y, full of grace! * The Lord is with you.

Blessed are you a - mong wo-men, al - le - lu - ia.

Psalm 25 (24V)

1, 2bc, 7bc, 8, 9, 14

16

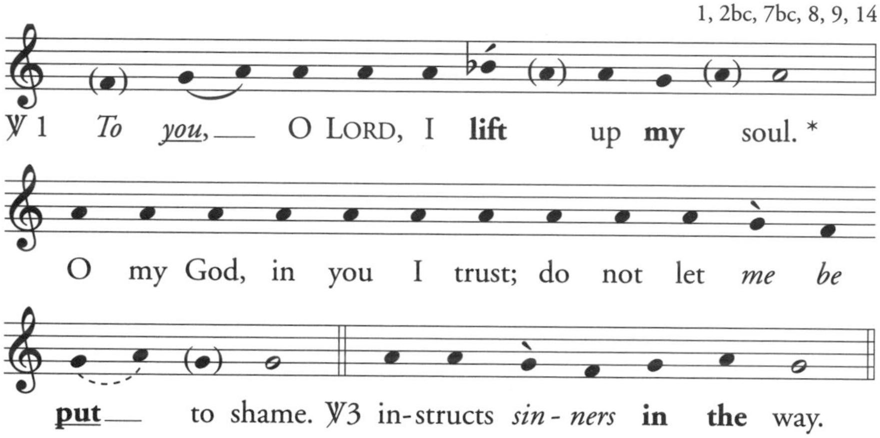

℣ 1 *To you,* — O LORD, I **lift** up **my** soul. *

O my God, in you I trust; do not let *me be*

put — to shame. ℣3 in-structs *sin - ners* **in the** way.

2   *accord*ing to your steadfast **lóve** remember me, *
   for your *gòodness'* **sake**, O LORD!

3   *Good* and **úp**right **is** the LORD; *
   therefore he instructs *sìnners* **in the** way.

4   *He leads* the **húm**ble in **what** is right, *
   and teaches the *hùmble* **his** way.

5   *The friend*ship of the LORD is for **thóse** who **fear** him, *
   and he makes his covènant **known** to them.

Communion Antiphon

Psalm 85 (84V):1a

17 VI F

Lord, you have blessed your — land. —

Psalm 85 (84V)

8–13 (followed by 1–7; see Performance Notes)

18

℣ 1 *Let me* hear what God the **LORD** will speak, †

for he will speak peace to *his* **peo** - ple, *

to his faith - ful, to those who turn *to him* **in** their hearts.

2 *Sure*ly his salvation is at hand for those *whò* **fear** him, *
that his glory *mày dwell* **in** our land.

3 *Stead*fast love and faithfulness *wìll* **meet;** *
righteousness and peace *wìll kiss each* **oth**er.

4 *Faith*fulness will spring up from *thè* **ground,** *
and righteousness will *lòok down* **from** the sky.

5 *The LORD* will give what *ìs* **good,** *
and our land *wìll yield its* **in**crease.

6 *Right*eousness will go *bèfore* him, *
and will make *à path* **for** his steps.

7 *LORD,* you were favorable to *yòur* **land;** *
you restored the *fòrtunes of* **Ja**cob.

8 *You for*gave the iniquity of *yòur* **peo**ple; *
you par*dòned all* **their** sin.

9 *You with*drew all *yòur* **wrath;** *
you turned *fròm your hot* **an**ger.

10 *Restore* us again, O God of our *sàlva*tion, *
and put away your in*dìgnation* **t'ward** us.

11 *Will you* be angry with us *fòre*ver? *
Will you prolong your anger to *àll gener*ations?

12 *Will you* not revive us *àgain,* *
so that your people may *rèjoice* **in** you?

13 *Show us* your stead*fàst* **love,** O LORD, *
and grant *ùs your salva*tion.

Christmas

Solemnity

Entrance Antiphon

Psalm 2:7

19 II D

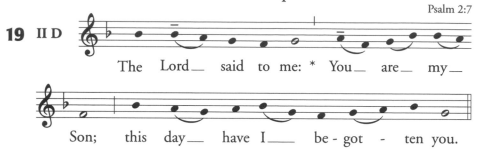

The Lord said to me: * You are my Son; this day have I be-got - ten you.

Psalm 2

1, 6, 8–12ae (See Performance Notes)
or

20

℣1 *Why do* the na-tions con-**spire**, * and the peo-*ples* **plot** in vain?

2 *"I have* set my king on **Zí**on, * *mỳ* **ho**ly hill.

3 *Ask of* me, and I will make the nations your **hér**itage, * and the ends of the earth your *pòs***ses**sion.

4 *You shall* break them with a rod of **í**ron, * and dash them in pieces like a pot*tèr's* **ves**sel."

5 *Now there*fore, O kings, be **wíse;** * be warned, O rulers *òf* **the** earth.

6 *Serve the* LORD with fear, with trembling **kíss** his feet. * Happy are all who take ref*ùge* **in** him.

Responsorial Psalm C 3 g   **Psalm 110 (109V)**

(3bc) 3, 1–2, 4–5, 7

21

℣1 Your peo-ple will of - fer them-selves **will**-ing-ly * on the day

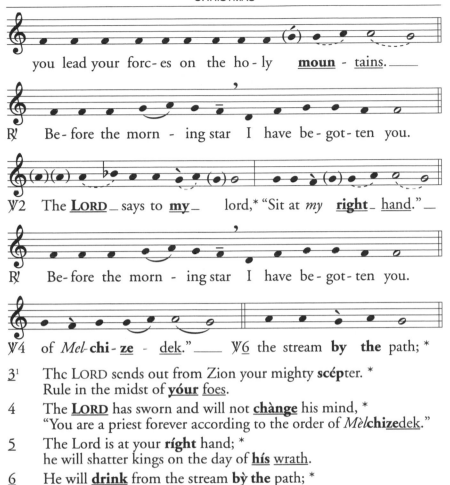

you lead your forc- es on the ho - ly **moun** - tains.____

℟ Be- fore the morn - ing star I have be - got- ten you.

℣2 The **LORD** _ says to **my** _ lord,* "Sit at *my* **right** _ hand." _

℟ Be- fore the morn - ing star I have be - got- ten you.

℣4 of *Mel-* **chi- ze** - dek." ____ ℣6 the stream **by the** path; *

3¹ The LORD sends out from Zion your mighty **scép**ter. *
Rule in the midst of **yóur** foes.

4 The **LORD** has sworn and will not **chànge** his mind, *
"You are a priest forever according to the order of *Mèl*chizedek."

5 The Lord is at your **ríght** hand; *
he will shatter kings on the day of **hís** wrath.

6 He will **drink** from the stream **bỳ the** path; *
therefore he will lift *ùp* **his** head.

Alleluia **Psalm 98 (97V)**
1ab, 2

III g

22

Al- le- lu- ia, __ al- le- lu - ia, __ al- le - lu - ia.

All repeat: Alleluia, alleluia, alleluia.

¹ Odd numbered verses are chanted on the first chanting note (fa); even numbered verses,
on the second chanting note (la).

13

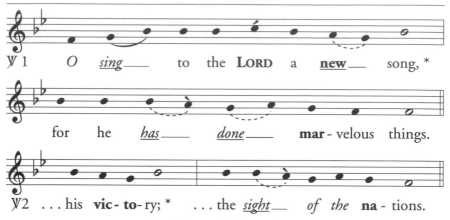

℣ 1 O sing___ to the **LORD** a **new**___ song, *

for he *has*___ *done*___ **mar**- velous things.

℣2 ...his **vic- to-**ry; * ...the *sight*___ of *the* **na**- tions.

All: Alleluia, alleluia, alleluia.

2 *The* <u>LORD</u> has made **knówn** his **victo**ry; *
he has revealed his vindication in the *sight* of *the* **na**tions.

All: Alleluia, alleluia, alleluia.

or **Alleluia Psalm** C 4   Psalm 98 (97V)

1–4

23

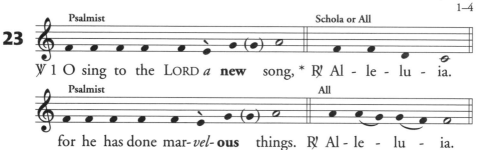

℣ 1 O sing to the LORD *a* **new** song, * ℟ Al - le - lu - ia.

for he has done mar-*vel-* **ous** things. ℟ Al - le - lu - ia.

2 His right hand and *his* **ho**ly arm *
have gotten *him* **vic**tory.

3 The LORD has made known *his* **vic**tory; *
he has revealed his vindication in the sight of *the* **na**tions.

4 He has remembered *his* **stead**fast love *
and faithfulness to the house *of* Israel.

<u>5</u> All the ends of the *earth* **have** seen *
the victory *of* **our** God.

<u>6</u> Make a joyful noise to the LORD, *all* **the** earth; *
break forth into joyous song and *sing* **prais**es.

Preparation of the Gifts Antiphon

Psalm 96 (95V):11ab, 13ab

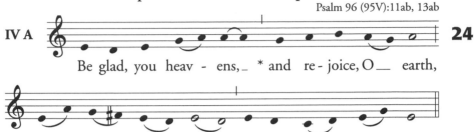

IV A

Be glad, you heav - ens, _ * and re - joice, O _ earth,

be - fore _ the _ Lord: _ for the Lord _ has _ come.

Psalm 96 (95V)

1–3, 8bc–9a, 13de

or

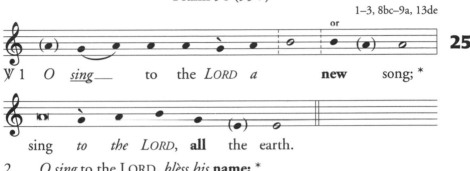

℣ 1 O sing __ to the LORD a **new** song; *

sing *to* *the* LORD, **all** the earth.

2 O sing to the LORD, *blèss his* **name;** *
tell of his sal*vàtion from* **day** to day.

3 *Declare* his glory a*mòng the* **na**tions, *
his marvelous works a*mòng all the* **peo**ples.

4 *bring* an offering, and come in*tò his* **courts.** *
Worship the LORD *ìn holy* **splen**dor

5 *He will* judge the *wòrld with* **righ**teousness, *
and the *pèoples with* **his** truth.

Communion Antiphon

Psalm 98 (97V):3b

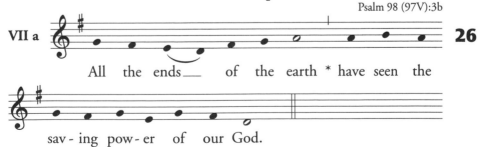

VII a

All the ends __ of the earth * have seen the

sav - ing pow - er of our God.

Psalm 98 (97V)

27

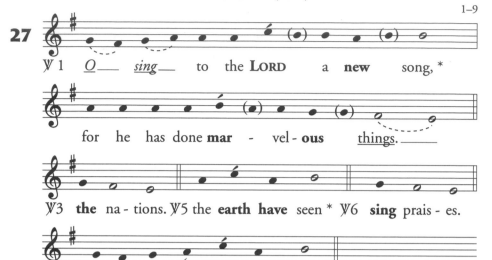

2   *His right* **hánd** and his **ho**ly arm *
have **gót**ten him **vic**to_ry._

3   *The* _LORD_ has made **knówn** his **vic**tory; *
he has revealed his vindication in the **síght** of **the** nations.

4   *He has* re**mém**bered his **stead**fast love *
and faithfulness to the **hóuse** of Isra_el._

5   *All the ends* of the **éarth have** seen *
the **víc**tory **of** our _God._

6   *Make a joy*ful noise to the **LÓRD**, all **the** earth; *
break forth into joyous **sóng** and **sing** praises.

7   *Sing prais*es to the **LÓRD** with **the** lyre, *
with the lyre and the **sóund** of mel_ody._

8   *With trum*pets and the **sóund** of **the** horn *
make a joyful noise be**fóre** the **King**, the _LORD._

9   *Let the sea* roar, and **áll** that **fills** it; *
the world and **thóse** who **live** in _it._

10   *Let the floods* **cláp their** hands; *
let the hills sing to**géth**er **for** _joy_

11   *at the* **prés**ence of **the** LORD, *
for he is **cóm**ing to **judge** the _earth._

12   *He will judge* the **wórld** with **right**eousness, *
and the **péo**ples with equi_ty._

16

Holy Family

Feast

Entrance Antiphon I

Matthew 1:16

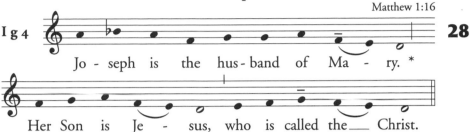

28

Jo - seph is the hus - band of Ma - ry. *

Her Son is Je - sus, who is called the___ Christ.

Entrance Antiphon II

Matthew 2:21

29

Jo - seph a - rose, * took the child and his moth-er,

and went to the land of Is - ra - el.

Psalm 128 (127V)

1–6 (See Performance Notes)

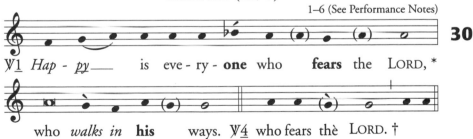

30

℣1 *Hap - py*___ is eve - ry - **one** who **fears** the LORD, *

who *walks in* **his** ways. ℣4 who fears thè LORD. †

2   *You shall* eat the fruit of the **lá**bor of **your** hands; *
you shall be happy, and it *shàll go* **well** with you.

3   *Your wife* will be like a fruitful **víne** within **your** house; *
your children will be like olive shoots aròund your **ta**ble.

4   *Thus shall* the man be blessed who fears thè LORD. †
The LORD **bléss** you from **Zion**. *
May you see the prosperity of Jerusalem all the *dàys of* **your** life.

5   *May you* see your **chíl**dren's **chil**dren. *
Peace be *ùpon* **Is**rael!

Responsorial Psalm D 1 b   Psalm 84 (83V)

(2a) 1–4, 8–9, 11–12 (See Performance Notes)

or

31

℣ 1 How love-ly is your dwell-ing place, O **LORD** of hosts! *

My soul longs, in-deed it faints for the courts of **the** LORD;

℟ I long for the courts___ of the LORD.

2   my heart and my **flésh** *
    sing for joy to the **lìv**ing God.

3   Even the sparrow **fínds** a home, *
    and the swallow a nest for herself, where she may **làl̀y** her young,

4   at your altars, O **LÓRD** of hosts, *
    my King and **mỳ** God.

5   Happy are those who live in **yóur** house, *
    ever singing **yòur** praise.

6   O LORD God of hosts, **héar** my prayer; *
    give ear, O God of **Jà**cob!

7   Behold our **shíeld,** O God; *
    look on the face of your an**ò̀in**ted.

8   For the LORD God is a **sún** and shield; *
    he bestows favor and **hòn**or.

9   No good thing does the LORD withhold from those who walk
       úprightly. *
    O LORD of hosts, happy is everyone who **trùsts** in you.

Alleluia   Psalm 27 (26V)

4

32 IV E

Al-le-lu - ia, al-le-lu-ia,___ al-le-lu - ia.

All repeat: Alleluia, alleluia, alleluia.

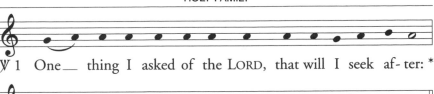

℣ 1 One— thing I asked of the LORD, that will I seek af-ter: *

to live in the house of the LORD all the days— of my— life,

All: Alleluia, alleluia, alleluia.

℣ 2 to be - hold___ the beau - ty of the LORD *

and to in - quire in his___ tem - ple.

All: Alleluia, alleluia, alleluia.

or **Alleluia Psalm C 1**   **Psalm 27 (26V)**

1, 4–5ab, 7–9ab, 13 (See Performance Notes)

or

33

℣ 1 The LORD is my light and my sal - **va** - tion; *

whom *shall* **I** fear? ℟ Al - le - lu-ia, al - le - lu - ia.

2 The LORD is the stronghold of my **lífe;** *
 of whom shall I *bè* **afraid?**

3 One thing I asked of the LORD, that will I seek **áfter:** *
 to live in the house of the LORD all the days *òf* **my** life,

4 to behold the beauty of the **LÓRD,** *
 and to inquire in *hìs* **tem**ple.

5 For he will hide me in his shelter in the day of **tróu**ble; *
 he will conceal me under the cover *òf* **his** tent.

6 Hear, O LORD, when I **crý** aloud, *
 be gracious to me *ànd* **an**swer me!

7 "Come," my heart says, "**séek** his face!" *
Your face, LORD, *dò* **I** seek.

8 Do not hide your **fáce** from me. *
Do not turn your servant away in anger, you who have
bèen **my** help.

9 Do not **cást** me off, *
do not forsake me, O God of my *sálva*tion!

10 I believe that I shall see the goodness of the **LÓRD** *
in the land of *thè* **liv**ing.

Preparation of the Gifts Antiphon

Luke 2:33

34 VIII G

The things___ that were said of Je -

sus_____ * filled__ his par - ents with won - der.

Psalm 40 (39V)

1, 6b–8, 16

35

℣ 1 *I wait-* ed pa-tient-ly for the **LORD;** *   he in-

clined to *me and* **heard** my cry. *Flex:* not re-quired. †

2 *Burnt of*fering and sin offering you have not rèquired. †
Then I said, "**Hére** I am; *
in the scroll of the book it is *written* **of** me.

3 *I de*light to do your will, O my **Gód;** *
your law *is with***in** my heart."

4 *May all* who seek you rejoice and be **glád** in you; *
may those who love your salvation say continually, "*Grèat*
is **the** LORD!"

Communion Antiphon

Luke 2:19

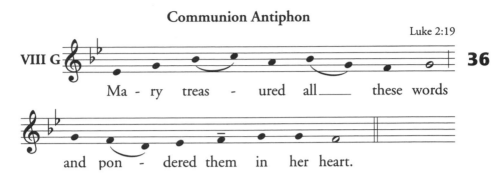

Ma - ry treas - ured all____ these words and pon - dered them in her heart.

Psalm 78 (77V)

1–4, 23–25, 29, 70–71

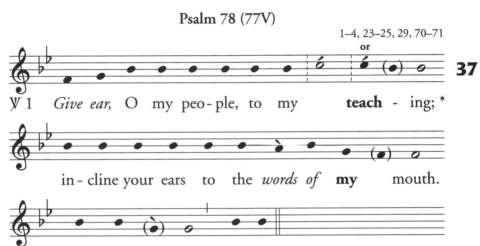

℣ 1 *Give ear,* O my peo-ple, to my **teach** - ing; *
in - cline your ears to the *words of* **my** mouth.

Flex: their chil - dren; †

2 *I will* open my mouth in a **pár**able; *
  I will utter dark *sàyings* **from** of old,

3 *things that* we have **héard** and known, *
  that our ances*tòrs have* **told** us.

4 *We will* not hide them from their childrèn; †
    we will tell to the coming generátion *
  the glorious deeds of the LORD, and his might, and the wondèrs
  that **he** has done.

5 *God com*manded the **skíes** above, *
  and opened the *dòors of* **heav**en;

6 *he rained* down on them manna to **éat,** *
  and gave them the *gràin of* **heav**en.

7 *Mortals* ate of the bread of **án**gels; *
  he sent them food *in* **a**bundance.

21

8   *And they* ate and were **wéll** filled, *
     for he *gàve them* **what** they craved.

9   *God brought* David to be the shepherd of his people **Já**cob, *
     of Israel, *hìs in*heritance.

10   *With up*right heart he **ténd**ed them, *
     and guided *thèm with* **skill**ful hand.

January 1

The Solemnity of Mary Mother of God

Use the Common of the Blessed Virgin Mary, p. 252.

Epiphany

Solemnity

Entrance Antiphon

Psalm 95 (94V):6a and 7a

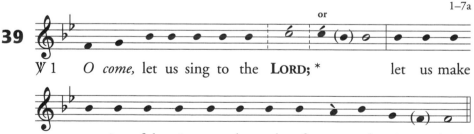

O — come, — * let — us — wor-ship him,

for he is the Lord our God.

Psalm 95 (94V)

1–7a

℣ 1   O *come,* let us sing to the **LORD;** *   let us make

a joy-ful noise to the rock of *our sal* - **va** - tion!

2   *Let us* come into his presence with thanks**gív**ing; *
     let us make a joyful noise to *hìm with* **songs** of praise!

3   *For the* LORD is a great **Gód,** *
     and a great *Kìng a***bove** all gods.

4   *In his* hand are the depths of the **éarth;** *
     the heights of the mountains *àre his* **al**so.

5   *The sea* is his, for he **máde** it, *
     and the dry land, *whìch his* **hands** have formed.

6   *O come,* let us worship and **bów** down, *
     let us kneel before the *LÒRD, our* **Mak**er!

7   *For he* is our **Gód,** *
     and we are the people of his pasture, and the *shèep of* **his** hand.

Responsorial Psalm E 5   **Psalm 72 (71V)**
                                                (11b) 11a, 1–4ab, 10–13, 17

40

℣ 1 To the king, O God, give your **jus** - tice, *
and to a king's son *your* **right-eous** - ness.
℟ All the na - tions will come to serve him.

℣ 2 May he **judge** your peo-ple with **right** - eous-ness, *
and your poor *with* **jus** - tice.
℟ All the na - tions will come to serve him.

3[1]   May the mountains yield prosperity for the **péo**ple, *
       and the hills, in *ríght***eous**ness.

4   **May** he defend the cause of the poor of the **pèo**ple, *
     give deliverance to *thè* **need**y.

5   May the kings of Tarshish and of the isles render him **tríb**ute, *
     may the kings of Sheba and *Séba* **bring** gifts.

[1] Odd numbered verses are chanted on the first chanting note (mi); even numbered verses, on the second chanting note (la).

6   May **all** kings fall down be**fòre** him, *
    all nations give *hìm* **ser**vice.

7   For he delivers the needy **whén** they call, *
    the poor and those who have *nó* **help**er.

8   **He** has pity on the weak and the **nèed**y, *
    and saves the lives of *thè* **need**y.

9   May his name endure for**év**er, *
    his fame continue as *lóng* **as the** sun.

10 May **all** nations be **blèssed** in him; *
    may they pronounce *hìm* **hap**py.

Alleluia   **Psalm 29 (28V)**
                                                      2, 11

41   III g

Al- le- lu- ia, ___   al- le- lu - ia, ___   al- le - lu - ia.

All repeat: Alleluia, alleluia, alleluia.

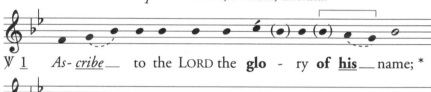

℣ 1   As- *cribe* ___ to the LORD the **glo** - ry **of his** ___ name; *

wor-ship the LORD in   *ho* - *ly* ___ **splen** - dor.

All: Alleluia, alleluia, alleluia.

2   *May the* LORD give **stréngth** to his **peo**ple! *
    May the LORD bless his *pèople* **with** peace!

All: Alleluia, alleluia, alleluia.

or **Alleluia Psalm** C 4   **Psalm 29 (28V)**
                                          1–5, 10–11 (See Performance Notes)

42

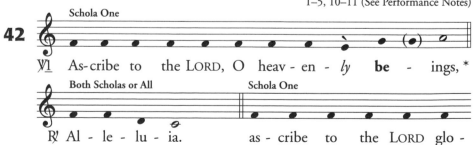

Schola One

℣1   As-cribe to   the LORD, O heav - en - *ly*   **be** - ings, *

Both Scholas or All   Schola One

℟ Al - le - lu - ia.   as - cribe   to   the LORD glo -

-ry **and** strength. ℟ Al - le - lu - ia.

2 Ascribe to the LORD the glory *òf* **his** name; *
   worship the LORD in ho*ly* **splen**dor.

3 The voice of the LORD is over the waters; '
      the God of glo*ry* **thun**ders, *
   the LORD, over migh*ty* **wa**ters.

4 The voice of the LORD *is* **pow**erful; *
   the voice of the LORD is full *òf* **maj**esty.

5 The voice of the LORD breaks *thè* **ce**dars; *
   the LORD breaks the cedars *òf* **Leb**anon.

6 The LORD sits enthroned o*vèr* **the** flood; *
   the LORD sits enthroned as king *fòre*ver.

7 May the LORD give strength to *his* **peo**ple! *
   May the LORD bless his peo*plè* **with** peace!

Preparation of the Gifts Antiphon

Psalm 72 (71V):10

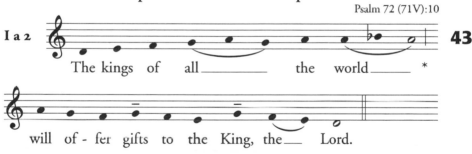

I a 2

The kings of all ____ the world ____ *

will of - fer gifts to the King, the __ Lord.

Psalm 72 (71V)

7a–9, 15–16ab

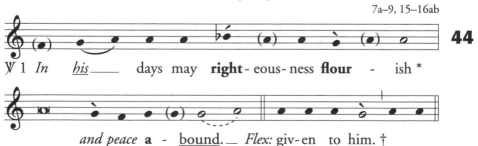

℣ 1 *In* *his* ___ days may **right** - eous- ness **flour** - ish *

and peace **a** - bound. __ *Flex:* giv- en to him. †

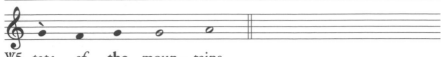

℣5 *tops* *of* **the** moun - tains.

2 *May* he have do**mín**ion from **sea** to sea, *
   and from the River to the *ènds of* **the** <u>earth</u>.

3 *May* his foes bow **dówn** be**fore** him, *
   and his en*èmies* **lick** the <u>dust</u>.

4 *Long* may he live! May gold of Sheba be given to hìm. †
      May prayer be made for **hím** con**tin**ually, *
   and blessings invoked for *hìm all* **day** <u>long</u>.

5 *May* there be abundance of **gráin** in **the** land; *
   may it wave on the *tòps of* **the** mountains.

Communion Antiphon

Matthew 2:2

45 IV E

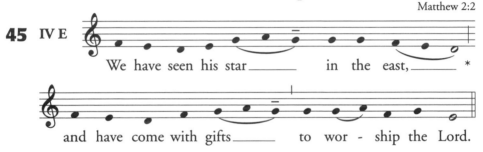

We have seen his star_____ in the east,_____ *

and have come with gifts_____ to wor - ship the Lord.

Psalm 96 (95V)

1–4, 6–13 (See Performance Notes)
or

46

℣ 1 *O* *sing*__ to the Lord *a new* **song;** * sing

to the <u>Lord</u>, _ **all** __ the earth. *Flex:* earth re- joice;†

2 *Sing* to the Lord, *blèss his* **name;** *
   tell of his salva*tìon from* <u>day</u> **to** day.

3 *Declare* his glory a*mòng the* **na**tions, *
   his marvelous works *among all the* **peo**ples.

4 *For* <u>great</u> is the Lord, and greatly *tò be* **praised;** *
   he is to be re*vèred a<u>bove</u>* **all** gods.

5   _Hon_or and majesty _àre be**fore**_ him; *
      strength and beauty are _ìn his sanctu_ary.

<u>6</u>   _As<u>cribe</u>_ to the LORD, O families _òf the_ **peo**ples, *
      ascribe to _thè_ LORD _glory_ **and** strength.

<u>7</u>   _As<u>cribe</u>_ to the LORD the _glòry_ **due** his name; *
      bring an offering, _ànd come into_ **his** courts.

8   _<u>Wor</u>_ship the LORD in _hòly_ **splen**dor; *
      tremble be_fòre him, all_ **the** earth.

9   _<u>Say</u>_ among the na_tìons, "The_ **LORD** is king! *
      He will judge the peo_plès with_ e<u>qui</u>ty."

<u>10</u>   _Let the <u>heav</u>_ens be glad, and let the earth _rèjoice;_ †
       let the sea roar, and _àll that_ **fills** it; *
      let the field exult, and _èverything_ **in** it.

<u>11</u>   _Then shall <u>all</u>_ the trees of the forest sing for joy before the LÒRD; †
       for _hè is_ **com**ing, *
      for he is com_ìng to <u>judge</u>_ **the** earth.

<u>12</u>   _He will <u>judge</u>_ the _wòrld with_ **right**eousness, *
      and the _pèoples <u>with</u>_ **his** truth.

Baptism of the Lord

Feast

As above, for the Epiphany of the Lord, p. 22, except for:

The entrance antiphon, _With the spirit of the Lord_, **493,** with Psalm 19.

Psalm 19 (18V)

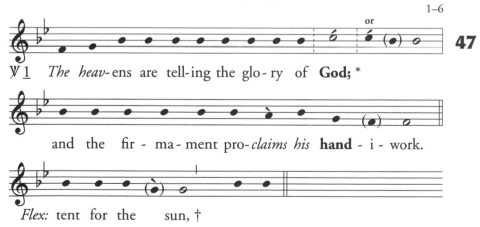

2   _Day to_ day pours forth **spéech**, *
      and night to night _dèclares_ **know**ledge.

<u>3</u>   *There is* no speech, nor **áre** there words; *
     their *vòice is* **not** heard;

<u>4</u>   *yet their* voice goes out through **áll** the earth, *
     and their words to the *ènd of* **the** world.

<u>5</u>   *In the* heavens he has set a tent for the sùn †
        which comes out like a bridegroom from his wedding **cán**opy, *
     and like a strong man *rùns its* **course** with joy.

<u>6</u>   *Its ris*ing is from the end of the heavèns, †
        and its circuit to the **énd** of them; *
     and nothing is *hìd from* **its** heat.

The preparation of the gifts antiphon, *Christ is the light of nations,* **298,** with its psalm, **299.**

The communion antiphon, *Justice you love,* **116,** with its psalm, **117.**

After the feast of Baptism of the Lord, Ordinary Time begins. Any of the nine suites (or "formularies") of antiphons and psalms for Ordinary Time, beginning on p. 148, may be used during this time, "according to what seems best for the occasion. Some parts may even be chosen from one formulary and some from another (see **Performance Notes,** p. 421). At communion time the singing of Psalm 34 (33V) *I will bless the Lord,* with the response *Alleluia* or *Taste and See,* is always permitted [see pp. 382–386]. But other suitable chants may be chosen at will [see p. 386]" (Introduction to the *Graduale Simplex,* §21).

Ash Wednesday

Entrance Antiphon

Psalm 57 (56V):1ab

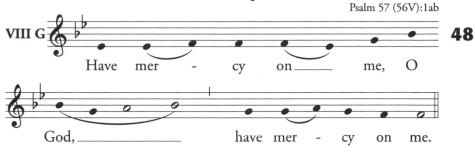

48

Have mer - cy on me, O God, have mer - cy on me.

Psalm 57 (56V)

1de, 2–3, 5, 7–11
or

49

In the shad-ow of your wings I will take **ref** - uge, *

un- til the de-*stroy-ing* **storms** pass by. *Flex:* and save me, †

2 *I cry* to God Most **Hígh,** *
  to God who fulfills his *pùrpose* **for** me.

3 *He will* send from heaven and **save** mè, †
    he will put to shame those who trample on **mé.** *
  God will send forth his steadfast love *ànd his* **faith**fulness.

4 *Be ex*alted, O God, above the **héav**ens. *
  Let your glory be *òver* **all** the earth.

5 *My heart* is steadfast, O God, my heart is **stéad**fast. *
  I will sing *ànd make* **mel**ody.

6 *Awake,* my soul! Awake, O **hárp** and lyre! *
  I *wìll* *a***wake** the dawn.

7 *I will* give thanks to you, O Lord, among the **péo**ples; *
  I will sing praises to you a*mòng the* **na**tions.

8 *For your* steadfast love is as high as the **héav**ens; *
  your faithfulness ex*tènds to* **the** clouds.

9 *Be ex*alted, O God, above the **héav**ens. *
  Let your glory be *òver* **all** the earth.

or as desired:

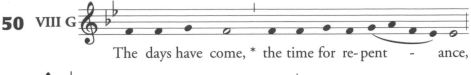

50 VIII G

The days have come, * the time for re-pent - ance,

to re-deem us from our sins___ and to save_____ us.

with Psalm 69 (68V), *Save me, O God,* **218,** or with the following canticle :

Canticle of Wisdom
Wisdom 11:21–12:2 (See Performance Notes)

51 1   *O Lord,* it is always in your power to show great **stréngth,** *
and who can withstand the *mìght of* **your** arm.

2   *Because* the whole world before you is like a speck that **típs**
the scales, *
and like a drop of morning dew that *fàlls on* **the** ground.

3   *But you* are merciful to àll, †
for you can do **áll** things, *
and you overlook people's sins, so *thàt they* **may** repent.

4   *For you* love all things that exìst, †
and detest none of the things that **yóu** have made, *
for you would not have made anything if *yòu had* **hat**ed it.

5   *How would* anything have endured if you had not **wílled** it? *
Or how would anything not called forth by *yòu have* **been**
preserved?

6   *You spare* all things for they are yours, Ò Lord, †
you who love the **lív**ing. *
For your immortal spirit *ìs in* **all** things.

7   *Therefore* you correct little by little those who trespàss, †
and you remind and warn them of the things through
which they **sín,** *
so that they made be freed from their wickedness, and put
their *trùst in* **you,** O Lord.

The following is the arrangement of the chants between the readings:

When there are two readings before the gospel, the chants are arranged as follows: One of the two responsorial psalms is sung after the first reading; after the second reading, either the other responsorial psalm is sung, or the tract or the acclamation antiphon.

Whenever there is only one reading before the gospel, a single chant from among the following may be chosen at will.

Responsorial Psalm I C 2 g

Psalm 51 (50V)
(1a) 1–3, 7–12

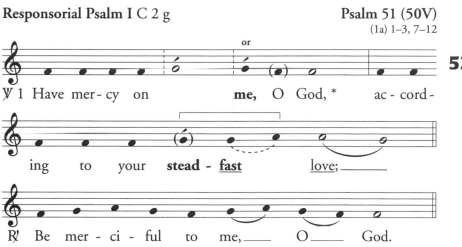

52

℣ 1 Have mer-cy on **me,** O God, * ac-cord-ing to your **stead - fast** love;

℟ Be mer - ci - ful to me, O God.

2 according to your abundant **mér**cy *
   blot out my trans**gré**ssions.

3 Wash me thoroughly from my in**í**quity, *
   and cleanse me **fróm my** sin.

4 For I know my trans**gré**ssions, *
   and my sin is ever be**fóre** me.

5 Purge me with hyssop, and I **sháll** be clean; *
   wash me, and I shall be whiter **thán** snow.

6 Let me hear joy and **glád**ness; *
   let the bones that you have crushed **ré**joice.

7 Hide your face **fróm** my sins, *
   and blot out all my in**í**quities.

8 Create in me a clean **héart,** O God, *
   and put a new and right spirit with**ín** me.

9 Do not cast me away from your **prés**ence, *
   and do not take your holy spirit **fróm** me.

10 Restore to me the joy of your salv**á**tion, *
   and sustain in me a willing **spír**it.

Responsorial Psalm II E 1

Psalm 79 (78V)
(9b) 9a, 4–5, 8, 10a, 11, 13

53

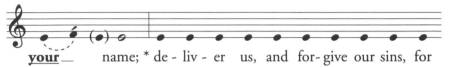

℣ 1 Help us, O God of our sal - va - tion, for the glo - ry of

your__ name; * de - liv - er us, and for - give our sins, for

your__ **name's__** sake. ℟ Deal kind - ly with us

sin - ners, deal kind - ly. ℣5 *"Where__* **is their** God?"

℣7 will give *thanks to* **you for** - ev - er;

2　We have become a taunt to our **néigh**bors, *
　　mocked and derided by *thóse a***round** us.

3　How long, O LORD? Will you be angry for**é**ver? *
　　Will your jealous wrath *búrn* **like** fire?

4　Do not remember against us the iniquities of our ancestors; '
　　　let your compassion come speedily to **méet** us, *
　　for we are *bróught* **very** low.

5　Why should the **ná**tions say, *
　　"*Where* **is their** God?"

6　Let the groans of the prisoners come be**fóre** you; *
　　according to your great power preserve those *dóomed* **to** die.

7　Then we your people, the flock of your **pás**ture, *
　　will give *thánks to* **you for**ever;

8　from generation to gener**á**tion *
　　we will re*cóunt* **your** praise.

or **Tract** C *

Psalm 79 (78V)

9, 4, 5, 8, 13

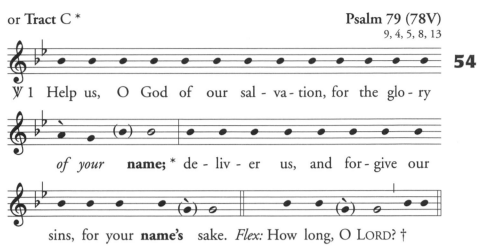

℣ 1 Help us, O God of our sal - va - tion, for the glo - ry

of your **name;** * de - liv - er us, and for - give our

sins, for your **name's** sake. *Flex:* How long, O LORD? †

2 We have become a taunt *tò our* **neigh**bors, *
mocked and derided by those a**round** ùs.

3 How long, Ò LORD? †
    Will you be an*grỳ fore*ver? *
Will your jealous wrath burn **like** fire?

4 Do not remember against us the iniquities of our ancèstors; †
    let your compassion come speedi*lỳ to* **meet** us, *
for we are brought **verỳ** low.

5 Then we your people, the flock of your pastùre, †
    will give thanks to *yòu fore*ver; *
from generation to generation we will recount **your** pràise.

Blessing and Distribution of Ashes

When the presider begins to distribute ashes, the following chant is immediately sung:

Psalm 51 (50V):1b

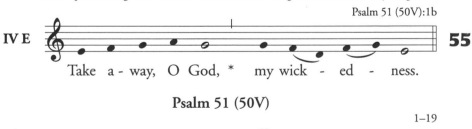

IV E

Take a - way, O God, * my wick - ed - ness.

Psalm 51 (50V)

1–19

or

Have mer - cy on *me,* O **God,** * ac - cord-*ing to*

54

55

56

your **stead - fast** love; ℣11 and *blot out all my*

in - iq - ui - ties. ℣16 a-*loud of your de -* **liv** - 'rance.

℣20 re - build the walls *of Je -* *ru* - **sa** - lem,

2   *accord*ing to your a*bùn*dant **mer**cy *
    blot *òut my* *transgres*sions.

3   *Wash* me thoroughly from *mỳ in***iq**uity, *
    and *clèanse me* *from* **my** sin.

4   *For I* know *mỳ trans***gres**sions, *
    and my sin *ìs ever be***fore** me.

5   *Against* you, you alone, *hàve I* **sinned,** *
    and done what is *èvil in* **your** sight,

6   *so that* you are justified *ìn your* **sen**tence *
    and blameless *whèn you pass* **judg**ment.

7   *Indeed,* I *wàs born* **guil**ty, *
    a sinner *whèn my mother* **conceived** me.

8   *You de*sire truth in the *ìnward* **be**ing; *
    therefore teach me *wìsdom in my* **secret** heart.

9   *Purge* me with hyssop, and I *shàll be* **clean;** *
    wash me, and I *shàll be whiter* **than** snow.

10   *Let* me hear *jòy and* **glad**ness; *
    let the bones that *yòu have crushed* **re**joice.

11   *Hide* your face *fròm my* **sins,** *
    and *blòt out all my* **iniqui**ties.

12   *Create* in me a clean *hèart, O* **God,** *
    and put a new *ànd right spirit* **within** me.

13   *Do not cast* me away *fròm your* **pres**ence, *
    and do not take your *hòly spirit* **from** me.

14   *Restore* to me the joy of *yòur sal***va**tion, *
    and sustain in *mè a willing* **spir**it.

15   *Then I* will teach transgres*sòrs your* **ways,** *
    and sinners *wìll re*turn **to** you.

16 *Deliv*er me from bloodshed, O God, O God of *my salva*tion, *
and my tongue will sing a*loud of your de**liv**'*rance.

17 *O Lord*, op*èn my* **lips,** *
and my mouth *will declare* **your** praise.

18 *For you* have no de*light in* **sac**rifice; *
if I were to give a burnt offering, *you would not* **be** pleased.

19 *The sac*rifice acceptable to God is a *bròken* **spir**it; *
a broken and contrite heart, O God, *you will not* **de**spise.

20 *Do good* to Zion in *yòur good* **pleas**ure; *
rebuild the walls *òf Jerusa*lem,

21 *then you* will delight in right sacrifices, in burnt offerings and
whòle burnt **of**ferings; *
then bulls will be *òffered on your* **al**tar.

Preparation of the Gifts Antiphon

Psalm 30 (29V):11b

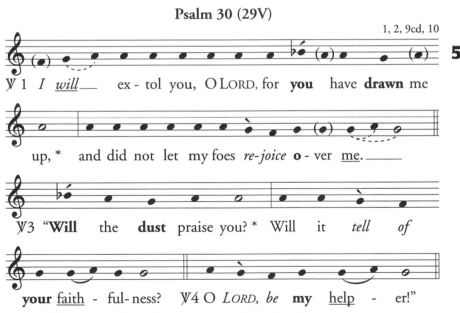

I g 2

57

The Lord— has come to help me.

Psalm 30 (29V)

1, 2, 9cd, 10

58

℣ 1 *I will*— ex - tol you, O LORD, for **you** have **drawn** me

up, * and did not let my foes *re-joice* **o** - ver me.—

℣3 "**Will** the **dust** praise you? * Will it *tell* of

your faith - ful-ness? ℣4 O LORD, *be* **my** help - er!"

2 *O LORD* my God, I **crìed** to **you** for help, *
and *yòu have* **healed** me.

35

3 "**Will** the **dust** praise you? *
Will it *tell of* **your** <u>faith</u>fulness?

4 *<u>Hear,</u>* O LORD, and be **gra**cious **to** me! *
O *LORD, be* **my** <u>help</u>er!"

Communion Antiphon

Psalm 60 (59V):11a

59 **II D**

O give us, Lord, ____ * your help ___ in time of suf- f'ring.

Psalm 60 (59V)

1–5, 11, 12

60

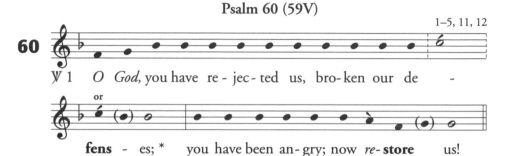

℣ 1 *O God,* you have re - jec- ted us, bro- ken our de -

or

fens - es; * you have been an- gry; now *re-* **store** us!

2 *You hav*e caused the land to quake; you have torn it **ó**pen; *
repair the cracks in it, for it *is* **tot**tering.

3 *You have* made your people suffer **hárd** things; *
you have given us wine to drink *thàt* **made** us reel.

<u>4</u> *You have* set up a banner for those who **féar** you, *
to rally to it out *òf* **bow**shot.

<u>5</u> *Give vic*tory with your right hand, and **án**swer us, *
so that those whom you love may *bè* **res**cued.

<u>6</u> *O grant* us help a**gáinst** the foe, *
for human help *is* **worth**less.

<u>7</u> *With God* we shall do **vál**iantly; *
it is he who will *trèad* **down** our foes.

These songs may be used on all weekdays of Lent.

First Sunday of Lent

Entrance Antiphon

Isaiah 58:9ab

61 **VII a**

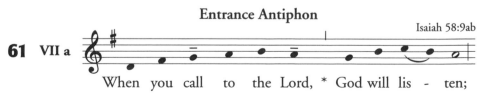

When you call to the Lord, * God will lis - ten;

when you cry___ out,   God will say: here___ I am.

Psalm 91 (90V)

1–2, 4–6, 9–13 (See Performance Notes)

℣ 1 *You___ who___* live in the shel-ter **of** the **Most**

High, * who a - bide in the shad - ow **of** the

Al - might - y,   *Flex:* with his pin - ions, †

2   *You will* say to the LORD, "My refuge **ánd** my **for**tress; *
    my **Gód**, in **whom** I <u>trust</u>."

3   *The LORD* will cover you with his pinìons, †
    and under his wings you **wíll** find **ref**uge; *
    his faithfulness is a **búck**ler **and** <u>shield</u>.

4   *You will* not fear the **tér**ror **of** the night, *
    or the **ár**row that **flies** by <u>day</u>,

5   *or the* pestilence that **stálks** in **dark**ness, *
    or the destruction that **wástes** at **noon**<u>day</u>.

6   *Because* you have made the **LÓRD** your **refuge**, *
    the Most **Hígh** your **dwell**ing <u>place</u>,

7   *no evil* **sháll** be**fall** you, *
    no **scóurge** come **near** your <u>tent</u>.

8   *For he* will command his **án**gels con**cern**ing you*
    to **gúard** you in **all** your <u>ways</u>.

9   *On their* hands **théy** will **bear** you up, *
    so that you will not dash your **fóot** a<u>gainst</u> a <u>stone</u>.

10 *You will* tread on the lion **ánd** the **ad**der, *
    the young lion and the serpent you will **trám**ple **un**der <u>foot</u>.

Responsorial Psalm I E 5   Psalm 91 (90V)

(4b) 4ab, 10–16 (See Performance Notes)

63

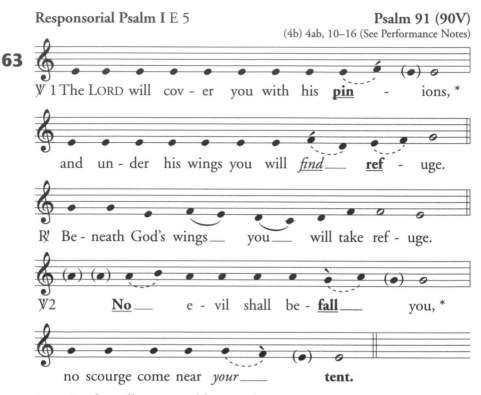

℣ 1 The LORD will cov - er you with his **pin** - ions, *

and un - der his wings you will *find* **ref** - uge.

℟ Be - neath God's wings you will take ref - uge.

℣ 2 **No** e - vil shall be - **fall** you, *

no scourge come near *your* **tent**.

3¹   For he will command his angels con**cerning** you*
      to guard you in *àll* **your** ways.

4   On their **hands** they will **bèar** you up, *
      so that you will not dash your *foot àgainst* a stone.

5   You will tread on the lion and the **ád**der, *
      the young lion and the serpent you will *trámple* **under** foot.

6   Those who **love** me, I will de**lìv**er; *
      I will protect those *whò* **knòw** my name.

7   When they call to me, I will answer them; '
      I will be with them in **tróu**ble, *
      I will rescue them and *hónor* them.

8   With **long** life I will satis**fȳ** them, *
      and show them my *sàl***va**tion.

Or, if desired, Responsorial Psalm I, Psalm 122 (121V), as in Advent II, **12.**

---

¹ Odd numbered verses are chanted on the first chanting note (mi); even numbered verses, on the second chanting note (la).

Responsorial Psalm II D 1 g   Psalm 41 (40V)
(4b) 4–9

℣ 1 As for me, I said, * "O LORD, be gra-cious to

me and **heal** me." ℟ Be-cause I have sinned a-gainst you.

2 My enemies wonder in **mál**ice *
when I will die, and my name **per**ish.

3 And when they come to see me, they utter empty words, '
while their hearts gather **mís**chief; *
when they go out, they tell it a**bròad**.

4 All who hate me whisper together a**bóut** me; *
they imagine the **worst** for me.

5 They think that a deadly thing has fastened on **mé**, *
that I will not rise again from **where** I lie.

6 Even my bosom friend in whom I trusted, '
who ate of **mý** bread, *
has lifted the heel a**gainst** mè.

Gospel Acclamation Antiphon

Mark 4:11

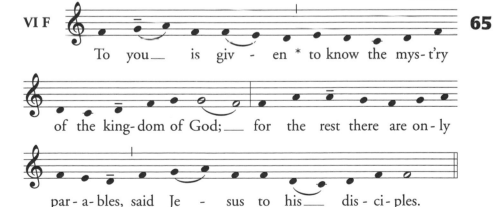

VI F

To you is giv-en * to know the mys-t'ry

of the king-dom of God; for the rest there are on-ly

par-a-bles, said Je-sus to his dis-ci-ples.

When the acclamation antiphon is used, at least one verse of one of the preceding responsorial psalms, which has not already been sung, is added (see Performance Notes).

or **Tract**

Psalm 41 (40V)

4–7, 12

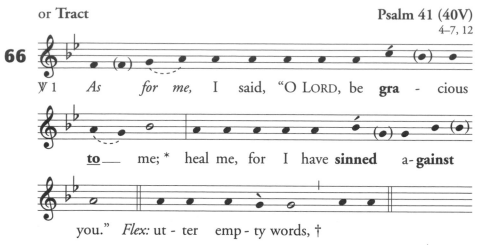

℣ 1 *As for me,* I said, "O LORD, be **gra** - cious **to** me; * heal me, for I have **sinned** a-**gainst** you." *Flex:* ut - ter emp - ty words, †

2 My enemies wonder in **má**lice when **I will** die, *
   and **mý** name **per**ish.

3 And when they come to see me, they utter emptỳ words, †
   while their hearts **gáth**er **mis**chief; *
   when they go out, they **téll** it abroad.

4 All who hate me whisper to**géth**er a**bout** me; *
   they im**ág**ine the **worst** for me.

5 But you have upheld me because of **mý** in**teg**rity, *
   and set me in your **prés**ence for**ev**er.

Preparation of the Gifts Antiphon

Matthew 6:3

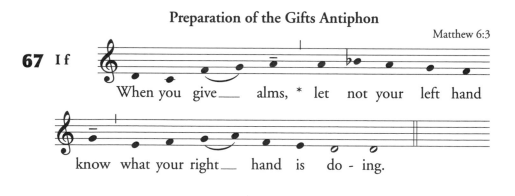

If When you give alms, * let not your left hand know what your right hand is do - ing.

Psalm 51 (50V)

1–3

℣ 1 *Have mer* - cy **on** me, **O** God, * ac-cord-

- ing *to your* **stead** - fast <u>love;</u> _____

2   *accord*ing to your a**bún**dant **mer**cy *
    blot out *mỳ trans***gres**sions.

3   <u>*Wash*</u> me thoroughly **fróm** my in**iq**uity, *
    and *clèanse me* **from** my <u>sin.</u>

4   *For I* **knów** my trans**gres**sions, *
    and my sin is ev*èr be***fore** <u>me.</u>

Communion Antiphon

Psalm 5:1b

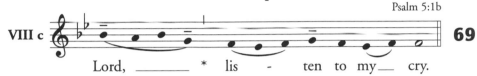

VIII c

Lord, _____ * lis - ten to my__ cry.   **69**

Psalm 5

1–8, 11–12

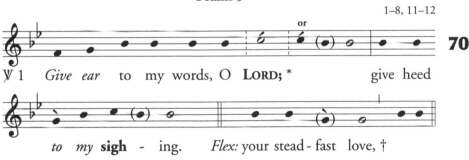

℣ 1   *Give ear* to my words, O **LORD;** *   give heed

    to my **sigh** - ing.   *Flex:* your stead - fast love, †   **70**

2   *Listen* to the sound of my cry, my King and my **Gód,** *
    for *tò you* **I** pray.

3   *O LORD,* in the morning you **héar** my voice; *
    in the morning I plead my *càse to* **you,** and watch.

4   *For you* are not a God who delights in **wíck**edness; *
    evil will not *sòjourn* **with** you.

5   *The boast*ful will not stand be**fóre** your eyes;*
    you hate all *èvil***do**ers.

6   *You de*stroy those who speak **líes;** *
    the LORD abhors the bloodthirsty *ànd de***ceit**ful.

7   *But I,* through the abundance of your steadfàst love, †
    will enter your **hóuse,** *
    I will bow down toward your holy tem*plè in* **awe** of you.

8   *Lead me,* O LORD, in your rightèousness †
      because of my **én**emies; *
    make your way *stràight be***fore** me.

9   *But let* all who take refuge in you re**jóice;** *
    let them *èver* **sing** for joy.

10 *Spread your* protection **ó**ver them, *
    so that those who love your name *mày* ex**ult** in you.

11 *For you* bless the righteous, O **LÓRD;** *
    you cover them with fa*vòr as* **with** a shield.

Second Sunday of Lent

See the Feast of Transfiguration of the Lord, p. 214. After the second reading, sing Responsorial Psalm II from the Mass of the Third Sunday of Lent, **74,** and/or the Acclamation Antiphon, **75.**

Third Sunday of Lent

Entrance Antiphon

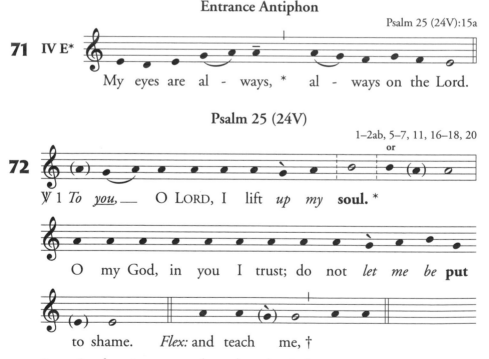

Psalm 25 (24V):15a

71 IV E*

My eyes are al - ways, * al - ways on the Lord.

Psalm 25 (24V)

1–2ab, 5–7, 11, 16–18, 20
or

72

℣ 1 *To you,* ___ O LORD, I lift *up my* **soul.** *

O my God, in you I trust; do not *let me be* **put**

to shame.   *Flex:* and teach   me, †

2   *Lead* me in your truth, and teach mè, †
      for you are the God of *mỳ sal***va**tion; *
    for *yòu I wait* **all** day long.

3   *Be <u>mind</u>ful of your mercy, O LÒRD,* †
        and of your *stèadfast* **love,** *
     for *thèy have been* **from** of old.

4   *Do <u>not</u> remember the sins of my youth or my transgressìons;* †
        according to your steadfast *lòve re<u>mem</u>*ber me, *
     for *yòur goodness'* **sake,** O LORD!

5   *For <u>your</u> name's sàke, O* **LORD,** *
     pardon *mỳ guilt, for* **it** is great.

6   <u>*Turn*</u> *to me and be gracìous to* **me,** *
     for I am lone*lỳ and a*<u>*fflic*</u>ted.

7   <u>*Relieve*</u> *the troubles òf my* **heart,** *
     and bring *mè out of* **my** distress.

8   *Con<u>sid</u>er my affliction ànd my* **trou**ble, *
     ànd forgive **all** my sins.

9   *O <u>guard</u> my life, and delivèr me;* †
        do not let *mè be* **put** to shame, *
     for I *tàke refuge* **in** you.

Responsorial Psalm I D 1 b   **Psalm 38 (37V)**
                                        (22b) 22a, 1–4, 6–10

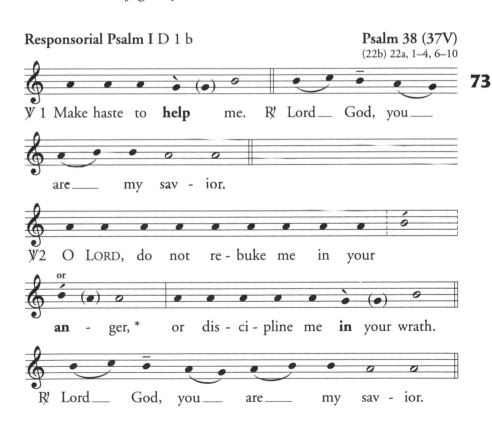

73

𝒱 1 Make haste to **help**   me.   ℟ Lord___ God, you___ are___ my sav - ior.

𝒱 2 O LORD, do not re - buke me in your **an** - ger, * or dis - ci - pline me **in** your wrath.

℟ Lord___ God, you___ are___ my sav - ior.

3   For your arrows have sunk ínto me, *
     and your hand has come **dòwn** on me.

4   There is no soundness in my flesh because of your indignátion; *
     there is no health in my bones because of **mỳ** sin.

5   For my iniquities have gone over my **héad;** *
     they weigh like a burden too heavy **fòr** me.

6   I am utterly bowed down and **prós**trate; *
     all day long I go around **mòurn**ing.

7   For my loins are filled with **búrn**ing, *
     and there is no soundness **ìn** my flesh.

8   I am utterly spent and **crúshed;** *
     I groan because of the tumult **òf** my heart.

9   O Lord, all my longing is **knówn** to you; *
     my sighing is not hidden **fròm** you.

10   My heart throbs, my strength **fáils** me; *
     as for the light of my eyes—it also has **gòne** from me.

Responsorial Psalm II D 1 g   **Psalm 123 (122V)**

(3a) 3b, 1–4

74

℣1 Have mer - cy up - on us, **O**   LORD, ℟ Have mer -

or

cy on us. ℣2 To you I lift up my **eyes,** *

O you who are en-throned in the **heav** - ens!

℟ Have mer - cy on us.

3   As the eyes of servants look to the hand of their **más**ter, *
     as the eyes of a maid to the hand of her **mis**trèss,

4   so our eyes look to the LORD our **Gód,** *
     until he has mercy up**on** ùs.

5   Have mercy upon us, O LORD, have mercy up**ón** us, *
     for we have had more than enough of **con**tèmpt.

6   Our soul has had more than its fill of the scorn of those who
         are at **éase,** *
     of the contempt of **the** pròud.

At the end, verse 1 and the response may be repeated: ℣ "Have mercy on us, O Lòrd.
℟ Have mercy on us."

Gospel Acclamation Antiphon

Matthew 4:4

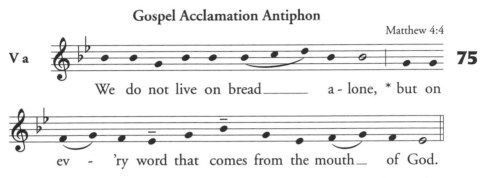

V a   75

We do not live on bread_____ a - lone, * but on

ev - 'ry word that comes from the mouth__ of God.

When the acclamation antiphon is used, at least one verse of one of the preceding
responsorial psalms, which has not already been, sung is added (see Performance Notes).

or **Tract**   Psalm 125 (124V)
                                                        1–5

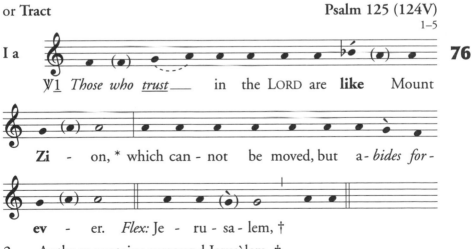

I a   76

℣1 *Those who trust___* in the LORD are **like** Mount

Zi - on, * which can - not be moved, but a - *bides for-*

ev - er. *Flex:* Je - ru - sa - lem, †

2   As the mountains surround Jerusàlem, †
         so the LORD sur**róunds** his **peo**ple, *
     from this time on *ànd fore***ver**more.

45

3 For the scepter of wickedness shall not rest on the land allotted **tó**
the **right**eous, *
so that the righteous might not stretch out their *hànds to* **do** wrong.

4 Do good, O LORD, to **thóse** who **are** good, *
and to those who are up*rìght in* **their** hearts.

5 But those who turn aside to their own crookèd ways †
the LORD will lead away with **é**vil**do**ers. *
Peace be *ùpon* **Is**rael!

Preparation of the Gifts Antiphon

Isaiah 58:7

77 IV E

Break your__ bread__ with the hun - gry, * and

bring the poor and home - less in - to your__ house.

Psalm 112 (111V)

1bc, 3, 5, 9 (See Performance Notes)

or

78

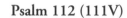

℣ 1   *Hap* - py are those who *fear the* **LORD**, *

who great - ly de - *light in his com* - **mand** - ments.

2 *Wealth* and riches are *ìn their* **hous**es, *
and their righteous*nèss endures* **for**ever.

3 *It is well* with those who deal generous*lỳ and* **lend**, *
who conduct *thèir affairs* **with jus**tice.

4 *They have* distributed freely, they have given *tò the* **poor;** *
their righteousness endures forever; their horn *is exalted* **in hon**or.

Communion Antiphon

Psalm 27 (26V):1ab

VIII c

The Lord__ is my light * and my sal - va - tion. **79**

Psalm 27 (26V)

1cd–5ab, 7–8, 13–14

or

℣ 1 *The* LORD is the strong-hold of my **life;** * **80**

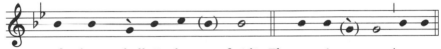

of whom *shall I* **be** a - fraid? *Flex:* a- gainst me, †

2 *When e*vildoers assail me to devour my **flésh,** *
they shall *stùmble* **and** fall.

3 *Though an* army encamp against mè, †
  my heart shall not **féar;** *
though war rise up against me, yet I *wìll be* **con**fident.

4 *One thing* I asked of the LORD, that will I seek **áf**ter: *
to live in the house of the LORD all the *dàys of* **my** life,

5 *to be*hold the beauty of the **LÓRD,** *
and to inquire *ìn his* **tem**ple.

6 *For he* will hide me in his shelter in the day of **tróu**ble; *
he will conceal me under the *còver* **of** his tent.

7 *Hear,* O LORD, when I **crý** aloud, *
be gracious to *mè and* **an**swer me!

8 *"Come," my* heart says, "seek his **fáce!"** *
Your face, *LÒRD, do* **I** seek.

9 *I be*lieve that I shall see the goodness of the **LÓRD** *
in the land *òf the* **liv**ing.

10 *Wait for* the LORD; be **stróng,** *
and let your heart take courage; *wàit for* **the** LORD!

Fourth Sunday of Lent

Entrance Antiphon

Psalm 118 (117V):5

81 VII c

In my___ dis - tress * I called out to the Lord;___ God heard my cry and set me free.

Psalm 118 (117V)

1, 4, 7–12, 14, 17 (See Performance Notes)

82

℣ 1 *O___ give___* thanks to the **LORD,** for **he** is good; *
his stead - fast **love** en - **dures** for - ev - er!

℣4 *It is bet - ter* to... put **cón** - fi - dence **in** mor - tals.

2 *Let those* who **féar** the **LORD** say, *
"His steadfast **lóve** en**dures** forever."

3 *The LORD* is on my **síde** to **help** me; *
I shall look in triumph on **thóse** who **hate** me.

4 *It is better* to take **réfuge in** the LORD *
than to put **cónfidence in** mortals.

5 *It is better* to take **réfuge in** the LORD *
than to put **cónfidence in** princes.

6 *All natíons* surround**ed** me; *
in the name of the **LÓRD** I **cut** them **off**!

7 *They surrounded* me, surrounded **mé** on **every** side; *
in the name of the **LÓRD** I **cut** them **off**!

8 *They surrounded* me like bees; they **blázed** like a **fire** of thorns; *
in the name of the **LÓRD** I **cut** them **off**!

9 *The LORD* is my **stréngth** and **my** might; *
he has be**cóme** my **sal**vation.

48

10   *I shall* not **díe,** but **I** shall live, *
     and recount the **déeds** of **the** Lord.

Responsorial Psalm I E 4   **Psalm 9**

(9) 1–3, 7–8, 10–11, 13, 18

℣ 1 The Lord is a strong-hold for the **op** - pressed.

℟ The Lord___ is our help in time of dis - tress.

℣2 I will give thanks to the Lord with my **whole** heart; *

I will tell of all your won - der - **ful** deeds.

℟ The Lord___ is our help in time of dis - tress.

83

3   I will be glad and exùlt in you; *
     I will sing praise to your name, **Ò** Most High.

4   When my enemies **tùrned** back, *
     they stumbled and perished befòre you.

5   But the Lord sits enthroned forèver, *
     he has established his throne for **jùdg**ment.

6   He judges the world with **rìght**eousness; *
     he judges the peoples with **è**quity.

7   Sing praises to the Lord, who dwells in **Zì**on. *
     Declare his deeds among the **pèo**ples.

8   Those who know your name put their **trùst** in you, *
     for you, O Lord, have not forsaken those **whò** seek you.

9   Be gracious to **mè**, O Lord. *
     See what I suffer from those **whò** hate me;

10   For the needy shall not always be forgòtten, *
     nor the hope of the poor perish fòrever.

Responsorial Psalm II C 2 g

Psalm 130 (129V)
(2a) 1–8 (See Performance Notes)

84

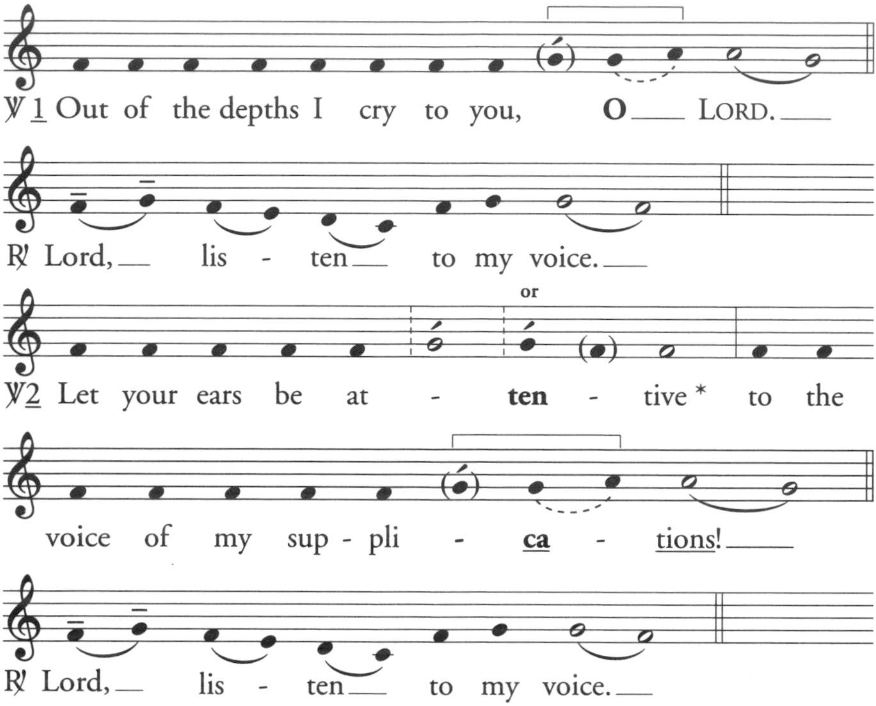

℣ 1 Out of the depths I cry to you, O___ LORD.___

℟ Lord,___ lis - ten___ to my voice.___

or

℣ 2 Let your ears be at - **ten** - tive * to the

voice of my sup - pli - **ca** - tions!___

℟ Lord,___ lis - ten___ to my voice.___

3   If you, O LORD, should mark in**í**quities, *
    Lord, who **cóuld** stand?

4   But there is forgiveness with **yóu,** *
    so that you may **bé re**vered.

5   I wait for the LORD, '
        my soul **wáits,** *
    and in his word **Í** hope;

6   my soul waits for the Lord '
        more than those who watch for the **mórn**ing, *
    more than those who watch for the **mórn**ing.

7   O Israel, hope in the LORD! '
        For with the LORD there is **stéad**fast love, *
    and with him is great pow**ér to re**deem.

8   It is he who will redeem **Í**srael *
    from all its in**í**quities.

Gospel Acclamation Antiphon

Cf. Luke 8:15

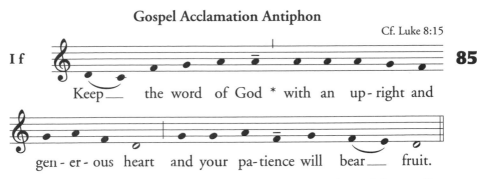

I f

Keep___ the word of God * with an up-right and

gen-er-ous heart and your pa-tience will bear___ fruit.

85

When the acclamation antiphon is used, at least one verse of one of the preceding responsorial psalms, which has not already been sung is added (see Performance Notes).

or **Tract**

Psalm 130 (129V)
1–6a (See Performance Notes)

I a

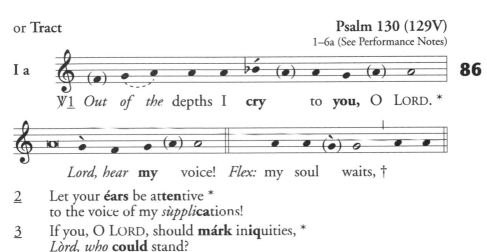

℣1 *Out of the* depths I **cry** to **you,** O LORD. *

Lord, hear **my** voice! *Flex:* my soul waits, †

86

2   Let your **éars** be atten**tive** *
    to the voice of my *sùppli***ca**tions!

3   If you, O LORD, should **márk** in**iq**uities, *
    Lòrd, who **could** stand?

4   But there is for**gíve**ness **with** you, *
    so that *yòu may* **be** revered.

5   I wait for the LORD, my soul wàits, †
    and in **hís** word **I** hope; *
    my soul *wàits for* **the** Lord.

Preparation of the Gifts Antiphon

Psalm 92 (91V):1a

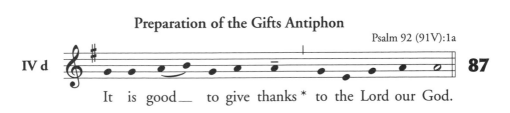

IV d

It is good___ to give thanks * to the Lord our God.

87

51

Psalm 92 (91V)

2, 4–5, 12

88

℣ 1   To de - _clare___   your stead - fast love   _in   the_

or

morn - ing, * and your _faith - ful - ness_ **by** night.

2   _For you,_ O LORD, have made me glad _by your_ **work;** *
at the works of _your hands I_ **sing** for joy.

3   _How great_ are your _works,_ O **LORD!** *
Your thoughts are **ver**y deep!

4   _The right_eous flourish _like the_ **palm** tree, *
and grow like a _cèdar in_ **Leb**anon.

Communion Antiphon

Psalm 43:4ab

89   IV A

I___   will go *   to   the   al - tar   of God,   the

God___ of my glad - ness, the God___ of my joy.

Psalm 43, 42 (42, 41V)

43:1–5; 42:1–6a (See Perfomance Notes)

90

℣ 1   _Vin_ - di - cate me, O   God, † and de - fend my

or

cause a - gainst an un - _god - ly_   **peo** - ple; * from those

who are de - ceit - ful and _un - just de_ - **liv** - er me!

2   *For you* are the God in whom I take refuge; †
      why *have you* **cast** me off? *
    Why must I walk about mournfully because of the oppres*sion of
      the* **en**emy?

3   O *send* out your light and your truth; *let them* **lead** me; *
    let them bring me to your holy hill *and to your* **dwel**ling.

4   *Then I* will go to the altar of Gòd, †
      to God my ex*cèeding* **joy;** *
    and I will praise you with *thè harp,* O **God,** my God.

5   *Why* are you cast down, O my sòul, †
      and why are you disquiet*èd within* me? *
    Hope in God; for I shall again praise him, *mỳ help and* **my** God.

6   As a *deer* longs for *flòwing* **streams,** *
    so my *sòul longs for* **you,** O God.

7   *My soul* thirsts for God, for the *living* **God.** *
    When shall I come and *bèhold the* **face** of God?

8   *My tears* have been my food *dày and* **night,** *
    while people say to me contin*uàlly,* "*Where* **is** your God?"

9   *These* things I remember, as I pour out my sòul: †
      how I went with the throng, and led them in procession *tò the*
        house of God, *
    with glad shouts and songs of thanksgiving, a multi*tùde keeping*
      festival.

10 *Why* are you cast down, O my sòul, †
      and why are you disquiet*èd within* me? *
    Hope in God; for I shall again praise him, *mỳ help and* **my** God.

Fifth Sunday of Lent

Entrance Antiphon

Psalm 71 (70V):19

VIII c

O God, my God, _____ * res - cue me from __ the hands _____ of the wick - ed.

91

Psalm 71 (70V)

1–3ab, 10–15ab, 24

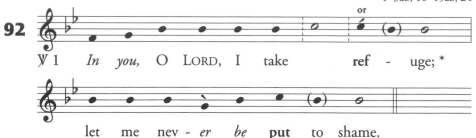

92 ℣ 1 *In you,* O LORD, I take **ref** - uge; *

let me nev - *er be* **put** to shame.

2   *In your* righteousness deliver me and **rés**cue me; *
     incline your ear to *mè and* **save** me.

3   *Be to* me a rock of **réf**uge, *
     a strong for*trèss, to* **save** me,

4   *For my* enemies speak con**cérn**ing me, *
     and those who watch for my life con*sùlt to***geth**er.

5   *They say,* "Pursue and seize that person whom God has for**sák**en, *
     for there is no one *tò de***liv**er."

6   *O God,* do not be **fár** from me; *
     O my God, make *hàste to* **help** me!

7   *Let my* accusers be put to shame and con**súmed;** *
     let those who seek to hurt me be covered with *scòrn and* **dis**grace.

8   *But I* will hope con**tín**ually, *
     and will praise *yòu yet* **more** and more.

9   *My mouth* will tell of your **ríght**eous acts, *
     of your deeds of sal*vàtion* **all** day long,

10   *All day* long my tongue will talk of your **ríght**eous help, *
     for those who tried to do me harm have been put to *shàme, and*
        disgraced.

Responsorial Psalm I D 1 g   **Psalm 22 (21V)**

(Cf. 19) 19a, 1, 6–8, 11, 15, 16c–17a, 22

93 ℣ 1 O my help, do not be **far** a - way!

℞ LORD,_____ come to my de - fense.

℣ 2 My God, my God, why have you for - sak - en me? * Why are you so far from help - ing me, ' from the words of my **groan** - ing?

℟ LORD, _____ come to my de - fense.

3   But I am a worm, and not **hú**man; *
scorned by others, and despised by the **peo**plè.

4   All who see me **móck** at me; *
they make mouths at me, they shake **their** hèads;

5   "Commit your cause to the LORD; let him de**lív**er— *
let him rescue the one in whom **he** dèlights!"

6   Do not be far from me, for trouble is **néar** *
and there is no one **to** hèlp.

7   my heart is like **wáx;** *
it is melted within **my** brèast;

8   my mouth is dried up like a potsherd, '
and my tongue sticks to my **jáws;** *
you lay me in the **dust** òf death.

9   My hands and feet have **shrív**eled; *
I can count **all** mỳ bones.

10   I will tell of your name to my brothers and **sís**ters; *
in the midst of the congregation I will **praise** yòu.

Responsorial Psalm II C *

Psalm 129 (128V)
(2a) 1, 3–8 (See Performance Notes)

94

℣ 1 "Of - ten have they at - tacked me *from my*

youth" * — let Is - ra - el **now** say—

℞ They have op- pressed me from my youth.

2 The plowers plowed *òn my* **back;** *
they made their **fur**ròws long."

3 The *LÒRD is* **right**eous; *
he has cut the cords of the **wick**èd.

4 May all *whò hate* **Zi**on *
be put to shame and turned **back**wàrd.

5 Let them be like the grass *òn the* **house**tops *
that withers before it **grows** ùp,

6 with which reapers do not *fill their* **hands** *
or binders of sheaves **their** àrms,

7 while those who pass by do not say, '
   "The blessing of the LORD *bè up***on** you! *
We bless you in the name of **the** LÒRD!"

Gospel Acclamation Antiphon

John 8:51

95 I f

Be - lieve me___ when I tell you this: *

if you keep my word,___ you will

nev - er taste__ death.

When the acclamation antiphon is used, at least one verse of one of the preceding responsorial psalms, which has not already been sung is added (see Performance Notes).

or Tract

Psalm 129 (128V)
1–5, 8b-c (See Performance Notes)

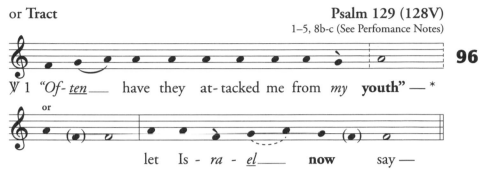

℣ 1 *"Of- ten* have they at- tacked me from *my* **youth"** — *

or

let Is - ra - *el* **now** say —

2 "often have they attacked me from *mỳ* **youth,** *
   yet they have not *prèvailed against* me.

3 The plowers plowed on *mỳ* **back;** *
   they made *their furrows* long."

4 The LORD *ìs* **right**eous; *
   he has cut the *còrds of the* **wick**ed.

5 May all who *hàte* **Zi**on *
   be put to shame *ànd turned* **back**ward.

6 "The blessing of the LORD be up*òn* **you!** *
   We bless you in *thè name* **of** the LORD!"

Preparation of the Gifts Antiphon

Cf. Psalm 43:1

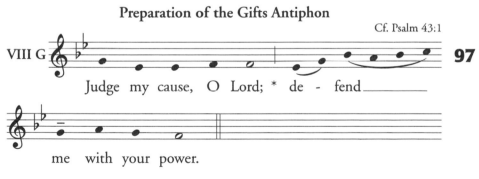

VIII G

Judge my cause, O Lord; * de - fend

me with your power.

Psalm 22 (21V)

1, 2, 20–21

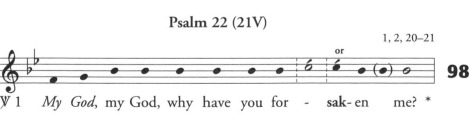

℣ 1 *My God,* my God, why have you for - sak- en me? *

Why are you so far from help-ing me, from the words

of my **groan** - ing?

2 *O my* God, I cry by day, but you do **nót** answer; *
and by *nìght, but* **find** no rest.

3 *Deliv*er my soul from the **swórd,** *
my life from the *pòwer* **of** the dog!

4 *Save me* from the mouth of the **líon!** *
From the horns of the wild oxen *yòu have* **res**cued me.

Communion Antiphon

Matthew 24:42

99 VIII c

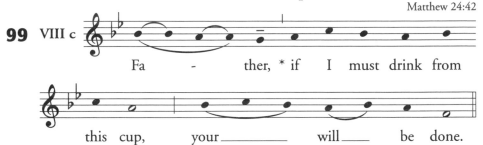

Fa - ther, * if I must drink from

this cup, your_____ will_____ be done.

Psalm 116 (115V)

10–19

100

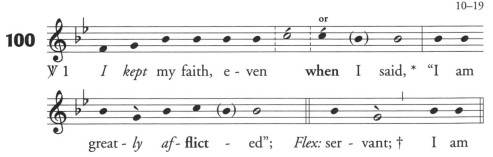

℣ 1 *I kept* my faith, e - ven **when** I said, * "I am

great - *ly af*- **flict** - ed"; *Flex:* ser - vant; † I am

2 *I said* in my conster**ná**tion, *
"Everyone *ìs a* **li**ar."

3 *What shall* I return to the **LÓRD** *
for all his *bòunty* **to** me?

<u>4</u>   *I will* lift up the cup of salvátion *
and call on the *nàme of* **the** LORD,

<u>5</u>   *I will* pay my vows to the **LÓRD** *
in the presence of *àll his* **peo**ple.

6   *Precious* in the sight of the **LÓRD** *
is the death *òf his* **faith**ful ones.

7   *O Lord,* I am your sèrvant; †
      I am your servant, the child of your **sérv**ing girl. *
Yòu have **loosed** my bonds.

8   *I will* offer to you a thanksgiving **sác**rifice *
and call on the *nàme of* **the** LORD.

9   *I will* pay my vows to the **LÓRD** *
in the presence of *àll his* **peo**ple,

10   *in the* courts of the house of the **LÓRD** *
in your midst, *Ò Jeru*salem.

The Communion Antiphon, *I will take the cup,* with its psalm (from Holy Thursday, **124, 125**) may be sung as an alternative.

Passion Sunday (Palm Sunday)

The Commemoration of the Lord's Entry into Jerusalem

Gathering Antiphon

As the presider and ministers approach the gathered assembly, the following antiphon and psalm is sung:

Matthew 21:9

101 VII a

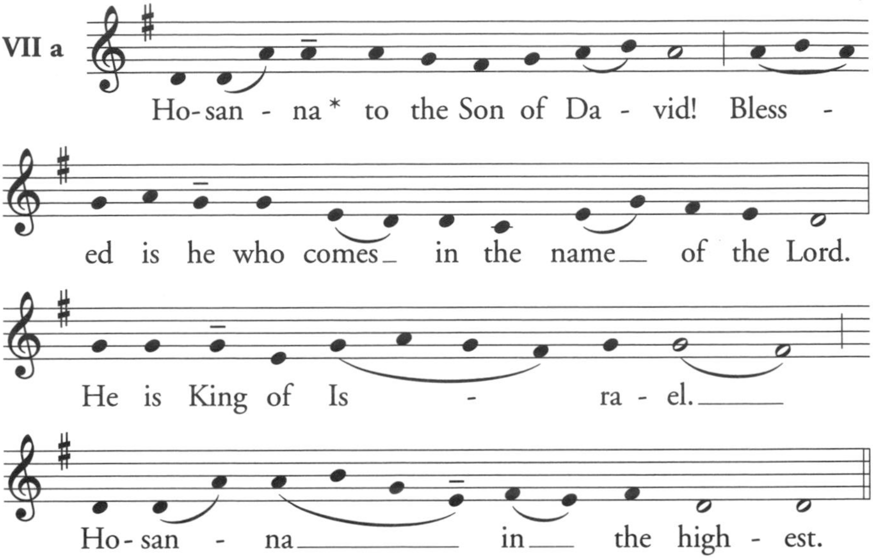

Ho-san - na * to the Son of Da - vid! Bless -

ed is he who comes_ in the name_ of the Lord.

He is King of Is - ra - el.___

Ho-san - na____ in__ the high - est.

Psalm 118 (117V)

1, 22–23, 27–28 (See Performance Notes)

102

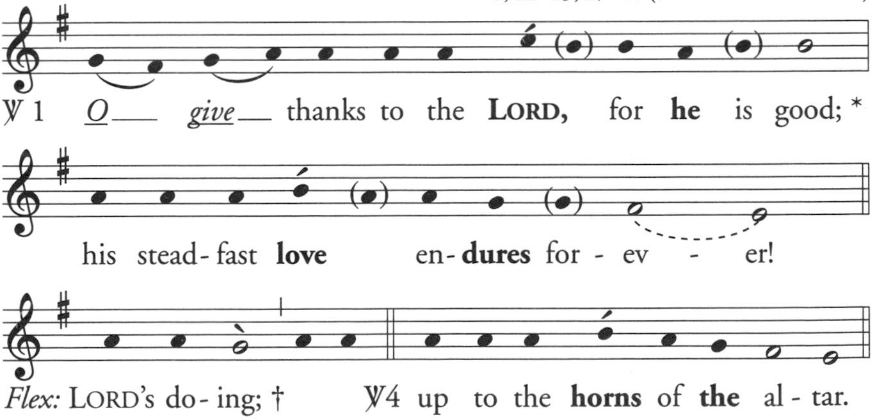

℣ 1 *O_ give_* thanks to the **LORD,** for **he** is good; *

his stead- fast **love** en- **dures** for - ev - er!

Flex: LORD's do- ing; †   ℣4 up to the **horns** of **the** al - tar.

2   *The* stone that the **búild**ers re**jec**ted *
has be**cóme** the chief **cor**nerstone.

3   *This is* the LORD's doìng; †
    it is **már**velous **in** our eyes. *
    The LORD is God, and he has **giv**en **us** light.

4   *Bind the* festal procéssion with **branches**, *
    up to the **hórns** of **the** altar.

5   *You are* my God, and Í will give **thanks** to you; *
    you are my God, I **wíll** ex**tol** you.

Procession

A deacon or the presider sings:

Let us go for-ward in peace.

All answer:

In the name of Christ. A - men.

103

Procession Antiphon I

John 12:13

If

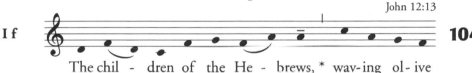

The chil - dren of the He - brews, * wav-ing ol-ive

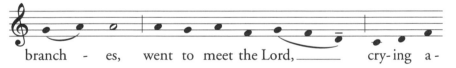

branch - es, went to meet the Lord,_____ cry-ing a-

loud:_____ Ho-san - na_____ in the high - est.

104

Psalm 24 (23V)

1–10

After the antiphon is repeated by all, the cantor(s) and choir sing each verse. The beginning of each verse is intoned.

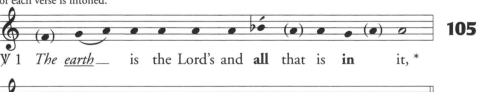

℣ 1 *The earth*___ is the Lord's and **all** that is **in** it, *

the world, and *those who* **live**___ in it;___

105

Flex: and pure hearts, †

2   *for he* has **fóund**ed it **on** the seas, *
    and established it *òn the* <u>riv</u>ers.

3   <u>*Who*</u> shall ascend the **híll** of the LORD? *
    And who shall stand *in his* <u>ho</u>ly <u>place</u>?

4   <u>*Those*</u> who have clean hands and pure hèarts, †
    who do not lift up their **sóuls** to **what** is false, *
    and do not *swèar de*<u>**ceit**</u>fu<u>lly</u>.

5   *They* <u>*will*</u> receive **bléss**ing **from** the LORD, *
    and vindication from the God of *thèir sal*<u>va</u>tion.

6   <u>*Such*</u> is the company of **thóse** who **seek** him, *
    who seek the face of the *Gòd of* <u>Ja</u>cob.

7   *Lift* <u>*up*</u> your heads, O gàtes! †
    and be lifted **úp**, O **an**cient doors! *
    that the King of glor*ỳ may* **come** in.

8   <u>*Who*</u> is the King of glorỳ? †
    The LORD, **stróng** and **migh**ty, *
    the LORD, migh*tỳ in* <u>**bat**</u>tle.

9   *Lift* <u>*up*</u> your heads, O gàtes! †
    and be lifted **úp**, O **an**cient doors! *
    that the King of glor*ỳ may* **come** in.

10 <u>*Who*</u> is this **Kíng** of glory? *
    The LORD of hosts, he is the *Kìng of* <u>**glo**</u>ry.

Procession Antiphon II

Matthew 21:9

106 I f

The He-brew peo-ple * spread their gar-ments on the

road and shout - ed, Ho-san-na to the Son of Da-vid:

Bless-ed is he who comes___ in the name_ of the Lord.

This antiphon may be repeated after each verse.

Psalm 47 (46V)

1–9 (See Performance Notes)

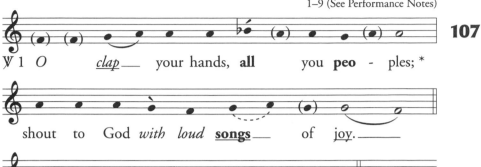

107

℣ 1 O *clap* your hands, **all** you **peo** - ples; *

shout to God *with loud* **songs** of joy.

℣3 and *na - tions* **un - der** our feet.

2 *For the LORD,* the Most **High,** is **awe**some, *
a great king *òver* **all** the earth.

3 *He sub<u>dued</u>* **péo**ples **un**der us, *
and *nàtions* **under** our feet.

4 *He chose* our **hér**itage **for** us, *
the pride of *Jàcob* **whom** he loves.

5 *God* has gone **úp** with **a** shout, *
the LORD with the sound *òf a* **trum**pet.

6 *Sing praises* to **Gód,** sing **prais**es; *
sing praises to our *Kìng, sing* **prais**es.

7 *For God* is the **kíng** of **all** the earth; *
sing *pràises* **with** a psalm.

8 *God is king* **ó**ver the **na**tions; *
God sits *òn his* **ho**ly throne.

9 *The prin*ces of the peoples gather as the people of the **Gód** of
Abraham. *
For the shields of the earth belong to God; he is high*ly* *ex*<u>al</u>ted.

According to the time available, sing the following hymn, repeating the refrain after every verse:

108 I

℟ Glo - ry and hon - or and praise— be to you, King Christ the Re - deem - er.

Chil - dren long a - go, in their— win - ning way,— raised their lov - ing cry:— "Ho - san - na."

℣ 1 Is - ra - el's King———— you— are,— and the glor - ious off - spring of Da - vid. You come, O King——— most— blessed,— in the Lord's— strong and ho - ly Name.

℣ 2 Glo - ry to you———— on——— high,——— the heav'n - ly con - gre - ga - tion is sing - ing;

glo - ry to you_____ here be - low_____

from your mor - tal chil-dren and all cre - at - ed things.

℣ 3 Your own be - lov - ed peo - ple___ came to

meet you with palms and ol-ive branch-es; now we are here__ be-

fore__ you,__ sing-ing hymns of praise and of- f'ring prayers.

℣ 4 They made their gift___ of praise to you___ on the

eve__ of__ your__ pas - sion; we sing our joy - ful

hymn to you,__ now re-joic - ing in heav - en.

℣ 5 As your own na - tion pleased you then,__ may our de-

vo - tion__ please you now. O King, so good,__ so

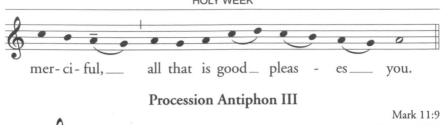

mer-ci-ful, ___ all that is good__ pleas - es__ you.

Procession Antiphon III

Mark 11:9

109

Ho-san-na in the high-est. Bless-ed is the one

who comes in the name of the LORD. _____

℟ Ho-san-na in the high - est.

Psalm 118 (117V)

26–29 (See Performance Notes)

110

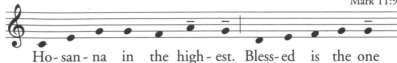

℣1 We bless you from the house *of* **the** LORD. ℟ Ho-san-na

in the high - est. ℣2 *The* LORD is God, ' and he has giv-

en **us** light. ℟ Ho - san - na in the high - est.

3   *Bind the* festal procession with branches, '
     up to the horns of *thè* **al**tar.

4   *You are* my God, and I will give thanks to you; '
     you are my God, I will *èx***tol** you.

5   *O give* thanks to the LORD, for he is good, '
     for his steadfast love endures *fore***ver**.

The rest of the chants for this liturgy are from the Fifth Sunday of Lent above, except for the Entrance Antiphon, which is omitted, as is the Penitential Rite. The Communion Antiphon to be sung is *Father, if I must drink from this cup*, **99**, with its psalm, **100**.

Holy Thursday

CHRISM MASS

Entrance Antiphon

Psalm 4:7

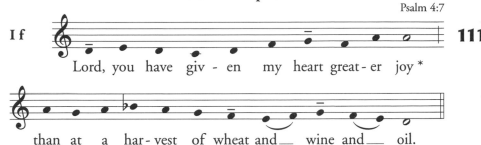

I f Lord, you have giv-en my heart great-er joy *

than at a har-vest of wheat and__ wine and__ oil.

111

Psalm 4

1–3, 5–6, 8 (See Performance Notes)

℣ 1 An-*swer*__ me when I call, O **God** of **my** right! *

112

You gave me room when *I was* **in**__ dis-tress. __

℣ 2 Be **gra**-cious **to** me, * *and* **hear**__ my prayer. __

3   *How long,* you people, shall my **hón**or **suf**fer shame? *
How long will you love vain *wòrds, and* **seek** after lies?

4   *But know* that the LORD has set apart the **fáithful for** himself; *
the LORD hears *whèn I* **call** to him.

5   Offer right **sác**rifices, *
and *pùt your* **trust** in the LORD.

6   *There are* many who say, "O **thát** we might **see** some good! *
Let the light of your face shine *òn us,* **O** LORD!"

7   *I will both* lie **dówn** and **sleep** in peace; *
for you alone, O LORD, make me lie *dòwn in* **safe**ty.

Responsorial Psalm I E 3 **Psalm 89 (88V)**
(Cf. 1a) 1a, 20–21, 24, 26 (See Performance Notes)

113

℣ 1 Of your stead-fast **love**, O LORD, ℟ I will sing— for ev - er.

℣ 2 "I have found my ser - vant **Da** - vid; *

with my ho - ly oil I have a - **noint**-ed him;

℟ I will sing— for ev - er.

3   my hand shall always re**main** with him; *
     my arm also shall **strèngth**en him.

4   My faithfulness and steadfast love shall **be** with him; *
     and in my name his horn shall be exàlted.

5   He shall cry to me, 'You are my **Fath**èr, *
     my God, and the Rock of my salvàtion!'"

Responsorial Psalm II C 2 g **Psalm 33 (32V)**
(1b) 1, 3, 5, 12–13, 18–22

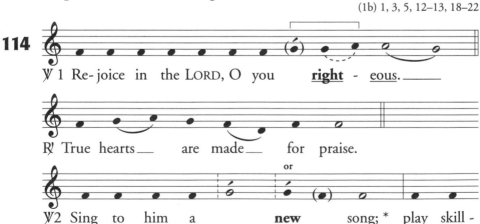

114

℣ 1 Re-joice in the LORD, O you **right** - eous.___

℟ True hearts___ are made___ for praise.

or

℣ 2 Sing to him a **new** song; * play skill -

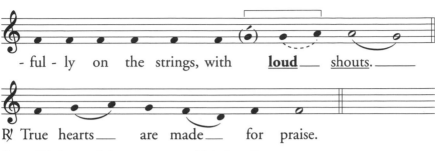

-ful - ly   on   the   strings, with   **loud** __ shouts. _____

℞ True hearts __ are made __ for   praise.

3   He loves righteousness and **jús**tice; *
    the earth is full of the steadfast love **óf the** LORD.

4   Happy is the nation whose God is the **LÓRD,** *
    the people whom he has chosen as his **hérit**age.

5   The LORD looks down from **héav**en; *
    he sees all **húman**kind.

6   Truly the eye of the LORD is on those who **féar** him, *
    on those who hope in his **stéadfast** love,

7   to deliver their soul from **déath,** *
    and to keep them alive in **fá**mine.

8   Our soul waits for the **LÓRD;** *
    he is our **hélp and** shield.

9   Our heart is **glád** in him, *
    because we trust in his **hóly** name.

10 Let your steadfast love, O LORD, be up**ón** us, *
    even as we **hópe in** you.

The Preparation of the Gifts

As the procession moves through the church, the schola or choir, with all the people answering, sing the hymn, *O Redeemer,* instead of the usual Preparation of the Gifts antiphon and psalm.

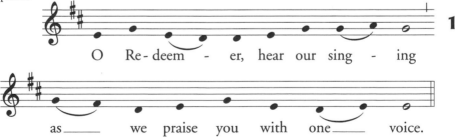

115

O   Re - deem - er,   hear   our   sing - ing

as __ we   praise   you   with   one __ voice.

All repeat *O Redeemer, hear …,* at this point and after each of the stanzas sung by the schola or choir.

1 Sun - light makes the ol - ive fruit - ful,
2 In your kind - ness, King im - mor - tal,
3 May all peo - ple, men and wom - en,
4 When our minds are cleansed by wa - ter,
5 Born of love of God the Fath - er,
6 May we keep this feast for - ev - er

1 From the fruit the___ oil___ is___ pressed;
2 con - se - crate this___ ol - ive___ oil:
3 Through this Chrism___ be___ made___ new,
4 Let our sins be___ put___ to___ flight;
5 Dwell - ing in the___ Vir - gin's___ womb,
6 As a ho - ly___ day___ of___ days;

1 Sav - ior___ of the___ gen - er - a - tions,
2 May it___ be a___ sign___ and___ safe - guard,
3 That the___ wound to___ their___ first___ glo - ry
4 When our___ fore - heads___ are___ a - noint - ed,
5 Give us___ light who___ share___ this___ Chrism; ___
6 May our___ hearts grow___ nev - er wear - y

1 Now___ we bring___ it___ to be___ blessed.
2 And___ the schemes___ of___ Sa - tan___ foil.
3 May___ be healed,___ O___ Lord, by___ you.
4 May___ we share___ your___ Spir - it's___ might.
5 Close___ the door___ of___ death's dark___ tomb.
6 As___ we sing___ its___ fit - ting___ praise.

Communion Antiphon

Psalm 45 (44V):7

VIII G

Jus- tice you love * and wick-ed-ness you hate: There- fore

God_ has a- noint- ed you _ with the oil of glad- ness.

116

Psalm 45 (44V)

1–6, 8, 16–17

℣ 1 *My heart* o - ver- flows with a good - ly theme; †

117

or

I ad - dress my vers - es to the **king;** *

my tongue is like the pen *of a* **read** - y scribe.

2 *You are* the most handsome of mèn; †
   grace is poured upon your **líps;** *
   therefore God has blessed *yòu fore*ver.

3 *Gird your* sword on your thigh, O **mígh**ty one, *
   in your glor*ỳ and* **maj**esty.

4 *In your* majesty ride on victoriously †
   for the cause of truth and to de**fénd** the right; *
   let your right hand *tèach you* **dread** deeds

5 *Your ar*rows are sharp in the heart of the king's **én**emies; *
   the peo*plès fall* **un**der you.

6 *Your throne,* O God, endures forever and **év**er. *
   Your royal scepter is a scep*tèr of* **eq**uity.

7 *Your robes* are all fragrant with myrrh and aloes and **cás**sia. *
   From ivory palaces stringed in*strùments* **make** you glad;

8 *In the* place of ancestors you, O king, shall have **sóns;** *
   you will make them princ*ès in* **all** the earth.

9 *I will* cause your name to be celebrated in all gener**á**tions; *
   therefore the peoples will praise you forev*èr and* **ev**er.

THE SACRED TRIDUUM OF THE PASSION AND RESURRECTION OF THE LORD

Evening Mass of the Lord's Supper

Entrance Antiphon

Galatians 6:14

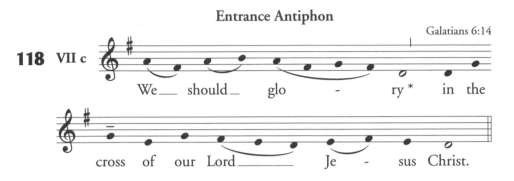

118 VII c

We should glo - ry * in the cross of our Lord Je - sus Christ.

Psalm 67 (66V)

1–7 (See Performance Notes)

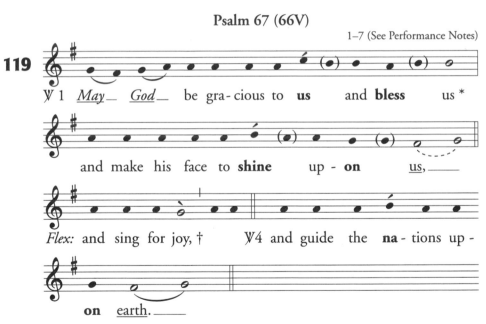

119

℣ 1 *May God* be gra-cious to **us** and **bless** us *

and make his face to **shine** up - **on** us, ___

Flex: and sing for joy, † ℣4 and guide the **na** - tions up -

on earth. ___

2 *that your* way may be **knówn** up**on** earth, *
   your saving power a**móng** all **na**tions.

3 *Let the* peoples **práise** you, **O** God; *
   let all the **péo**ples **praise** you.

4 *Let the* nations be glad and sing for jòy, †
   for you judge the **péo**ples with **equ**ity *
   and guide the **ná**tions up**on** earth.

5 *Let the* peoples **práise** you, **O** God; *
let all the **péo**ples praise <u>you</u>.

6 *The earth* has **yíeld**ed its **in**crease; *
God, our **Gód,** has **blessed** <u>us</u>.

<u>7</u> *May God* con**tí**nue to **bless** us; *
let all the ends of the **éarth** re**vere** <u>him</u>.

Or, as desired, the Entrance Antiphon *Priest forever,* **202.**

Responsorial Psalm I D *   Psalm 23 (22V)
                (2) 1, 2b–6 (See Performance Notes)

℣ 1 The LORD is my **shep** - herd, * I **shall** not want. ⎯

℟ In green⎯ pas-tures the LORD⎯⎯⎯ gives me rest.

℣ 2 He leads me be - side **still** wa - ters; *

he re - *stores*⎯ **my**⎯ soul.⎯

℟ In green⎯ pas-tures the LORD⎯⎯⎯ gives me rest.

120

3[1] He leads me in right **páths** *
for his **nàme's** <u>sake</u>.

4 Even though I walk through the darkest **vál**ley, *
I *féar* **no** evil;

5 for you are **wíth** me; *
your rod and your staff—they **com**fort <u>me</u>.

6 You prepare a table be**fóre** me *
in the presence *óf my* **en**<u>emies</u>;

[1] Odd numbered verses are chanted on the first chanting note (do); even numbered verses,
on the second chanting note (sol).

7   you anoint my head with **óil;** *
my cup ovèr<u>flows</u>.

8   Surely goodness and mercy shall **fól**low me *
all the _dáys_ **of** my <u>life</u>,

9   and I shall dwell in the house of the **LÓRD** *
my **whole** life <u>long</u>.

Responsorial Psalm II

Psalm 145 (144V) _I will extol you,_ with ℟ _I will bless your name,_ **204.**

The Washing of the Feet

Antiphon

John 13:14

121 **III a**

A new com- mand- ment I give you: * Love one

an - oth - er as I have loved___ you.

Psalm 119 (118V)
1, 15, 32, 40, 45, 47, 97, 103, 105, 129 (See Performance Notes)

122

℣ 1   _Hap_ - py are those whose **way** is **blame -**

less, * who walk in the law _of_ **the** LORD.___

℣ 7 Oh, **how** I **love** <u>your</u>___ law! *

2   _I will_ meditate **ón** your **pre**cepts, *
and fix my eyes _òn your_ <u>ways</u>.

3   _I run_ the way of **yóur** com**mand**ments, *
for you enlarge _mỳ_ **un**derstanding.

4   *See,* I have **lónged** for your **pre**cepts; *
    in your righteous*nèss* **give** me <u>life</u>.

5   *I shall* **wálk** at **liber**ty, *
    for I *hàve* **sought** your precepts.

6   *I find* my delight in **yóur** com**mand**ments, *
    because *I* **love** <u>them</u>.

7   Oh, **hów** I **love your** law! *
    It is my medita*tìon* **all** day <u>long</u>.

8   *How <u>sweet</u>* are your **wórds** to **my** taste, *
    sweeter than honey *tò* **my** <u>mouth</u>!

9   *Your <u>word</u>* is a **lámp** to **my** feet *
    and a light *tò* **my** <u>path</u>.

10 *<u>Your</u>* de**crées** are **wonder**ful; *
    therefore *mỳ* **soul** keeps <u>them</u>.

The Liturgy of the Eucharist

During the procession with the gifts, the following chant is sung in the place of the antiphon and psalm for the preparation of the gifts:

Ubi Caritas

The chant is sung thus: The antiphon *Where we live as friends* is sung in its entirety by the cantors and then is repeated by all. Depending on circumstances, the entire chant may be sung by all. It may also be divided between two choirs singing responsorially or between the cantors and the choir singing responsorially. Whenever the antiphon is repeated, it is to be sung by all.

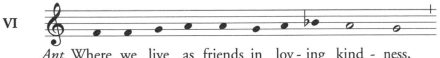

VI   *Ant.* Where we live as friends in lov - ing kind - ness,

123

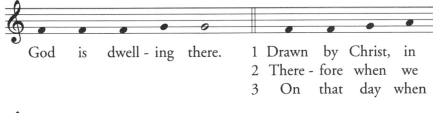

God is dwell - ing there.

1 Drawn by Christ, in
2 There - fore when we
3 On that day when

1 love we meet to - geth - er in his great name.
2 con - gre - gate to - geth - er to break the bread,
3 we will meet in heav - en with all the blessed,

1 Let us then re - joice and give the Fa - ther glo - ry
2 Let us then be care - ful lest dis - sent or quar - rels
3 May our glo - ry be to look up - on your face, ___

1 as he de - serves. Let us u - nite in
2 drive us a - part. Let all mis - un - der -
3 O Christ our God. So may we all par -

1 rev - 'rent love to wor - ship the liv - ing God.
2 stand-ing now be end - ed, all fight - ing cease.
3 take of heav-en's glo - ry, joy un - sur-passed,

1 And let us live our love for one an - oth - er with
2 And may the Lord ___ Christ, our God, now come ___ and
3 The gift of per - fect peace and bound-less love ___ to-

1 hearts ___ that are ___ sin - cere. *(to Antiphon)*
2 make ___ his dwell-ing with us. *(to Antiphon)*
3 geth-er for ev - er. A - men. ___

Communion Antiphon

Psalm 116 (115V):13

124 II D

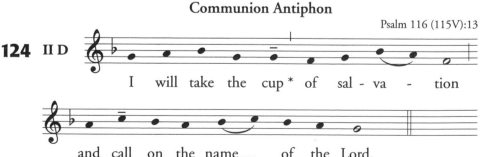

I will take the cup * of sal - va - tion

and call on the name ___ of the Lord.

Psalm 116 (115V)

10–12, 14–19

℣ 1 *I* *kept* my faith, e-ven when I **said,** *

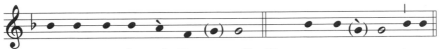

"I am great-ly *af-* **flict** - ed"; *Flex:* your ser - vant; †

2 *I said* in my conster**ná**tion, *
   "Everyone is *à* **li**ar."

3 *What shall* I return to the **LÓRD** *
   for all his boun*tỳ* **to** me?

4 *I will* pay my vows to the **LÓRD** *
   in the presence of all *hìs* **peo**ple.

5 *Precious* in the sight of the **LÓRD** *
   is the death of *hìs* **faith**ful ones.

6 *O LORD,* I am your ser**vànt;** †
      I am your servant, the child of your **sérv**ing girl. *
   You *hàve* **loosed** my bonds.

7 *I will* offer to you a thanksgiving **sá**crifice *
   and call on the name *òf* **the** LORD.

8 *I will* pay my vows to the **LÓRD** *
   in the presence of all *hìs* **peo**ple,

9 *in the* courts of the house of the **LÓRD** *
   in your midst, O *Jè*ru**sa**lem.

Transfer of the Holy Eucharist

During the procession, the following may be sung:

III

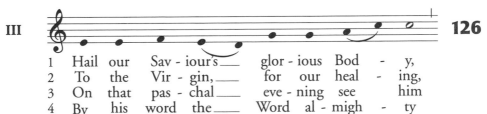

126

1 Hail our   Sav - iour's___   glor - ious Bod - y,
2 To   the   Vir - gin, ___   for   our   heal - ing,
3 On   that pas - chal___   eve - ning see   him
4 By   his   word the___   Word al - migh - ty

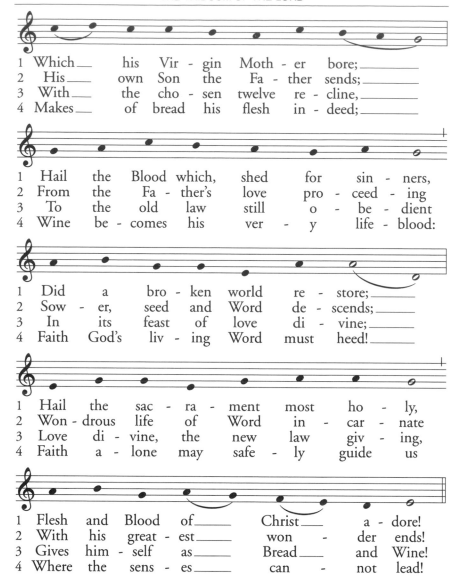

1 Which___ his Vir - gin Moth - er bore;___
2 His___ own Son the Fa - ther sends;___
3 With___ the cho - sen twelve re - cline,___
4 Makes___ of bread his flesh in - deed;___

1 Hail the Blood which, shed for sin - ners,
2 From the Fa - ther's love pro - ceed - ing
3 To the old law still o - be - dient
4 Wine be - comes his ver - y life - blood:

1 Did a bro - ken world re - store;___
2 Sow - er, seed and Word de - scends;___
3 In its feast of love di - vine;___
4 Faith God's liv - ing Word must heed!___

1 Hail the sac - ra - ment most ho - ly,
2 Won - drous life of Word in - car - nate
3 Love di - vine, the new law giv - ing,
4 Faith a - lone may safe - ly guide us

1 Flesh and Blood of___ Christ___ a - dore!
2 With his great - est___ won - der ends!
3 Gives him - self as___ Bread___ and Wine!
4 Where the sens - es___ can - not lead!

When the procession reaches the place of reposition, the hymn *Down in Adoration Falling*, **648**, is then sung. It is also permitted to sing another eucharistic hymn in the place of the foregoing hymn.

78

Good Friday
Celebration of the Lord's Passion
Part I: Liturgy of the Word

Responsorial Psalm after the First Reading C 3 a Psalm 31 (30V)
(5a) 1, 5, 9, 11–12, 14–16

127

℣ 1 In you, O LORD, I seek ref- uge; ' do not let me ev- er be

or

put to shame; * in your right-eous- ness de - **liv** - er me.

℟ Fa- ther, I put my life ___ in - to your ___ hands. ___

℣2 In - to **your** ___ hand I com-mit my **spir** - it; *

you have re - deemed me, O *LORD*, **faith - ful** ___ God.

℟ Fa- ther, I put my life ___ in - to your ___ hands. ___

3¹ Be gracious to me, O **LORD,** *
    for I am **ín dís**tress;

4 **I** am the scorn of all my adversaries, '
    a horror to my **nèigh**bors, *
    an object of dread to my *àc***quain**tances;

5 I have passed out of mind like one who is **déad;** *
    I have become like a broken **vés**sel.

6 But I **trust** in **yòu,** O LORD; *
    I say, "*Yòu* **are my** God."

¹ Odd numbered verses are chanted on the first chanting note (fa); even numbered verses, on the second chanting note (la).

79

7 My times are in your **hánd;** *
deliver me from the hand of my enemies and perse**cú**tors.

8 Let your **face** shine upon your **sèr**vant; *
save me in *yòur* **steadfast** love.

Responsorial Psalm after the Second Reading

Psalm 43 (42V) *Vindicate me, O God* with ℟ *My Savior and my God,* **232.**

Part II: Veneration of the Cross
Unveiling of the Cross

128

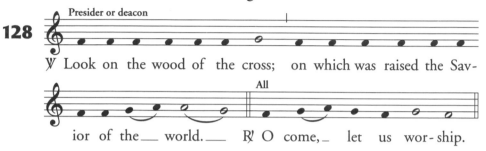

℣ Look on the wood of the cross; on which was raised the Sav-
ior of the __ world. __ ℟ O come, __ let us wor-ship.

This is sung three times; the presider or deacon raises the pitch each time.

Veneration of the Cross

129 IV A

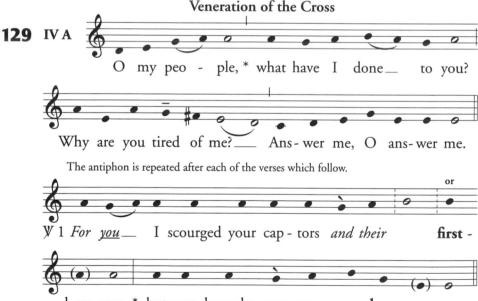

O my peo - ple, * what have I done __ to you?
Why are you tired of me? __ Ans-wer me, O ans-wer me.

The antiphon is repeated after each of the verses which follow.

℣ 1 *For you* __ I scourged your cap - tors *and their* **first** -
born sons, * but you brought *your scourg - es* **down** on me.

2 *I led* you from slavery to freedom and drowned your captors
in the **sea,** *
but you handed me *òver to* **your** high priests.

3   *I opened the sèa befòre* you, *
        but you opened *mỳ side with* **a** spear.

4   *I lèd* you on your way in a pil*làr of* **cloud,** *
        but you *lèd me to* **Pi**late's court.

5   *I bòre* you up with manna *ìn the* **des**ert, *
        but you struck *mè down and* **scourged** me.

6   *I gàve* you saving water *fròm the* **rock,** *
        but you gave me gall *ànd vine***gar** to drink.

7   *For yòu* I struck down the *kìngs of* **Can**aan, *
        but you *strùck my head* **with** a reed.

8   *I gàve* you a *ròyal* **scep**ter, *
        but you *gàve me a* **crown** of thorns.

9   *I ràised* you to the *hèight of* **maj**esty, *
        but you have *ràised me high* **on** a cross.

Then the following antiphon is sung:

IV E   Your cross, O Lord, * we wor - ship; your res - ur - rec - tion we praise and glo - ri - fy;___ through the wood of the cross joy has come_ to all__ the world.   **130**

Ps. 67 (66V):2 May God__ be gra-cious to us and bless us * and make his face to shine___ up - on___ us.

The antiphon is then repeated.

Part III: Holy Communion

While the Blessed Sacrament is being carried to the altar, all are silent. Appropriate songs may be sung during the distribution of communion.

The Easter Vigil

VIGIL OF THE LORD'S RESURRECTION

Part II: Liturgy of the Word

Responsorial Psalm I(A) C *   Psalm 104 (103V)
                                                    (Cf. 30) 1–2a, 5–6, 10, 12–14, 24, 35bc

131

℣ 1 Bless the LORD, O my soul. * O LORD my God,

you are **ver**-y great. ℟ Lord, send out your Spir - it,

and re-new the face of the earth.

2   You are clothed with honòr *and* **maj**esty, *
     wrapped in light as with a **gar**mènt.

<u>3</u>   You set the earth on *its found*ations, *
     so that it shall never be **shak**èn.

4   You cover it with the deep as *with a* **gar**ment; *
     the waters stood above the **moun**tàins.

<u>5</u>   You make springs gush forth *in the* **val**leys; *
     they flow bet**ween** thè hills,

<u>6</u>   By the streams the birds of the air have their *hàbi*tation; *
     they sing among the **branch**ès.

7   From your lofty abode you wat*èr the* **moun**tains; *
     the earth is satisfied with the fruit of **your** wòrk.

8   You cause the grass to grow for the cattle, '
        and plants for peo*plè to* **use,** *
     to bring forth food from **the** èarth,

9   O LORD, how manifold are your works! '
        In wisdom you have *màde them* **all;** *
     the earth is full of your **crea**tùres. *

<u>10</u>   Bless the LORD, *Ò my* **soul.***
     Praise thè LORD!

82

Responsorial Psalm I(B) E 1 **Psalm 33 (32V)**
(5b) 4–7, 12–13, 20–22

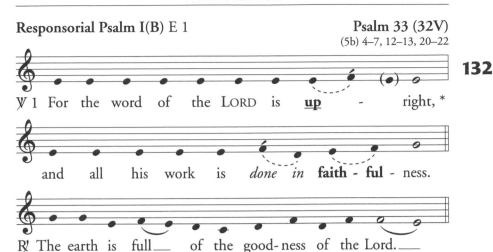

132

℣ 1 For the word of the LORD is **up** - right, *
and all his work is *done in* **faith - ful** - ness.

℟ The earth is full___ of the good-ness of the Lord.___

2 He loves righteousness and **jús**tice; *
the earth is full of the steadfast *lóve* **of the** LORD.

3 By the word of the LORD the heavens **wére** made, *
and all their host by the *bréath* **of his** mouth.

4 He gathered the waters of the sea as in a **bót**tle; *
he put the deeps in *stóre***hous**es.

5 Happy is the nation whose God **is thé** LORD, *
the people whom he has chosen as *hís* **heri**tage.

6 The LORD looks down from **héav**en; *
he sees *áll* **human**kind.

7 Our soul waits **for thé** LORD; *
he is our *hélp* **and** shield.

8 Our heart is **glád** in him, *
because we trust in his *hó***ly** name.

9 Let your steadfast love, O LORD, be up**ón** us, *
even as we *hópe* **in** you.

Responsorial Psalm II D 1 e **Psalm 16 (15V)**
(1) 5, 8–11(See Performance Notes)

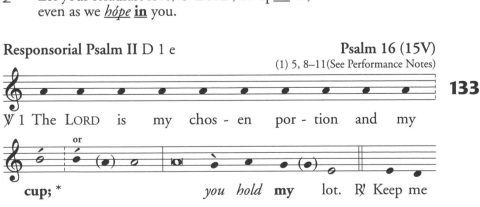

133

℣ 1 The LORD is my chos - en por - tion and my
cup; * *you hold* **my** lot. ℟ Keep me

safe, O God,___ you___ are my hope.

2   I keep the LORD always be**fóre** me; *
    because he is at my right hand, *I shall* **not** be moved.

3   Therefore my heart is glad, '
        and my soul re**jói**ces; *
    my body *also* **rests** secure.

4   For you do not give me up to **Shé**ol, *
    or let your faith*ful one* **see** the Pit.

5   You show me the path of life. '
        In your presence there is fullness of **jóy;** *
    in your right hand are plea*sùres* **fo**revermore.

Responsorial Psalm III E 3   **Canticle of Moses**

Exodus 15: (1b) 1b–4a, 8–10, 21(See Performance Notes)

134

℣ 1 I will sing to the LORD, for he has tri-umphed **glo**- rious-

ly; * horse and rid- er he has thrown in - to **the** sea.

℟ Let us sing to the Lord in his glo - rious tri- umph.

2   The LORD is my strength and **my** mìght, *
    and he has become my sal**và**tion;

3   this is my God, and I will **praise** hìm, *
    my father's God, and I will ex**à**lt him.

4   The LORD is a warrior; '
        the LORD is **his** nàme. *
    "Pharaoh's chariots and his army he cast into **thè** sea;

5   At the blast of your nostrils the waters piled up, '
        the floods stood up in **a** hèap; *
    the deeps congealed in the heart of **thè** sea.

6   The enemy said, 'I will pursue, I will overtake, I will divide
      the spoil, '
      my desire shall have its **fill** òf them. *
    I will draw my sword, my hand shall de**stròy** them.'

7   You blew with your wind, the sea **cov**èred them; *
    they sank like lead in the mighty **wà**ters.

8   Sing to the LORD, for he has triumphed **glor**ìously; *
    horse and rider he has thrown into **thè** sea.

Responsorial Psalm IV D 1 e   **Psalm 30 (29V)**
                                          (1) 1, 3–5, 10, 11a and 12b

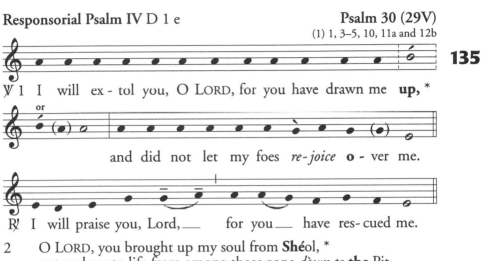

℣ 1 I will ex-tol you, O LORD, for you have drawn me **up,** *

         and did not let my foes *re-joice* **o** - ver me.

℟ I will praise you, Lord, ___ for you ___ have res-cued me.

2   O LORD, you brought up my soul from **Shé**ol, *
    restored me to life from among those gone *dòwn* to **the** Pit.

3   Sing praises to the LORD, O you his **fáith**ful ones, *
    and give thanks *tò his* **ho**ly name.

4   For his anger is but for a **mó**ment; *
    his favor is *fòr a* **life**time.

5   Weeping may linger for the **níght,** *
    but joy comes *wìth the* **morn**ing.

6   Hear, O LORD, and be gracious to **mé!** *
    O LORD, *bè my* **help**er!"

7   You have turned my mourning into **dán**cing; *
    O LORD my God, I will give thanks to *yòu fore*ever.

Responsorial Psalm V(A) C *   **Canticle of Isaiah**
                                                  Isaiah (12:3) 12:2–6

℣ 1 Sure-ly God is *my sal-* **va** - tion; *   I will

trust, and will not be a - fraid, ℟ You will draw wa-

ter joy-ful-ly from the springs of sal-va - tion.

2   for the LORD GOD is my strength *ànd my* **might;** *
he has become my sal**vat**ion.

3   With joy you *will draw* **wa**ter *
from the wells of sal**vat**ion.

4   And you will say in that day: '
    Give thanks *tò the* **LORD,** *
call on **his** nàme;

5   make known his deeds a*mòng the* **na**tions; *
proclaim that his name is ex**alt**èd.

6   Sing praises to the LORD, '
    for he *hàs done* **glo**riously; *
let this be known in **all** thè earth.

7   Shout aloud and sing for joy, O *ròyal* **Zi**on, *
for great in your midst is the Holy One of **Is**ràel.

Responsorial Psalm V(B) C *   **Canticle of Isaiah**
                                                Isaiah (5:7a) 5:1–7a

137

℣ 1 Let me sing for *my be-* **lov** - ed * my love-

song con-cern-ing his **vine** - yard: ℟ The vine-yard

of the Lord is the house_ of Is - ra - el._

2   My beloved had a vineyard on a very fertile hill. '
    He dug it and cleared *ìt of* **stones,** *
and planted it with **choice** vìnes;

3   he built a watchtower *ìn the* **midst** of it, *
and hewed out a wine vat **in** ìt;

4   he expected it *tò yield* **grapes,** *
but it yielded **wild** gràpes.

5   And now, inhabitants of Jerusalem and peo*plè of* **Ju**dah, *
judge between me and my **vine**yàrd.

6   What more was there to do for my vineyard that I *hàve not* **done**
       in it? *
When I expected it to yield grapes, why did it yield **wild** gràpes?

7   And now I will tell you what I will do to my vineyard. '
       I will remove its hedge, and it shall *bè de*voured; *
I will break down its wall, and it shall be **tram**plèd down.

8   I will make it a waste; '
       it shall not be *prùned or* **hoed,** *
and it shall be overgrown with briers **and** thòrns;

9   I will also com*mànd the* **clouds** *
that they rain no rain up**on** ìt.

10   For the vineyard of the *LÒRD of* **hosts** *
is the house of Is**ra**èl.

Responsorial Psalm VI(A) E 4   **Psalm 19 (18V)**
                                       (John 6:68) 7–10

℣1 The law of the LORD **is** per-fect, * re - viv- ing **the** soul;

℟ Lord, you have the words of ev - er - last - ing life.

2   the decrees of the LORD **àre** sure, *
making wise **thè** simple;

3   the precepts of the LORD **àre** right, *
rejoicing **thè** heart;

4   the commandment of the LORD **ìs** clear, *
enlightening **thè** eyes;

5   the fear of the LORD **ìs** pure, *
enduring for**è**ver;

6   the ordinances of the LORD **àre** true *
and righteous alto**gèth**er.

7   More to be desired are they **thàn** gold, *
even much **fìne** gold;

8   sweeter also **thàn** honey, *
and drippings of the **hòn**eycomb.

Responsorial Psalm VI(B) C 2 g **Canticle of Moses**
Deuteronomy 32: (Cf. 3) 1–2a, 3–4a, 8a and c, 9–12

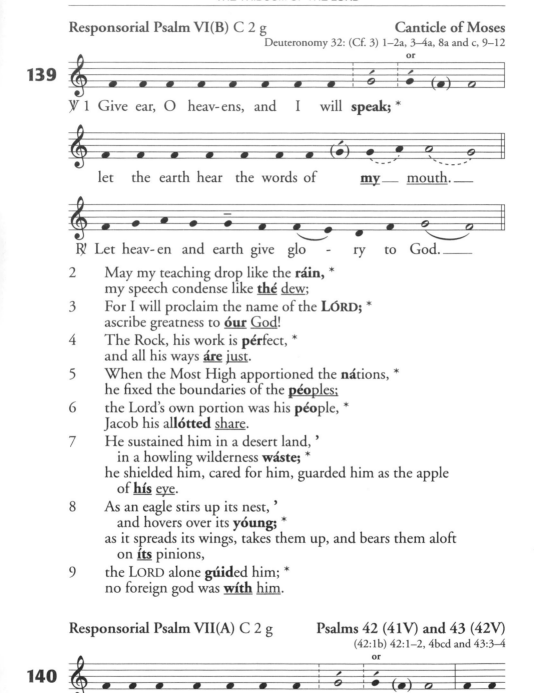

℣ 1 Give ear, O heav-ens, and I will **speak;** *
let the earth hear the words of **my** mouth.

℟ Let heav-en and earth give glo - ry to God.

2   May my teaching drop like the **ráin,** *
    my speech condense like **thé** dew;

3   For I will proclaim the name of the **LÓRD;** *
    ascribe greatness to **óur** God!

4   The Rock, his work is **pér**fect, *
    and all his ways **áre** just.

5   When the Most High apportioned the **ná**tions, *
    he fixed the boundaries of the **péo**ples;

6   the Lord's own portion was his **péo**ple, *
    Jacob his al**lótted** share.

7   He sustained him in a desert land, '
      in a howling wilderness **wáste;** *
    he shielded him, cared for him, guarded him as the apple
      of **hís** eye.

8   As an eagle stirs up its nest, '
      and hovers over its **yóung;** *
    as it spreads its wings, takes them up, and bears them aloft
      on **íts** pinions,

9   the LORD alone **gúid**ed him; *
    no foreign god was **wíth** him.

Responsorial Psalm VII(A) C 2 g **Psalms 42 (41V) and 43 (42V)**
(42:1b) 42:1–2, 4bcd and 43:3–4

℣ 1 As a deer longs for flow-ing **streams,** * so my

soul longs for **you**, **O** ___ God. ___ ℞ My soul ___
is long-ing for you, ___ O ___ God. ___

2 My soul thirsts for God, for the **lí**ving God. *
   When shall I come and behold the **fáce of** God?

3 I went with the throng, '
       and led them in procession to the **hóuse** of God, *
   with glad shouts and songs of thanksgiving, a multitude
       keeping **fésti**val.

4 O send out your light and your **trúth;** *
   let them **léad** me;

5 let them bring me to your holy **híll** *
   and to your **dwéll**ing.

6 Then I will go to the altar of **Gód,** *
   to God my ex**céed**ing joy;

7 and I will praise you with the **hárp,** *
   O **Gód, my** God.

Responsorial Psalm VII(B) D 1 g   Psalm 51 (50V)
                                                        (10) 10–13,16–17

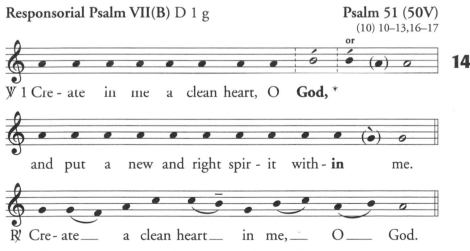

℣ 1 Cre-ate in me a clean heart, O **God,** *

and put a new and right spir-it with-**in** me.

℞ Cre-ate ___ a clean heart ___ in me, ___ O ___ God.

2 Do not cast me away from your **prés**ence, *
   and do not take your holy spirit **from** mè.

3   Restore to me the joy of your salvátion, *
     and sustain in me a willing **spir**ìt.

4   Then I will teach transgressors your **wáys,** *
     and sinners will re**turn** tò you.

5   For you have no delight in sacrifice; '
       if I were to give a burnt **óf**fering, *
     you would not **be** plèased.

6   The sacrifice acceptable to God is a broken **spí**rit; *
     a broken and contrite heart, O God, you will **not** dèspise.

After the final reading from the Hebrew Scriptures with its psalm response, the hymn *Glory to God in the highest* is sung.

After the reading from the Letter to the Romans, the psalmist sings:

142

Al-le-lu-ia, al-le-lu - ia, al-le - lu - ia.____

which is repeated by all. (This may be sung three times, the psalmist raising the pitch each time.) Then the psalmist continues:

Alleluia Psalm   **Psalm 118 (117V)**
                                                            1–4 (See Performance Notes)

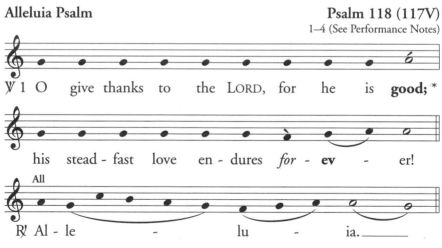

℣ 1 O give thanks to the LORD, for he is **good;** *

his stead - fast love en - dures *for* - **ev** - er!

All

℟ Al - le - lu - ia.____

2   Let Israel **sáy,** *
     "His steadfast love endures *fore*ver."

3   Let the house of Aaron **sáy,** *
     "His steadfast love endures *fore*ver."

4   Let those who fear the LORD **sáy,** *
     "His steadfast love endures *fore*ver."

The Litany of the Saints

The litany is chanted by two cantors. All stand (because it is the Easter season) and respond.

If there are none to be baptized and if the font is not to be blessed, the litany is omitted and the liturgy proceeds to the antiphon, *Springs of water,* **144.**

The names of other saints (for example, patrons of the place, titular saints of churches, and patrons of those who are to be baptized) and petitions suitable to the occasion may be added to the litany in the appropriate places (consult the Litany for Solemn Occasions, p. 404, for an indication of these places).

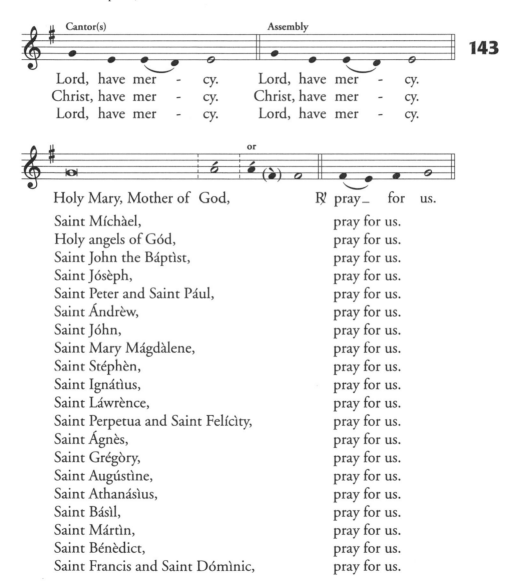

143

Lord, have mer - cy.	Lord, have mer - cy.
Christ, have mer - cy.	Christ, have mer - cy.
Lord, have mer - cy.	Lord, have mer - cy.

or

Holy Mary, Mother of God,	℟ pray for us.
Saint Míchàel,	pray for us.
Holy angels of Gód,	pray for us.
Saint John the Báptìst,	pray for us.
Saint Jósèph,	pray for us.
Saint Peter and Saint Pául,	pray for us.
Saint Ándrèw,	pray for us.
Saint Jóhn,	pray for us.
Saint Mary Mágdàlene,	pray for us.
Saint Stéphèn,	pray for us.
Saint Ignátìus,	pray for us.
Saint Láwrènce,	pray for us.
Saint Perpetua and Saint Felícìty,	pray for us.
Saint Ágnès,	pray for us.
Saint Grégòry,	pray for us.
Saint Augústìne,	pray for us.
Saint Athanásìus,	pray for us.
Saint Básìl,	pray for us.
Saint Mártìn,	pray for us.
Saint Bénèdict,	pray for us.
Saint Francis and Saint Dómìnic,	pray for us.

Saint Francis Xávìer,	pray for us.
Saint John Mary Viánnèy,	pray for us.
Saint Cáthèrine,	pray for us.
Saint Terésà,	pray for us.
All holy men and wómèn,	pray for us.

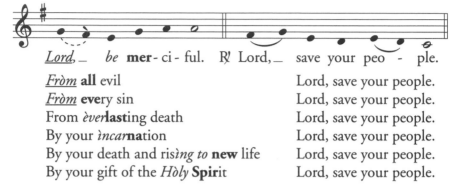

Lord, __ *be* **mer**-ci-ful. ℟ Lord, __ save your peo - ple.

Fròm **all** evil	Lord, save your people.
Fròm **eve**ry sin	Lord, save your people.
From *èver***last**ing death	Lord, save your people.
By your *ìncar***na**tion	Lord, save your people.
By your death and ris*ìng to* **new** life	Lord, save your people.
By your gift of the *Hòly* **Spir**it	Lord, save your people.

Lord, be merci - *ful* **to** us. ℟ Lord, hear our prayer.

If there are candidates to be baptized:

Give new life to these chosen ones by the *gràce* **of** baptism,	Lord, hear our prayer.
(Give new life to these chosen ones by the grace of baptism ' and pour out your Ho*lý* **Spir**it,	Lord, hear our prayer.)
(Give new life to these chosen ones by the grace of baptism, ' pour out your Spirit, ' and feed them with your Bod*ý* **and** Blood,	Lord, hear our prayer.)

If there is no one to be baptized:

By your grace bless this font where your children *wìll* **be** reborn,	Lord, hear our prayer.
Jesus, Son of *thè* **liv**ing God,	Lord, hear our prayer.

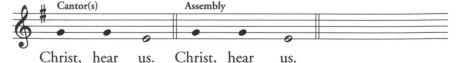

Cantor(s)   Assembly

Christ, hear us. Christ, hear us.

Lord Je-sus, hear our prayer. Lord Je-sus, hear our prayer.

After the renewal of baptismal promises, the presider sprinkles the whole assembly with the blessed baptismal water, while all sing:

Antiphon
Cf. Daniel 3:77–79 and 3:57 (See Performance Notes)

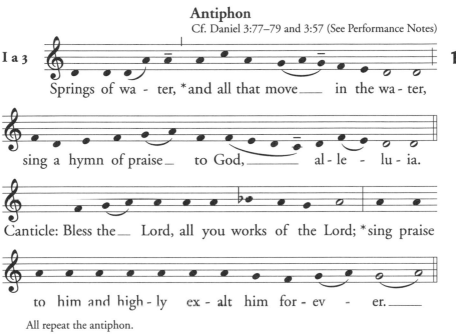

144

Springs of wa - ter, *and all that move___ in the wa - ter,

sing a hymn of praise_ to God,_____ al - le - lu - ia.

Canticle: Bless the_ Lord, all you works of the Lord; *sing praise

to him and high - ly ex - alt him for - ev - er.___

All repeat the antiphon.

The profession of faith is omitted.

Preparation of the Gifts Antiphon
Psalm 118 (117V):16

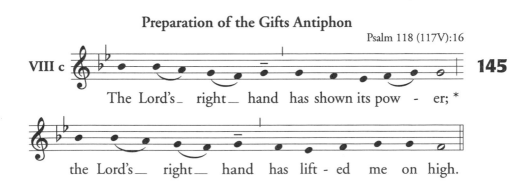

145

The Lord's_ right_ hand has shown its pow - er; *

the Lord's_ right_ hand has lift - ed me on high.

Psalm 118 (117V)

21–23, 27b

146 ℣ 1 *I thank* you that you have **an** - swered me *

and have be - come *my sal* - **va** - tion.

2   *The stone* that the builders re**jéc**ted *
    has become *thè chief* **cor**nerstone.

3   *This is* the **Lórd's** doing; *
    it is mar*vèlous* **in** our eyes.

4   *Bind the* festal procession with **bránch**es, *
    up to the horns *òf the* **al**tar.

For the Communion Procession Song, see the antiphon *Alleluia,* **156,** with Psalm 105 (104V), *O give thanks to the Lord,* **157.**

At the dismissal, all respond to the greeting of the deacon or presider with the following:

147 Thanks   be   to   God,   al - le - lu - ia,
        Or: De - *o grá* - *ti* - *as.*

al - le - lu - ia.____

Easter Sunday

MASS DURING THE DAY

Entrance Song

Cantor
Al - le - lu - ia.___ This is the day the Lord has made— ℟ Al - le - lu - ia—

Schola/Choir or All **Cantor**
let us re - joice and be glad.

All
℟ Al - le - lu - ia, al - le - lu - ia.

℣2 Al - le - lu - ia.___ The stone has been rolled a - way— ℟ Al - le - lu - ia— from the door of the tomb.

℟ Al - le - lu - ia, al - le - lu - ia.

℣3 Al - le - lu - ia.___ They have tak - en a - way my Lord,— ℟ Al - le - lu - ia— and I know not where they have laid___ him. ℟ Al - le - lu - ia, al - le - lu - ia.

℣4 Al - le - lu - ia.___ Ma - ry, why do you seek—

℟ Al - le - lu - ia— the liv - ing Christ a - mong the dead?

℟ Al - le - lu - ia, al - le - lu - ia.

℣5 Al - le - lu - ia.___ Ma - ry, do not weep;—

℟ Al - le - lu - ia— The Lord has ris - en a - gain.

℟ Al - le - lu - ia, al - le - lu - ia.

℣6 Al - le - lu - ia.___ He who hung up - on the cross—

℟ Al - le - lu - ia— has ris - en from the grave.

℟ Al - le - lu - ia, al - le - lu - ia.

℣7 Al - le - lu - ia.___ Tell us, Ma - ry,—

℟ Al - le - lu - ia— what did you see on your way?

℟ Al - le - lu - ia, al - le - lu - ia.

℣8 Al - le - lu - ia.___ I saw two an - gels robed in white,— ℟ Al - le - lu - ia— and I saw the shroud.

℟ Al - le - lu - ia, al - le - lu - ia.

℣9 Al - le - lu - ia.___ Christ my hope has ris - en;—

℟ Al - le - lu - ia— He goes be - fore you in - to Gal - i - lee.

℟ Al - le - lu - ia, al - le - lu - ia.

Responsorial Psalm C 3 g Psalm 118 (117V) and Psalm 107 (106V)
Psalm 118 (117V):1–2; Psalm 107 (106V):2–3; Psalm 118 (117V):16, 22–23, 26a and 27a
(See Performance Notes)

or

149

℣ 1 O give thanks to the LORD, for he is **good;** *

97

his stead-fast love en-dures for - **ev** - er!_____

℞ To - day_____ is the day the Lord has made.

℣2 Let **Is** - ra - el say, "His stead-fast love en-dures for-

ev - er." * Let the re-deemed of the LORD say

so, ' those he re - deemed *from* **trou** - ble_____

℞ To - day_____ is the day the Lord has made.

3[1]   and gathered in from the lands, '
    from the east and from the **wést,** *
    from the north and from **thé** south.

4   "The **right** hand of the LORD is exàlted; *
    the right hand of the LORD *dòes* **valiant**ly."

5   The stone that the builders rejected has become the chief
    córnerstone. *
    This is the Lord's doing; it is marvelous in **óur** eyes.

6   **Bless**ed is the one who comes in the **nàme of** the LORD. *
    The LORD is God, and he has givèn **us** light.

Alleluia Psalm   **Psalm 114 (113A V) and Psalm 115 (113B V)**
                Psalm 114 (113A V):1–8; Psalm 115 (113B V):17–18

150

℣1 When Is - ra - el went out from E-gypt,* the house_

[1] Odd numbered verses are chanted on the first chanting note (fa); even numbered verses, on the second chanting note (la).

of Ja - cob from a peo - ple of strange lan - guage,

℟ Al - le - lu - ia, al - le - lu - ia.

℣2 Ju - dah be - came God's sanc - tu - a - ry, *

Is - ra - el his do - min - ion. _____

℟ Al - le - lu - ia, _____ al - le - lu - ia, al - le - lu - ia.

℣3 The sea _____ looked _____ and fled; * Jor - dan turned back.

℟ Al - le - lu - ia, al - le - lu - ia.

℣4 The moun - tains skipped like rams, * the hills like _____ lambs. _____

℟ Al - le - lu - ia, _____ al - le - lu - ia, al - le - lu - ia.

℣5 Why is _____ it, O sea, that _____ you flee? *

O Jor - dan, that you turn back?

R⁊ Al - le - lu - ia, al - le - lu - ia.

℣6 O moun - tains, that you skip _ like rams?* hills, like _ lambs? _

R⁊ Al - le - lu - ia, _ al - le - lu - ia, al - le - lu - ia.

℣7 Trem - ble, _ O earth, at the pres - ence of the LORD, *

at the pres - ence of the God of Ja - cob,

R⁊ Al - le - lu - ia, al - le - lu - ia.

℣8 who turns _ the rock in - to a pool of wa - ter, *

the flint _ in - to a spring _ of wa - ter.

R⁊ Al - le - lu - ia, _ al - le - lu - ia, al - le - lu - ia.

℣9 The dead do not praise the LORD, *

nor do an - y that go down in - to si - lence.

℟ Al - le - lu - ia, al - le - lu - ia.

℣10 But we will bless the LORD *

from this time on and for - ev - er - more.

℟ Al - le - lu - ia, al - le - lu - ia, al - le - lu - ia.

Sequence

I

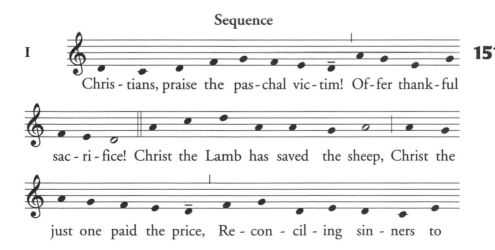

Chris - tians, praise the pas - chal vic - tim! Of - fer thank - ful

sac - ri - fice! Christ the Lamb has saved the sheep, Christ the

just one paid the price, Re - con - cil - ing sin - ners to

151

the Fa - ther. Death and life fought bit - ter - ly For this

won - drous vic - to - ry; The Lord of life who died reigns

glo - ri - fied! O Ma - ry, come and say __ what you saw

at break of day. "The emp - ty tomb of my liv - ing

Lord! I saw Christ Je - sus ri - sen and a - dored!

Bright an - gels tes - ti - fied, __ Shroud and grave clothes

side by side! Yes, Christ my hope rose glo - ri - ous - ly.

He goes be - fore __ you in - to Ga - li - lee." Share the

good news, sing joy - ful - ly: His death is vic - to - ry!

Lord Je - sus, Vic - tor King, Show us mer - cy.

Preparation of the Gifts Antiphon

Psalm 76 (75V):8b–9a

VIII c

The earth — trem - bled,* then all _____ was — still,

when God a - rose for judg- ment, al - le - lu - ia.

152

Psalm 76 (75V)

1–5a

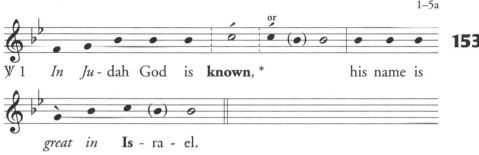

℣ 1   *In Ju* - dah God is **known,** *   his name is

great in **Is** - ra - el.

153

2   *His a*bode has been established in **Sá**lem, *
    his dwelling *plàce in* **Zi**on.

3   *There he* broke the flashing **ár**rows, *
    the shield, the sword, and the *wèapons of* war.

4   *Glorious* are you, more majestic than the everlasting **móun**tains. *
    The stouthearted were *strìpped of* **their** spoil.

From the two psalms and antiphons that follow, one as desired is chosen.

Communion Antiphon I

1 Corinthians 5:7–8

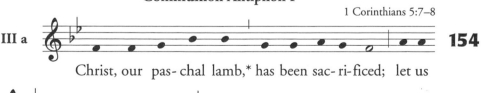

III a

Christ, our pas- chal lamb,* has been sac - ri -ficed; let us

keep this feast with joy: al - le - lu - ia, al - le - lu - ia.

154

Psalm 66 (65V)

1–2, 4–6, 8–9, 16, 20

155

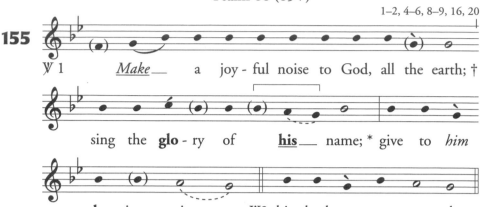

℣ 1 _Make_ a joy-ful noise to God, all the earth; †

sing the **glo**-ry of **his** name; * give to _him_

glor-ious praise. ℣3 his deeds a-**mong** mor-tals.

2 _All_ the earth worshìps you; †
   they sing **práis**es **to** you, *
   sing praises _tò_ **your** name.

3 _Come_ and **sée** what God **has** done: *
   he is awesome in his deeds _à_**mong** mortals.

4 _He turned_ the sea into dry lànd; †
   they passed through the **rív**er **on** foot. *
   There we re_jòic_ed **in** him,

5 _Bless our_ God, O peoplès, †
   let the sound of **hís** praise **be** heard, *
   who has kept us among the living, and has not let _òur_ **feet** slip.

6 _Come_ and hear, all **yóu** who **fear** God, *
   and I will tell what he _hàs_ **done** for me.

7 _Blessed_ be God, because he has not re**jéct**ed **my** prayer *
   or removed his stead_fàst_ **love** from me.

or **Communion Antiphon II**

156 VI F

Al-le-lu-ia, * al - le-lu-ia, al-le - lu - ia.

Psalm 105 (104V)

1–11, 40–45ab

157

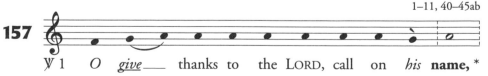

℣ 1 O _give_ thanks to the LORD, call on _his_ **name**, *

make known his deeds *a-mong the* **peo** - ples.

2   *Sing* to him, sing praises *tò* **him;** *
    tell of all *hìs wonder***ful** works.

3   *Glo*ry in *hìs* **ho**ly name; *
    let the hearts of those who seek *thè* <u>LORD</u> re*joice.

4   *Seek* the LORD and *hìs* **strength;** *
    seek his *prèsence con***tin**ually.

5   *Remem*ber the wonderful works he *hàs* **done,** *
    his miracles, and the judg*mènts* <u>he</u> **ut**tered,

6   O *off*spring of his ser*vànt* **Abraham,** *
    children of Ja*còb,* <u>his</u> **cho**sen ones.

7   *He* <u>is</u> the LORD *òur* **God;** *
    his judgments are *ìn* <u>all</u> **the** earth.

8   *He* <u>is</u> mindful of his covenant *fòr*ever, *
    of the word that he commanded, for a thou*sànd gener*ations,

9   *the cov*enant that he made *wìth* **Abr**aham, *
    his sworn pro*mìse* <u>to</u> **Isaac,**

10 *which* <u>he</u> confirmed to Jacob as *à* **stat**ute, *
    to Israel as an ev*èrlasting* **cov**enant:

11 *"To* <u>you</u> I will give the land *òf* **Canaan***
    as your portion *fòr an in***her**itance."

12 *They* <u>asked,</u> and he *bròught* **quails,** *
    and gave them food from heav*èn in a***bun**dance.

13 *He* *o*pened the rock, and water *gùshed* **out;** *
    it flowed through the des*èrt like a* **riv**er.

14 *For* <u>he</u> remembered his ho*lỳ***prom**ise,*
    and Abra*hàm,* <u>his</u> **ser**vant.

15 *So* <u>he</u> brought his people out *wìth* **joy,** *
    his chosen *ònes* <u>with</u> **sing**ing.

16 *He* <u>gave</u> them the lands of *thè* **na**tions, *
    and they took possession of the *wèalth of the* **peo**ples,

17 *that* <u>they</u> might keep *hìs* **stat**utes *
    and *òb*<u>serve</u> **his** laws.

Easter Season I

Entrance Antiphon

John 10:16–17b

158 III a

I am __ the good __ shep - herd, * I
pas - ture my sheep, and for my sheep I lay down my
life and take it up a - gain, al - le - lu - ia.

Psalm 23 (22V)

1–6 (See Performance Notes)

159

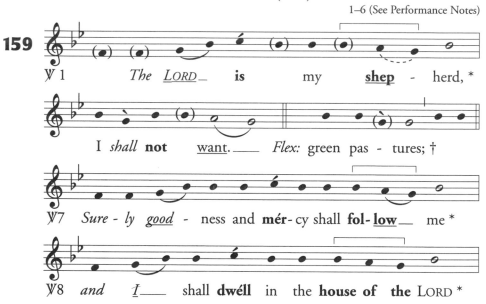

℣ 1 *The* L**ORD** __ **is** my **shep** - herd, *
I *shall* **not** want. __ *Flex:* green pas - tures; †

℣ 7 *Sure - ly* good - ness and **mér**- cy shall **fol- low** __ me *

℣ 8 *and* I __ shall **dwéll** in the **house of** the LORD *

2 *He makes* me lie down in green pastures; †
   he leads me be**síde** still **wa**ters; *
   he re*stòres* **my** soul.

3 He **léads** me in **right** paths *
   for *his* **name's** sake.

4   *Even though* I walk through the darkest vallèy, †
        I fear no evil; for **yóu** are **with** me; *
    your rod and your staff—*thèy* **com**fort <u>me</u>.

5   *You pre<u>pare</u>* a **tá**ble be**fore** me *
    in the presence of *mỳ* **en**<u>emies</u>;

6   you an**óint** my **head** <u>**with**</u> oil; *
    my cup *òverflows*.

7   *Surely <u>good</u>*ness and **mér**cy shall **fol<u>low</u>** me *
    all the days *òf* **my** <u>life</u>,

8   *and <u>I</u>* shall **dwéll** in the **house of the** LORD *
    my *whòle* **life** <u>long</u>.

When there are two readings before the gospel, the chants between the readings are arranged as follows: Alleluia Psalm I is sung after the first reading; after the second reading, either Alleluia Psalm II or the antiphon *Alleluia* with its own verses are sung.

Whenever there is only a single reading before the gospel, a single chant may be chosen as desired from those appropriate to the reading.

At least five verses of a psalm, chosen at will, are always sung, whenever more than five are given.

This applies to all of the Easter season.

Alleluia Psalm I D 1 b   Psalm 107 (106V)

1, 4–9

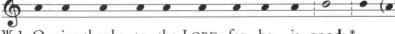

℣ 1 O give thanks to the LORD, for he   is **good;** *

for   his stead-fast love en-dures for-**ev** - er.

160

℟ Al - le - lu - ia,___   al - le - lu - ia.

2   Some wandered in **dés**ert wastes, *
    finding no way to an inhabitèd town;

3   hungry and **thírs**ty, *
    their soul fainted withìn them.

4   Then they cried to the LORD in their **tróu**ble, *
    and he delivered them from **thèir** distress;

5   he led them by a **stráight** way, *
    until they reached an inhabitèd town.

6   Let them thank the LORD for his **stéad**fast love, *
    for his wonderful works to **hù**mankind.

7   For he satisfies the **thírst**y, *
    and the hungry he fills with **gòod** things.

Alleluia Psalm II D 1 b   Psalm 107 (106V)
                                                    1, 10–16

161

℣ 1 O give thanks to the LORD, for he is **good;** *

for his stead-fast love en-dures for - **ev** - er.

℟ Al - le - lu - ia,___ al - le - lu - ia.

2   Some sat in darkness and in **glóom,** *
    prisoners in misery and **ìn** irons,

3   for they had rebelled against the words of **Gód,** *
    and spurned the counsel of the **Mòst** High.

4   Their hearts were bowed down with **hárd** labor; *
    they fell down, with no one **tò** help.

5   Then they cried to the LORD in their **tróu**ble, *
    and he saved them from **thèir** distress;

6   he brought them out of darkness and **glóom,** *
    and broke their bonds a**sùn**der.

7   Let them thank the LORD for his **stéad**fast love, *
    for his wonderful works to **hù**mankind.

8   For he shatters the doors of **brónze,** *
    and cuts in two the **bàrs** of iron.

or Alleluia   Psalm 107 (106V)
                                                1, 8, 9, 16, 22, 32

162 VIII G

Al- le - lu - ia, al-le-lu - ia, al - le-lu- ia.

All repeat: Alleluia, alleluia, alleluia.

℣ 1 O *give* thanks to the LORD, for he is **good;** *

for his stead-fast love en - *dures for* - **ev** - er.

All: Alleluia, alleluia, alleluia.

2 *Let them* thank the LORD for his **stéad**fast love, *
for his wonderful *wòrks to* **hu**mankind.
All: Alleluia, alleluia, alleluia.

3 *For he* satisfies the **thírst**y, *
and the hungry he *fílls with* **good** things.
All: Alleluia, alleluia, alleluia.

4 *For he* shatters the doors of **brónze,** *
and cuts in *twò the* **bars** of iron.
All: Alleluia, alleluia, alleluia.

5 *And let* them offer thanksgiving sacrí**fíc**es, *
and tell of his *dèeds with* **songs** of joy.
All: Alleluia, alleluia, alleluia.

6 *Let them* extol him in the congregation of the **péo**ple, *
and praise him in the assembly *òf the* **eld**ers.
All: Alleluia, alleluia, alleluia.

Preparation of the Gifts Antiphon

Psalm 63 (62V):1

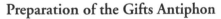

VII a

For you I watch, O God,* I long to gaze on you to

be-hold your glo - ry and your pow-er, al-le-lu-ia.

163

Psalm 63 (62V)

1–4

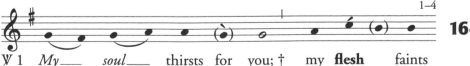

℣ 1 *My__ soul__* thirsts for you; † my **flesh** faints

164

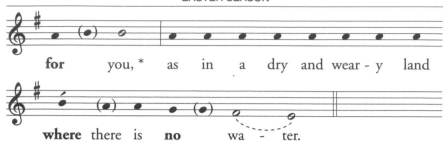

for you, * as in a dry and wear-y land

where there is **no** wa - ter.

2 *So I* have looked upon **yóu** in the **sanc**tuary, *
beholding your **pów**er **and** glory.

3 *Because* your steadfast love is **bét**ter **than** life, *
my **líps** will **praise** you.

4 *So I* will bless you as **lóng** as **I** live; *
I will lift up my hands and **cáll** on **your** name.

Communion Antiphon

Mark 16:7

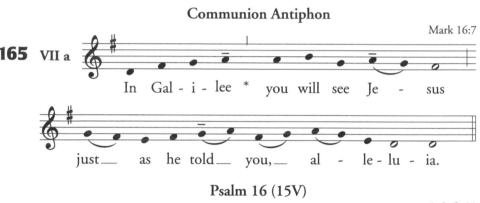

165 VII a

In Gal - i - lee * you will see Je - sus

just___ as he told___ you,___ al - le - lu - ia.

Psalm 16 (15V)

1–2, 5–11

166

℣ 1 *Pro - tect*___ me, O God, for in you I take

ref - uge. † I say to the LORD, "**You** are **my**

Lord; * I have no **good** a - **part** from you." ___

2 *The LORD* is my chosen **pór**tion and **my** cup; *
yóu hold **my** lot.

3   *The bound*ary lines have fallen for me in **pléas**ant **plac**es; *
    I have a **góod**ly **her**itage.

4   *I bless* the LORD who **gíves** me **coun**sel; *
    in the night also my **héart** in**structs** me.

5   *I keep* the LORD **ál**ways be**fore** me; *
    because he is at my right hand, **Í** shall **not** be moved.

6   *Therefore* my heart is glad, and my **sóul** re**joic**es; *
    my body **ál**so **rests** se<u>cure</u>.

7   *For you* do not give me **úp** to **She**ol, *
    or let your **fáith**ful one **see** the <u>Pit</u>.

8   *You show* me the path òf life. †
        In your presence there is **fúll**ness **of** joy; *
    in your right hand are **pléas**ures for<u>ever</u>more.

Easter Season II

Entrance Antiphon

Psalm 98 (97V):1a and 3c

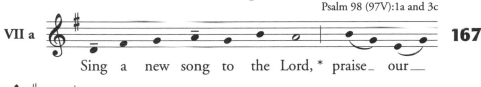

167

Sing a new song to the Lord, * praise our God from the ends of the earth, al - le - lu - ia.

Psalm 98 (97V)

1cd, 6, 8–12ae (See Performance Notes)

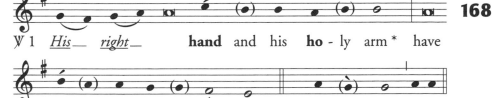

168

℣ 1 *His right* **hand** and his **ho** - ly arm * have **got**-ten him **vic** - to - <u>ry</u>. *Flex:* clap their hands;†

2   *The LORD* has made **knówn** his **vic**tory; *
    he has revealed his vindication in the **síght** of the <u>nations</u>.

3   *He has* remembered his steadfast **lóve** and **faith**fulness *
    to the **hóuse** of Isr<u>ael</u>.

4   *All the* **énd**s of the **éarth** have seen *
    the **victory of** our <u>God</u>.

5   *Make a* joyful noise to the **LÓRD,** all **the** earth; *
    break forth into joyous **sóng** and sing **prais**<u>es</u>.

6   *Sing prais*es to the **LÓRD** with **the** lyre, *
    with the lyre and the **sóund** of mel<u>ody</u>.

7   *With trum*pets and the **sóund** of **the** horn *
    make a joyful noise be**fóre** the **King,** the <u>LORD</u>.

8   *Let the* sea roar, and **áll** that **fills** it; *
    the world and **thóse** who **live** in <u>it</u>.

9   *Let the* floods clap thèir hands; †
    let the hills sing to**géth**er **for** joy *
    at the **prés**ence **of** the <u>LORD</u>,

10 *for he* is coming to judge thè earth. †
    He will judge the **wórld** with **right**eousness, *
    and the **péo**ples with **equi**<u>ty</u>.

Alleluia Psalm I D 1 b   **Psalm 107 (106V)**
                                         1, 17–22

169

℣ 1   O give thanks to the LORD, for he   is **good;** *

for   his   stead - fast   love   en - dures   for - **ev** - er.

℞   Al - le - lu - ia, ___   al - le - lu - ia.

2   Some were sick through their **sín**ful ways, *
    and because of their iniquities endured af**flì**ction;

3   they loathed any kind of **fóod,** *
    and they drew near to the **gàtes** of death.

4   Then they cried to the LORD in their **tróu**ble, *
    and he delivered them from **thèir** distress;

5   he sent out his word and **héaled** them, *
    and delivered them from de**strùc**tion.

6   Let them thank the LORD for his **stéad**fast love, *
    for his wonderful works to **hù**mankind.

7   And let them offer thanksgiving sacrifíces, *
    and tell of his deeds with sòngs of joy.

Alleluia Psalm II D 1 b   Psalm 107 (106V)
                                                      1, 23–32

Ⅴ 1 O give thanks to the LORD, for he is **good;** *

for   his   stead-fast   love   en-dures   for - **ev** - er.

R/ Al - le - lu - ia,___   al - le - lu - ia.

2   Some went down to the sea in **shíps,** *
    doing business on the mighty **wàters;**

3   they saw the deeds of the **LÓRD,** *
    his wondrous works in **thè** deep.

4   For he commanded and raised the **stórm**y wind, *
    which lifted up the waves of **thè** sea.

5   They mounted up to heaven, '
        they went down to the **dépths;** *
    their courage melted away in their calàmity;

6   they reeled and staggered like **drúnk**ards, *
    and were at their **wìts'** end.

7   Then they cried to the LORD in their **tróu**ble, *
    and he delivered them from **thèir** distress;

8   he made the storm be **stíll,** *
    and the waves of the **sèa** were hushed.

9   Then they were glad because they had **qúi**et, *
    and he brought them to their desired **hà**ven.

10 Let them thank the LORD for his **stéad**fast love, *
    for his wonderful works to **hù**mankind.

11 Let them extol him in the congregation of the **péo**ple, *
    and praise him in the assembly of the **èld**ers.

or *Alleluia* as in Easter Season I, **162.**

Preparation of the Gifts Antiphon

Psalm 47 (46V):1b

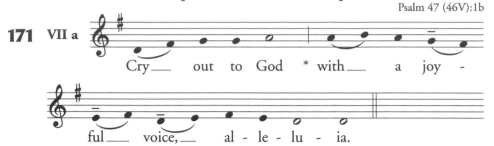

171 VII a

Cry___ out to God * with___ a joy -
ful___ voice,___ al - le - lu - ia.

Psalm 47 (46V)

1–4, 6

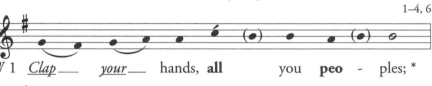

172

℣ 1 *Clap___ your___* hands, **all** you **peo** - ples; *
shout to **God** with loud **songs** of joy.___

2 *For the* LORD, the Most **Hígh,** is **awe**some, *
a great king **óver all** the earth.

3 *He subdued péoples under us, *
and nations **únder our** feet.

4 *He chose* our **hér**itage **for** us, *
the pride of **Jácob whom** he loves.

5 *Sing praises* to **Gód,** sing **praises;** *
sing praises to **óur** King, **sing** praises.

Communion Antiphon

Psalm 96 (95V):2

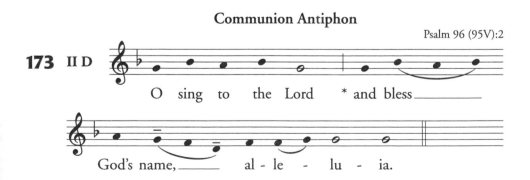

173 II D

O sing to the Lord * and bless___
God's name,___ al - le - lu - ia.

Psalm 96 (95V)

1, 3, 6–13

174

℣ 1 *O sing* to the LORD a new **song;** * sing to the

LORD, *all* **the** earth. *Flex:* "The LORD is king! †

2 *Declare* his glory among the **ná**tions, *
his marvelous works among all *thè* **peo**ples.

3 *Honor* and majesty are be**fóre** him; *
strength and beauty are in *hìs* **sanc**tuary.

4 *Ascribe* to the LORD, O families of the **péo**ples, *
ascribe to the LORD glo*rỳ* **and** strength.

5 *Ascribe* to the LORD the glory due his **náme;** *
bring an offering, and come in*tò* **his** courts.

6 *Worship* the LORD in holy **splén**dor; *
tremble before *hìm,* **all** the earth.

7 *Say a*mong the nations, "The LORD *ìs* king! †
The world is firmly established; it shall never be **móved.** *
He will judge the peoples *wìth* **equi**ty."

8 *Let the* heavens be glad, and let the earth rè**joice;** †
let the sea roar, and all that **fills** it; ʳ
let the field exult, and eve*rỳ***thing** in it.

9 *Then shall* all the trees of the forest sing *fòr* joy †
before the LORD; for he is **cóm**ing, *
for he is coming *tò* **judge** the earth.

10 *He will* judge the world with **ríght**eousness, *
and the peo*plès* **with** his truth.

115

The Ascension of the Lord

Solemnity

Entrance Antiphon I

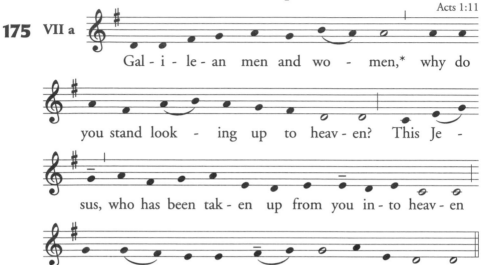

175 VII a

Acts 1:11

Gal - i - le - an men and wo - men,* why do you stand look - ing up to heav - en? This Je - sus, who has been tak - en up from you in - to heav - en will come___ in the same___ way, al - le - lu - ia.

Entrance Antiphon II

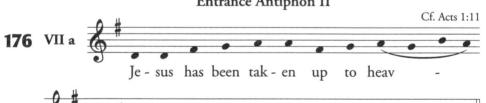

176 VII a

Cf. Acts 1:11

Je - sus has been tak - en up to heav - en * and he will___ come a - gain,___ al - le - lu - ia.

Psalm 68 (67V)

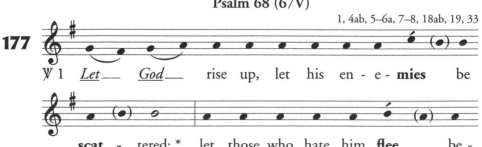

177

1, 4ab, 5–6a, 7–8, 18ab, 19, 33

℣ 1 *Let___ God___* rise up, let his en - e - **mies** be **scat** - tered; * let those who hate him **flee** be -

116

- **fore** him. _Flex:_ to his name; †

2 *Sing to* God, sing praises to his nàme; †
      lift up a song to him who **rídes** up**on** the clouds— *
   his **náme** is **the** LORD.

3 *Father* of orphans and protector of widòws †
      is God in his holy **hábitation.** *
   God gives the desolate a **hóme** to **live** in;

4 *O God,* when you went out be**fóre** your **peo**ple, *
   when you **márched** through the **wil**derness,

5 *the earth* quaked, the heavens poured down ràin †
      at the presence of God, the **Gód** of Sinai, *
   at the presence of God, the **Gód** of Israel.

6 *You as*cended the high mòunt, †
      leading **cáp**tives **in** your train *
   and recéiving gifts **from** people.

7 *Blessed* be the Lord, who **dái**ly **bears** us up; *
   Gód is our **sal**vation.

8 *O rid*er in the heavens, the **án**cient **heav**ens; *
   listen, he sends out his **vóice,** his **migh**ty voice.

Alleluia Psalm I   Psalm 47 (46V)
                                                              1–9

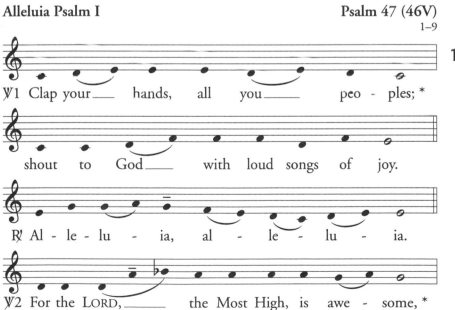

℣1 Clap your hands, all you peo - ples; *

shout to God with loud songs of joy.

℟ Al - le - lu - ia, al - le - lu - ia.

℣2 For the LORD, the Most High, is awe - some, *

178

117

a great___ king o - ver all___ the earth.___

℟ Al - le - lu - ia,___ al - le - lu - ia, al - le - lu - ia.

℣3 He sub - dued___ peo - ples un - der us, *

and na - tions un - der our feet.

℟ Al - le - lu - ia, al - le - lu - ia.

℣4 He chose___ our her - i - tage for___ us, *

the pride___ of Ja - cob whom he___ loves.___

℟ Al - le - lu - ia,___ al - le - lu - ia, al - le - lu - ia.

℣5 God has gone___ up with___ a shout, *

the LORD___ with the sound of a trum - pet.

℟ Al - le - lu - ia, al - le - lu - ia.

℣6 Sing prais - es to God, sing prais - es; *

sing prais - es to our King, sing prais - es._____

℟ Al - le - lu - ia,__ al - le - lu - ia, al - le - lu - ia.

℣7 For God__ is the king of all__ the earth; *

sing prais - es with a psalm.

℟ Al - le - lu - ia, al - le - lu - ia.

℣8 God is king__ o - ver the na - tions; *

God sits__ on his__ ho - ly throne.__

℟ Al - le - lu - ia,__ al - le - lu - ia, al - le - lu - ia.

℣9 The princ - es of the peo - ples gath-er *

as the peo - ple of the God of A - bra-ham.

℟ Al - le - lu - ia, al - le - lu - ia.

℣10 For the shields____ of the earth be - long__ to God; *

he____ is high - ly ex - alt - ed._____

℟ Al - le - lu - ia,__ al - le - lu - ia, al - le - lu - ia.

Alleluia Psalm II E 2 d   Psalm 24 (23V)
                                                3, 7–10

179

℣ 1 Who shall as - cend the hill **of the** LORD? *

And who shall stand in his **ho** - ly place?

℟ Al - le - lu - ia, al - le - lu - ia.

2   Lift up your heads, O gates! '
       and be lifted up, O **án**cient doors! *
    that the King of glory may **come** ìn.

3   Who is the King of glory? '
       The LORD, strong and **mígh**ty, *
    the LORD, mighty in **batt**lè.

4   Lift up your heads, O gates! '
       and be lifted up, O **án**cient doors! *
    that the King of glory may **come** ìn.

5   Who is this King of glory? '
       The **LÓRD** of hosts, *
    he is the King of **glo**rỳ.

Preparation of the Gifts Antiphon

Psalm 47 (46V):5

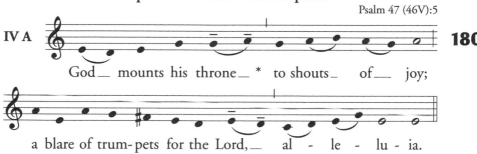

180

God mounts his throne * to shouts of joy;
a blare of trum-pets for the Lord, al - le - lu - ia.

Psalm 47 (46V)

1–2, 6, 8

181

℣ 1 *Clap your hands, all you* **peo** - ples; *
shout to *God with loud* **songs** *of* joy.

2   *For the LORD, the Most High, is* **awe**some, *
    a great *kìng over* **all** the earth.

3   *Sing prais*es to *Gòd, sing* **prais**es; *
    sing praises to *òur King, sing* **prais**es.

4   *God is king ovèr the* **na**tions; *
    God *sìts on his* **ho**ly throne.

Communion Antiphon

Psalm 110 (109V):1a

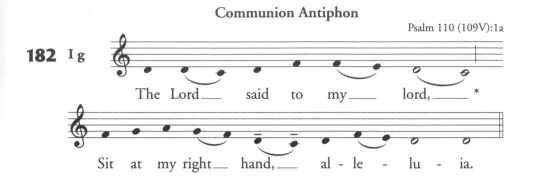

182 I g

The Lord___ said to my___ lord,___ *

Sit at my right___ hand,___ al - le - lu - ia.

Psalm 110 (109V)

1–5, 7

183

℣ 1 *The LORD_* says to my lord, † "**Sit** at my **right** hand *

un - til I make your en - e - *mies your* **foot** - stool."

℣ 3 will **of** - fer them - selves **will** - ing - ly.

2   *The LORD* sends out from Zion your **míght**y **scep**ter. *
      Rule in the *mìdst of* **your** foes.

3   *Your peo*ple will **óf**fer themselves **will**ingly *
      on the day you lead your forces on the *hòly* **moun**tains.

4   *From* the **wómb** of the **morn**ing, *
      like dew, your *yòuth will* **come** to you.

5   *The LORD* has sworn and will not change his mìnd, †
      "You are a **príest** for**ev**er *
      according to the order *òf Mel***chi**zedek."

6   *The Lord* is **át** your **right** hand; *
      he will shatter kings on the *dày of* **his** wrath.

7   *He* will drink from the **stréam** by **the** path; *
      therefore he will *lìft up* **his** head.

These same songs are used for the Mass of the Sunday after the Ascension (the Seventh
Sunday of Easter).

Pentecost

Solemnity

Entrance Antiphon

Cf. Acts 2:1

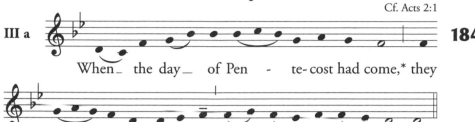

184

When the day of Pen - te-cost had come,* they were all to-geth - er, sing - ing al-le - lu - ia.

Psalm 104 (103V)

1ab, 30–31, 33–35 (See Performance Notes)

185

℣ 1 *Bless* the **LORD,** O **my** soul. * O LORD my God, you *are* **ver** - y great. — *Flex:* from the earth,†

2 *When you send* forth your spirit, **théy** are cre**at**ed; *
and you renew the face *òf* **the** ground.

3 *May* the glory of the LORD en**dúre** for**ev**er; *
may the LORD rejoice *ìn* **his** works.

4 *I will sing* to the LORD as **lóng** as **I** live; *
I will sing praise to my God while *Ì* **have** being.

5 *May* my meditation be **pléas**ing **to** him, *
for I re*jòice* **in** the LORD.

6 *Let sin*ners be consumed from the èarth, †
and let the **wíck**ed be **no** more. *
Bless the LORD, *Ò* **my** soul.

Or, if desired, the entrance song as in the votive Mass of the Holy Spirit, **493.**

Alleluia Psalm I

Psalm 68 (67V)

1–2, 4, 9, 26, 28–29, 32, 34

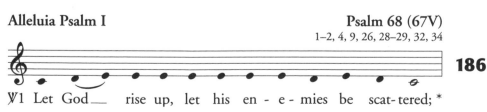

186

℣1 Let God rise up, let his en - e - mies be scat-tered; *

let those___ who hate him flee be - fore him.

℟ Al - le - lu - ia, al - le - lu - ia. ℣2 As_smoke_

is driv-en a-way, so drive them_ a-way; * as wax_ melts be-

fore the fire, let the wick-ed per-ish be-fore_ God.___

℟ Al - le - lu - ia,___ al - le - lu - ia, al - le - lu - ia.

℣3 Sing to God,___ sing prais - es to his name; *

lift up___ a song to him who rides up-on the clouds—

℟ Al - le - lu - ia, al - le - lu - ia.

℣4 his name_____ is___ the LORD— *

be ___ ex - ult - ant be - fore_ him.___

℟ Al-le-lu - ia, ___ al-le-lu - ia, al - le - lu - ia.

℣5 Rain ___ in a-bun-dance, O God, you show-ered a-broad; *

you re-stored ___ your her - it - age when it lan-guished;

℟ Al - le - lu - ia, al - le - lu - ia.

℣6 "Bless ___ God in the great con-gre-ga-tion, the ___ LORD, *

O you ___ who are of Is - ra - el's foun - tain!" ___

℟ Al - le-lu - ia, ___ al-le-lu - ia, al - le - lu - ia.

℣7 Sum - mon your might, O God; show ___ your strength, *

O God, ___ as you have done for us be - fore.

℟ Al - le-lu - ia, al - le - lu - ia.

125

℣8 Be - cause— of your tem-ple at Je - ru - sa-lem *

kings———— bear— gifts—— to you.————

℟ Al-le-lu - ia,—— al-le-lu - ia, al - le - lu - ia.

℣9 Sing———— to God, O king-doms of the earth; *

sing prais - es to the Lord.

℟ Al - le-lu - ia, al - le - lu - ia.

℣10 As - cribe— pow-er to God, whose maj-es-ty is o-ver

Is - ra-el; * and whose pow - er is in— the skies.——

℟ Al-le-lu - ia,—— al-le-lu - ia, al - le - lu - ia.

Alleluia Psalm II E 2 d

Psalm 50 (49V)
1–6, 14–15, 23

℣ 1 The might-y one, God the LORD,' speaks and sum-**mons the**

earth * from the ris-ing of the sun to its **set** - ting.

℟ Al - le - lu - ia, al - le - lu - ia.

187

2 Out of Zion, the perfection of **béau**ty, *
God **shines** fòrth.

3 Our God comes and does not keep silence, '
before him is a de**vóur**ing fire, *
and a mighty tempest all a**round** hìm.

4 He calls to the heav**ens á**bove *
and to the earth, that he may judge his **peo**plè:

5 "Gather to me my **fáith**ful ones, *
who made a covenant with me by **sac**rìfice!"

6 The heavens declare his **right**eousness, *
for God himself **is** jùdge.

7 "Offer to God a sacrifice of thanks**gív**ing, *
and pay your vows to the **Most** Hìgh.

8 Call on me in the day of **tróu**ble; *
I will deliver you, and you shall glori**fy** mè.

9 Those who bring thanksgiving as their sacrifice **hón**or me; *
to those who go the right way I will show the salvation **of** Gòd."

Sequence

I

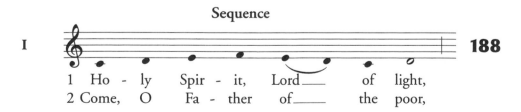

1 Ho - ly Spir - it, Lord___ of light,
2 Come, O Fa - ther of___ the poor,

188

From your clear ce - les - tial height,
Come with treas - ures that en - dure;

Your pure beam - ing ra - diance give.
Come, O Light of all that live.

3 You, of all con - sol - ers best,
4 You in work are com - fort sweet,

You the soul's de - light - ful guest,
Pleas - ant cool - ness in the heat,

Sweet re - fresh - ing peace be - stow.
Sol - ace in the midst of woe.

5 Light im - mor - tal, Light div - ine,
6 If you take your grace a - way,

Show your love to hu - man - kind,
Noth - ing pure in us will stay;

And our in - most be - ing fill.
All our good is turned to ill.

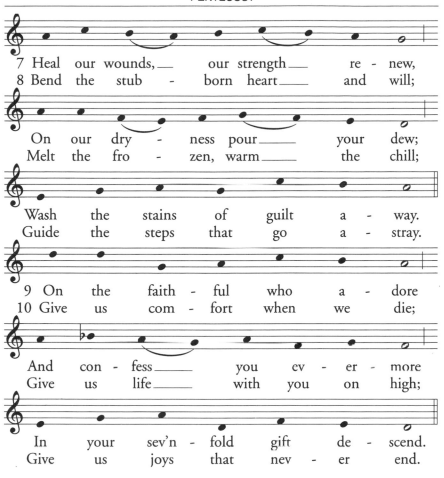

7 Heal our wounds, __ our strength __ re - new,
8 Bend the stub - born heart __ and will;

On our dry - ness pour __ your dew;
Melt the fro - zen, warm __ the chill;

Wash the stains of guilt a - way.
Guide the steps that go a - stray.

9 On the faith - ful who a - dore
10 Give us com - fort when we die;

And con - fess __ you ev - er - more
Give us life __ with you on high;

In your sev'n - fold gift de - scend.
Give us joys that nev - er end.

Preparation of the Gifts Antiphon

Psalm 68 (67V):28b–29

VIII c   **189**

Con-firm, O God, __ * what you have

done for us, from __ your ho - ly tem - ple in Je-

- ru - sa - lem, al - le - lu - ia, al - le - lu - ia.

Psalm 68 (67V)

1, 21, 24, 35

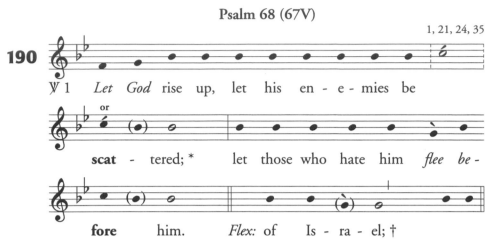

190

℣ 1 *Let God* rise up, let his en-e-mies be **scat** - tered; * let those who hate him *flee be-* **fore** him. *Flex:* of Is - ra - el; †

2 *But God* will shatter the heads of his **én**emies, *
the hairy crown of those who walk *ìn their* **guilt**y ways.

3 *Your sol*emn processions are **séen,** O God, *
the processions of my God, my King, in*tò the* **sanc**tuary—

4 *Awesome* is God in his sanctuary, the God of Isràel; †
he gives power and strength to his **péo**ple. *
Blèssed **be** God!

Communion Antiphon

John 14:26

191 VIII G

The Spir - it * who pro-ceeds from the Fa - ther, al - le - lu - ia, will re - veal__ my__ glo - ry, al - le - lu - ia, al - le - lu - ia.

Psalm 78 (77V)

1, 4b, 5c–7, 20, 23–25, 28–29
or

192

℣ 1 *Give ear,* O my peo-ple, to my **teach** - ing; *

in - cline your ears to the *words of* **my** mouth.

Flex: gen - er - a - tion †

2 *We will* tell to the coming generàtion †
   the glorious deeds of the LORD, and his **míght,** *
   and the wond*èrs that* **he** has done.

3 *He com*manded our ancestors to teach to their **chíl**dren; *
   that the next genera*tìon might* **know** them,

4 *the child*ren yet un**bórn,** *
   and rise up and tell them *tò their* **chil**dren,

5 *so that* they should set their hope in Gòd, †
   and not forget the works of **Gód,** *
   but keep *hìs com*mand**ments;**

6 "*Even* though God struck the rock so that water gushed out
   and torrents overflòwed, †
   can he also give **bréad,** *
   or provide meat *fòr his* **peo**ple?"

7 *Yet he* commanded the **skíes** above, *
   and opened the *dòors of* **heav**en;

8 *he rained* down on them manna to **éat,** *
   and gave them the *gràin of* **heav**en.

9 *Mortals* ate of the bread of **án**gels; *
   he sent them food *ìn a***bun**dance.

10 *he let* them fall with**ín** their camp, *
   all aròund *their* **dwell**ings.

11 *And they* ate and were well **fílled,** *
   for he *gàve them* **what** they craved.

Or, if desired, the communion song as in the votive Mass of the Holy Spirit, **496, 497,** and **498.**

131

Trinity Sunday

Solemnity

Entrance Antiphon

193 II D

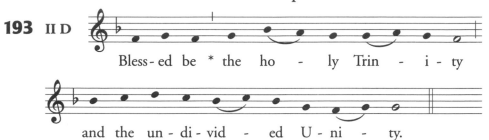

Bless-ed be * the ho - ly Trin - i - ty
and the un - di - vid - ed U - ni - ty.

Psalm 8

1, 3–9

194

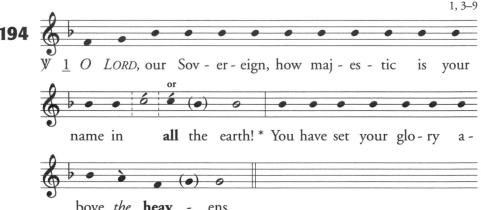

℣ 1 O LORD, our Sov - er - eign, how maj - es - tic is your name in **all** the earth! * You have set your glo - ry a - bove *the* **heav** - ens.

2 *When I* look at your heavens, the work of your **fín**gers, *
   the moon and the stars that you have *ès***tab**lished;

3 *what are* human beings that you are mindful of **thém,** *
   mortals that *yòu* **care** for them?

4 *Yet you* have made them a little lower than **Gód,** *
   and crowned them with glory *ànd* **hon**or.

5 *You have* given them dominion over the works of your **hánds;***
   you have put all things un*dèr* **their** feet,

6 *all sheep* and **óx**en, *
   and also the beasts *òf* **the** field,

7 *the birds* of the air, and the fish of the **séa,** *
   whatever passes along the paths *òf* **the** seas.

8 *O LORD,* our **Só**vereign, *
   how majestic is your name *ìn* **all** the earth!

The chants between the readings are sung according to the rules for Ordinary Time, p. 149.

Responsorial Psalm C 2 g

Psalm 148
(1)1–3, 5–6, 11–14

195

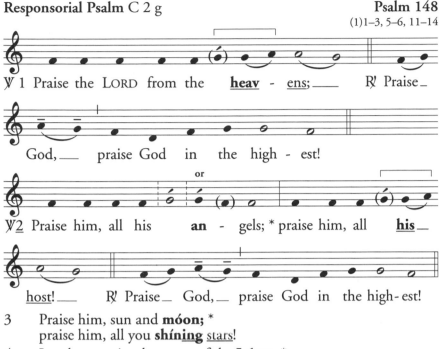

℣ 1 Praise the LORD from the **heav** - ens; ___ ℟ Praise ___ God, ___ praise God in the high - est!

or

℣2 Praise him, all his **an** - gels; * praise him, all **his** ___ host! ___ ℟ Praise ___ God, ___ praise God in the high- est!

3   Praise him, sun and **móon;** *
    praise him, all you **shíning** stars!

4   Let them praise the name of the **LÓRD,** *
    for he commanded and they were creáted.

5   He established them forever and éver; *
    he fixed their bounds, which cannot **bé** passed.

6   Kings of the earth and all **péo**ples, *
    princes and all rulers of **thé** earth!

7   Young men and women alíke, *
    old and young togéther!

8   Let them praise the name of the LORD, ’
        for his name alone is exálted; *
    his glory is above earth and **héa**ven.

9   He has raised up a horn for his people, ’
        praise for all his **fáith**ful, *
    for the people of Israel who are **clóse to** him.

Alleluia

Psalm 150
1b, 3 (See Performance Notes)

196

VII a

Al-le-lu - ia, al - le-lu - ia, al-le-lu - ia.

All repeat: Alleluia, alleluia, alleluia.

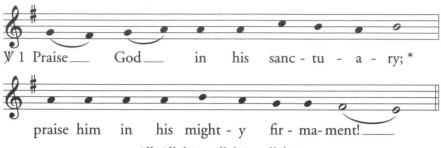

℣ 1 Praise___ God___ in his sanc - tu - a - ry; *

praise him in his might - y fir - ma - ment!___

All: Alleluia, alleluia, alleluia.

℣ 2 Praise___ him___ with trum - pet sound; * praise him

with lute___ and harp!___

All: Alleluia, alleluia, alleluia.

or **Alleluia Psalm** E *

Psalm 150

1b–6 (See Performance Notes)

197

℣ 1 Praise God in his **sanc**-tu - a - ry; * praise him in his *might-y*

fir- ma- ment! ℟ Al - le - lu - ia,___ al - le - lu - ia.

2 Praise him for his mighty **déeds;** *
   praise him according to his sur*passìng* **great**ness!

3 Praise him with **trúm**pet sound; *
   praise him with lute *ànd* **harp!**

4 Praise him with tambourine and **dánce;** *
   praise him with strings *ànd* **pipe!**

5 Praise him with clanging **cým**bals; *
   praise him with loud *clashìng* **cym**bals!

6 Let everything that **bréathes** *
   praise *thè* **LORD!**

Preparation of the Gifts Antiphon

Daniel 3:56

I a 2

Bless-ed are you, O God,* in the fir-ma-ment_ of the

198

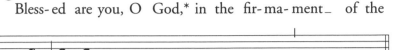

heav-ens, and to be sung_ and glo - ri-fied for-ev - er.

Canticle of the Three Young Men

Daniel 3:57, 58a, 59a, 84a, 85a, 86a, 87a

℣1 *Bless_* the Lord, all you **works** of **the** Lord; * sing

199

praise to him and high-ly ex-alt *him for-ev* - *er.*___

2   *Bless* the Lord, you **án**gels **of** the Lord, *
     Bless the *Lòrd, you* **heav**<u>ens</u>,

3   *Bless* the Lord, you **príests** of **the** Lord, *
     Bless the Lord, you *sèrvants* of the <u>Lord</u>,

4   *Bless* the Lord, spirits and **sóuls** of the **right**eous, *
     Bless the Lord, you who are holy and *hùmble* **of** <u>heart</u>,

5   *Let <u>us</u>* bless the Father and the Son and the **Hóly Spir**it, *
     let us praise and highly exalt *hìm for*<u>ev</u>er.

Communion Antiphon

Psalm 148:1bc

I a

Praise____ the Lord of heav-en for ev - er!

200

Canticle of David

1 Chronicles 29:10b–18 (See Performance Notes)

℣ 1 "*Bless-ed* <u>*are*</u>_ you, O Lᴏʀᴅ, the God of our **an**-ces-tor

201

Is- ra- el, * for- ev- *er and* **ev** - er.   *Flex:* the great - ness,†

2   *Yours, O* LORD, are the greatnèss, †
        the power, the glory, the victory, **ánd** the **maj**esty; *
    for all that is in the heavens and on *thè earth* **is** yours;

3   *yours is* the **kíng**dom, **O** LORD, *
    and you are exalted as *hèad above* all.

4   *Rich*es and **hón**or **come** from you, *
    and *yòu rule* **o**ver all.

5   *In your* hand are **pów**er **and** might; *
    and it is in your hand to make great and *tò give* **strength** to all.

6   *And now,* our God, **wé** give **thanks** to you *
    and *pràise your* **glo**rious name.

7   *O* LORD our God, all this abundance that we have providèd †
        for building you a **hóuse** for your **ho**ly name *
    comes from your hand *ànd is* **all** your own.

8   *I know,* my **Gód,** that you **search** the heart, *
    and take pleas*ùre in* **up**rightness;

9   *in* the **úp**rightness **of** my heart *
    I have freely *òffered* **all** these things,

10 *and now* I have seen your people, **whó** are **pres**ent here, *
    offering freely and joy*òusly* **to** you.

11 *O* LORD, the God of Abraham, Isaac, and Israel, our ancèstors, †
        keep forever such purposes and thoughts in the **héarts** of
        your **peo**ple, *
    and direct *thèir hearts* **toward** you."

The Body and Blood of Christ

Solemnity

Entrance Antiphon

Cf. Hebrews 6:20–7:28

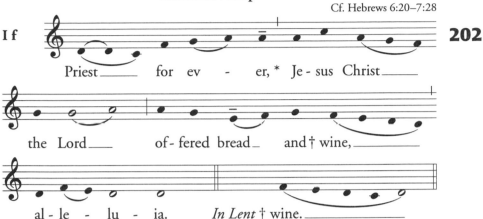

202

Priest for ev - er, * Je - sus Christ

the Lord of- fered bread and † wine,

al - le - lu - ia. *In Lent* † wine.

Psalm 110 (109V)

1–5, 7

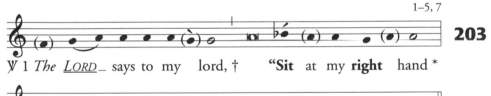

203

℣ 1 *The LORD* says to my lord, † **"Sit** at my **right** hand *

un - til I make your en - e- *mies your* **foot** - stool." __

2   *The LORD* sends out from Zion your **mígh**ty **scep**ter. *
   Rule in the *mìdst of* **your foes.**

3   *Your peo*ple will **óf**fer themselves **will**ingly *
   on the day you lead your forces on the *hòly* **moun**tains.

4   *From* the **wómb** of the **morn**ing, *
   like dew, your *yòuth will* **come** to you.

5   *The LORD* has sworn and will not change his mìnd, †
     "You are a **príest** for**ev**er *
   according to the order *òf Mel***chi**zedek."

6   *He* will drink from the **stréam** by **the** path; *
   therefore he will *lìft up* **his** head.

137

Responsorial Psalm E 5

Psalm 145 (144V)
(1b) 1, 3–4, 9, 15–17, 19–21

204

℣ 1 I will ex-**tol** you, * my _God_ **and** King.

℟ I will bless your name, O Lord.

℣ 2 **Great** is the LORD, and great-ly **to be** praised; *

his great-ness is _un_ - **search**-a-ble.

℟ I will bless your name, O Lord.

3[1]   One generation shall laud your works to an**óth**er, *
     and shall declare your _mígh_ty acts.

4   The **LORD** is **gòod** to all, *
     and his compassion is over _all thàt_ **he** has made.

5   The eyes of all **lóok** to you, *
     and you give them their food _in due_ **seas**on.

6   You **o**pen **yòur** hand, *
     satisfying the desire of _everỳ_ **liv**ing thing.

7   The LORD is just in **áll** his ways, *
     and kind in _áll his_ **do**ings.

8   **He** fulfills the desire of all who **fèar** him; *
     he also hears their cry, _ànd_ **saves** them.

9   The LORD watches over all who **lóve** him, *
     but all the wicked he _wíll_ **de**stroy.

10   My **mouth** will speak the praise **òf the** LORD, *
     and all flesh will bless his holy name forever _ànd_ **ev**er.

[1] Odd numbered verses are chanted on the first chanting note (mi); even numbered verses, on the second chanting note (la).

Alleluia   Psalm 78 (77V)
1, 3

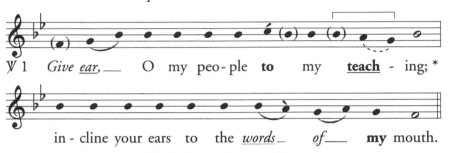

III g   **205**

Al-le-lu-ia,⎯ al-le-lu - ia,⎯ al-le - lu - ia.

All repeat: Alleluia, alleluia, alleluia.

℣ 1 *Give ear,* ⎯ O my peo-ple **to** my **teach** - ing; *

in - cline your ears to the *words*⎯ *of*⎯ **my** mouth.

All: Alleluia, alleluia, alleluia.

2   *things* that **wé** have **heard and** known, *
       that our ances*tòrs have* **told** us.

               All: Alleluia, alleluia, alleluia.

or **Alleluia Psalm C 4**   Psalm 78 (77V)
1, 3, 4b, 7, 24–25, 29, 35, 38

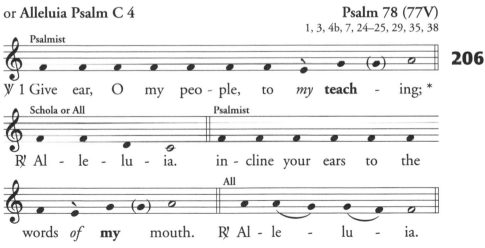

Psalmist   **206**

℣ 1 Give ear, O my peo - ple, to *my* **teach** - ing; *

Schola or All   Psalmist

℟ Al - le - lu - ia.   in - cline your ears to the

                               All

words *of* **my** mouth. ℟ Al - le - lu - ia.

2   things that we *hàve* **heard** and known, *
       that our ancestors *hàve* **told** us.

3   We will tell to the coming generation ’
       the glorious deeds of the LORD, *ànd* **his** might, *
       and the wonders that *hè* **has** done.

4   so that they should set their hope in God, '
      and not forget *thè* **works** of God, *
    but keep his *còm***mand**ments;

5   he rained down on them man*nà* **to** eat, *
    and gave them the grain *òf* **heav**en.

6   Mortals ate of the bread *òf* **an**gels; *
    he sent them food in *à***bun**dance.

7   And they ate and *wère* **well** filled, *
    for he gave *thèm* **what** they craved.

8   They remembered that God *wàs* **their** rock, *
    the Most High God their *rè***deem**er.

9   He, being compassionate, forgave their *ìniq*uity, *
    and did not *dè***stroy** them.

For the Sequence
(optional)

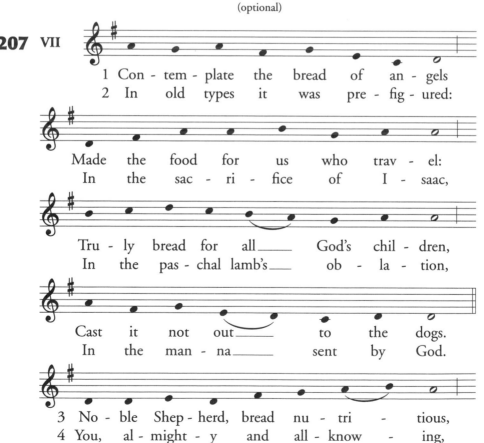

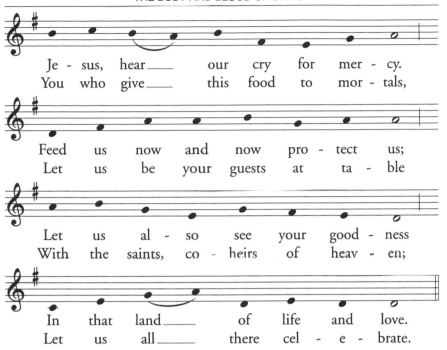

Je - sus, hear___ our cry for mer - cy.
You who give___ this food to mor - tals,

Feed us now and now pro - tect us;
Let us be your guests at ta - ble

Let us al - so see your good - ness
With the saints, co - heirs of heav - en;

In that land___ of life and love.
Let us all___ there cel - e - brate.

Preparation of the Gifts Antiphon

Cf. Psalm 78 (77V):24–25

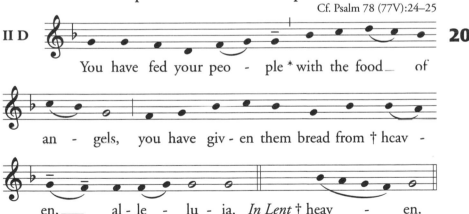

II D   **208**

You have fed your peo - ple * with the food___ of

an - gels, you have giv - en them bread from † heav -

en,___ al - le - lu - ia. *In Lent* † heav - en.

Psalm 84 (83V)

1–2, 3c–4

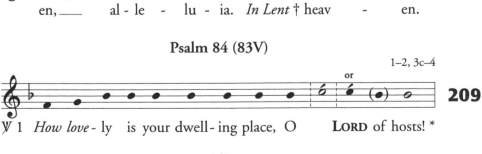

209

℣ 1 *How love-* ly is your dwell- ing place, O **LORD** of hosts! *

My soul longs, in- deed it faints for the courts *of* **the** LORD;

2   *my heart* and my **flésh** *
sing for joy to *thè* **liv**ing God.

3   *at your* altars, O **LÓRD** of hosts, *
my King *ànd* **my** God.

4   *Happy* are those who live in your **hóuse,** *
ever sing*ìng* **your** praise.

Communion Antiphon

John 6:51

210   I f

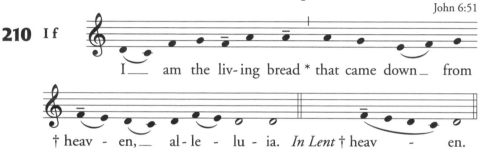

I ___ am the liv-ing bread * that came down ___ from
† heav - en, ___ al - le - lu - ia. *In Lent* † heav - en.

Psalm 23 (22V)

1–6

211

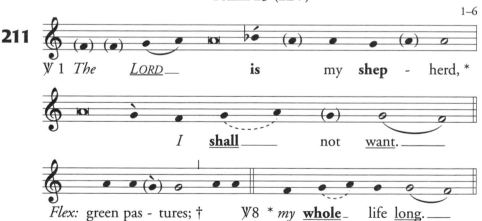

℣ 1 *The* LORD ___ **is** my **shep** - herd, *
I **shall** ___ not want. ___
Flex: green pas - tures; †   ℣8 * *my* **whole** ___ life long. ___

2   *He <u>makes</u>* me lie down in green pastùres; †
he leads me be**síde** still **wat**ers; *
*hè re***<u>stores</u>** my <u>soul</u>.

3   *He <u>leads</u>* **mé** in **right** paths *
fòr his **<u>name's</u>** <u>sake</u>.

4   *Even though* I walk through the darkest vallèy, †
    I fear no evil; for **yóu** are **with** me; *
    your rod and your *stàff—they* **com**fort me.

5   *You prepare* a **tá**ble be**fore** me *
    in the presence *of my* **en**emies;

6   *you anoint* **mý** head **with** oil; *
    mỳ cup **o**verflows.

7   *Surely good*ness and **mér**cy shall **fol**low me *
    all the *dàys of* **my** life,

8   *and I* shall dwell in the **hóuse** of **the** LORD *
    my **whole** life long.

If there is to be the procession, sing the hymn *Sing My Tongue,* **126** ending with **648.**

Friday after the Second Sunday after Pentecost

Sacred Heart

Solemnity

Entrance Antiphon

Matthew 11:29

Learn_____ from_____ me, * for I am gen - tle and low - ly of heart.

Psalm 33 (32V)

1, 5, 8–9, 11–12, 14–15, 18, 20–21 (See Performance Notes)

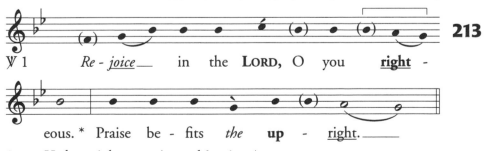

℣ 1 *Re - joice*___ in the **LORD,** O you **right** -
      eous. * Praise be - fits *the* **up** - right.___

2   *He loves* righteous**néss** and **jus**tice; *
    the earth is full of the steadfast love *òf* **the** LORD.

143

3   Let **áll** the earth **fear the** LORD; *
    let all the inhabitants of the world stand *in* **awe** of <u>him</u>.

4   For he **spóke,** and it **came to** be; *
    he commanded, and *it* **stood** <u>firm</u>.

5   *The* <u>coun</u>sel of the LORD **stánds** for<u>ev</u>er, *
    the thoughts of his heart to all gen<u>è</u><u>ra</u>tions.

6   <u>Hap</u>py is the nation whose **Gód** is **the** LORD, *
    the people whom he has chosen as *hìs* **her**<u>itage</u>.

7   From where **hé** sits **en**throned *
    he watches all the inhabitants *òf* **the** <u>earth</u>—

8   *he* who fashions the **héarts** of <u>**them**</u> all, *
    and observes *àll* **their** <u>deeds</u>.

9   <u>Tru</u>ly the eye of the LORD is on **thóse** who <u>**fear**</u> him, *
    on those who hope in *hìs* **stead**fast <u>love</u>,

10 Our **héart** is **glad** <u>**in**</u> him, *
    because we trust in *hìs* **ho**ly <u>name</u>.

11 *Let* <u>your</u> steadfast love, O **LÓRD,** be up<u>**on**</u> us, *
    even as *wè* **hope** in <u>you</u>.

Responsorial Psalm C 2 g   Psalm 25 (24V)
                                (9b) 1–2ab, 4–6, 8, 10, 14–15, 20

214

℣ 1 To you, O LORD, I lift up my soul. ' O my God, in you

I **trust;** *   do not let me be **put** <u>**to**</u> <u>shame;</u>

℟ The Lord will teach the low - ly<u></u> his<u></u> ways. <u></u>

2   Make me to know your ways, O **LÓRD;** *
    teach me <u>**yóur**</u> paths.

3   Lead me in your truth, and teach me, '
        for you are the God of my salv<u>á</u>tion; *
    for you I wait **áll** <u>**day**</u> long.

4   Be mindful of your mercy, O LORD, '
        and of your **stéad**fast love, *
    for they have been **fróm** <u>of</u> old.

5 Good and upright is the **LÓRD;** *
therefore he instructs sinners in **thé** <u>way</u>.

6 All the paths of the LORD are steadfast love and **fáith**fulness, *
for those who keep his covenant and his <u>dé</u><u>crees</u>.

7 The friendship of the LORD is for those who **féar** him, *
and he makes his covenant **knówn** **to** <u>them</u>.

8 My eyes are ever toward the **LÓRD,** *
for he will pluck my feet out **óf** **the** <u>net</u>.

9 O guard my life, and deliver me; '
do not let me be put to **sháme,** *
for I take re**fúge** **in** <u>you</u>.

Alleluia   Psalm 103 (102V)
                                                              1, 8

II D   **215**

Al - le - lu - ia, al - le - lu - ia,___ al - le - lu - ia.

All repeat: Alleluia, alleluia, alleluia.

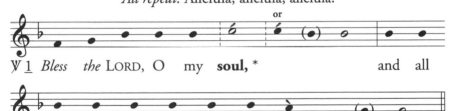

℣ 1 *Bless* *the* LORD, O my **soul,** *   and all

that is with - in me, bless *his* **ho** - ly name.

All: Alleluia, alleluia, alleluia.

2 *The* LORD is merciful and **gra**cious, *
slow to anger and abounding *in* **stead**fast love.

All: Alleluia, alleluia, alleluia.

or **Alleluia Psalm E** *   Psalm 103 (102V)
                                                  1–2, 6, 8–10, 13, 17–19

                                                                  216

℣1 Bless the LORD, O my **soul,** *   and all

that is with - in me, bless *his*___ **ho** - ly name.

145

℟ Al - le - lu - ia, _____ al - le - lu - ia.

2 Bless the LORD, O my **soul,** *
   and do not forget all _his_ **ben**efits—

3 The LORD works vindication and **jús**tice *
   for all who are _òp_**pressed.**

4 The LORD is merciful and **grá**cious, *
   slow to anger and abounding _in_ **stead**fast love.

5 He will not always ac**cúse,** *
   nor will he keep his anger _for_**e**ver.

6 He does not deal with us according to our **síns,** *
   nor repay us according to our _ìn_**iqui**ties.

7 As a father has compassion for his **chíl**dren, *
   so the LORD has compassion for those _whò_ **fear** him.

8 But the steadfast love of the **LÓRD** *
   is from everlasting to everlasting on those _whò_ **fear** him,

9 and his righteousness to children's **chíl**dren, *
   to those who keep his covenant and remember to do his
   còm**mand**ments.

10 The LORD has established his throne in the **héav**ens, *
   and his kingdom _rùles_ **o**ver all.

Preparation of the Gifts Antiphon

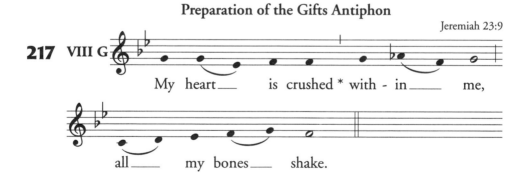

Jeremiah 23:9

217 VIII G

My heart___ is crushed * with - in ___ me,

all ___ my bones ___ shake.

Psalm 69 (68V)

1, 13, 20ab, 30

218

℣ 1 _Save me,_ O **God,** *   for the wa - ters have

146

come up **to** my neck.   *Flex:* to you, O L<small>ORD</small>. †

2   *But as* for me, my prayer is to you, Ò L<small>ORD</small>. †
     At an acceptable time, O **Gód,** *
  in the abundance of your stead*fàst love,* **an**swer me.

3   *Insults* have broken my hèart, †
     so that I am in des**páir.** *
  I looked for pi*tỳ, but* **there** was none;

4   *I will* praise the name of God with a **sóng;** *
  I will magnify him *wìth thanks***giv**ing.

Communion Antiphon

John 19:34

VII c

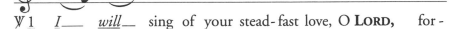

219

One of the sol - diers * pierced his_ side with a

spear, and at once blood_ and wa - ter came out.

Psalm 89 (88V)

1–2, 8, 14–16, 35–36, 47–48, 52

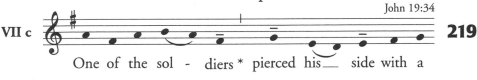

220

℣ 1 *I_ will_* sing of your stead-fast love, O **L**ord, for -

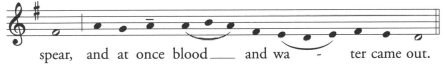

ev - er; * with my mouth I will pro-claim your faith-ful-

ness to **all** gen-er - a-<u>tions</u>._   *Flex:* the fes - tal shout,†

2   *I de*clare that your steadfast love is es**táb**lished for**ev**er; *
  your faithfulness is as **fírm** as **the** heavens.

3   *O* <u>L</u><small>ORD</small> God of hosts, who is as **míght**y as **you,** O L<small>ORD</small>? *
  Your faithful**néss** sur**rounds** <u>you</u>.

4   *Righteous*ness and justice are the found**á**tion of **your** throne; *
    steadfast love and faithfulness **gó** be**fore** you.

5   *Happy* are the people who know the festàl shout, †
      who walk, O LORD, in the **líght** of your **coun**tenance; *
    they exult in your **náme** all **day** long,

6   *Once and* for all I have sworn by my holìness; †
      I will not **líe** to **Da**vid. *
    His line shall con**tín**ue forev*er*,

7   *Remem*ber how **shórt** my **time** is— *
    for what vanity you have cre**á**ted **all** mortals!

8   *Who can* live and **né**ver **see** death? *
    Who can escape the **pówer** of **She**ol?

9   *Blessed* be the **LÓRD** forever. *
    Am**én** and Amen.

For the solemnity of Christ the King, see below, **296–301.**

Ordinary Time I

Entrance Antiphon

Psalm 66 (65V):4

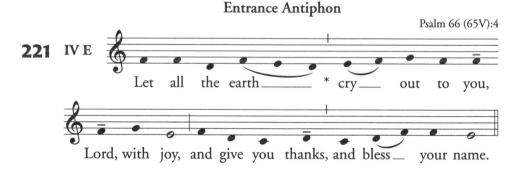

221   IV E

Let all the earth ___ * cry ___ out to you,
Lord, with joy, and give you thanks, and bless ___ your name.

Psalm 66 (65V)

1–2, 8–10, 13–14a, 16–20

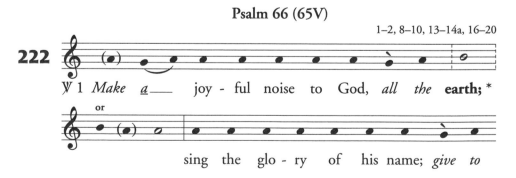

222

℣ 1 *Make* *a* ___ joy - ful noise to God, *all* *the* **earth;** *
or
sing the glo - ry of his name; *give to*

him__ **glo-rious__** praise. *Flex:* burnt of-fer-ings; †

2   *Bless* our *Gòd, O* **peo**ples, *
    let the sound *òf his praise* **be** heard,

3   *who has* kept us a*mòng the* **liv**ing, *
    and *hàs not let* **our feet** slip.

4   *For you, O Gòd, have* **tes**ted us; *
    you have tried *ùs as silver* **is** tried.

5   *I will* come into your house with burnt offerings; †
    I will *pày you* **my** vows, *
    those *thàt my lips* **ut**tered.

6   *Come* and hear, all you *whò fear* **God,** *
    and I will tell what *hè has done* **for** me.

7   *I cried* al*òud to* **him,** *
    and he *wàs extolled* **with my** tongue.

8   *If I* had cherished iniquity *in my* **heart,** *
    the *Lòrd would not have* **lis**tened.

9   *But truly Gòd has* **lis**tened; *
    he has given heed *tò the words* **of my** prayer.

10 *Blessèd* be God, because he has not rejec*tèd my* **prayer** *
    or removed *his steadfast* **love from** me.

When there are two readings before the gospel, the chants between the readings are arranged as follows: The responsorial psalm is sung after the first reading; after the second reading, the alleluia psalm or the antiphon Alleluia with its own verses.

Whenever there is only a single reading before the gospel, a single chant may be chosen at will from those provided.

At least five verses of a psalm, chosen at will, are always sung, whenever more than five are given.

This applies throughout Ordinary Time.

Responsorial Psalm C 2 a
Psalm 66 (65V)

(2), 1–7, 22

223

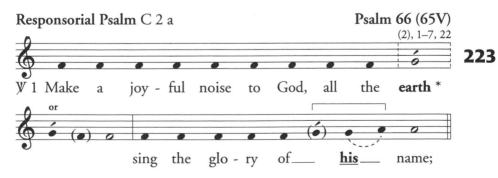

℣ 1 Make a joy-ful noise to God, all the **earth** *

or

sing the glo-ry of__ **his__** name;

℟ Give God glo - rious praise.

2. Say to God, "How awesome are your **déeds!** *
Because of your great power, your enemies cringe be**fóre** you.

3. All the earth worships you; they sing praises to **yóu,** *
sing praises to **yóur** name."

4. Come and see what God has **dóne:** *
he is awesome in his deeds among **mór**tals.

5. He turned the sea into dry land; '
they passed through the river on **fóot** *
There we rejoiced **ín** him,

6. who rules by his might forever, '
whose eyes keep watch on the **ná**tions— *
let the rebellious not exalt **thém**selves.

7. Blessed be God, because he has not rejected my **práyer** *
or removed his steadfast love **fróm** me.

Alleluia Psalm 97 (96V)

1, 6

224 VIII c

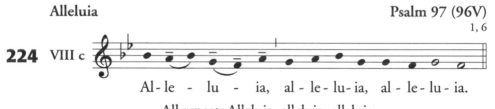

Al - le - lu - ia, al - le - lu - ia, al - le - lu - ia.

All repeat: Alleluia, alleluia, alleluia.

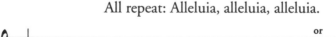

℣ 1 *The* LORD is king! Let the **earth** re - joice; *

let the man - y *coast - lands* **be** glad!

All repeat: Alleluia, alleluia, alleluia.

2. *The heav*ens proclaim his **right**eousness; *
and all the peoples be*hòld his* **glo**ry.

All repeat: Alleluia, alleluia, alleluia.

Alleluia Psalm E *   Psalm 97 (96V)
1–4, 6–9, 12

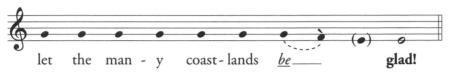

℣ 1 The LORD is king! Let the earth re-**joice;** *

let the man-y coast-lands *be*____ **glad!**

℟ Al-le-lu - ia,____ al-le-lu - ia.

225

2   Clouds and thick darkness are all **aróund** him; *
    righteousness and justice are the foundation of *hìs* **throne.**

3   Fire goes be**fóre** him, *
    and consumes his adversaries on *everỳ* **side.**

4   His lightnings light up the **wórld;** *
    the earth sees *ànd* **trem**bles.

5   The heavens proclaim his **rígh**teousness; *
    and all the peoples behold *hìs* **glo**ry.

6   All worshipers of images are put to shame, '
        those who make their boast in worthless **í**dols; *
    all gods bow down be*fòre* **him.**

7   Zion hears and is glad, and the towns of Judah re**jóice,** *
    because of your judgments, *Ò* **God.**

8   For you, O LORD, are most high over **áll** the earth; *
    you are exalted far above *àll* **gods.**

9   Rejoice in the LORD, O you **rígh**teous, *
    and give thanks to his *holỳ* **name!**

Preparation of the Gifts Antiphon

Psalm 47 (46V):1b

VII a

Cry out to God with joy,* with_ a voice of ex-ul-ta-tion.

226

Psalm 47 (46V)

2, 6–8

227

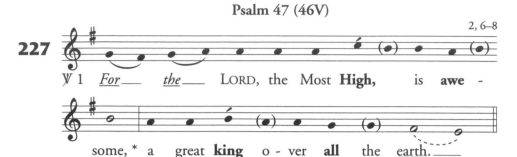

℣ 1 *For* _ *the* _ LORD, the Most **High,** is **awe** -

some, * a great **king** o - ver **all** the earth. _

2 *Sing prais*es to **Gód,** sing **prais**es; *
   sing praises **tó** our King, **sing** praises.

3 *For God* is the **kíng** of **all** the earth; *
   sing **prái**ses **with** a psalm.

4 *God is* king **óv**er the **na**tions; *
   God **síts** on his **hol**y throne.

Communion Antiphon

Luke 4:22

228 I f

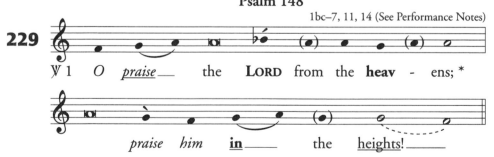

And all the peo - ple mar - velled * at the

words _ that came from the mouth _ of the Lord.

Psalm 148

1bc–7, 11, 14 (See Performance Notes)

229

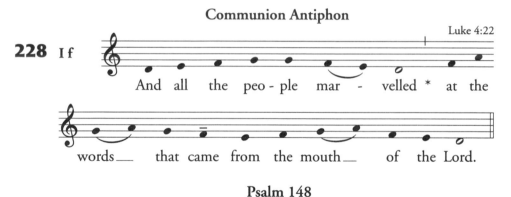

℣ 1 O *praise* _ the **LORD** from the **heav** - ens; *

praise him **in** _ the heights! _

2 *O praise* him, **áll** his **an**gels; *
   prà ise him, **all** his host!

3 O **prái**se him, **sun** and moon; *
   praise him, *àll you* **shin**ing stars!

152

4   *O praise* him, you **high**est **heav**ens, *
and you wa*tèrs a***bove** the heavens!

5   *O let* them praise the **náme** of **the** LORD, *
for he commanded *ànd they* **were** created.

6   *He es*tablished them for**év**er and **ev**er; *
he fixed their bounds, *whìch can***not** be passed.

7   *O praise* the **LÓRD** from **the** earth, *
you sea mon*stèrs and* **all** deeps,

8   *O kings* of the **éarth** and all **peo**ples, *
princes and all *rùlers* **of** the earth!

9   *He has* raised up praise for **áll** his **faith**ful, *
for the people of Israel *whò are* **close** to him.

Ordinary Time II

Entrance Antiphon

Psalm 18 (17V):Cf. 18b

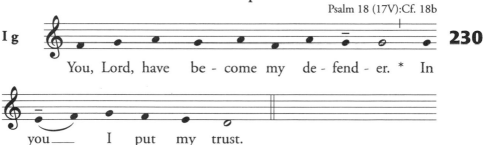

230

You, Lord, have be - come my de - fend - er. * In you — I put my trust.

Psalm 18 (17V)

(Cf. 18b) 1–4, 6, 16, 18, 20, 49

231

℣ 1 *I love* — **you,** O **LORD,** my strength. * The LORD is my rock, my for - tress, and *my de* - **liv** - er - er,

2   *my God,* my rock in **whóm** I take **ref**uge, *
my shield, and the horn of my salva*tìon, my* **strong**hold.

3   *I call* upon the LORD, who is **wór**thy to **be** praised, *
so I shall be saved *fròm my* **en**emies.

4 *The <u>cords</u> of* **déath** *encom*passed me; *
   the torrents of perdi*tìon as***sailed** me;

5 *In <u>my</u>* distress I **called** upon the LORD; *
   to my *Gòd I* **cried** for help.

6 *<u>From</u> his* **tém**ple he **heard** my voice, *
   and my cry *tò him* **reached** his ears.

7 *He <u>reached</u>* down from on **hígh,** he **took** me; *
   he drew me out of *mìghty* **wa**ters.

8 *They confront*ed me in the day of **mý** ca**lam**ity; *
   but the *LÒRD wàs* **my** support.

9 *The <u>LORD</u>* rewarded me according **tó** my **right**eousness; *
   according to the cleanness of my hands he *rècom***pensed** me.

10 *For <u>this</u>* I will extol you, O LORD, a**móng** the **na**tions, *
   and sing prais*ès to* **your** name.

Responsorial Psalm C 2 g   **Psalm 43 (42V)**
                                                   (5d) 1–5

232
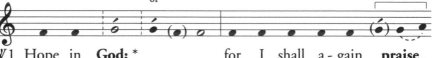
℣1 Hope in **God;** *   for I shall a-gain **praise**.

him,___ ℟ My Sav - ior and___ my___ God.___

2 Vindicate me, O God, '
      and defend my cause against an ungodly **péo**ple; *
   from those who are deceitful and unjust de**lí**ver <u>me</u>!

3 For you are the God in whom I take refuge; '
      why have you **cást** me off? *
   Why must I walk about mournfully because of the oppression
      of the **éne**<u>my</u>?

4 O send out your light and your truth; '
      let them **léad** me; *
   let them bring me to your holy hill and to your **dwéll**ing.

5 Then I will go to the altar of God, '
      to God my ex**céed**ing joy; *
   and I will praise you with the harp, O **Gód, my** <u>God</u>.

6 Why are you cast down, O my **sóul,** *
   and why are you disquieted with**ín** <u>me</u>?

154

7 Hope in **Gód;** *
for I shall again **práise** him.

Alleluia   **Psalm 9**
                                                                 1, 10

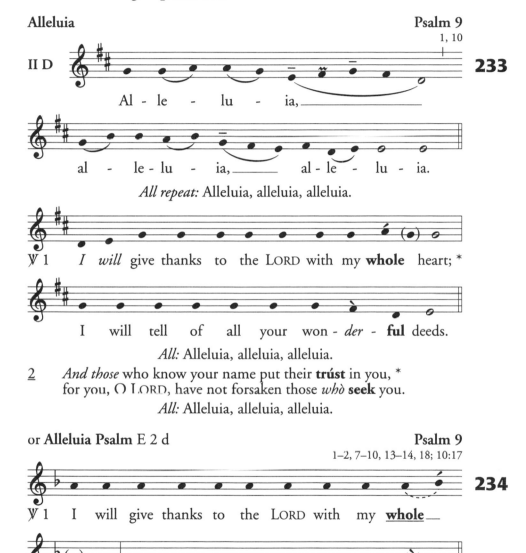

Al - le - lu - ia, _____

al - le - lu - ia, _____ al - le - lu - ia.

All repeat: Alleluia, alleluia, alleluia.

℣ 1   *I will* give thanks to the LORD with my **whole** heart; *

I will tell of all your won - *der* - **ful** deeds.

All: Alleluia, alleluia, alleluia.

2   *And those* who know your name put their **trúst** in you, *
for you, O LORD, have not forsaken those *whò* **seek** you.

All: Alleluia, alleluia, alleluia.

or **Alleluia Psalm** E 2 d   **Psalm 9**
                                        1–2, 7–10, 13–14, 18; 10:17

℣ 1 I will give thanks to the LORD with my **whole** __

heart; * I will tell of all your won - der - **ful** deeds.

℟ Al - le - lu - ia, al - le - lu - ia.

155

2   I will be glad and ex**últ** in you; *
     I will sing praise to your name, O **Most** Hìgh.

3   But the LORD sits enthroned for**é**ver, *
     he has established his throne for **judg**mènt.

4   He judges the world with **right**eousness; *
     he judges the peoples with **eq**ùity.

5   The LORD is a stronghold for **the óp**pressed, *
     a stronghold in times of **trou**blè.

6   And those who know your name put their **trúst** in you, *
     for you, O LORD, have not forsaken those who **seek** yòu.

7   Be gracious to me, O LORD. '
        See what I suffer from those who **háte** me; *
     you are the one who lifts me up from the **gates** òf death,

8   so that I may recount all your **práis**es, *
     and, in the gates of daughter Zion, rejoice in your de**liv**èrance.

9   For the needy shall not always be for**gót**ten, *
     nor the hope of the poor perish for**ev**èr.

10   O LORD, you will hear the desire **of thé** meek; *
     you will strengthen their heart, you will incline **your** èar.

Preparation of the Gifts Antiphon

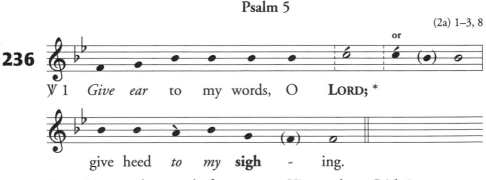

Psalm 5:2a

235 VIII G

Hear my cry for help, * my King_____ and my God.

Psalm 5

(2a) 1–3, 8

236

℣ 1 *Give ear* to my words, O **LORD;** *

or

give heed *to my* **sigh** - ing.

2   *Listen to* the sound of my cry, my King and my **Gód,** *
     for to **you** I pray.

156

3 *O LORD,* in the morning you **héar** my voice; *
   in the morning I plead my *càse to* **you,** and watch.

4 *Lead me,* O LORD, in your righteousness because of my **én**emies; *
   make your way *stràight be***fore** me.

Communion Antiphon

Psalm 13 (12V):6

II D

237

Let me sing to you, Lord,* for all _ your good-ness to me.

Psalm 13 (12V)

1–5 (See Performance Notes)

238

℣ 1 *How long,* O LORD? Will you for - get me for -

or

ev - er? * How long will you hide *your* **face** from me?

Flex: pain in my soul, †

2 *How long* must I bear pain in my sòul, †
   and have sorrow in my heart **áll** day long? *
   How long shall my enemy be exalt**èd** over me?

3 *Consid*er and answer me, O **LÓRD** my God! *
   Give light to my eyes, or I will sleep *thè* **sleep** of death,

4 *and my* enemy will say, "I have pre**váiled**"; *
   my foes will rejoice because I *àm* **shak**en.

5 *But I* trusted in your **stéad**fast love; *
   my heart shall rejoice in your *sàl***va**tion.

Ordinary Time III

Entrance Antiphon

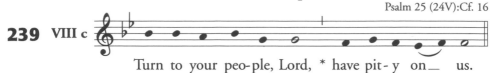

Psalm 25 (24V):Cf. 16

239 VIII c

Turn to your peo-ple, Lord, * have pit-y on us.

Psalm 25 (24V)

1–2, 4–6, 7bc–10, 15–16

240

℣ 1 *To you,* O LORD, I lift up my **soul.** *

O my God, in you I trust; do not let *me be*

put to shame. *Flex:* and teach me, †

2 *Make me* to know your **wáys,** O LORD; *
   tèach me **your** paths.

3 *Lead me* in your truth, and teach mè, †
   for you are the God of my salvátion; *
   for you *Ì wait* **all** day long.

4 *Be mind*ful of your mercy, O LORD, and of your **stéad**fast love, *
   for they *hàve been* **from** of old.

5 *Accord*ing to your steadfast love remémber me, *
   for your *gòodness'* **sake,** O LORD!

6 *Good and* upright is the **LÓRD;** *
   therefore he instructs *sìnners* **in** the way.

7 *He leads* the humble in what is **ríght,** *
   and teaches the *hùmble* **his** way.

8 *All the* paths of the LORD are steadfast love and **fáith**fulness, *
   for those who keep his *covenànt and* **his** decrees.

9 *My eyes* are ever toward the **LÓRD,** *
   for he will pluck my *fèet out* **of** the net.

10 *Turn to* me and be gracious to **mé,** *
   for I am lonely *ànd af***flic**ted.

158

Responsorial Psalm E 4

Psalm 55 (54V)

(2a) 1, 4, 6–7, 16–19, 22

241

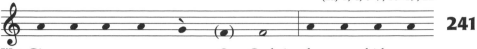

℣ 1 Give ear to my **prayer,** O God; * do not hide your-

self from my sup - pli - **ca** - tion. ℟ Turn __

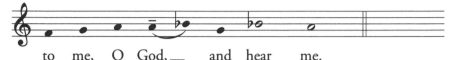

to me, O God, __ and hear me.

2 My heart is in anguish with**ìn** me, *
   the terrors of death have fallen up**òn** me.

3 And I say, "O that I had wings **lìke** a dove! *
   I would fly away and **bè** at rest;

4 truly, I would flee **fàr** away; *
   I would lodge in the **wìl**derness."

5 But I call up**òn** God, *
   and the LORD will **sàve** me.

6 Evening and morning and at noon I utter my com**plàint**
      and moan, *
   and he will **hèar** my voice.

7 He will redeem me unharmed from the battle that **Ì** wage, *
   for many are arrayed a**gàinst** me.

8 God, who is enthroned **fròm** of old, *
   will hear, and will **hùm**ble them.

9 Cast your burden on the LORD, '
      and he will sus**tàin** you; *
   he will never permit the righteous to **bè** moved.

Alleluia

Psalm 31 (30V)

1–2

VII a

242

Al - le - lu - ia, al - le - lu - ia, al - le - lu - ia.

All repeat: Alleluia, alleluia, alleluia.

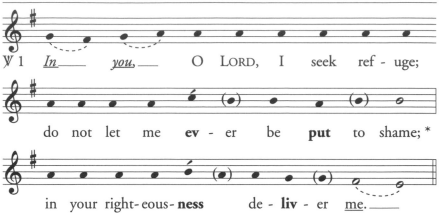

℣ 1 *In you,* O LORD, I seek ref - uge; do not let me **ev** - er be **put** to shame; * in your right-eous-**ness** de - **liv** - er me.

All: Alleluia, alleluia, alleluia.

2   *Incline* your ear to me; **rés**cue me **speed**ily. *
    Be a rock of refuge for me, a strong **fór**tress to **save** me.

All: Alleluia, alleluia, alleluia.

or **Alleluia Psalm** D 1 b   **Psalm 31 (30V)**
                                               1–3, 5–7, 19, 24

243

℣ 1 In you, O LORD, I seek ref- uge; do not let me ev - er be

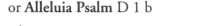

put to shame; * in your right-eous- ness de - **liv**- er me.

℟ Al - le - lu - ia, ____ al - le - lu - ia.

2   Incline your ear to me; rescue me **spéed**ily. *
    Be a rock of refuge for me, a strong fortress to **sàve** me.

3   You are indeed my rock and my **fór**tress; *
    for your name's sake lead me and **gùide** me,

4   Into your hand I commit my **spír**it; *
    you have redeemed me, O LORD, **faith**ful God.

5   I trust in the **LÓRD**. *
    I will exult and rejoice in your **stèad**fast love,

6   because you have seen my afflíction; *
    you have taken heed of my ad**vèr**sities,

7   O how abundant is your **góod**ness *
that you have laid up for those who **fèar** you,

8   Be strong, and let your heart take **cóur**age, *
all you who wait **fòr** the LORD.

Preparation of the Gifts Antiphon

Psalm 54 (53V):4

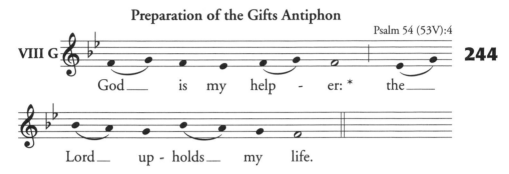

God___ is my help - er: * the___
Lord___ up - holds___ my life.

VIII G   244

Psalm 54 (53V)

1–2, 6–7

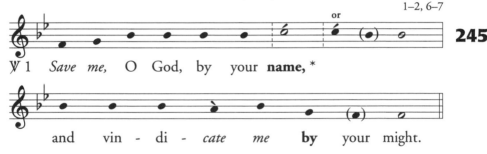

or

℣ 1 *Save me,* O God, by your **name,** *
and vin - di - *cate me* **by** your might.

245

2   *Hear my* prayer, O **Gód;** *
give ear to the *wòrds of* **my** mouth.

3   *With a* freewill offering I will sacrifice to **yóu;** *
I will give thanks to your name, O *LÒRD, for* **it** is good.

4   *For he* has delivered me from every **tróu**ble, *
and my eye has looked in triumph *òn my* **en**emies.

Communion Antiphon

Matthew 6:33

I g

Seek first God's king - dom * and God's___
jus - tice: and all the rest will be giv - en to you.

246

Psalm 37 (36V)

1, 3–6, 16, 18, 23–25 (See Performance Notes)

247

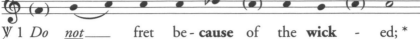

℣ 1 *Do* _not___ fret be - **cause** of the **wick** - ed; *

do not be en - *vious* *of* **wrong** - doers,

Flex: and now am old, †

2 *Trust* in the **LÓRD,** and **do** good; *
so you will live in the land, and en*jòy se***cur**ity.

3 *Take* de**líght** in **the** LORD, *
and he will give you the de*sìres of* **your** heart.

4 *Commit* your **wáy** to **the** LORD; *
trust in *hìm, and* **he** will act.

5 *He* _will_ make your vindication **shíne** like **the** light, *
and the justice of your cause *lìke the* **noon**day.

6 *Better is* a little that the **ríght**eous **per**son has *
than the abundance of *màny* **wick**ed.

7 *The* LORD knows the **dáys** of the **blame**less, *
and their heritage will a*bìde for***ev**er;

8 *Our* _steps_ are made **fírm** by **the** LORD, *
when he de*lìghts in* **our** way;

9 *though* _we_ stumble, we shall **nót** fall **head**long, *
for the LORD *hòlds us* **by** the hand.

10 *I* _have_ been young, and now àm old, †
    yet I have not seen the **ríght**eous forsaken *
or their *chìldren* **beg**ging bread.

Ordinary Time IV

Entrance Antiphon

Psalm 48 (47):9

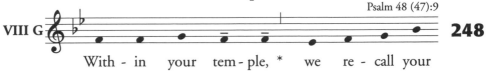

VIII G **248**

With - in your tem - ple, * we re - call your lov - ing kind - ness, O God, our God.

Psalm 48 (47)

1–2, 4–5, 8, 11–14 (See Performance Notes)
or

249

℣ 1 *Great is* the LORD and great - ly to be **praised** *

in the *cit - y* **of** our God. *Flex:* so have we seen †

2 *His ho*ly mountain, beautiful in eleváted, *
   is the *jòy of* **all** the earth,

3 *Mount Zi*on, in the **fár** north, *
   the city *òf the* **great** King.

4 *Then the* kings as**sém**bled, *
   they came *òn to***geth**er.

5 *As soon* as they saw it, they were as**tóund**ed; *
   they were in pan*ìc, they* **took** to flight;

6 *As we* have heard, so have wè seen †
      in the city of the **LÓRD** of hosts, *
   in the city of our God, which God establish*ès for*ever.

7 *Let Mount* Zion be **glád**, *
   let the towns of Judah rejoice because *òf your* **judg**ments.

8 *Walk a*bout Zion, go all a**róund** it, *
   còunt its **tow**ers,

9 *consid*er well its rampàrts; †
      go through its **cí**tadels, *
   that you may tell the next *gèner*ation

10 *that this* is God, our God forever and **év**er. *
    He will be our *gùide for*ever.

Responsorial Psalm C 2 g

Psalm 92 (91V)
(1b) 1–6, 12–15

250

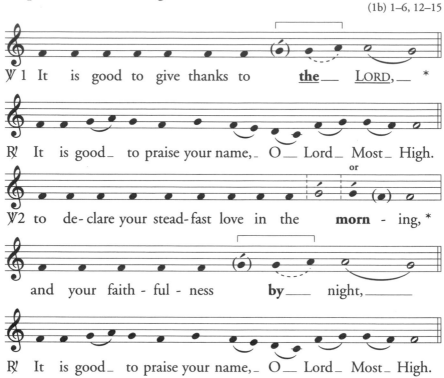

℣ 1 It is good to give thanks to **the** LORD, *

℟ It is good to praise your name, O Lord Most High.

℣ 2 to de-clare your stead-fast love in the **morn** - ing, *

and your faith - ful - ness **by** night,

℟ It is good to praise your name, O Lord Most High.

3   to the music of the lute and the **hárp,** *
     to the melody of **thé** lyre.

4   For you, O LORD, have made me glad by your **wórk;** *
     at the works of your hands I sing **fór** joy.

5   How great are your works, O **LÓRD!** *
     Your thoughts are **véry** deep!

6   The dullard cannot **knów,** *
     the stupid cannot under**stánd** this.

7   The righteous flourish like the **pálm** tree, *
     and grow like a cedar in **Léba**non.

8   They are planted in the house of the **LÓRD;** *
     they flourish in the courts of **our** God.

9   In old age they still produce **frúit;** *
     they are always green and **fúll of** sap,

10   showing that the LORD is **úp**right; *
     he is my rock, and there is no unrighteousness **ín** him.

Alleluia Psalm 65 (64V)
1, 2

251

Al - le - lu - ia, al - le - lu - ia,— al - le - lu - ia.

All repeat: Alleluia, alleluia, alleluia.

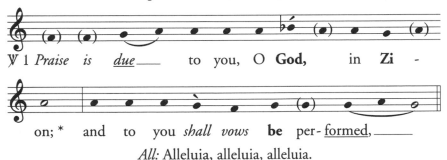

℣ 1 *Praise is due*— to you, O **God,** in **Zi** -

on; * and to you *shall vows* **be** per- formed, ____

All: Alleluia, alleluia, alleluia.

2 O **yóu** who **an**swer prayer! *
To you *àll flesh* **shall** come.

All: Alleluia, alleluia, alleluia.

or **Alleluia Psalm** D 1 b Psalm 65 (64V)
1–2, 4–7, 9–10
or

252

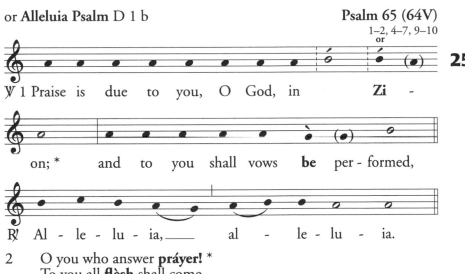

℣ 1 Praise is due to you, O God, in **Zi** -

on; * and to you shall vows **be** per - formed,

℟ Al - le - lu - ia,— al - le - lu - ia.

2 O you who answer **práyer!** *
To you all **flèsh** shall come.

3 Happy are those whom you choose and bring **néar** *
to live **ìn** your courts.

4 We shall be satisfied with the goodness of your **hóuse,** *
your holy **tèm**ple.

5   By awesome deeds you answer us with deliverance, O God of our
        salvá́tion; *
     you are the hope of all the ends of the earth and of the **far**thest seas.

6   By your strength you established the **móun**tains; *
     you are girded **with** might.

7   You silence the roaring of the seas, '
        the roaring of their **wáves,** *
     the tumult of the **pèo**ples.

8   You visit the earth and **wá**ter it, *
     you greatly en**rìch** it;

9   the river of God is full of water; '
        you provide the people with **gráin,** *
     for so you have pre**pàred** it.

<u>10</u>   You water its furrows a**bún**dantly, *
     settling its ridges, softening it with showers, and blessing **ìts** growth.

Preparation of the Gifts Antiphon

Psalm 140 (139V):Cf. 8a, 7

253 IV E

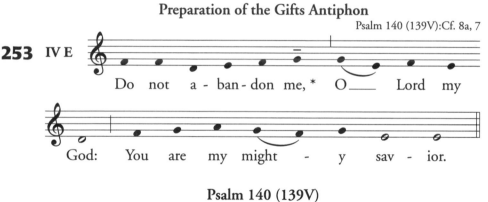

Do not a - ban - don me, * O___ Lord my

God: You are my might - y sav - ior.

Psalm 140 (139V)

1, 4, 6, 13

254

℣ 1 *De-liv* - er me, O LORD, from *e - vil* - **do** - ers; *

pro - tect me from *those who are*___ **vi - o** - lent,

℣4 the up-*right shall live in* **your pres** - ence.

166

2 _Guard_ me, O LORD, from the hands *òf the* **wick**ed; *
protect me from the violent *whò have* _planned_ **my** **down**fall.

3 *I* _say_ to the LORD, *"Yòu are* **my** God; *
give ear, O LORD, to the voice *òf my* suppli**ca**tions."

4 _Sure_ly the righteous shall give thanks *tò your* **name;** *
the up*rìght shall live in* **your** **pres**ence.

Communion Antiphon I

Psalm 96 (95V):Cf. 9a

Psalm 96 (95V)

(9a)1–5, 7–9, 11–13

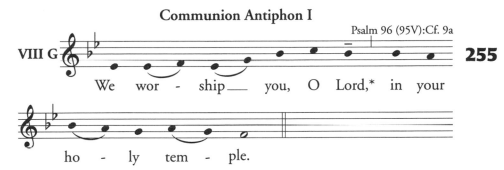

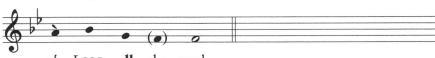

2 *Sing to* the LORD, bless his **náme;** *
tell of his salva*tion from* **day** to day.

3 *Declare* his glory among the **ná**tions, *
his marvelous works among *àll the* **peo**ples.

4 *For great* is the LORD, and greatly to be **práised;** *
he is to be re*vèred a***bove** all gods.

5 *For all* the gods of the peoples are **í**dols, *
but the LORD *màde the* **heav**ens.

6 *Ascribe* to the LORD, O families of the **péo**ples, *
ascribe to the LORD *glòry* **and** strength.

7 *Ascribe* to the LORD the glory due his **náme;** *
bring an offering, and come *ìnto* **his** courts.

8 *Worship* the LORD in holy **splén**dor; *
tremble be*fòre him,* **all** the earth.

9   *Let the* heavens be glad, and let the **éarth** rejoice; *
let the sea roar, and *àll that* **fills** it;

10   *let the* field exult, and everything **ín** it. *
Then shall all the trees of the *fòrest* **sing** for joy

11   *before* the LORD; for he is **cóm**ing, *
for he is com*ìng to* **judge** the earth.

12   *He will* judge the world with **rígh**teousness, *
and the *pèoples* **with** his truth.

or **Communion Antiphon II**

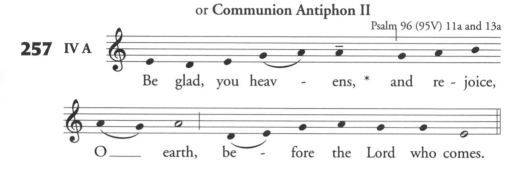

Psalm 96 (95V) 11a and 13a

257 IV A

Be glad, you heav - ens, * and re - joice,
O___ earth, be - fore the Lord who comes.

Psalm 96 (95V)

1–5, 7–9, 11–13
or

258

℣ 1 O *sing*___ to the LORD a **new**
song; * sing *to* *the* LORD, **all** the earth.

2   *[O] sing* to the LORD, *blèss his* **name;** *
tell of his sal*vàtion from* **day** to day.

3   *Declare* his glory a*mòng the* **na**tions, *
his marvelous works a*mòng all the* **peo**ples.

4   *For great* is the LORD, and greatly *tò be* **praised;** *
he is to be *rèvered a***bove** all gods.

5   *For all* the gods of the peo*plès are* **idols,** *
but the LÒRD *made the* **heav**ens.

6   *Ascribe* to the LORD, O families *òf the* **peo**ples, *
ascribe to the LÒRD *glory* **and** strength.

7   *Ascribe* to the LORD the glory *dùe his* **name;** *
    bring an offering, and *còme into* **his** courts.

8   *Wor*ship the LORD in *hòly* **splen**dor; *
    tremble *bèfore him,* **all** the earth.

9   *Let the heav*ens be glad, and *lèt the* **earth** rejoice; *
    let the sea roar, *ànd all that* **fills** it;

10 *let the field* exult, and ever*ỳthing* **in** it. *
    Then shall all the trees of *thè forest* **sing** for joy

11 *before* the LORD; for *hè is* **com**ing, *
    for he is *còming to* **judge** the earth.

12 *He* will judge the *wòrld with* **right**eousness, *
    and *thè peoples* **with** his truth.

Ordinary Time V

Entrance Antiphon I

Psalm 86 (85V):1

I g 3   In-cline your ear, O Lord,__ * and__ an-swer__ me.   **259**

or Entrance Antiphon II

Psalm 86 (85V):10

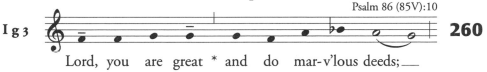

I g 3   Lord, you are great * and do mar-v'lous deeds;__   **260**

you a-lone are__ God.

Psalm 86 (85V)

1–7, 9–10, 12

℣ 1   *In-cline*__ your ear, O **LORD,** and **an-**swer me, *   **261**

for I am *poor and* **need** - y. *Flex:* shall come †

2   *Preserve* my life, for I am de**vó**ted **to** you; *
    save your ser**vànt** *who* **trusts** in you.

3   *You are* my God; be **grá**cious to **me,** O Lord, *
    for to you do *Ì cry* **all** day long.

4   *Glad*den the **sóul** of your **ser**vant, *
    for to you, O Lord, I *lìft up* **my** soul.

5   *For you,* O Lord, are **góod** and for**giv**ing, *
    abounding in steadfast love to *àll who* **call** on you.

6   *Give ear,* O **LÓRD,** to **my** prayer; *
    listen to my cry of *sùppli***ca**tion.

7   *In the day* of my **tróu**ble I **call** on you, *
    for *yòu will* **an**swer me.

8   *All the na*tions you have made shall còme †
    and bow down be**fó**re you, **O** Lord, *
    and shall glo*rìfy* **your** name.

9   *For you* are **gréat** and do **won**drous things; *
    you *àlone* **are** God.

10 *I give thanks* to you, O Lord my **Gód,** with my **whole** heart, *
    and I will glorify your *nàme* for**ev**er.

Responsorial Psalm E 4   Psalm 17 (16V)
                                      (1b) 1–2, 4–9, 15

262

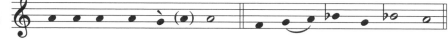

℣ 1 Hear a just cause, **O**   LORD; ℟ O Lord,— hear my plead-ing.

℣ 2 give ear to **my** prayer * from lips free **of** de - ceit.

℟   O Lord,— hear my plead - ing.

3   From you let my vindi**cà**tion come; *
    let your eyes **sèe** the right.

4   As for what others do, by the word of **yòur** lips *
    I have avoided the ways of the **vìo**lent.

5   My steps have held fast to **yòur** paths; *
    my feet have **nòt** slipped.

170

6 I call upon you, for you will answer **mè,** O God; *
incline your ear to me, **hèar** my words.

7 Wondrously show your **stèad**fast love, *
O savior of those who seek refuge from their adversaries
at your **rìght** hand.

8 Guard me as the apple **òf** the eye; *
hide me in the shadow of **yòur** wings,

9 from the wicked who de**spòil** me, *
my deadly enemies who sur**ròund** me.

10 As for me, I shall behold your face in **rìght**eousness; *
when I awake I shall be satisfied, beholding your **lìke**ness.

Alleluia   Psalm 95 (94V)
1, 3 (See Performance Notes)

IV E   **263**

Al - le - lu - ia, al - le - lu - ia,___ al - le - lu - ia.

All repeat: Alleluia, alleluia, alleluia.

℣ 1 O *come,*___ let us sing *to the* LORD; *   let us make

a joy-ful noise to the *rock of our*___ **sal - va** - tion!

All: Alleluia, alleluia, alleluia.

2 For the LORD *is a* **great** God, *
and a great *King above* **all** gods.

All: Alleluia, alleluia, alleluia.

or **Alleluia Psalm C 1**   Psalm 95 (94V)
1–5, 7

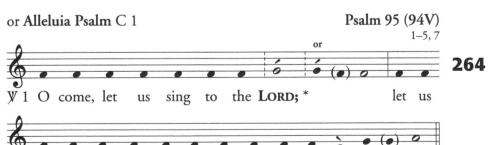

264

℣ 1 O come, let us sing to the LORD; *   let us

make a joy - ful noise to the rock of our *sal - va* - tion!

℟ Al - le - lu - ia, al - le - lu - ia.

2   Let us come into his presence with thanks**gí**ving; *
     let us make a joyful noise to him *wìth* **songs** of praise!

3   For the LORD is a **gréat** God, *
     and a great King a*bòve* **all** gods.

4   In his hand are the depths of the **éarth;** *
     the heights of the mountains are *hìs* **al**so.

5   The sea is his, for he **máde** it, *
     and the dry land, which *hìs* **hands** have formed.

6   We are the people of his **pás**ture, *
     and the sheep *òf* **his** hand.

Preparation of the Gifts Antiphon

Psalm 13 (12V):3b

265 VIII c

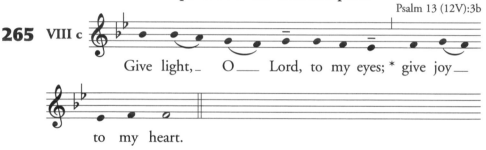

Give light, _ O ___ Lord, to my eyes; * give joy ___

to   my   heart.

Psalm 13 (12V)

1–3a, 5b–6 (See Performance Notes)

or

266

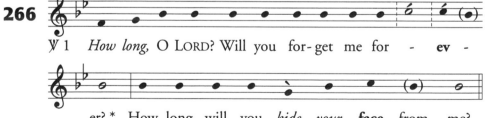

℣ 1   *How long,* O LORD? Will you for-get me for - **ev** -

er? * How long will you *hide* *your* **face** from   me?

2   *How long* must I bear pain in my **sóul,** *
     and have sorrow in *mỳ heart* **all** day long?

3   *How long* shall my enemy be exalted **ó**ver me? *
     Consider and answer me, *Ò LORD* **my** God!

4   *My heart* shall rejoice in your sal**vá**tion. *
     I will sing to the LORD, because he has dealt boun*tìfully* **with** me.

172

Communion Antiphon

Psalm 147 (146V):Cf. 1

VIII c

We sing to you, God, * for you are good; it is

267

right to praise you.

Psalm 147 (146V)

1bc, 2–9, 11
or

℣ 1 *How good* it is to sing prais- es to our **God;** *

268

for *he is* **gra** - cious. *Flex:* heav-ens with clouds,†

2 *The* LORD builds up Jerúsalem; *
he gathers the out*càsts of* **Is**rael.

3 *He heals* the broken**héart**ed, *
and *bìnds up* **their** wounds.

4 *He de*termines the number of the **stárs;** *
he gives to all *òf them* **their** names.

5 *Great is* our Lord, and abundant in **pówer;** *
his understanding is *bèyond* **meas**ure.

6 *The Lord* lifts up the **dówn**trodden; *
he casts the *wìcked* **to** the ground.

7 *Sing to* the LORD with thanks**gív**ing; *
make melody to our *Gòd on* **the** lyre.

8 *He cov*ers the heavens with clòuds, †
prepares rain for the **éarth,** *
makes grass *gròw on* **the** hills.

9 *He gives* to the animals their **fóod,** *
and to the young *ràvens* **when** they cry.

10 *The* LORD takes pleasure in those who **féar** him, *
in those who hope *ìn his* **stead**fast love.

Ordinary Time VI

Entrance Antiphon

269 II D

Give peace, O Lord, * in our ___ days;
may all who love you dwell se - cure.

Psalm 122 (121V)

1–9 (See Performance Notes)

270

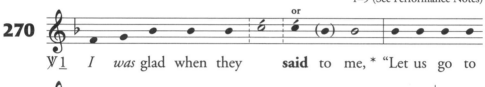

℣1 *I was* glad when they **said** to me, * "Let us go to
the house *of* **the** LORD!" *Flex:* of the LORD, †

2.   *Our feet* are **stánd**ing *
within your gates, O *Jè*ru*salem.

3.   *Jerus*alem—built as a **cí**ty *
that is bound firmly *tò*geth*er.

4.   *To it* the tribes go up, the tribes of the LÒRD, †
as was decreed for **Ís**rael, *
to give thanks to the name *òf* **the** LORD.

5.   *For there* the thrones for judgment were set **úp**, *
the thrones of the house *òf* **Da**vid.

6.   *Pray for* the peace of Jerú*salem: *
"May they prosper *whò* **love** you.

7.   *Peace be* within your **wálls**, *
and security within *yòur* **tow**ers."

8.   *For the* sake of my relatives and friends I will **sáy**, *
"Peace be *wìth***in** you."

9.   *For the* sake of the house of the **LÓRD** our God, *
I *wìll* **seek** your good.

The Responsorial Psalm, Alleluia, and/or Alleluia Psalm may be taken from Ordinary Time II, **232, 233,** and **234,** or Ordinary Time III, **241, 242,** and **243.**

Preparation of the Gifts Antiphon

Psalm 125 (124V):4

VIII c

O Lord,___ be kind * to the good and up-right.

271

Psalm 125 (124V)

1–5 (See Performance Notes)
or

℣ 1 *Those who* trust in the LORD are like Mount **Zi** - on, *

272

which can-not be moved, but a - *bides for* - **ev** - er.

Flex: Je - ru - sa-lem, †

2 *As the* mountains surround Jerusàlem, †
  so the LORD surrounds his **péo**ple, *
  from this time on *and fore*vermore.

3 *For the* scepter of wickedness shall not rest on the land allotted
    to the **ríght**eous, *
  so that the righteous might not stretch out their *hànds to* **do**
    wrong.

4 *But those* who turn aside to their own crookèd ways †
    the LORD will lead away with evil**dó**ers. *
  Peace be *ùpon* **Is**rael!

Communion Antiphon

Psalm 119 (118V):117

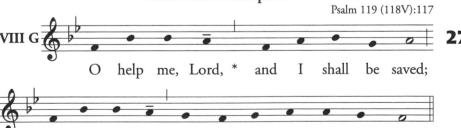

VIII G

O help me, Lord, * and I shall be saved;

O give me life, and I will keep your com-mands.

273

Psalm 119 (118V)

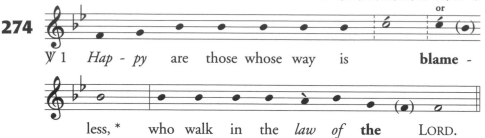

1–2, 12, 17, 25, 27, 35–36, 48–49

274 ℣ 1 *Hap - py* are those whose way is **blame** - less, * who walk in the *law of* **the** LORD.

2 *Happy* are those who keep his de**crées,** *
who seek him *with their* **whole** heart,

3 *Blessed* are you, O **LÓRD;** *
teach *mè your* **stat**utes.

4 *Deal boun*tifully with your **sér**vant, *
so that I may live *ànd observe* your word.

5 *My soul* clings to the **dúst;** *
revive me accord*ìng to* **your** word.

6 *Make me* understand the way of your **pré**cepts, *
and I will meditate *òn your* **won**drous works.

7 *Lead me* in the path of your com**mánd**ments, *
for *Ì de***light** in it.

8 *Turn my* heart to your de**crées,** *
and *nòt to* **sel**fish gain.

9 *I re*vere your commandments, which I **lóve,** *
and I will meditate *òn your* **stat**utes.

10 *Remem*ber your word to your **sér**vant, *
in which *yòu have* **made** me hope.

Ordinary Time VII

Entrance Antiphon

Psalm 123 (122V):1b and 3a

275 VIII G

Lord God in heav - en,* have mer - cy on us.

Psalm 123 (122V)

1–4 (See Performance Notes)

276

℣ 1 *To you* I lift up my **eyes,** * O you who are

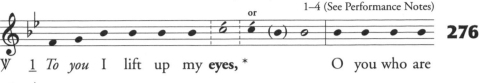

en- throned *in the* **heav** - ens! *Flex:* than its fill †

2 *As the* eyes of servants look to the hand of their **más**ter, *
as the eyes of a maid to the hand *òf her* **mis**tress,

3 *so our* eyes look to the **LÓRD** our God, *
until he has mer*cỳ up*on us.

4 *Have mer*cy upon us, O LORD, have mercy up**ón** us, *
for we have had more than en*òugh of* **con**tempt.

5 *Our soul* has had more than its fill †
of the scorn of those who are at **éase,** *
of the con*tèmpt of* **the** proud.

The Responsorial Psalm, Alleluia, and/or Alleluia Psalm may be taken from Ordinary Time IV, **250, 251,** and **253,** or Ordinary Time V, **262, 263,** and **264.**

Preparation of the Gifts Antiphon

Psalm 128 (127V):1

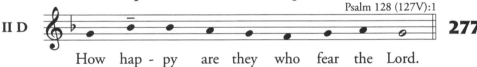

II D

277

How hap - py are they who fear the Lord.

Psalm 128 (127V)

2, 4–6 (See Performance Notes)
or

278

℣ 1 *You shall* eat the fruit of the la- bor of your **hands;** *

you shall be hap - py, and it shall *go* **well** with you.

2 *Thus shall* the man be **bléssed** *
who *fears* **the** LORD.

3 *The* LORD bless you from **Zíon.** *
May you see the prosperity of Jerusalem all the days *òf* **your** life.

4   *May you* see your children's **chíl**dren. *
Peace be up*òn* **Is**rael!

Communion Antiphon

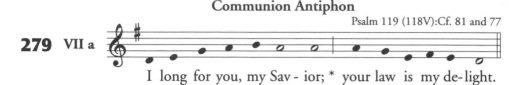

Psalm 119 (118V):Cf. 81 and 77

279 VII a

I long for you, my Sav - ior; * your law is my de-light.

Psalm 119 (118V)

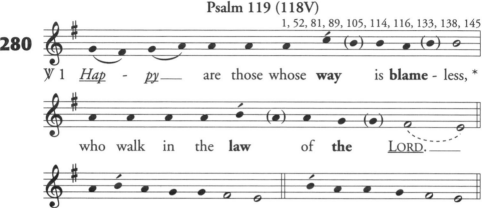

1, 52, 81, 89, 105, 114, 116, 133, 138, 145

280

℣ 1 *Hap - py* are those whose **way** is **blame** - less, *

who walk in the **law** of **the** LORD.

℣4 is **firm**-ly **fixed** in heav-en. ℣10 **I** will keep **your** stat-utes.

2   *When I* think of your **órd**inances **from** of old, *
I take **cóm**fort, **O** LORD.

3   *My soul* languishes for **yóur** sal**va**tion; *
I **hópe** in **your** word.

4   *The LORD* ex**ísts** for**ev**er; *
your word is **fírm**ly **fixed** in heaven.

5   *Your word* is a **lámp** to **my** feet *
and a **líght** to **my** path.

6   *You are* my hiding **pláce** and **my** shield; *
I **hópe** in **your** word.

7   *Uphold* me according to your **próm**ise, that **I** may live, *
and let me not be put to **sháme** in **my** hope.

8   *Keep my* steps steady according **tó** your **prom**ise, *
and never let iniquity have do**mín**ion **ov**er me.

9   *You have* appointed your de**crées** in **right**eousness *
and **ín** all **faith**fulness.

10   *With my* whole heart I cry; **án**swer me, **O** LORD. *
I will keep **your** statutes.

Ordinary Time VIII

Entrance Antiphon

Psalm 113 (112V):2

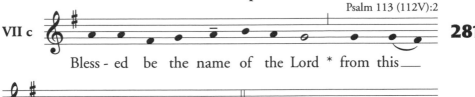

VII c

281

Bless - ed be the name of the Lord * from this___

time and for ev - er.

Psalm 113 (112V)

1, 3–9

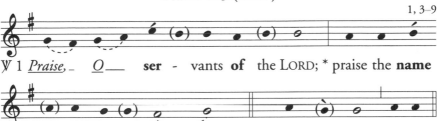

282

℣ 1 *Praise,*_ *O*__ **ser** - vants **of** the LORD; * praise the **name**

of **the** LORD.___ *Flex:* LORD our God, †

℣3 his **glo**-ry a-**bove** the **heav**-ens. ℣7 the **princ**-es **of**

his peo - ple. ℣8 joy - ous **moth**-er **of** chil - dren.

2   *From the* rising of the **sún** to its **setting** *
    the name of the **LÓRD** is **to** be <u>praised</u>.

3   *The* <u>LORD</u> is high a**bóve** all **na**tions, *
    and his **gló**ry a**bove** the heavens.

4   *Who* <u>is</u> like the LORD òur God, †
    who is **séat**ed **on** high, *
    who looks far down on the **héav**ens **and** the <u>earth</u>?

5   *He* <u>rais</u>es the **póor** from **the** dust, *
    and lifts the needy **fróm** the **ash** <u>heap</u>,

6   *to* <u>make</u> them **sít** with **princ**es,*
    with the **prín**ces **of** his people.

7   *He gives* the barren **wóm**an a home, *
making her the joyous **móth**er **of** children.

Responsorial Psalm E 4   Psalm 106 (105V)
(1b) 1a, 2–4, 6, 8, 44–45, 47

283

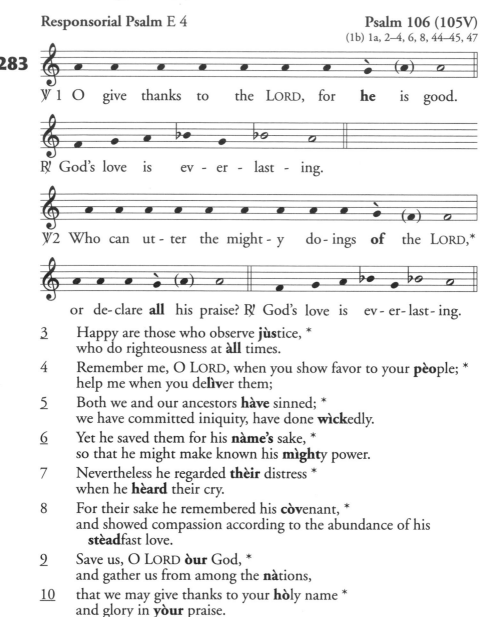

℣ 1 O give thanks to the LORD, for **he** is good.

℟ God's love is ev - er - last - ing.

℣ 2 Who can ut - ter the might - y do - ings **of** the LORD,*

or de - clare **all** his praise? ℟ God's love is ev - er - last - ing.

3   Happy are those who observe **jùs**tice, *
who do righteousness at **àll** times.

4   Remember me, O LORD, when you show favor to your **pèo**ple; *
help me when you de**lìv**er them;

5   Both we and our ancestors **hàve** sinned; *
we have committed iniquity, have done **wìck**edly.

6   Yet he saved them for his **nàme's** sake, *
so that he might make known his **mìght**y power.

7   Nevertheless he regarded **thèir** distress *
when he **hèard** their cry.

8   For their sake he remembered his **còv**enant, *
and showed compassion according to the abundance of his
stèadfast love.

9   Save us, O LORD **òur** God, *
and gather us from among the **nà**tions,

10   that we may give thanks to your **hòl**y name *
and glory in **yòur** praise.

Alleluia Psalm 145 (144V)

1–2

VIII c

Al - le - lu - ia,   al - le - lu - ia,   al - le - lu - ia.

All repeat: Alleluia, alleluia, alleluia.

284

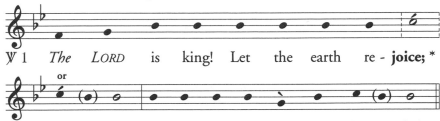

℣ 1   *The* LORD   is   king! Let   the   earth   re - **joice;** *

or

let   the   man - y   *coast-lands*   **be**   glad!

All: Alleluia, alleluia, alleluia.

2   *The heav*ens proclaim his **right**eousness; *
     and all the peoples be*hòld his* **glo**ry.

All: Alleluia, alleluia, alleluia.

or **Alleluia Psalm** C 1 Psalm 145 (144V)

1–4, 8, 15–16, 18–19, 21

or

285

℣ 1   I   will   ex - tol you,   my   God   and   **King,** *

and   bless   your   name   for - ev - er   *and*   **ev** -   er.

℟ Al -   le -   lu - ia,   al - le -   lu -   ia.

2   Every day I will **bléss** you, *
     and praise your name forever *ànd* **ev**er.

3   Great is the LORD, and greatly to be **práised;** *
     his greatness is *ùn***search**able.

4   One generation shall laud your works to an**óth**er, *
     and shall declare *yòur* **might**y acts.

5 The LORD is gracious and **mér**ciful, *
slow to anger and abounding *ìn* **stead**fast love.

6 The eyes of all **lóok** to you, *
and you give them their food in *dùe* **sea**son.

7 You open your **hánd,** *
satisfying the desire of eve*rỳ* **liv**ing thing.

8 The LORD is near to all who **cáll** on him, *
to all who call *òn* **him** in truth.

9 He fulfills the desire of all who **féar** him; *
he also hears their cry, *ànd* **saves** them.

10 My mouth will speak the praise of the **LÓRD,** *
and all flesh will bless his holy name forever *ànd* **ev**er.

Preparation of the Gifts Antiphon

Psalm 113 (112V):3

286 IV E

From sun-rise to sun - set * praise the name of the Lord.

Psalm 113 (112V)

1–2, 4–6

287

or

℣ 1 *Praise, O__ ser-vants of the* **LORD;** *

praise the name__ **of the__** LORD.

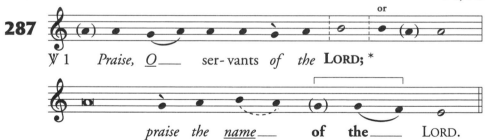

2 *Blessed* <u>*be*</u> *the name* *òf the* **LORD** *
from this time on *ànd for*<u>*ev*</u>*er*more.

<u>3</u> *The* <u>LORD</u> *is high a*bòve all **na**tions, *
and his glo*rỳ above the* **heav**ens.

4 *Who is* <u>*like*</u> the LORD our God, who is seat*èd on* **high,** *
who looks far down *òn the heavens* **and** <u>**the**</u> earth?

Communion Antiphon

Psalm 34 (33V), *I will bless the* LORD, with ℟ *Taste and See,* **645,** or another appropriate chant as listed on p. 386.

182

Ordinary Time IX: Last Weeks in Ordinary Time

Entrance Antiphon

Revelation 2:10

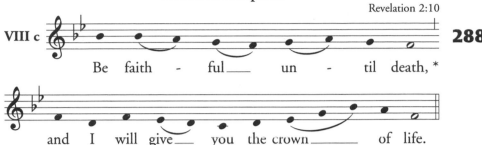

288

VIII c

Be faith - ful___ un - til death, *
and I will give___ you the crown___ of life.

Canticle of Revelation

Revelation 2:17, 26, 28; 3: 5, 10–12, 21

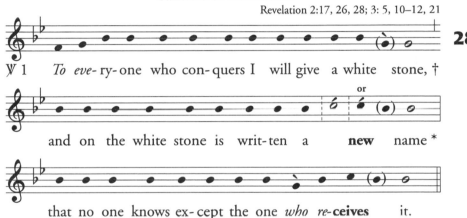

289

℣ 1 *To eve-*ry-one who con-quers I will give a white stone, †
and on the white stone is writ-ten a **new** name *
that no one knows ex-cept the one *who re-***ceives** it.

2 *To every*one who conquers and continues to do my works
to the ènd, †
I will give authority over the **ná**tions, *
even as I also received authority *fròm my* **Fa**ther.

3 *To the* one who **cón**quers *
I will also *give the* **morn**ing star.

4 *If you* conquer, you will be clothed in **whíte** robes, *
and I will not blot your name out *òf the* **book** of life;

5 *I will* confess your name before my **Fá**ther *
and be*fòre his* **an**gels.

6 *Because* you have kept my word of patient en**dúr**ance, *
I will keep you from the *hòur of* **tri**al.

7 *I am* coming sòon; †
hold fast to what you **háve,** *
so that no *òne may* **seize** your crown.

8   *If you* conquer, I will make you a pillar in the temple of my **Gód;** *
you will nev*èr go* **out** of it.

9   *To the* one who conquers I will give a place with me on **mý** throne, *
just as I myself conquered and sat down with my Fa*thèr on* **his**
throne.

The Responsorial Psalm may be taken from Easter Vigil Responsorial Psalm II, **133,** or
Easter Vigil Responsorial Psalm VII(A), **140.**

Alleluia   **Psalm 146 (145V)**

290   IV E

Al - le - lu - ia, al - le - lu - ia, al - le - lu - ia.

All repeat: Alleluia, alleluia, alleluia.

℣ 1 *I will praise* the LORD as long *as* I **live;** *

I will sing prais- es to *my God all my* **life** long.

All: Alleluia, alleluia, alleluia.

2   *The LORD* will *rèign fore*ver, *
your God, O Zion, *for all gener*ations.

All: Alleluia, alleluia, alleluia.

or **Alleluia Psalm** C 1   **Psalm 146 (145V)**

291

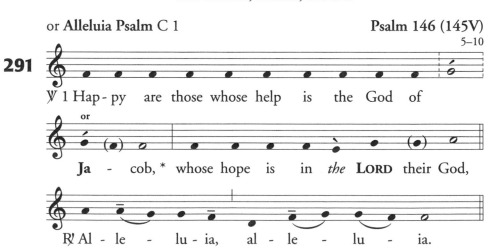

℣ 1 Hap - py are those whose help is the God of

Ja - cob, * whose hope is in *the* **LORD** their God,

℟ Al - le - lu - ia, al - le - lu - ia.

184

2   who made heaven and earth, the sea, and all that is **in** them; *
    who keeps faith *fòre*ver;

3   who executes justice for the op**pressed;** *
    who gives food to *thè* **hun**gry.

<u>4</u>   The Lord sets the prisoners **free;** *
    the Lord opens the eyes *òf* **the** blind.

<u>5</u>   The Lord lifts up those who are bowed **down;** *
    the Lord loves *thè* **right**eous.

<u>6</u>   The Lord watches over the strangers; '
      he upholds the orphan and the **wid**ow, *
    but the way of the wicked *hè* **brings** to ruin.

7   The Lord will reign for**ev**er, *
    your God, O Zion, for all gen*èra*tions.

Preparation of the Gifts Antiphon

Matthew 24:42, 44

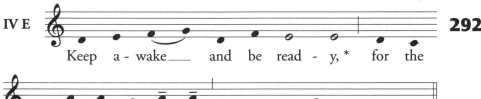

Keep a - wake___ and be read - y, * for the Son of Man is com - ing at an un - ex - pec - ted hour.

Canticle of Revelation

Revelation 2:7, 17a; 3:13, 20

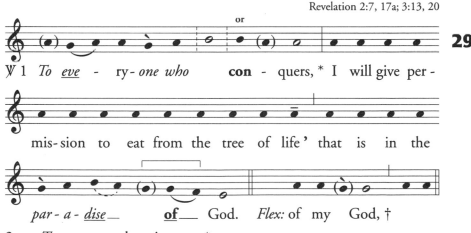

℣ 1 *To eve - ry-one who* **con** - quers, * I will give per - mis-sion to eat from the tree of life ' that is in the par - a - *dise*___ **of**___ God. *Flex:* of my God, †

2   *To eve*ryone who **cón**quers *
    I will give some *òf the hidden* **man**na,

3   *I will* write on you the name of my Gòd, †
     and the name of the city of my God, '
     the new Jerusalem that comes down from my God òut
     of **heav**en, *
ànd my own new name.

4   *Lis*ten! I am standing at the door, knockìng; †
     if you hear my voice and o*pèn the* **door,** *
     I will come in to you and eat with *yòu, and you* **with** me.

Communion Antiphon

Revelation 22:17, 19:9

294 I D 2

The Spir - it and the Bride___ say, "Come."___ How

hap- py those in- vit- ed to the wed- ding feast__ of the Lamb!

Canticle of Revelation

Revelation 19:6c–7a, 7b–8a, 11ab, 13, 16; 21: 1–2, 3b–5a, 6; 22:17, 20 (See Performance Notes)

295

℣ 1 *"Hal - le -* lu - jah! For the Lord our **God** the Al -

might-y reigns. *Let us re- joice and ex- ult and give *him the*

glo - ry, *Flex:* has come, †   ℣ 9 **Death** will **be** no more; *

2   *for the mar*riage of the Lamb has còme, †
     and his bride has **made** herself **ready;** *
     to her it has been granted to be clothed with fine *lìnen,* **bright**
        and pure."

3   *Then I saw* heaven opened, and **thére** was a **white** horse! *
     Its rider is called *Fàithful* **and** True.

4   *He is clothed* in a **róbe** dipped **in** blóod, *
     and his name is *càlled The* **Word of** God.

5   *On his <u>robe</u> he* **hás** a **name** inscribed, *
       "King of *kìng*s *and* **Lord** **of** lords."

6   *Then I <u>saw</u>* a new heaven and a new èarth; †
       and I saw the holy city, the **néw** Jerusalem, *
     coming down out of heaven from God, '
       prepared as a bride adorned *for her* **hus**band.

7   *"See, the <u>home</u>* of God is among mortàls. †
       He will **dwéll** with them **as** their God; *
     they will be his peoples, ' and God himself *wìll be* **with** them;

8   *he will <u>wipe</u>* every tear from their èyes. †
       Déath will **be** no *more;* *
     mourning and crying and pain will be no more, '
       for the first *thìngs have* **passed** away."

9   *And the <u>one</u>* who was seated **ón** the **throne** sáid, *
       "See, I am *màking* **all** **things** new."

10   *Then he <u>said</u>* to me, "It is dòne! †
       I am the Alpha and the Omega, the begínning **and** the end. *
     To the thirsty I will give water as a gift from the spring of the
     wàter **of** life."

11   *The <u>Spiri</u>t* **ánd** the **bride** say, "Cóme." *
       And let everyòne *who* **hears** <u>say</u>, "Come."

12   *And let <u>eve</u>ryone* **whó** is **thirst**y come. *
       Let anyone who wishes take the water *òf life* **as** <u>a</u> gift.

13   *The <u>one</u>* who testifies to these things sàys, †
       "Surely **Í** am **com**ing soon." *
     Amèn. Cóme, **Lord** **Je**sus!

Christ the King

Solemnity

Entrance Antiphon

Daniel 7:27

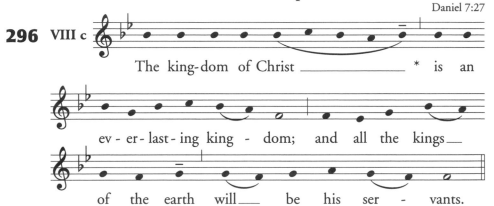

296 VIII c

The king-dom of Christ _____ * is an ev-er-last-ing king - dom; and all the kings___ of the earth will___ be his ser - vants.

Psalm 72 (71V)

1–2, 4, 7–8, 10–13, 17cd

297

℣ 1 *Give the* king your jus-tice, O **God,** * and your right-eous-ness *to a* **king's** son. *Flex:* the peo - ple, †

2 *May he* judge your people with **right**eousness, *
and your *pòor with* **jus**tice.

3 *May he* defend the cause of the poor of the peoplè, †
give deliverance to the **néed**y, *
and crush *thè op***pres**sor.

4 *In his* days may righteousness flourish and peace a**bóund,** *
until the *mòon is* **no** more.

5 *May he* have dominion from **séa** to sea, *
and from the River to the *ènds of* **the** earth.

6 *May the* kings of Tarshish and of the isles render him **tríb**ute, *
may the kings of Sheba and *Sèba* **bring** gifts.

7 *May all* kings fall down be**fóre** him, *
all nations *gìve him* **ser**vice.

8   *For he* delivers the needy when they **cáll,** *
    the poor and those who *hàve no* **help**er.

8   *For he* delivers the needy when they **cáll,** *
    the poor and those who *hàve no* **help**er.

9   *He has* pity on the weak and the **néed**y, *
    and saves the lives *òf the* **need**y.

<u>10</u>   *May all* nations be blessed in **hím;** *
    may they pro*nòunce him* **hap**py.

For the Responsorial Psalm, Alleluia, and Alleluia Psalm, see the solemnity of the Epiphany, **40, 41,** and **42.**

Preparation of the Gifts Antiphon

Isaiah 49:6

298

Christ is the light of nations, * to bring salvation to the ends of the earth.

Psalm 47 (46V)

1, 6–8

299

℣ 1 *Clap your* hands, all you **peo** - ples; *
shout to God *with loud* **songs** of joy.

<u>2</u>   *Sing prais*es to God, sing **práis**es; *
    sing praises to our *Kìng, sing* **prais**es.

<u>3</u>   *For God* is the king of all the **éarth;** *
    sing *pràises* **with** a psalm.

4   *God is* king over the **ná**tions; *
    God sits *òn his* **ho**ly throne.

Communion Antiphon

Micah 5:4c–5a

300

Christ will ex - tend his pow'r * through

all the earth, and be the Prince of Peace.

Canticle of David

1 Chronicles 29:10b–18 (See Performance Notes)

301

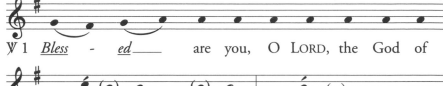

℣ 1 *Bless - ed*____ are you, O LORD, the God of

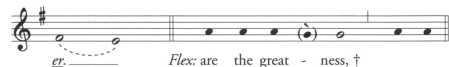

our **an**-ces - tor **Is** - ra - el, * for - **ev** - er and **ev** -

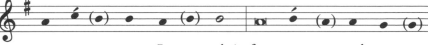

er. _____ *Flex:* are the great - ness, †

2 *Yours, O* LORD, are the greatnèss, †
  the power, the glory, the **víc**tory, and the **maj**esty; *
  for all that is in the heavens and **ón** the **earth** is <u>yours</u>;

3 *yours is* the **kíng**dom, O LORD, *
  and you are exalted as **héad** a**bove** <u>all</u>.

4 *Riches* and **hón**or **come** from you, *
  and **yóu** rule **o**ver <u>all</u>.

5 *In your* hand are **pów**er **and** might; *
  and it is in your hand to make great and to **gíve** strength **to** <u>all</u>.

6 *And now,* our God, **wé** give **thanks** to you *
  and **práise** your **glo**rious <u>name</u>.

7 *O LORD* our God, all this abundance that we have providèd †
  for building you a **hóuse** for your **ho**ly name *
  comes from your **hánd** and is **all** your <u>own</u>.

8 *I know,* my **Gód,** that you **search** the heart, *
  and take **pléas**ure in **up**right<u>ness</u>;

9 *in the* **úp**rightness **of** my heart *
  I have freely **óf**fered **all** these <u>things</u>,

10 *and now* I have seen your people, **whó** are **pres**ent here, *
  offering freely and **jóy**ously to <u>you</u>.

11 *O LORD,* the God of Abraham, Isaac, and Israel, our ancèstors, †
  keep forever such purposes and thoughts in the **héarts** of your
  people, *
  and dir**éct** their **hearts** toward <u>you</u>.

The Proper of Saints

February 2

Presentation of the Lord

Feast

Blessing of Candles

As the candles are being lighted, the following antiphon is sung:

Cf. Isaiah 35:4–5

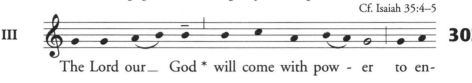

III **302**

The Lord our __ God * will come with pow - er to en-

light - en the eyes of his ser - vants, al - le - lu - ia.

The Procession

A deacon or the presider sings:

303

Let us go for-ward in peace.

All answer:

In the name of Christ. A - men.

Procession Antiphon I

Cf. Luke 2:32

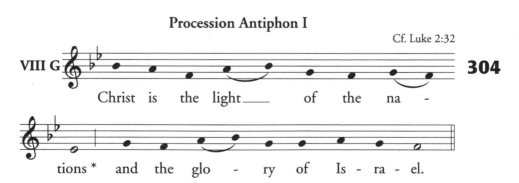

VIII G **304**

Christ is the light __ of the na -

tions * and the glo - ry of Is - ra - el.

191

Canticle of Simeon

Luke 2:29–32

305

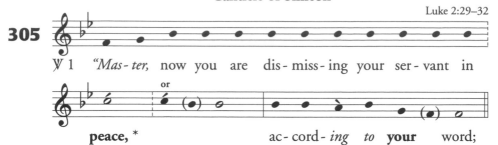

℣ 1 "*Mas-ter,* now you are dis-miss-ing your ser-vant in

peace, * ac-cord-*ing to* **your** word;

2 *for my* eyes have seen your salvá-tion, *
which you have prepared in the presence *òf all* **peo**ples,

3 *a light* for revelation to the **Gén**tiles *
and for glory to your *pèople* **Is**rael."

Procession Antiphon II

Cf. Luke 2:22a, 24a

306 VIII G

They brought_ him_ up_ to Je-ru-sa-lem *

to pre-sent him to the Lord and of-fer sac-ri-fice for him.

Psalm 24 (23V)

1–10

307

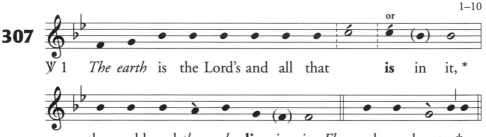

℣ 1 *The earth* is the Lord's and all that **is** in it, *

the world, and *those who* **live** in it; *Flex:* and pure hearts, †

2 *for he* has founded it on the **séas,** *
and established it *òn the* **riv**ers.

3 *Who shall* ascend the hill of the **LÓRD?** *
And who shall stand *ìn his* **ho**ly place?

4 *Those who* have clean hands and pure hearts, †
who do not lift up their souls to what is **fálse,** *
and do not *swèar* **deceit**fully.

192

5 *They will* receive blessing from the **LÓRD,** *
and vindication from the God of *thèir salva*tion.

6 *Such is* the company of those who **seek** him, *
who seek the face of the *Gòd of* **Ja**cob.

7 *Lift up* your heads, O **gà**tes! †
  and be lifted up, O ancient **dóors!** *
that the King of glo*rỳ may* **come** in.

8 *Who is* the King of **gló**ry? *
The LORD, strong and mighty, the LORD, migh*tỳ in* **bat**tle.

9 *Lift up* your heads, O **gà**tes! †
  and be lifted up, O ancient **dóors!** *
that the King of glo*rỳ may* **come** in.

10 *Who is* this King of **gló**ry? *
The LORD of hosts, he is the *Kìng of* **glo**ry.

Or, as desired, Responsorial Psalm 84 (83V) *How lovely is your dwelling place,* **31,** as in the feast of the Holy Family.

As the procession enters the church, the following is sung:

Entrance Antiphon

Psalm 48 (47):9

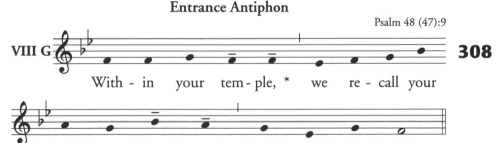

With - in your tem - ple, * we re - call your lov - ing kind - ness, O God, our God.

308

Psalm 48 (47)

1–2, 4–5, 8, 11–14
or

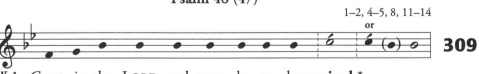

℣ 1 *Great is* the LORD and great - ly to be **praised** * in the *cit - y* **of** our God. *Flex:* so have we seen †

309

2 *His ho*ly mountain, beautiful in elevátion, *
is the *jòy of* **all** the earth,

3   *Mount Zi*on, in the **fár** north, *
     the city *òf the* **great** King.

4   *Then the* kings as**sém**bled, *
     they came *òn toget*her.

5   *As soon* as they saw it, they were as**tóund**ed; *
     they were in pan*ìc, they* **took** to flight;

6   *As we* have heard, so have wè seen †
          in the city of the **LÓRD** of hosts, *
     in the city of our God, which God establish*ès fore*ver.

7   *Let Mount* Zion be **glád,** *
     let the towns of Judah rejoice because *òf your* **judg**ments.

8   *Walk a*bout Zion, go all a**róund** it, *
     còunt its **tow**ers,

9   *consid*er well its ram**pàrts;** †
          go through its **cít**adels, *
     that you may tell the next *gèner*ation

10   *that this* is God, our God forever and **év**er. *
     He will be our *gùide fore*ver.

The Penitential Rite is omitted and the hymn *Glory to God* is sung.

The Responsorial Psalm is from the feast of the Immaculate Conception, **396.**

Alleluia   **Psalm 87 (86V)**
                                                        1–2, 6

310 IV E

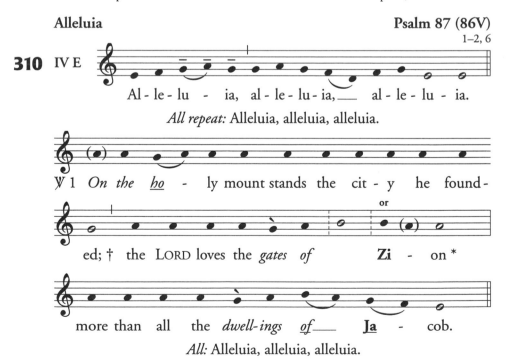

Al - le - lu - ia, al - le - lu - ia, ___ al - le - lu - ia.

All repeat: Alleluia, alleluia, alleluia.

℣ 1 *On the* <u>ho</u> - ly mount stands the cit - y he found-

                                                    or

ed; † the LORD loves the *gates of* Zi - on *

more than all the *dwell-ings of*___ **Ja** - cob.

All: Alleluia, alleluia, alleluia.

2   *The <u>LORD</u> records, as he regist*èrs *the* **peo**ples, *
"*Thìs one <u>was</u>* **born** there."

         All: Alleluia, alleluia, alleluia.

or **Alleluia Psalm** E 2 d   **Psalm 87 (86V)**

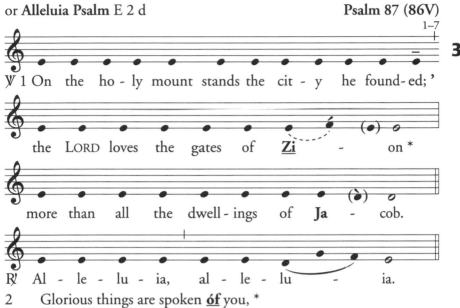

311

℣ 1 On the ho-ly mount stands the cit-y he found-ed; '
the LORD loves the gates of **Zi** - on *
more than all the dwell-ings of **Ja** - cob.
℟ Al - le - lu - ia, al - le - lu - ia.

2   Glorious things are spoken **óf** you, *
O city **of** Gòd.

3   Among those who know me I mention Rahab and Babylon; '
        Philistia too, and Tyre, with Ethiópia— *
"This one was born there," **they** sày.

4   And of Zion it shall be said, "This one and that one were **bórn** in it"; *
for the Most High himself will es**tab**lish it.

5   The LORD records, as he registers the **péo**ples, *
"This one was **born** thère."

6   Singers and dancers a**líke** say, *
"All my springs are **in** yòu."

Preparation of the Gifts Antiphon

                              Psalm 45 (44V):2bc

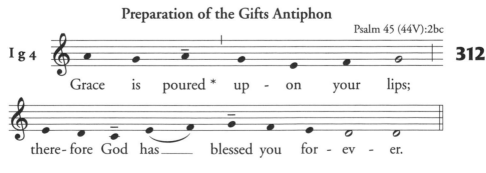

I g 4   **312**

Grace is poured * up - on your lips;
there-fore God has____ blessed you for - ev - er.

Psalm 45 (44V)

1, 4, 6–7

313

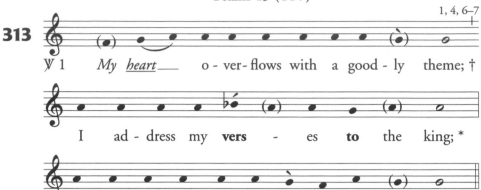

℣ 1 *My heart*___ o - ver- flows with a good - ly theme; †

I ad - dress my **vers** - es **to** the king; *

my tongue is like the pen *of* *a* **read** - y scribe.

2   *In* your majesty ride on victorìously †
     for the cause of truth and **tó** de**fend** the right; *
     let your right hand *tèach you* **dread** deeds.

3   *Your throne*, O God, endures forever and evèr. †
     Your royal scepter is a **scép**ter of **eq**uity; *
     you love righteousness *ànd hate* **wick**edness.

4   *Therefore* God, your **Gód,** has a**noin**ted you *
     with the oil of gladness beyond *yòur com***pan**ions.

Communion Antiphon

Luke 2:28

314   VII a

Sim - e - on re - ceived the child in his

arms ___ * and gave praise___ to God.

Canticle of Simeon

Luke 2:29–32

315

℣ 1 *"Mas* - *ter,*___ now you are dis - miss - ing your **ser** -

vant **in** peace, * ac - **cord** - ing to **your** word;___

2   *for my* eyes have **séen** your sal**va**tion, *
    which you have prepared in the **prés**ence of **all** peoples,

3   *a light* for revelation **tó** the **Gen**tiles *
    and for glory to your **péo**ple Isra<u>el</u>."

Then, if necessary, Ps. 34 (33V), **645** or **646,** is added, or another chant as listed on p. 386.

March 19

St. Joseph, Husband of Mary

Solemnity

Entrance Antiphon

Matthew 1:20

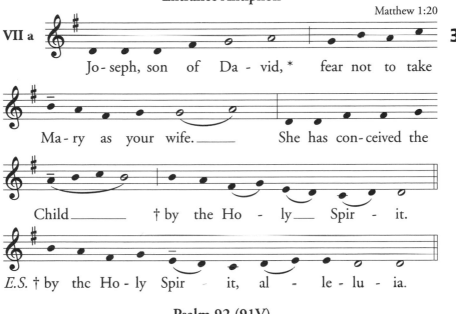

VII a

Jo - seph, son of Da - vid, * fear not to take
Ma - ry as your wife.____ She has con-ceived the
Child____ † by the Ho - ly__ Spir - it.
E.S. † by the Ho - ly Spir - it, al - le - lu - ia.

316

Psalm 92 (91V)

1–2, 4–5, 12–15

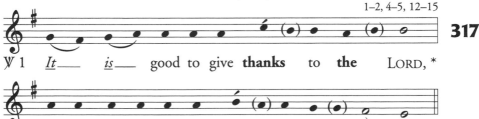

℣ 1 *It__ is__* good to give **thanks** to **the** L<small>ORD</small>, *
     to sing prais-es to your **name,** O **Most** High;__

317

2   *to de*clare your steadfast **lóve** in the **morn**ing, *
    and your **fáith**fulness by <u>night</u>,

197

3 *For you*, O LORD, have made me **glád** by **your** work; *
at the works of your **hánds** I **sing** for joy.

4 *How great* **áre** your **works**, O LORD! *
Your **thóughts** are **ver**y deep!

5 *The right*eous flourish **like** the **palm** tree, *
and grow like a **cé**dar in **Leb**anon.

6 *They are* planted in the **hóuse** of **the** LORD; *
they flourish in the **cóurts** of **our** God.

7 *In old* age they **stíll** pro**duce** fruit; *
they are always **gréen** and **full** of sap,

8 *showing* that the LORD is upright; **hé** is **my** rock, *
and there is no un**rígh**teous**ness** in him.

The Responsorial Psalm, the Alleluia, and the Alleluia Psalm are taken from the feast of the
Holy Family, **31**, **32**, and **33**.

Preparation of the Gifts Antiphon

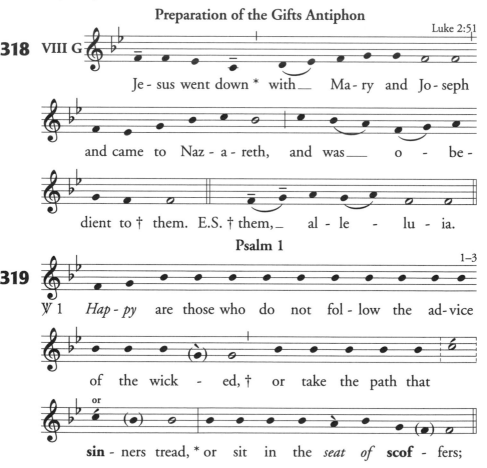

Luke 2:51

318 VIII G

Je - sus went down * with __ Ma - ry and Jo - seph
and came to Naz - a - reth, and was __ o - be -
dient to † them. E.S. † them, __ al - le - lu - ia.

Psalm 1

1–3

319

℣ 1 *Hap - py* are those who do not fol - low the ad - vice
of the wick - ed, † or take the path that
sin - ners tread, * or sit in the *seat of* **scof** - fers;

198

2 *but their* delight is in the law of the **LÓRD**, *
and on his law they medi*tàte day* **and** night.

<u>3</u> *They are* like trees planted by streams of **wáter**, *
which yield their fruit *in its* **sea**son,

<u>4</u> *and their* leaves do not **wíth**er. *
In all that they *dò, they* **pros**per.

Communion Antiphon

Matthew 24:45

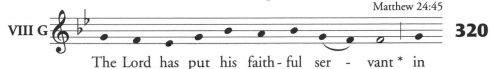

VIII G   **320**

The Lord has put his faith-ful ser - vant * in

charge of his house-† hold. *E.S.* † hold,_ al - le - lu - ia.

Psalm 21 (20V)

1–7, 13

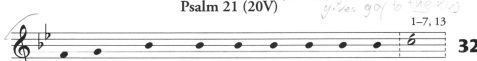

321

℣ 1 *In your* strength the king re - joic - es, O **LORD**, *

or

and in your help how *great-ly* **he** ex-ults!

2 *You have* given him his **héart's** desire, *
and have not withheld the re*quèst of* **his** lips.

3 *For you* meet him with rich **bléss**ings; *
you set a crown of *fine gold* **on** his head.

4 *He asked* you for life; you gave it to **hím**— *
length of days forev*èr and* **ev**er.

5 *His glo*ry is great through your **hélp**; *
splendor and majesty *yòu* be**stow** on him.

6 *You* be*stow* on him blessings for**év**er; *
you make him glad with the joy *òf your* **pres**ence.

7 *For the* king trusts in the **LÓRD**, *
and through the steadfast love of the Most High *hè shall*
not be moved.

8 *Be ex*alted, O LORD, in your **stréngth**! *
We will sing and *pràise your* **pow**er.

199

March 25

Annunciation of the Lord

Solemnity

Entrance Antiphon

Cf. Luke 1:30 and 38

322 If

An an-gel of the Lord __ * brought the good news to Ma-ry, and she__ con - ceived__ by the † Ho - ly__ Spir - it. *E.S.* † Ho - ly Spir - it, __ al - le - lu - ia.

Psalm 46 (45V)

1–10

323

℣ 1 *God* __ is our **ref** - uge **and** strength, * a ver-y pres-ent *help in* **trou** - ble. __ *Flex:* of the earth;†

2 *Therefore* we will not fear, **though** the **earth** should change, *
   though the mountains shake *in the* **heart of** the <u>sea</u>;

3 *though* its **wá**ters **roar** and foam, *
   though the mountains tremble *with its* **tu**<u>mult</u>.

4 *There <u>is</u>* a river whose streams make glad the **cí**ty **of** God, *
   the holy habitation *òf the* **Most** <u>High</u>.

5 *God* is in the midst of the city; **í**t shall **not** be moved; *
   God will help it *whèn the* **morn**ing <u>dawns</u>.

6 *The <u>na</u>*tions are in an uproar, the **kíng**doms **tot**ter; *
   he utters his *vòice, the* **earth** <u>melts</u>.

7 *The <u>LORD</u>* of **hósts** is **with** us; *
   the God of Jacob *ìs our* **refuge**.

8 *Come*, behold the **wórks** of **the** LORD; *
   see what desolations he *hàs brought* **<u>on</u>** the <u>earth</u>.

200

9   *He* <u>*makes*</u> wars cease to the end of the èarth; †
     he breaks the bow, and **shát**ters **the** spear; *
     he *bùrns the* <u>**shields**</u> with <u>fire</u>.

10   *"Be* <u>*still,*</u> and know that I àm God! †
     I am exalted a**món**g the **na**tions, *
     I am ex*àlted* **in** the <u>earth</u>."

The Responsorial Psalm, the Alleluia, and the Alleluia Psalm are taken from the Solemnity of the Immaculate Conception, **396, 397,** and **398.**

Preparation of the Gifts Antiphon

Luke 1:28 and 42

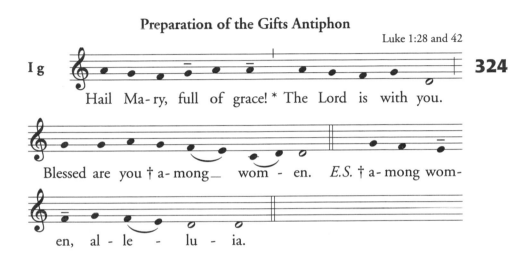

I g

324

Hail Ma-ry, full of grace! * The Lord is with you.

Blessed are you † a-mong___ wom - en. *E.S.* † a-mong wom-

en, al - le - lu - ia.

Psalm 85 (84V)

1, 10–12

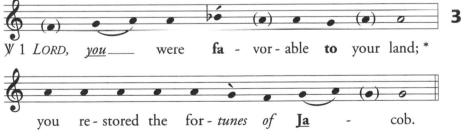

325

℣ 1 LORD, <u>*you*</u>___ were **fa** - vor-able **to** your land; *

you re-stored the for-*tunes of* <u>**Ja**</u> - cob.

2   *Steadfast* love and **fáith**fulness **will** meet; *
     righteousness and peace will *kìss each* **oth**er.

3   <u>*Faith*</u>fulness will spring **úp** from **the** ground, *
     and righteousness will *lòok down* <u>**from**</u> the sky.

4   *The* <u>LORD</u> will **gíve** what **is** good, *
     and our land will *yìeld its* <u>**in**</u>crease.

201

Communion Antiphon

Luke 1:38

326 VIII c

I am the serv - vant of the Lord: *

let it be done to me as you † have said.

E.S. † have said, al - le - lu - ia.

Psalm 96 (95V)

1–4, 6–9a, 11–13

327

or

℣ 1   *O sing* to the LORD a **new** song; *

sing to *the LORD,* **all** the earth. *Flex:* the earth re-jòice; †

2   *Sing to* the LORD, bless his **náme;** *
tell of his salvat*ion from* **day** to day.

3   *Declare* his glory among the **nát**ions, *
his marvelous works among *àll the* **peo**ples.

4   *For great* is the LORD, and greatly to be **práised;** *
he is to be rev*èred a***bove** all gods.

5   *Honor* and majesty are be**fóre** him; *
strength and beauty are *ìn his* **sanc**tuary.

6   *Ascribe* to the LORD, O families of the peoplès, †
ascribe to the LORD glory and **stréngth.** *
Ascribe to the LORD the *glòry* **due** his name;

7   *bring an* offering, and come into his **cóurts.** *
Worship the LORD in *hòly* **splen**dor

8   *Let the* heavens be glad, and let the earth rèjoice; †
let the sea roar, and all that **fílls** it; *
let the field exult, and *èvery***thing** in it.

9 *Then shall* all the trees of the forest sing for joy †
    before the LORD; for he is **cóm**ing, *
    for he is com*ing to* **judge** the earth.

10 *He will* judge the world with **rígh**teousness, *
    and the *pèoples* **with** his truth.

June 24

Birth of St. John the Baptist

Solemnity

Entrance Antiphon

Isaiah 49:1b

From my moth-er's womb * I was called by the Lord;

be-fore my birth____ God_ an - nounced my_ name.

Psalm 92 (91V)

1–5, 12–15

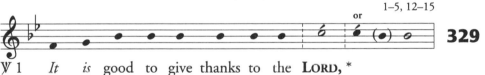

℣ 1 *It is* good to give thanks to the **LORD,** *

to sing prais - es to your *name,* O **Most** High;

2 *to de*clare your steadfast love in the **mórn**ing, *
    and your *fàithful***ness** by night,

3 *to the* music of the lute and the **hárp**, *
    to the melo*dỳ of* **the** lyre.

4 *For you,* O LORD, have made me glad by your **wórk;** *
    at the works of your *hànds I* **sing** for joy.

5 *How great* are your works, O **LÓRD!** *
    Your *thòughts are* **ver**y deep!

6 *The righ*teous flourish like the **pálm** tree, *
    and grow like a ce*dàr in* **Leb**anon.

7   *They are* planted in the house of the **LÓRD;** *
    they flourish in the *còurts of* **our** God.

8   *In old* age they still produce **frúit;** *
    they are always *grèen and* **full** of sap,

9   *showing* that the LORD is upright; he is my **róck,** *
    and there is no un*righteous***ness** in him.

Responsorial Psalm E 5   Psalm 71 (70V)
                                                             (1b) 1–8, 14–15

330

℣ 1 In you, O LORD, I *take*___ **ref** - uge; *

℟ Let me nev - er___ come to shame. ___

℣ 2 In your **right** - eous-ness de - liv - er me and **res** -

cue me; * in - cline your ear to me and *save*___ **me.**

℟ Let me nev - er___ come to shame. ___

℣ 3 Be to me a rock of ref - uge, a strong for - tress, to

save___ me, * for you are my rock *and my* **for** - tress.

℟ Let me nev - er___ come to shame. ___

204

4¹ **Res**cue me, O my God, from the hand of the wìck**ed**, *
    from the grasp of the un*jùst and* **cru**el.

5   For you, O Lord, are **mý** hope, *
    my trust, O LORD, *fròm* **my** youth.

6   Upon **you** I have leaned from my birth; '
    it was you who took me from my **mò**ther's womb. *
    My praise is continually *òf* **you**.

7   I have been like a portent to **mán**y, *
    but you are my *stròng* **ref**uge.

8   **My** mouth is filled with **yòur** praise, *
    and with your glo*rý* **all** day long.

9   But I will hope con**tín**ually, *
    and will praise you yet *mòre* **and** more.

10 My **mouth** will tell of your righteous acts, '
    of your deeds of salvation **àll** day long, *
    though their number is past *mỳ* **know**ledge.

Alleluia   Psalm 25 (24V)
                                                  1–2c, 4

I g 2

331

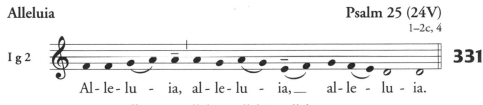

Al - le - lu - ia, al - le - lu - ia,__ al - le - lu - ia.

All repeat: Alleluia, alleluia, alleluia.

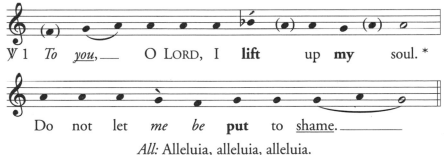

℣ 1 *To* *you*,__ O LORD, I **lift** up **my** soul. *

Do not let *me* *be* **put** to shame.____

All: Alleluia, alleluia, alleluia.

2   *Make* me to **knów** your **ways,** O LORD; *
    tèach me **your** paths.

All: Alleluia, alleluia, alleluia.

¹ Odd numbered verses are chanted on the first chanting note (mi); even numbered verses,
on the second chanting note (la).

or **Alleluia Psalm** C 4

Psalm 25 (24V)
1–2b, 4–6, 10, 15–17, 20–21

332

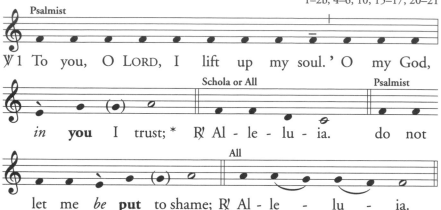

℣1 To you, O Lord, I lift up my soul.' O my God, in **you** I trust; * ℟ Al - le - lu - ia. do not let me *be* **put** to shame; ℟ Al - le - lu - ia.

2   Make me to know *yòur* **ways,** O Lord; *
    teach *mè* **your** paths.

3   Lead me in your truth, and teach me, '
       for you are the God of my *sàl*vation; *
    for you I wait *àll* **day** long.

4   Be mindful of your mercy, O Lord, and of *yòur* **stead**fast love, *
    for they have been *fròm* **of** old.

5   All the paths of the Lord are steadfast love *ànd* **faith**fulness, *
    for those who keep his covenant *ànd* **his** decrees.

6   My eyes are ev*èr* **toward** the Lord, *
    for he will pluck my feet out *òf* **the** net.

7   Turn to me and be gra*cìous* **to** me, *
    for I am lonely and *à***fflic**ted.

8   Relieve the troubles *òf* **my** heart, *
    and bring me out *òf* **my** distress.

9   May integrity and uprightness *prè***serve** me, *
    for *Ì* **wait** for you.

10 Redeem Isra*èl,* **O** God, *
    out of all *its* **trou**bles.

Preparation of the Gifts Antiphon

333 VII d

The child, ___ * who is born for us to - day,

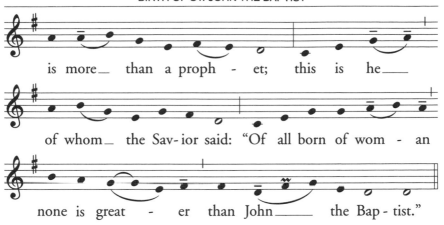

is more— than a proph - et; this is he—
of whom— the Sav-ior said: "Of all born of wom - an
none is great - er than John— the Bap - tist."

Psalm 65 (64V)

1, 4–5

334

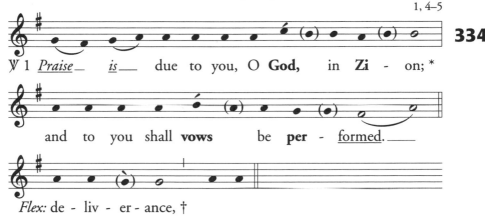

℣ 1 *Praise— is—* due to you, O **God,** in **Zi** - on; *
and to you shall **vows** be **per** - formed. ____

Flex: de - liv - er - ance, †

2 *Happy* are those whom you **chóose** and **bring** near *
   to **líve** in **your** courts.

3 *We shall* be satisfied with the **góod**ness **of** your house, *
   your **hó**ly **tem**ple.

4 *By awe*some deeds you answer us with delivèrance, †
      O God of **óur** salvation; *
   you are the hope of all the ends of the earth and **óf** the **fart**hest seas.

Communion Antiphon

Luke 1:76

335

III a

You,— my child,— *shall go be - fore the Lord

to pre-pare___ the way___ for him.

Canticle of Zechariah

Luke 1:68–75, 77–79

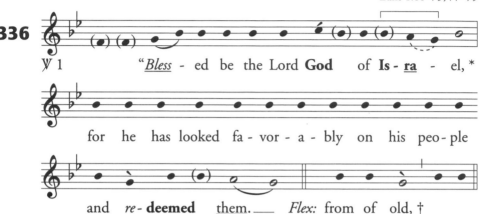

336

℣ 1 "*Bless* - ed be the Lord **God** of **Is** - **ra** - el, *

for he has looked fa - vor - a - bly on his peo - ple

and *re* - **deemed** them.___ *Flex:* from of old, †

2 *He has <u>raised</u>* up a mighty **sáv**ior **for** us *
in the house of his servànt **Da**vid,

3 *as he <u>spoke</u>* through the mouth of his holy prophets from of óld, †
that we would be **sáved** from our **ene**mies *
and from the hand of all *whò* **hate** us.

4 *<u>Thus</u>* he has shown the mercy promised **tó** our **<u>ances</u>**tors, *
and has remembered his hol*ỳ* **cove**nant,

5 *the <u>oath</u>* that he swore to our ancestor Abraham, to grant ùs †
that we, being rescued from the hands of our enemies, might
sérve him **without** fear, *
in holiness and righteousness before *hìm* **all** our <u>days</u>.

6 *to <u>give</u>* knowledge of salvation **tó** his **peo**ple *
by the forgiveness *òf* **their** <u>sins</u>.

7 *By the <u>ten</u>*der **mér**cy of **<u>our</u>** God, *
the dawn from on high will break *ùpon* us,

8 *to give <u>light</u>* to those who sit in darkness and in the **shád**ow **of**
death, *
to guide our feet into *thè* **way** of <u>peace</u>."

208

St. Peter and St. Paul, Apostles

Solemnity

Entrance Antiphon

Acts 12:11

337

VII c 2

The Lord sent his an - gel to Pe - ter *
and res - cued__ him from Her - od's__ pow - er,
al - le - lu - ia.

Psalm 19 (18V)

1–6 (See Performance Notes)

338

℣ 1 *The__ heav* - ens are tell-ing the **glo** - ry **of**

God; * and the fir - ma - ment pro-**claims** his

hand - i - work. _____ *Flex:* for the sun, †

2   Day to **dáy** pours **forth** speech, *
and night to **níght** de**clares** knowledge.

3   *There is* no **spéech**, nor **are** there words; *
their **vóice** is **not** heard;

4   *yet their* voice goes **óut** through **all** the earth, *
and their words to the **énd** of **the** world.

5   *In the* heavens he has set a tent for the sùn, †
which comes out like a bridegroom from his **wéd**ding **can**opy, *
and like a strong man **rúns** its **course** with joy.

6   *Its rising* is from the end of the heavèns, †
    and its circuit **tó** the **end** of them; *
    and nothing is **híd** from **its** heat.

Responsorial Psalm C 3 g   **Psalm 45 (44V) and Psalm 117 (116V)**
Psalm 45:16–17 (44V:16) and 117 (116V):1–2

339

℣ 1 You will make them **princ** - es___ ℟ In eve - ry

part of the earth.

℣2 In the **place**___ of **an** - ces - tors * *you*

shall have___ sons; ___ ℟ In eve - ry part of the earth.

℣3 I will cause your name to be cel - e - **brat** - ed * in all

gen- er - a - tions; ℟ In eve - ry part of the earth.

4[1] **there**fore the peoples will **pràise** you *
    forever *ànd* **ever**.

5   Praise the LORD, all you **nátions**! *
    Extol him, all you **péo**ples!

6   For **great** is his steadfast **lòve** toward us, *
    and the faithfulness of the LORD endures *fòr*ever.

___

[1] Odd numbered verses are chanted on the first chanting note (fa); even numbered verses, on the second chanting note (la).

Alleluia   Psalm 126 (125V)
                                                1–2b

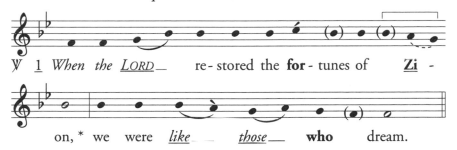

III g

Al-le-lu-ia,— al-le-lu - ia,— al-le - lu-ia.

All repeat: Alleluia, alleluia, alleluia.

℣ 1 When the LORD— re-stored the **for** - tunes of **Zi** -

on, * we were *like* *those*— **who** dream.

All: Alleluia, alleluia, alleluia.

2   *Then our <u>mouth</u> was* **filled** with **laugh**ter, *
   and our tongue *<u>with</u> <u>shouts</u>* **of** joy;

All: Alleluia, alleluia, allcluia.

or **Alleluia Psalm** C 4   Psalm 126 (125V)
                                                1–8 (See Perfomance Notes)

Schola One

℣1 When   the   LORD   re - stored   the   for - tunes   *of*

Schola Two or All   Schola One

Zi - on, * ℟ Al - le - lu - ia.   we   were   *like*

All

those   who   dream. ℟ Al - le   -   lu - ia.

2   Then our mouth was filled *with* **laugh**ter, *
   and our tongue *with* **shouts** of joy;

3   then it was said among *the* **na**tions, *
   "The LORD has done *great* **things** for them."

4   The LORD has done *great* **things** for us, *
   and **we** rejoiced.

5 Restore our for*tùnes,* **O** LORD, *
  like the watercourses in *thè* **Ne**geb.

6 May those *whò* **sow** in tears *
  reap *wìth* **shouts** of joy.

7 Those who go *òut* **weep**ing, *
  bearing the seed *fòr* **sow**ing,

8 shall come home *wìth* **shouts** of joy, *
  carry*ìng* **their** sheaves.

Preparation of the Gifts Antiphon

Cf. Psalm 45 (44V):16–17

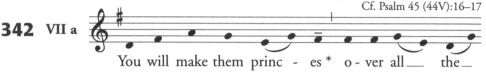

You will make them princ - es * o - ver all___ the___

world;___ they will cel - e - brate your name, O Lord.

Psalm 45 (44V)

1–2, 16–17

℣ 1 *My___ heart___* o - ver-flows with a good - ly theme; †

I ad - dress my **vers** - es **to** the king; *

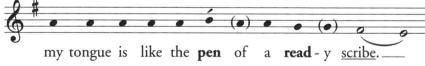

my tongue is like the **pen** of a **read** - y scribe. ___

2 *In your* majesty ride on victor*ìous*ly †
   for the cause of truth **ánd** to de**fend** the right; *
   let your right hand **téach** you **dread** <u>deeds</u>.

3 *In the* place of ancestors you, O **kíng,** shall **have** sons; *
   you will make them **prín**ces in **all** the <u>earth</u>.

4 *I will* cause your name to be celebrated in **áll** generations; *
   therefore the peoples will praise you for**é**ver and **ev**<u>er</u>.

Communion Antiphon

Matthew 16:18

VII c   **344**

You __ are __ Pe - ter, * the rock __

on which I will build __ my Church.

Canticle

Ephesians 1:3–10

345

℣ 1 *Bless - ed* __ be the God and Fath-er of **our** Lord Je-sus

Christ, * who has blessed us in Christ with eve - ry spir - it -

ual bless-ing in the **heav**-en - ly **plac** - es, __

2   *just as* he chose us in Christ before the found**á**tion **of** the world *
to be holy and blameless be**fóre** him **in** love.

3   *He des*tined us for adoption as his **chíl**dren through **Je**sus Christ, *
according to the good **pléas**ure of **his** will,

4   *to the* praise of his **gló**rious grace *
that he freely bestowed on **ús** in the **Be**loved.

5   *In him* we have re**démp**tion **through** his blood, *
the forgiveness **óf** our **tres**pass**es**,

6   *accord*ing to the **rích**es of **his** grace *
that he **láv**ished **on** us.

7   *With all* **wís**dom and **in**sight *
he has made known to us the **mý**stery of **his** will,

8   *accord*ing to his good pleasure that **hé** set **forth** in Christ, *
as a plan for the **fúll**ness **of** time,

9   *to gath*er up **áll** things **in** him, *
things in **héav**en and **things** on earth.

Transfiguration of the Lord

Feast

Entrance Antiphon

Matthew 17:1–2

346 II D

Je - sus took his dis - ci - ples * up the moun - tain and was trans - fig - ured in__ their__ pres - ence.

Psalm 84 (83V)

1–4, 8–11

347

℣ 1 *How love - ly* is your **dwell** - ing place, *

O **LORD** of hosts! *Flex:* spar - row finds a home, †

2 *My soul* longs, indeed it faints for the courts of the **LÓRD;** *
my heart and my flesh sing for joy to *thè* **liv**ing God.

3 *Even* the sparrow finds à home, †
and the swallow a nest for herself, where she may **láy** her young, *
at your altars, O LORD of hosts, my King *ànd* **my** God.

<u>4</u> *Happy* are those who live in your **hóuse,** *
ever sing*ìng* **your** praise.

5 *O LORD* God of hosts, **héar** my prayer; *
give ear, O God *of* **J**acob!

6 *Behold* our **shíeld,** O God; *
look on the face of your *à***noint**ed.

<u>7</u> *For a* day in your courts is better than a thousand elsewhère. †
I would rather be a doorkeeper in the house of my **Gód** *
than live in the tents *òf* **wick**edness.

8 *For the* LORD God is a sun *ànd* shield; †
he bestows favor and **hón**or. *
No good thing does the LORD withhold from those who walk
*ù***right**ly.

Responsorial Psalm C 2 g

Psalm 21 (20V)
(5) 1–7, 13

℣1 Splen-dor and maj-es-ty you **be-stów on** him;____ *

℟ His glo - ry is great through your help.

℣2 In your strength the king re - joic-es, **O** Lord, *

and in your help how great-ly **hé ex** - ults!____

℟ His glo - ry is great through your help.

3 You have given him his **héart's** desire, *
   and have not withheld the request of **hís** lips.

4 For you meet him with rích **bléss**ings; *
   you set a crown of fine gold on **hís** head.

5 He asked you for **lífe;** *
   you gave it to him—length of days forever and **éver.**

6 You bestow on him blessings for**éver;** *
   you make him glad with the joy of your **prés**ence.

7 For the king trusts in the **LÓRD,** *
   and through the steadfast love of the Most High he shall
      nót be moved.

8 Be exalted, O LORD, in your **stréngth!** *
   We will sing and praise your **pów**er.

Alleluia

Psalm 97 (96V)
1, 6

VII a

Al - le - lu - ia, al - le - lu - ia, al - le - lu - ia.

348

349

All repeat: Alleluia, alleluia, alleluia.

℣ 1 *The* LORD is king! **Let** the **earth** re-joice; *

let the man - y **coast** - lands **be** glad!

All: Alleluia, alleluia, alleluia.

2   *The heav*ens pro**cláim** his **right**eousness; *
and all the **péo**ples be**hold** his glory.

All: Alleluia, alleluia, alleluia.

Alleluia Psalm E 2 d   Psalm 97 (96V)
                                            1–6, 7c–8a, 8b–c, 11–12

350

℣1 The LORD is king! Let the **eárth** re-joice; *

let the man - y coast - lands **be** glad!

℟ Al - le - lu - ia, al - le - lu - ia.

2   Clouds and thick darkness are all a**roúnd** him; *
    righteousness and justice are the foundation of **his** thròne.

3   Fire goes be**fóre** him, *
    and consumes his adversaries on **everỳ** side.

4   His lightnings light **úp** the world; *
    the earth sees and **trem**blès.

5   The mountains melt like wax be**fóre** the LORD, *
    before the Lord of **all** thè earth.

6   The heavens proclaim his **ríght**eousness; *
    and all the peoples behold his **glo**rỳ.

7   All gods bow down be**fóre** him. *
    Zion hears and **is** glàd,

8   and the towns of Judah **ré**joice, *
       because of your judgments, **O** Gòd.

9   Light dawns for the **right**eous, *
       and joy for the upright **in** hèart.

<u>10</u>   Rejoice in the LORD, O you **right**eous, *
       and give thanks to his **holy** name!

Preparation of the Gifts Antiphon

Mark 9:5

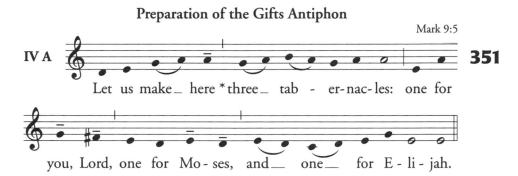

Let us make here *three tab-er-nac-les: one for you, Lord, one for Mo-ses, and one for E-li-jah.

Psalm 133 (132V)

1–3 (See Perfomance Notes)

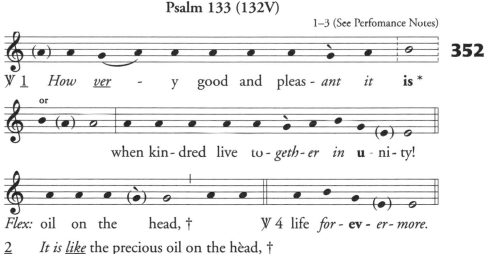

℣ 1 *How ver - y* good and pleas-*ant it* **is** *

or

when kin-dred live to-*geth-er in* u-ni-ty!

Flex: oil on the head, †   ℣ 4 *life for-ev-er-more.*

<u>2</u>   *It is <u>like</u>* the precious oil on the hèad, †
      running down upon the beard, on the *bèard of* **Aar**on, *
      running down over the *còllar of* **his** robes.

<u>3</u>   *It is <u>like</u>* the *dèw of* **Her**mon, *
      which falls on the *mòuntains of* **Zi**on.

<u>4</u>   *For <u>there</u>* the LORD or*dàined his* **bless**ing, *
      life *fóre*vermore.

217

Communion Antiphon

Matthew 17:9

353 I f

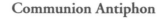

Tell no one of the vis - ion you have seen____ *

un - til the Son of Man is ris - en from the dead.

Psalm 45 (44V)

1–7, 17 (See Performance Notes)

354

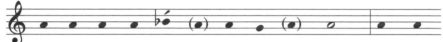

℣ 1 *My heart*__ o - ver- flows with a good - ly theme; †

I ad-dress my **vers** - es **to** the king; * my tongue

is like the pen *of a* **read** - y scribe.____

2 *You are* the most handsome of mèn; †
      grace is **póured** up**on** your lips; *
   therefore God has blessed *yòu forev*er.

3 *Gird* your sword on your **thígh,** O **migh**ty one, *
   in your glo*rỳ and* **maj**esty.

4 *In* your majesty ride on victoriouslỳ †
      for the cause of truth and **tó** de**fend** the right; *
   let your right hand *tèach you* **dread** deeds.

5 *Your ar*rows are sharp in the heart of the **én**emies **of** the king; *
   the peo*plès fall* **un**der you.

6 *Your throne,* O God, endures forever and evèr. †
      Your royal scepter is a **scép**ter of **eq**uity; *
   you love righteousness *ànd hate* **wick**edness.

7 *Therefore* God, your **Gód,** has a**noin**ted you *
   with the oil of gladness beyond *yòur com***pan**ions;

8 *I will* cause your name to be celebrated in **áll** generations; *
   therefore the peoples will praise you forevèr *and* **ev**er.

Assumption of Mary

Solemnity

Entrance Antiphon

VII A   **355**

Ma - ry has been tak - en up to heav - en; *

the an - gels re - joice and praise_____ the Lord.

Psalm 98 (97V)

1–9 (See Performance Notes)

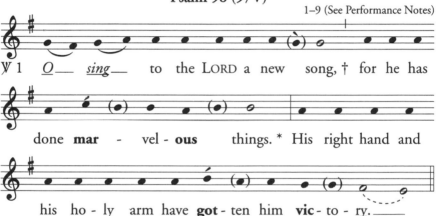

356

℣ 1 *O__ sing__* to the LORD a new song, † for he has

done **mar** - vel - **ous** things. * His right hand and

his ho - ly arm have **got** - ten him **vic** - to - ry.___

2   *The LORD* has made **knówn** his **vic**tory; *
    he has revealed his vindication in the **síght** of the **na**tions.

3   *He has* remembered his steadfast **lóve** and **faith**fulness *
    to the **hóuse** of Isra̲el.

4   *All the* **énd**s of the **éarth** have seen *
    the **vic**tory **of** our God.

5   *Make a* joyful noise to the **LÓRD**, all **the** earth; *
    break forth into joyous **sóng** and **sing** praises.

6   *Sing prais*es to the **LÓRD** with **the** lyre, *
    with the lyre and the **sóund** of melo̲dy.

7   *With trum*pets and the **sóund** of **the** horn *
    make a joyful noise be**fóre** the **King**, the LORD.

8   *Let the* sea roar, and **áll** that **fills** it; *
    the world and **thóse** who **live** in it.

9   *Let the* floods clap thèir hands; †
        let the hills sing to**géth**er **for** joy *
    at the **prés**ence **of** the <u>LORD</u>,

10   *for he* is coming to judge thè earth. †
        He will judge the **wórld** with **right**eousness, *
    and the **péo**ples with **equi**ty.

Responsorial Psalm E 5   **Song of Songs**

(4:8b) 4:8ab, 3:6, 5:1, 6:10, 2:10, 8:5, 6:9b, 2:13b–14, 7:6 (See Performance Notes)

357

℣ 1 Come with me from Leb - a - non, **my**____

bride; * come with *me from* **Leb** - a - non.

℟ Come,__ my be - lov - ed, re - ceive your crown.____

℣ 2 **What**____ is that com - ing up from the

wil - der - ness, * like a col - umn of smoke,

per - fumed with *myrrh and* **frank** - in - cense.

℟ Come,__ my be - lov - ed, re - ceive your crown.____

3[1]   I come to my garden, my sister, **mý** bride; *
        I gather my *mýrrh* **with** my spice.

[1] Odd numbered verses are chanted on the first chanting note (mi); even numbered verses, on the second chanting note (la).

4   Who is **this** that looks forth **like** the dawn, *
       fair as the moon, bright as the sun, terrible as an army
         with **ban**ners?

5   My beloved speaks and **sáys** to me: *
       "Arise, my love, my fair one, and _cóme_ **a**way."

6   Who is **that** coming up from the **wil**derness, *
       leaning upon _her bè_**lov**ed?

7   The maidens saw her and called her **háp**py; *
       the queens also, _ànd they_ **praised** her.

8   A**rise,** my love, my fair one, and **còme** away. *
       O my dove, let _mè_ **see** your face,

9   let me hear your voice; for your **vóice** is sweet, *
       and your _fáce is_ **love**ly.

10   How **fair** and pleasant you are, O **lòved** one, *
       delec_tablè_ **maid**en!

Alleluia   Psalm 45 (44V)
                                                         1, 9

358

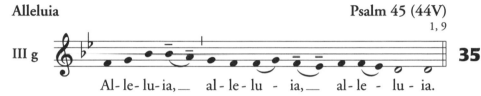

Al- le- lu- ia, _ al - le - lu - ia, _ al - le - lu - ia.

All repeat: Alleluia, alleluia, alleluia.

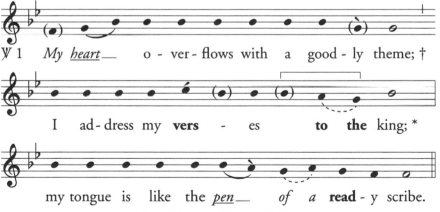

℣ 1   *My _heart_ _* o - ver- flows with a good - ly theme; †

I   ad - dress my **vers** - es **to the** king; *

my tongue is like the _pen_ _ of a **read** - y scribe.

All: Alleluia, alleluia, alleluia.

2   _Daugh_ters of kings are among your **lá**dies of **hon**or; *
       at your right hand stands the queen in _gòld of_ **O**phir.

All: Alleluia, alleluia, alleluia.

or **Alleluia Psalm**

Psalm 45 (44V)
1, 9–15, 17

359

℣1 My heart___ o-ver-flows with a good-ly theme; *

I ad-dress my vers-es to the king.___

℟ Al - le - lu - ia,___ al - le - lu - ia.

℣2 Daugh-ters of kings are a-mong your la-dies of hon-or; *

at your right hand stands the queen in gold of O - phir.

℟ Al - le - lu - ia, al-le-lu-ia,___ al - le - lu - ia.

℣3 Hear, O___ daugh-ter, con-sid-er and in-cline your ear; *

for - get your peo - ple and your fa - ther's house,___

℟ Al - le - lu - ia,___ al - le - lu - ia.

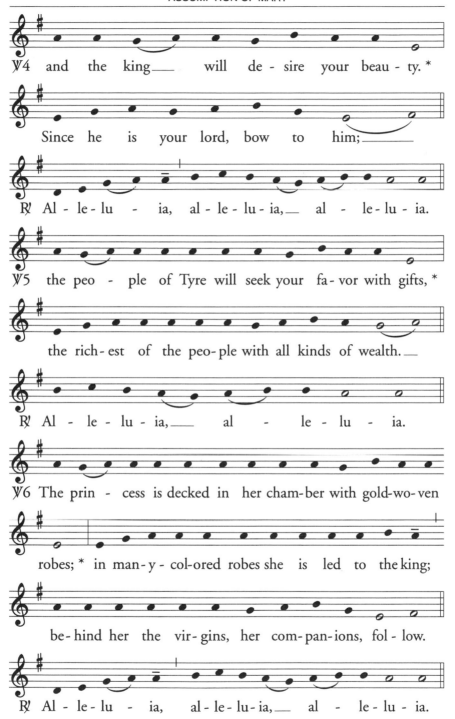

℣4 and the king___ will de - sire your beau - ty. *

Since he is your lord, bow to him;___

℟ Al - le - lu - ia, al - le - lu - ia,___ al - le - lu - ia.

℣5 the peo - ple of Tyre will seek your fa - vor with gifts, *

the rich - est of the peo - ple with all kinds of wealth.___

℟ Al - le - lu - ia,___ al - le - lu - ia.

℣6 The prin - cess is decked in her cham - ber with gold-wo-ven

robes; * in man-y - col-ored robes she is led to the king;

be- hind her the vir - gins, her com-pan-ions, fol - low.

℟ Al - le - lu - ia, al - le - lu-ia,___ al - le - lu - ia.

℣7 With joy — and glad-ness they are led a-long *

as they en-ter the pal-ace of the king. —

℟ Al-le-lu-ia, — al - le-lu - ia.

℣8 I will cause — your name to be cel - e - brat-ed

in all gen-er-a-tions; * there-fore the peo-ples will

praise you for - ev - er and ev - er.

℟ Al - le-lu - ia, al - le-lu-ia, — al - le-lu - ia.

Preparation of the Gifts Antiphon

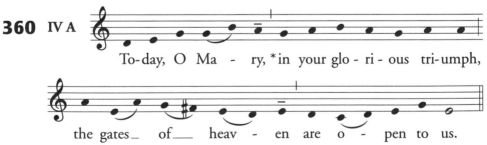

360 IV A

To-day, O Ma - ry, * in your glo - ri - ous tri-umph,

the gates — of — heav - en are o - pen to us.

Psalm 96 (95V)

1–3, 8b–9

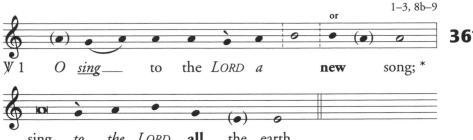

361

℣ 1 O _sing_— to the LORD a **new** song; *

sing _to the_ LORD, **all** the earth.

2 _Sing_ to the LORD, _blèss his_ **name;** *
tell of his sal_vàtion from_ **day** to day.

3 _Declare_ his glory a_mòng the_ **na**tions, *
his marvelous works a_mòng all the_ **peo**ples.

4 _Bring_ an offering, and come in_tò his_ **courts.** *
Worship the LORD _in holy_ **splen**dor.

Communion Antiphon

Luke 1:49 and 46

VIII G

362

All ag - es will call_ me bless - ed, * for the Al-

might - y has done great_ things for me,_ al - le-lu - ia.

The Canticle of Mary

Luke 1:46–55

363

℣ 1 _My soul_ mag - ni - fies the **Lord,** *

and my spir - it re - joic - es in _God my_ **Sav** - ior,

2 _for he_ has looked with favor on the lowliness of his **sér**vant. *
Surely, from now on all generations will _càll me_ **bless**ed;

3 _for the_ Mighty One has done great things for **mé,** *
and _hòly_ **is** his name.

4   *His mercy* is for those who **féar** him *
     from generation to *gèner*ation.

5   *He has* shown strength with his **árm;** *
     he has scattered the proud in the *thòughts of* **their** hearts.

6   *He has* brought down the powerful from their **thrónes,** *
     and lifted *ùp the* **low**ly;

7   *he has* filled the hungry with **góod** things, *
     and sent the rich *àway* **emp**ty.

8   *He has* helped his servant **Ís**rael, *
     in remembrance *òf his* **mer**cy,

9   *accord*ing to the promise he made to our **án**cestors, *
     to Abraham and to his descen*dànts fore*ver.

September 8

Birth of Mary

Feast

Entrance Antiphon

364 VII a

Of all wom - en * born in - to this world,

none can com-pare with you, O_____ Vir-gin Ma-ry.

Psalm 46 (45V)

1–10

365

℣ 1 *God_ is_* our **ref** - uge **and** strength, * a ver- y **pres-**

ent **help** in trou - ble. *Flex:* end of the earth; †

2   *Therefore* we will not fear, **thóugh** the **earth** should change, *
     though the mountains shake in the **héart of the** <u>sea;</u>

3   *though its* **wá**ters **roar** and foam, *
     though the mountains **trém**ble with **its** tumult.

4   *There is* a river whose streams make glad the **cí**ty **of** God, *
     the holy habitation **óf** the **Most** <u>High</u>.

5   *God is* in the midst of the city; it **sháll** not **be** moved; *
God will help it **whén** the **morn**ing <u>dawns</u>.

6   *The na*tions are in an uproar, the **kíng**doms **tot**ter; *
he utters his **vóice,** the **earth** <u>melts</u>.

7   *The* <u>LORD</u> of **hósts** is **with** us; *
the God of **Já**cob is **our** refuge.

8   *Come, be*hold the **wórks** of **the** LORD; *
see what desolations he has **bróught** on **the** <u>earth</u>.

9   *He makes* wars cease to the end of the èarth; †
      he breaks the bow, and **shát**ters **the** spear; *
he **búrns** the **shields** with <u>fire</u>.

10   *"Be still,* and **knów** that **I** am God! *
I am exalted among the nations, I am ex**ál**ted **in** the <u>earth</u>."

The Chants between the Readings are taken from the solemnity of the Immaculate Conception, **396–398.**

The Preparation of the Gifts Antiphon is *Hail Mary,* taken from the solemnity of the Annunciation, **324.**

Communion Antiphon

VIII G

366

How blest you— are, * O Vir - gin Ma - ry;

you bore the Son of the e - ter - nal † Fa - ther.

E.S. † Fa - ther,— al - le - lu - ia.

The Canticle of Mary

Luke 1:46–55

367

℣ 1 *My soul* mag - ni - fies the **Lord,** *

and my spir - it re - joic - es in *God my* **Sav** - ior,

227

2 *for he* has looked with favor on the lowliness of his **sér**vant. *
Surely, from now on all generations will *càll me* **bless**ed;

3 *for the* Mighty One has done great things for **mé,** *
and *hòly* **is** his name.

4 *His mer*cy is for those who **féar** him *
from generation to *gèner*ation.

5 *He has* shown strength with his **árm;** *
he has scattered the proud in the *thòughts of* **their** hearts.

6 *He has* brought down the powerful from their **thrónes,** *
and lifted *ùp the* **low**ly;

7 *he has* filled the hungry with **góod** things, *
and sent the rich *àway* **emp**ty.

8 *He has* helped his servant **Í**srael, *
in remembrance *òf his* **mer**cy,

9 *accord*ing to the promise he made to our **án**cestors, *
to Abraham and to his descen*dànts fore*ver.

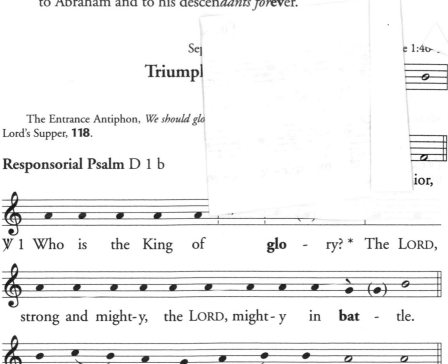

Se[...]   e 1:40

Triumpl[...]

The Entrance Antiphon, *We should glo[...]*
Lord's Supper, **118.**

Responsorial Psalm D 1 b

368

℣ 1 Who is the King of **glo** - ry? * The LORD,

strong and might-y, the LORD, might-y in **bat** - tle.

℟ The Lord___ is the king___ of glo - ry.

2 The earth is the LORD's and all that is **ín** it, *
the world, and those who **lìve** in it;

NATIVITY OF MARY

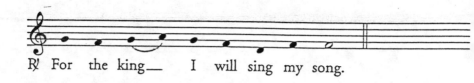

℟ For the king— I will sing my song.

℟ Al - le - lu - ia, al - le - lu - ia.

Communion Antiphon

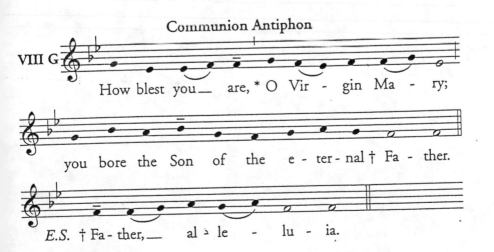

VIII G

How blest you— are, * O Vir - gin Ma - ry;

you bore the Son of the e - ter - nal † Fa - ther.

E.S. † Fa - ther,— al - le - lu - ia.

3   for he has founded it on the **séas,** *
and established it on the **rì**vers.

4   Who shall ascend the hill of the **LÓRD?** *
And who shall stand in his **hò**ly place?

5   Those who have clean hands and **púre** hearts, *
who do not lift up their souls to what is false, and do
    not swear de**cèit**fully.

6   They will receive blessing from the **LÓRD,** *
and vindication from the God of their sal**và**tion.

7   Such is the company of those who **séek** him, *
who seek the face of the God of **Ja**cob.

8   Lift up your heads, O gates! ’
    and be lifted up, O **án**cient doors! *
that the King of glory may **còme** in.

9   Who is this King of **gló**ry? *
The LORD of hosts, he is the King of **glò**ry.

Alleluia   Psalm 97 (96V)

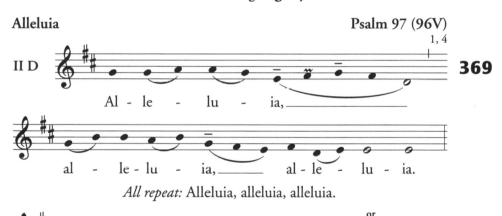

369

Al - le - lu - ia, _____

al - le - lu - ia, _____ al - le - lu - ia.

All repeat: Alleluia, alleluia, alleluia.

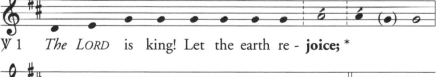

℣ 1   *The* LORD is king! Let the earth re - **joice;** *

let the man - y coast-*lands* be   glad!

All: Alleluia, alleluia, alleluia.

2   *His light*nings light up the **wórld;** *
the earth sees *ànd* **trem**bles.

All: Alleluia, alleluia, alleluia.

229

or **Alleluia Psalm** C 1

Psalm 97 (96V)
1–6, 9–12

370

℣ 1 The LORD is king! Let the earth re - **joice;** *

or

let the man - y coast-*lands* **be** glad!

℟ Al - le - lu - ia, al - le - lu - ia.

2   Clouds and thick darkness are all a**róund** him; *
     righteousness and justice are the foundation *òf* **his** throne.

3   Fire goes be**fóre** him, *
     and consumes his adversaries *òn* **eve**ry side.

4   His lightnings light up the **wórld;** *
     the earth sees *ànd* **trem**bles.

5   The mountains melt like wax before the **LÓRD,** *
     before the Lord of *àll* **the** earth.

6   The heavens proclaim his **ríght**eousness; *
     and all the peoples behold *hìs* **glo**ry.

7   For you, O LORD, are most high over **áll** the earth; *
     you are exalted far a**bòve** **all** gods.

8   The LORD loves those who hate evil; '
        he guards the lives of his **fáith**ful; *
     he rescues them from the hand of *thè* **wick**ed.

9   Light dawns for the **ríght**eous, *
     and joy for the up**rìght** **in** heart.

10   Rejoice in the LORD, O you **ríght**eous, *
     and give thanks to *hìs* **ho**ly name!

Preparation of the Gifts Antiphon

371 I f

The Lord_ is ex-alt - ed * on the cross;_____

230

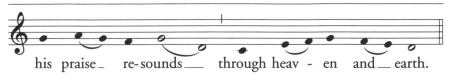

his praise‿ re-sounds‿ through heav - en and‿ earth.

Psalm 1

1–3 (See Performance Notes)

372

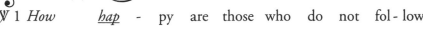

℣ 1 *How* <u>*hap*</u> - py are those who do not fol - low

the ad-**vice** of the **wick** - ed, * or take the path that sin-

ners tread, or sit in the *seat of* <u>**scof**</u> - fers; ‿

2   *but* <u>*their*</u> delight is in the **láw** of **the** LORD, *
    and on his law they med*ìtate* **day** and <u>night</u>.

3   *They are* <u>*like*</u> trees planted by **stréams** of **wa**ter, *
    which yield their fruit *ìn its* <u>**sea**</u>son,

4   *and* <u>*their*</u> **léaves** do not **with**er. *
    In all that they *dò, they* <u>**pros**</u>per.

Communion Antiphon

VIII c

373

By the sign‿ of the cross, ‿ *

de - liv - er us from our en - e - mies, O Lord our God.

Psalm 2

1–4, 6–8, 11, 12e (See Performance Notes)
or

374

℣ 1 *Why do* the na-tions con-**spire,** * and the *peo-ples*

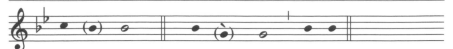

plot in vain? *Flex:* set them-selves, †

2 *The kings* of the earth set thèmselves, †
   and the rulers take counsel to**géth**er, *
   against the LORD and *hìs a*nointed,

3 *saying,* "Let us burst their bonds asúnder, *
   and *càst their* **cords** from us."

4 *He who* sits in the heavens **láughs;** *
   the LORD has them *ìn de*rision.

5 *"I have* set my king on **Zíon,** *
   *mỳ ho*ly hill."

6 *I will* tell of the decree of the LÒRD: †
   He said to me, "You are my **són;** *
   today I *hàve be***got**ten you.

7 *Ask of* me, and I will make the nations your **hér**itage, *
   and the ends of the earth *yòur pos***ses**sion."

8 *Serve the* LORD with fèar, †
   with trembling **kíss** his feet. *
   Happy are all who take *rèfuge* **in** him.

September 29

St. Michael, St. Gabriel, and St. Raphael, Archangels

Feast

Entrance Antiphon

Tobit 13:10

375 VIII G

Bless ____ the ___ Lord, ____ * all ___
you ___ his an - gels; make ___ the day ___
glad ____ with thanks-giv - ing to our ___ God.

Psalm 138 (137V)

1–8

℣ 1 *I give* you thanks, O LORD, with my whole heart, †

or

for you have heard the words of my **mouth;** *

376

be - fore the an - *gels* *I* **sing** your praise;

2   *I bow* down toward your holy templè †
    and give thanks to your name for your steadfast love and your
    faithfulness; *
    for you have exalted your name and your word *àbove* **eve**rything.

3   *On the* day I called, you **án**swered me, *
    you incrèased *my* **strength** of soul.

4   *All the* kings of the earth shall praise you, O **LÓRD,** *
    for they have heard the *wòrds of* **your** mouth.

5   *They shall* sing of the ways of the **LÓRD,** *
    for great is the glorỳ *of* **the** LORD.

6   *For though* the LORD is high, he regards the **lów**ly; *
    but the haughty he percèives *from* **far** away.

7   *Though I* walk in the midst of trouble, †
    you preserve me against the wrath of my **én**emies; *
    you stretch out your hand, and your right *hànd de***liv**ers me.

8   *The LORD* will fulfill his purpose for mè; †
    your steadfast love, O LORD, endures foréver. *
    Do not forsake the *wòrk of* **your** hands.

Responsorial Psalm E 5 *

Psalm 148

(2a) 1–6, 11–14

℣ 1 Praise the LORD from the **heav** - ens; *praise *him in*

377

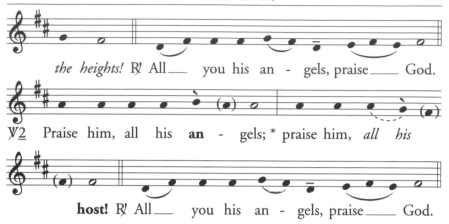

the heights! ℟ All___ you his an - gels, praise___ God.

℣2 Praise him, all his **an** - gels; * praise him, *all his*

host! ℟ All___ you his an - gels, praise___ God.

3[1] Praise him, **sún** and moon; *
    praise him, all *yóu shining stars!*

4 Praise him, you highest **héav**ens, *
    and you waters *above thè* **heav**ens!

5 Let them praise the name **of thé** LORD, *
    for he commanded and they *wére created.*

6 He established them forever and **év**er; *
    he fixed their bounds, which *cán***not** be passed.

7 Kings of the earth and all **péo**ples, *
    princes and all rul*érs of the earth!*

8 Young men and women **á**like, *
    old and *young tò***geth**er!

9 Let them praise the name of the LORD, '
        for his name alone is ex**ált**ed; *
    his glory is above *éarth and heaven.*

10 He has raised up a horn for his people, '
        praise for all his **fáith**ful, *
    for the people of Israel *who àre* **close** to him.

Alleluia   **Psalm 103 (102V)**
                                                        1, 20

378 III g

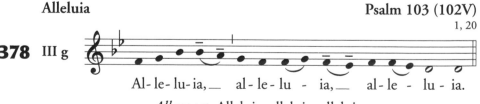

Al- le - lu - ia,___ al - le - lu - ia,___ al - le - lu - ia.

All repeat: Alleluia, alleluia, alleluia.

[1] Odd numbered verses are chanted on the first chanting note (mi); even numbered verses, on the second chanting note (sol).

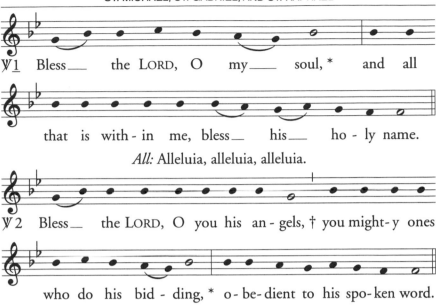

℣1 Bless__ the LORD, O my__ soul, * and all that is with-in me, bless__ his__ ho-ly name.

All: Alleluia, alleluia, alleluia.

℣2 Bless__ the LORD, O you his an-gels, † you might-y ones who do his bid-ding, * o-be-dient to his spo-ken word.

All: Alleluia, alleluia, alleluia.

or **Alleluia Psalm** C 4

Psalm 103 (102V)
1–6, 8, 20–22 (See Performance Notes)

379

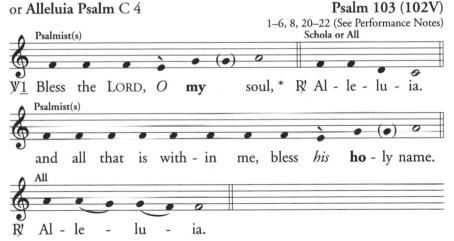

Psalmist(s) / Schola or All

℣1 Bless the LORD, O **my** soul, * ℟ Al - le - lu - ia.

Psalmist(s)

and all that is with - in me, bless *his* **ho** - ly name.

All

℟ Al - le - lu - ia.

2 Bless the Lord, *Ò* **my** soul, *
   and do not forget all *hìs* **ben**efits—

3 who forgives all your *ìniq*uity,*
   who heals all your *dì*seases,

4 who redeems your life *fròm* **the** Pit, *
   who crowns you with steadfast love *ànd* **mer**cy,

5 who satisfies you with good as long *às* **you** live *
   so that your youth is renewed like *thè* **eag**le's.

<u>6</u>   The LORD works vindication *ànd* **jus**tice *
    for all *whò* **are** oppressed.

7   The LORD is merciful *ànd* **gra**cious, *
    slow to anger and abounding *ìn* **stead**fast love.

8   Bless the LORD, O you *hìs* **an**gels, *
    you mighty ones who do his bidding, obedient to *hìs* **spo**ken word.

9   Bless the LORD, *àll* **his** hosts, *
    his ministers that *dò* **his** will.

10   Bless the LORD, all his works, '
    in all places of his *dò***min**ion. *
    Bless the LORD, *Ò* **my** soul.

Preparation of the Gifts Antiphon

Revelation 8:3

380 IV A

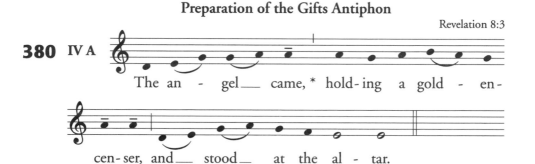

The an - gel__ came, * hold-ing a gold - en-cen-ser, and__ stood__ at the al - tar.

Psalm 141 (140V)

1–4a

381

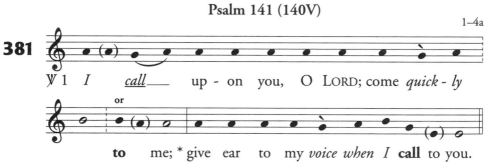

℣ 1 *I* <u>*call*</u>__ up - on you, O LORD; come *quick - ly*

or

to me; * give ear to my *voice when I* **call** to you.

2   *Let my* <u>*prayer*</u> be counted as in*cènse be***fore** you, *
    and the lifting up of my hands as *àn evening* **sac**rifice.

3   *Set a* <u>*guard*</u> over my *mòuth,* O **LORD;** *
    keep watch over *thè door of* **my** lips.

4   *Do* <u>*not*</u> turn my heart to *àny* **e**vil, *
    to busy myself with wicked deeds in company with those
        *whò work in***iq**uity.

Communion Antiphon

Cf. Psalm 148:1–2

V a   All_ you an - gels, * praise_ the Lord__ in heav- en.   **382**

Psalm 135 (134V)

1–6, 13, 19–21

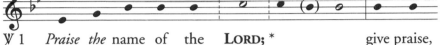

℣ 1   *Praise the* name of   the   **LORD;** *   give praise,   **383**

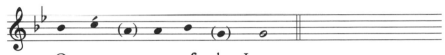

O   ser - vants **of**   the   LORD,

2   *you that* stand in the house of the **LÓRD,** *
in the courts of the **hóuse** of **our** God.

3   *Praise the* LORD, for the LORD is **góod;** *
sing to his name, for **hé** is **gra**cious.

4   *For the* LORD has chosen Jacob for him**sélf,** *
Israel as his **ówn** possession.

5   *For I* know that the LORD is **gréat;** *
our **Lórd** is a**bove** all gods.

6   *Whatev*er the LORD pleases he **dóes,** *
in heaven and on earth, in the **séas** and **all** deeps.

7   *Your name,* O LORD, endures for**éver,** *
your renown, O LORD, through**óut** all **ages.**

8   *O house* of Israel, bless the **LÓRD!** *
O house of **Áa**ron, **bless** the LORD!

9   *O house* of Levi, bless the **LÓRD!** *
You that **féar** the LORD, **bless** the LORD!

10   *Blessed* be the LORD from **Zíon,** *
he who re**sídes** in Jeru**sa**lem.

November 1

All Saints

Solemnity

Entrance Antiphon

Psalm 31 (30V):23

384 II D

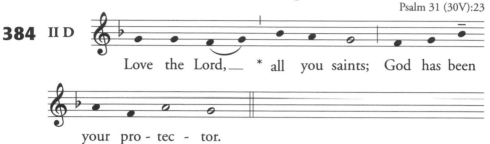

Love the Lord, — * all you saints; God has been

your pro - tec - tor.

Psalm 31 (30V)

1–3, 19–20a, 21, 24

385

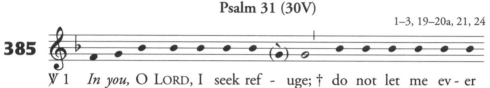

℣ 1 *In you,* O LORD, I seek ref - uge; † do not let me ev - er

or

be put to **shame;** * in your right-eous-ness *de-***liv**- er me.

2 *Incline* your **éar** to me; *
   rescue *mè* **speed**ily.

3 *Be a* rock of refuge for **mé,** *
   a strong fortress *tò* **save** me.

4 *You are* indeed my rock and my **fór**tress; *
   for your name's sake lead me *ànd* **guide** me,

5 *O how* abundant is your **góod**ness *
   that you have laid up for those *whò* **fear** you,

6 *and ac*complished for those who take refuge in **yóu,** *
   in the sight *òf* **eve**ryone!

7 *In the* shelter of your **prés**ence *
   you hide them *fròm* **hu**man plots;

8 *you hold* them safe under your **shél**ter *
   from *còn***ten**tious tongues.

9 *Blessed* be the LÒRD, †
   for he has wondrously shown his steadfast love to **mé** *
   when I was beset as a ci*tỳ* **un**der siege.

10 *Be strong,* and let your heart take **cóur**age, *
all you who wait *fòr* **the** LORD.

Responsorial Psalm C 3 g   **Psalm 150**
1b–6 (See Performance Notes)

386

℣ 1 Praise God in his **sanc** - tu - ar - y; *

praise him in his might - y **fir - ma** - ment!___

℟ Sing the Lord's___ praise___ with all___ the___ saints!___

℣ 2 **Praise**___ him for his **might** - y deeds; * praise him

ac - cord-ing to his sur - pass-*ing* **great** - ness!___

℟ Sing the Lord's___ praise___ with all___ the___ saints!___

3[1] Praise him with **trúm**pet sound; *
praise him with lute **ánd** **harp**!

4   **Praise** him with tambourine **ànd** dance; *
praise him *wìth* **strings** **and** pipe!

5   Praise him with clanging **cým**bals; *
praise him with loud **clásh**ing cymbals!

6   Let **eve**rything that breathes **pràise** the LORD! *
Pràise **the** **LORD**!

[1] Odd numbered verses are chanted on the first chanting note (fa); even numbered verses, on the second chanting note (la).

239

Alleluia Psalm 33 (32V)
1, 12

387 VIII c

Al - le - lu - ia, al - le - lu - ia, al - le - lu - ia.

All repeat: Alleluia, alleluia, alleluia.

℣ 1 *Re-joice* in the LORD, O you **right** - eous. * Praise be-

fits the **up** - right.

All: Alleluia, alleluia, alleluia.

2 *Happy* is the nation whose God is the **LÓRD,** *
   the people whom he has chosen *às his* **heri**tage.

All: Alleluia, alleluia, alleluia.

or **Alleluia Psalm C 4** Psalm 33 (32V)
1–2, 4–6, 12–13, 18–19, 22

388

℣ 1 Re-joice in the LORD, O *you* **right** - eous.* ℟ Al - le - lu - ia.

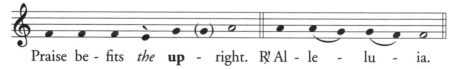

Praise be - fits *the* **up** - right. ℟ Al - le - lu - ia.

2 Praise the LORD *with* **the** lyre; *
   make melody to him with the harp *òf* **ten** strings.

3 For the word of the LORD *is* **up**right, *
   and all his work is done *in* **faith**fulness.

4 He loves righteousness *ànd* **ju**stice; *
   the earth is full of the steadfast love *òf* **the** LORD.

5 By the word of the LORD the heav*ens* **were** made, *
   and all their host by the breath *òf* **his** mouth.

6 Happy is the nation whose God *is* **the** LORD, *
   the people whom he has chosen as *hìs* **heri**tage.

7   The LORD looks down *fròm* **heav**en; *
     he sees *àll* **hu**mankind.

8   Truly the eye of the LORD is on those *whò* **fear** him, *
     on those who hope in *hìs* **stead**fast love,

9   to deliver *thèir* **soul** from death, *
     and to keep them alive *ìn* **fam**ine.

10   Let your stead*fàst* **love,** O LORD, *
     be upon us, even as *wè* **hope** in you.

Preparation of the Gifts Antiphon

Sirach 15:6

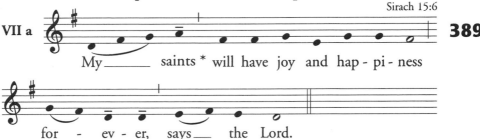

Psalm 5

1, 7bc, 11

2   *I will* **én**ter **your** house, *
     I will bow down toward your holy **tém**ple in **awe** of you.

3   *But let* all who take **réf**uge in **you** rejoice; *
     let them **év**er **sing** for joy.

4   *Spread your* pro**téc**tion **o**ver them, *
     so that those who love your **náme** may ex**ult** in you.

Communion Antiphon

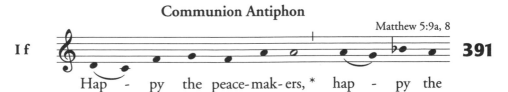

Matthew 5:9a, 8

241

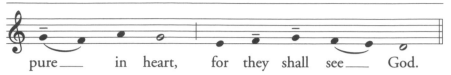

pure___ in heart, for they shall see___ God.

Psalm 126 (125V)

1–6 (See Performance Notes)

392

℣ 1 *When the LORD___* re-stored the **for** - tunes of **Zi** - on, * we

were like **those**_ who dream.___ ℣4 *and* **we**_ re- joiced.___

2   *Then our mouth* was **filled** with **laugh**ter, *
    and our *tòngue with* **shouts** of joy;

3   *then* it was said a**móng** the **nations,** *
    "The LORD has *dòne great* **things** for them."

4   *The LORD* has done **gréat** things **for** us, *
    ànd **we** rejoiced.

5   *Restore* our **fór**tunes, **O** LORD, *
    like the watercourses *ìn the* **Negeb.**

6   May **thóse** who **sow** in tears *
    rèap with **shouts** of joy.

7   *Those* who **gó** out **weep**ing, *
    bearing the *sèed for* **sow**ing,

8   *shall* come **hóme** with **shouts** of joy, *
    car*rỳing* **their** sheaves.

December 8

Immaculate Conception of Mary

Solemnity

Entrance Antiphon

393 I g 2

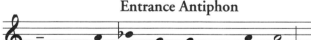

Ma - ry, you are all beau - ti - ful; * no stain was

ev - er found___ in___ you.

Canticle of Isaiah

61:10–62:3

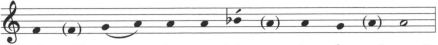

℣ 1 I will great - ly re - **joice** in **the** LORD, *

my whole be-ing shall ex - *ult* *in* **my** God;____

394

Flex: to spring up, †

2 *for he* has clothed me with the garments **óf** sal**va**tion, *
he has covered me with the *ròbe of* **right**eous<u>ness</u>,

3 *as a <u>bride</u>*groom decks him**sélf** with a **gar**land, *
and as a bride adorns *hèrself* **with** her <u>jew</u>els.

4 *For <u>as</u>* the **éarth** brings **forth** its shoots, *
and as a garden causes what is sown in *ìt to* **spring** <u>up</u>,

5 *so the <u>Lord</u>* GOD will cause **ríght**eousness **and** praise *
to spring up be*fòre all* **the** <u>na</u>tions.

6 *For <u>Zi</u>*on's sake I will **nót** keep **silent**, *
and for Jerusalem's sake *Ì will* **not** <u>rest</u>,

7 *un<u>til</u>* her vindication shines **óut** like **the** dawn, *
and her salvation *likè a* **burn**ing <u>torch</u>.

8 *The <u>na</u>*tions shall see your **vín**dication, *
and all *thè kings* **your** <u>glory</u>;

9 *and <u>you</u>* shall be **cálled** by a **new** name *
that the mouth *òf the* **LORD** will <u>give</u>.

10 *You shall <u>be</u>* a crown of beauty in the **hánd** of **the** LORD, *
and a royal diadem in the *hànd of* **your** <u>God</u>.

Responsorial Psalm C 2 a

or

Psalm 45 (44V)
(1b) 1–2, 7–15

℣ 1 My heart **o** - ver - flows * with a **good-<u>ly</u>**___ theme.

395

℟ For the king— I will sing my song.

 2 Grace is poured upon your **líps;** *
therefore God has blessed you for**év**er.

3 You love righteousness and hate wickedness. '
Therefore God, your God, has a**nóin**ted you *
with the oil of gladness beyond your **cómpan**ions;

4 Your robes are all fragrant with myrrh and aloes and **cás**sia. *
From ivory palaces stringed instruments make **yóu** glad;

5 Daughters of kings are among your ladies of **hón**or; *
at your right hand stands the queen in gold of **Ó**phir.

6 Hear, O daughter, consider, and in**clíne** your ear; *
forget your people and your **fáther's** house,

7 and the king will desire your **béau**ty. *
Since he is your lord, **bów to** him;

8 the people of Tyre will seek your favor with **gífts,** *
the richest of the people with all **kínds of** wealth.

9 The princess is decked in her chamber with gold-woven **róbes;** *
in many-colored robes she is led to **thé** king;

10 behind her the virgins, her companions, **fól**low. *
With joy and gladness they are led along as they enter the palace
of **thé** king.

Alleluia   **Song of Songs**
4:1, 12 (See Performance Notes)

396 IV E

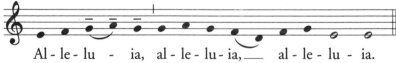

Al - le - lu - ia, al - le - lu - ia,— al - le - lu - ia.

All repeat: Alleluia, alleluia, alleluia.

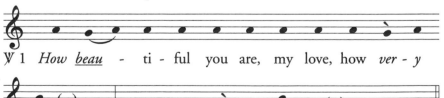

℣ 1 *How beau* - ti - ful you are, my love, how *ver - y*

beau-ti - ful! * Your eyes are *doves be- hind* **your** veil.

NATIVITY OF MARY

℟ For the king — I will sing my song.

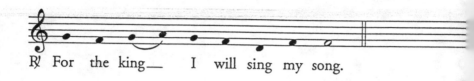

℟ Al - le - lu - ia, al - le - lu - ia.

Communion Antiphon

VIII G

How blest you — are, * O Vir - gin Ma - ry;

you bore the Son of the e - ter - nal † Fa - ther.

E.S. † Fa - ther, — al - le - lu - ia.

All: Alleluia, alleluia, alleluia.

2   *A gar*den locked is my *sister,* **my** bride, *
a garden *locked, a* <u>**foun**</u>**tain** sealed.

All: Alleluia, alleluia, alleluia.

or **Alleluia Psalm** E 2 d   **Song of Songs**
4:1, 2:11–12 and 13bc, 2:14, 4:11–12, 5:2cd, 6:4 (See Performance Notes)

397

℣ 1 How beau - ti - ful you are, my love, how ver - y

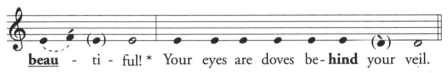

<u>**beau**</u> - ti - ful! * Your eyes are doves be-**hind** your veil.

℟ Al - le - lu - ia, al - le - lu - ia.

2   For now the winter **ís** past, *
    the rain is over **and** gòne.

3   The flowers appear **on thé** earth; *
    the time of singing **has** còme,

4   the voice of the turtledove is heard in **óur** land. *
    The vines are in blossom; they give forth **fra**grànce.

5   Let me hear **yóur** voice; *
    for your voice is sweet, and your face is **love**lỳ.

6   Your lips distill nectar, **mý** bride; *
    honey and milk are under **your** tòngue;

7   the scent of your **gár**ments *
    is like the scent of **Leb**ànon.

8   A garden locked is my sister, **mý** bride, *
    a garden locked, a **foun**tàin sealed.

9   Open to me, my sister, **mý** love, *
    my dove, my **per**fèct one;

10   You are beautiful, my love, comely as Je**rú**salem, *
    terrible as an army with **ban**nèrs.

Preparation of the Gifts Antiphon

Psalm 46 (45V):Cf. 4b

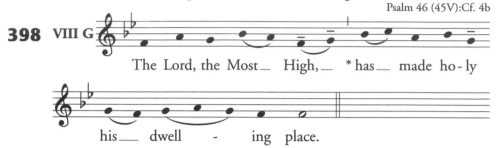

398 VIII G

The Lord, the Most High, * has made holy his dwelling place.

Psalm 46 (45V)

1, 5, 8, 11

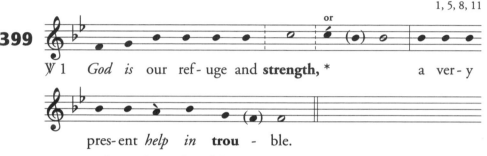

399

℣ 1 *God is* our ref-uge and **strength,** * a very pres-ent *help in* **trou** - ble.

2 *God is* in the midst of the city; it shall not be **móved;** *
God will help it *whèn the* **morn**ing dawns.

3 *Come, be*hold the works of the **LÓRD;** *
see what desolations he has *bròught on* **the** earth.

4 *The Lord* of hosts is **with** us; *
the God of Jacob *is our* **ref**uge.

Or, if desired, the Preparation of the Gifts Antiphon, *Hail Mary,* as on the solemnity of the Annunciation, **324,** with its psalm, **325.**

Communion Antiphon I

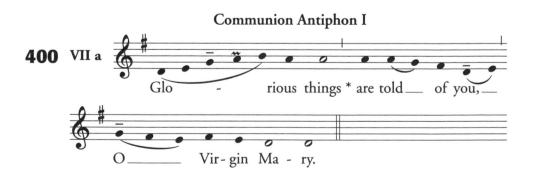

400 VII a

Glo - rious things * are told of you, O Virgin Ma - ry.

Communion Antiphon II

Luke 1:49

401

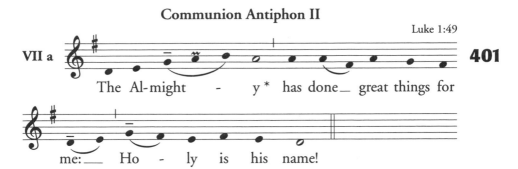

The Al-might - y * has done__ great things for me:__ Ho - ly is his name!

Canticle of Mary

Luke 1:46–55

402

℣ 1 *My__ soul__* **mag** - ni - **fies** the Lord,*

and my spir - it re - **joic** - es in **God** my Sav - ior,

2 *for he* has looked with favor on the lowliness **óf** his **ser**vant. *
Surely, from now on all gener**á**tions will **call** me blessed;

3 *for the* Mighty One has done **gréat** things **for** me, *
and **hól**y **is** his <u>name</u>.

4 *His <u>mer</u>*cy is for **thóse** who **fear** him *
from gener**á**tion to **gen**eration.

5 *He <u>has</u>* shown **stréngth** with **his** arm; *
he has scattered the proud in the **thóughts** of **their** <u>hearts</u>.

6 *He <u>has</u>* brought down the **pów**erful **from** their thrones, *
and **líft**ed up **the** lowly;

7 *he <u>has</u>* filled the **hún**gry with **good** things, *
and sent the **rích** a**way** empty.

8 *He <u>has</u>* helped his **sér**vant Israel, *
in re**mém**brance **of** his mercy,

9 *accord*ing to the promise he **máde** to our **an**cestors, *
to Abraham and to his des**cén**dants **for**ever.

Common of the Dedication of a Church

Entrance Antiphon

Psalm 5:7

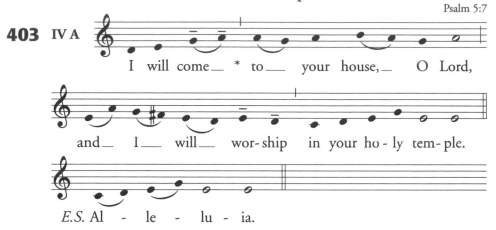

403 IV A

I will come __ * to __ your house, __ O Lord,

and __ I __ will __ wor-ship in your ho - ly tem-ple.

E.S. Al – le – lu – ia.

Psalm 5

1–5a, 8, 11–12

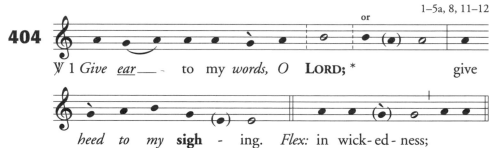

404

℣ 1 *Give ear __* - to my *words,* O **LORD;** *   give

heed to my **sigh** - ing.   *Flex:* in wick-ed-ness;

2   *Listen* to the sound of my cry, my *Kìng and* **my** God, *
     fòr to you **I** pray.

3   *O LORD,* in the mornìng you **hear** my voice; *
     in the morning I plead *mỳ case to* **you,** and watch.

4   *For you* are not a God who delights in wickèdness; †
         evil will *nòt sojourn* **with** you. *
     The boastful will *nòt stand be*fore your eyes.

5   *Lead* me, O LORD, in your righteousness because *òf my* **en**emies; *
     make your *wày straight be*fore me.

6   *But let all* who take refuge in *yòu re*joice; *
     let *thèm ever* **sing** for joy.

7   *Spread* your protèction **o**ver them, *
     so that those who love your *nàme may ex***ult** in you.

8   *For you bless* the rightèous, O **LORD;** *
     you cover them with favòr *as with* **a** shield.

248

The Responsorial Psalm is taken from the feast of the Holy Family, **31.**

Alleluia   **Psalm 122 (121V)**
1–2 (See Performance Notes)

℣ 1 I was glad when they said to me, * "Let us go to the house of the LORD!"

Al-le-lu-ia, al-le-lu-ia, al-le-lu-ia.

All repeat: Alleluia, alleluia, alleluia.

All: Alleluia, alleluia, alleluia.

℣ 2 Our feet are stand - ing * with-in your gates, O Je - ru - sa - lem.

All: Alleluia, alleluia, alleluia.

405

or **Alleluia Psalm** C 1   **Psalm 122 (121V)**
1–9 (See Performance Notes)

℣ 1 I was glad when they said to me, *

"Let us go to the house *of* **the** LORD!"

℟ Al - le - lu - ia, al - le - lu - ia.

406

249

2 Our feet are **stánd**ing *
   within your gates, O *Jè*ru**sa**lem.

3 Jerusalem—built as a **cí**ty *
   that is bound firmly *tò***geth**er.

4 To it the tribes go up, the tribes of the **LÓRD,** *
   as was decreed for Israel, to give thanks to the name *òf* **the** LORD.

5 For there the thrones for judgment were set **úp,** *
   the thrones of the house *òf* **Da**vid.

6 Pray for the peace of Je**rú**salem: *
   "May they prosper *whò* **love** you.

7 Peace be within your **wálls,** *
   and security within *yòur* **tow**ers."

8 For the sake of my relatives and friends I will **sáy,** *
   "Peace be *wìth***in** you.

9 For the sake of the house of the **LÓRD** our God, *
   I will *sèek* **your** good.

Preparation of the Gifts Antiphon

407 VIII c

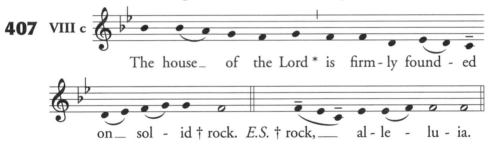

The house_ of the Lord * is firm-ly found-ed on_ sol-id † rock. *E.S.* † rock,__ al-le-lu-ia.

Psalm 138 (137V)

408

℣ 1 *I give* you thanks, O LORD, with my whole heart, †

for you have heard the words of my **mouth;** *

be-fore the an-*gels* *I* **sing** your praise;

250

2 *I bow* down toward your holy templè †
and give thanks to your name for your steadfast love and your
fáithfulness; *
for you have exalted your name and your word *àbove* **eve**rything.

3 *On the* day I called, you **án**swered me, *
you in**crèased** *my* **strength** of soul.

Communion Antiphon

Matthew 21:13

I D 2

409

My_ house_____ * shall be called_ a house_ of

† prayer._____ *E.S.* † prayer,_____ al - le - lu - ia.

Psalm 147

12–20 (See Performance Notes)

410

V1 *Praise* *the*___ LORD, **O** Je - **ru** - sa - lem! *

Praise your *God, O* **Zi** - on!

2 *For he* <u>strength</u>ens the **bárs** of **your** gates; *
he blesses your child*rèn withín* you.

3 *He* <u>grants</u> peace withín your **bor**ders; *
he fills you *wìth the* **finest** wheat.

4 *He* <u>sends</u> out his com**mánd** to **the** earth; *
his *wòrd runs* **swift**ly.

5 He **gíves** snow **like** wool; *
he scatters *fròst like* <u>ash</u>es.

6 He **húrls** down **hail** like crumbs— *
who can *stànd be*<u>**fore**</u> **his** cold?

7 *He* <u>sends</u> out his **wórd**, and **melts** them; *
he makes his wind blow, *ànd the* **waters** flow.

8 *He* <u>declares</u> his **wórd** to Jacob, *
his statutes and ordinanc*ès to* **Isra**el.

9 *He has* <u>not</u> dealt thus with any **óth**er **nation**; *
they do not know *hìs* ordi<u>**nan**</u>ces.

Common of the Blessed Virgin Mary

Entrance Antiphon

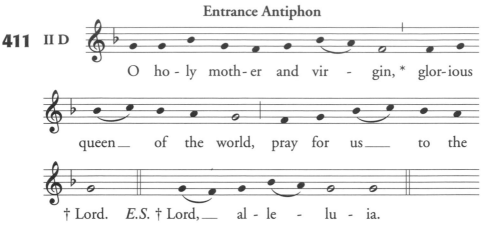

411 II D

O ho-ly moth-er and vir - gin, * glor-ious queen — of the world, pray for us — to the † Lord. *E.S.* † Lord, — al - le - lu - ia.

Psalm 46 (45V)

1–10

412

℣ 1 *God is* our ref - uge and **strength,** *

a ver - y pres - ent help *in* **trou** - ble.

Flex: end of the earth; †

2 *Therefore* we will not fear, though the earth should **chánge,** *
   though the mountains shake in the heart *òf* **the** sea;

3 *though its* waters **róar** and foam, *
   though the mountains tremble with *ìts* **tu**mult.

4 *There is* a river whose streams make glad the city of **Gód,** *
   the holy habitation of *thè* **Most** High.

5 *God is* in the midst of the city; it shall not be **móved;** *
   God will help it when *thè* **morn**ing dawns.

6 *The na*tions are in an uproar, the kingdoms **tót**ter; *
   he utters his voice, *thè* **earth** melts.

7 *The* LORD of hosts is **wíth** us; *
   the God of Jacob is *òur* **refuge.**

252

8   *Come, be*hold the works of the **LÓRD;** *
     see what desolations he has brought *òn* **the** earth.

9   *He makes* wars cease to the end of the *èarth;* †
        he breaks the bow, and shatters the **spéar;** *
     he burns the *shìelds* **with** fire.

10   *"Be still,* and know that **Í** am God! *
     I am exalted among the nations, I am exalted *ìn* **the** earth."

The Responsorial Psalm, the Alleluia, and/or the Alleluia Psalm are taken from the solemnity of the Immaculate Conception, **396–398**.

The Preparation of the Gifts Antiphon, *Hail Mary,* is taken from the solemnity of the Annunciation, **324**.

Communion Antiphon I, *How Blest You Are,* is taken from the feast of the Birth of Mary, **366**.

Communion Antiphon II

Cf. Luke 1:49 and 46

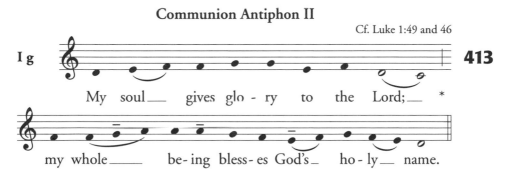

My soul___ gives glo - ry to the Lord;___ *
my whole_____ be-ing bless-es God's_ ho-ly__ name.

Canticle of Mary

Luke 1:46–55

℣ 1 *My soul*___ **mag** - ni - **fies** the Lord, * and my
spir - it re - joic - es in *God my* **Sav** - ior,

2   *for he* has looked with favor on the lowliness **óf** his **ser**vant. *
     Surely, from now on all generations will *càll me* **bless**ed;

3   *for the Migh*ty One has done **gréat** things **for** me, *
     and ho*lỳ is* **his** name.

4   *His mer*cy is for **thóse** who **fear** him *
     from generation to *gèner*ation.

253

5   *He has* shown **stréngth** with **his** arm; *
he has scattered the proud in the *thòughts of* **their** hearts.

6   *He has* brought down the **pów**erful **from** their thrones, *
and lifted *ùp the* **low**ly;

7   *he has* filled the **hún**gry with **good** things, *
and sent the rich *àway* **emp**ty.

8   *He has* helped his **sér**vant Israel, *
in remembrance *òf his* **mer**cy,

9   *accord*ing to the promise he **máde** to our **an**cestors, *
to Abraham and to his descen*dànts forev*er.

Common of Apostles

Entrance Antiphon I

Psalm 19:4

415 II D

Their voice goes out * through all the world; their message, to the ends of the † earth. *E.S.* † earth, al - le - lu - ia.

Entrance Antiphon II

John 20:21

416 II D

Peace be with you. * As the Fa - ther has sent me, so I send † you. *E.S.* † you, al - le - lu - ia.

Psalm 19 (18V)

1–6

417

℣ 1 *The heav-*ens are tell-ing the glo-ry of **God;** *

and the fir - ma-ment pro-claims *his* **hand** - i - work.

Flex: for the sun, †

2   *Day to* day pours forth **spéech,** *
    and night to night *dè*clares knowledge.

3   *There is* no speech, nor are there **wórds;** *
    their voice *ìs* **not** heard;

4   *yet their* voice goes out through **áll** the earth, *
    and their words to the end *òf* **the** world.

5   *In the* heavens he has set a tent for the sùn, †
        which comes out like a bridegroom from his wedding **cán**opy, *
    and like a strong man runs *ìts* **course** with joy.

6   *Its ri*sing is from the end of the heavèns, †
        and its circuit to the **énd** of them; *
    and nothing is hid *fròm* **its** heat.

The Responsorial Psalm, the Alleluia, and/or the Alleluia Psalm are taken from the solemnity of St. Peter and St. Paul, Apostles, **239–241**.

Preparation of the Gifts Antiphon

Luke 4:18

II D

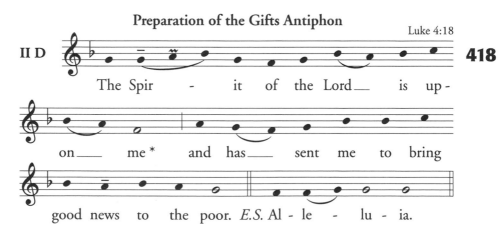

418

The Spir - it of the Lord__ is up-

on__ me * and has__ sent me to bring

good news to the poor. *E.S.* Al - le - lu - ia.

Canticle of Wisdom

Wisdom 3:7–9

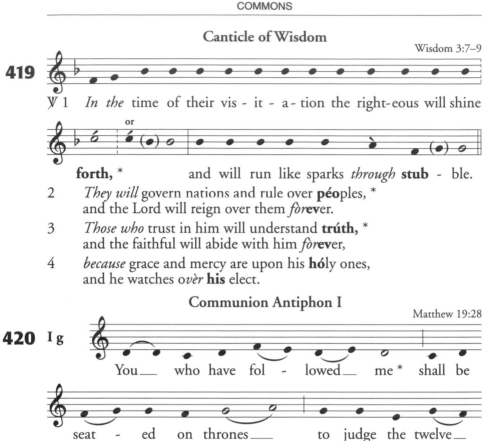

419

𝖵 1 *In the* time of their vis - it - a - tion the right-eous will shine

forth, *   and will run like sparks *through* **stub** - ble.

2 *They will* govern nations and rule over **péo**ples, *
and the Lord will reign over them *fóre*ver.

3 *Those who* trust in him will understand **trúth,** *
and the faithful will abide with him *fóre*ver,

4 *because* grace and mercy are upon his **hó**ly ones,
and he watches o*vèr* **his** elect.

Communion Antiphon I

Matthew 19:28

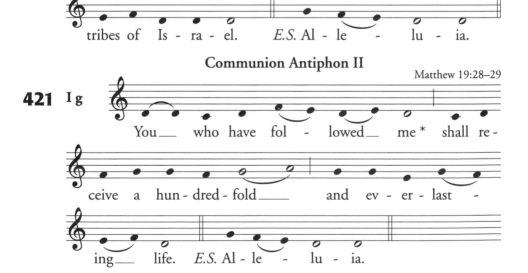

420 I g

You— who have fol - lowed— me * shall be
seat - ed on thrones— to judge the twelve—
tribes of Is - ra - el. *E.S.* Al - le - lu - ia.

Communion Antiphon II

Matthew 19:28–29

421 I g

You— who have fol - lowed— me * shall receive a hun - dred - fold— and ev - er - last -
ing— life. *E.S.* Al - le - lu - ia.

Psalm 139 (138V)

1–6, 17–18, 23–24

422

℣ 1 O LORD, ___ **you** have **searched** me *
and *you have* **known** ___ me.

2 *You know* when I sit down and **whén I rise** up; *
   you discern my *thòughts from* **far** away.

3 *You search* out my **páth** and my **ly**ing down, *
   and are acquain*tèd with* **all** my ways.

4 *E*ven before a word is **ón** my **tongue,** O LORD, *
   you know *it com***plete***ly.

5 *You hem* me in, be**hínd** and **be**fore, *
   and lay your *hànd up***on** me.

6 *Such know*ledge is too **wón**derful **for** me; *
   it is so high that I can*nòt a***ttain** it.

7 *How weigh*ty to me **áre** your **thoughts,** O God! *
   How vast *ìs the* **sum** of them!

8 *I try* to count them—they are **móre** than **the** sand; *
   I come to the end—*Ì am* **still** with you.

9 *Search* me, O **Gód,** and **know** my heart; *
   test *mè and* **know** my thoughts.

10 *See* if there is any **wíck**ed **way** in me, *
   and lead me in the way *èver***last**ing.

Common of Martyrs

Entrance Antiphon I

Revelation 7:14

I a

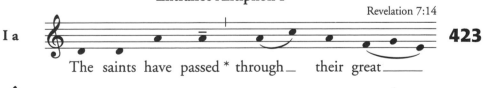

423

The saints have passed * through ___ their great ___
or - deal ___ and ___ washed ___ their ___ robes ___ in the

blood___ of the † Lamb. *E.S.* † Lamb, _ al - le - lu - ia.

Psalm 89 (88V)

1, 3–5, 19–24

424

℣ 1 *I will sing*___ of your stead-fast love, O **LORD,** for-

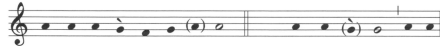

ev - er; * with my mouth I will pro-claim your faith-ful-

ness to all *gen-er-a* - tions. *Flex:* one, and said: †

2   *You said,* "I have made a covenant **with** my **cho**sen one, *
        I have sworn to my *sèrvant* **Da**vid:

3   *'I will* establish your de**scénd**ants for**ev**er, *
        and build your throne for all *gènera*tions.'"

<u>4</u>   *Let the heav*ens praise your **wón**ders, O LORD, *
        your faithfulness in the assembly *òf the* **ho**ly ones.

5   *Then* you spoke in a vision to your faithful one, and *sàid:* †
        "I have set the crown on **óne** who is **might**y, *
        I have exalted one chosen *fròm the* **peo**ple.

6   *I have found* my **sér**vant **Da**vid; *
        with my holy oil I *hàve a*noint**ed** him;

7   *my hand* shall **ál**ways re**main** with him; *
        my arm al*sò shall* **strength**en him.

8   *The en*emy shall **nót** out**wit** him, *
        the wicked *shàll not* **hum**ble him.

9   *I will crush* his **fóes** be**fore** him *
        and strike down *thòse who* **hate** him.

10   *My faith*fulness and steadfast **lóve** shall be **with** him; *
        and in my name his horn shall *bè ex*alt**ed**."

Entrance Antiphon II

Sirach 44:15

IV E

425

Peo-ples will re - call * the wis - dom＿ of the saints; the whole＿ Church will＿ sing＿ their＿ praise.

Psalm 33 (32V)

1–7, 9, 11

or

426

℣ 1 Re - *joice*＿ in the LORD, O you **right** - eous. *

Praise be - fits the **up** - right.

2 *Praise* the LORD *with the* **lyre;** *
   make melody to him *with the harp of* **ten** strings.

3 *Sing* to him *à new* **song;** *
   play skillfully *òn the strings, with* **loud** shouts.

4 *For the word* of the *LÒRD is* **up**right, *
   and all his work is *dòne in faithful*ness.

5 *He loves* righteous*nèss and* **jus**tice; *
   the earth is full of the *stèadfast love of* **the** LORD.

6 *By the word* of the LORD the heav*èns were* **made,** *
   and all their host *bỳ the breath of* **his** mouth.

7 *He gath*ered the waters of the sea as *ìn a* **bot**tle; *
   he put the *dèeps in* **store**hous*es.*

8 *For he spoke,* and it *càme to* **be;** *
   he command*èd, and it* **stood** firm.

9 *The coun*sel of the LORD *stànds for*ever, *
   the thoughts of his heart *tò all gener*ations.

Responsorial Psalm I C 2 g　　　　　　　　　　**Psalm 8**
(5b) 1–9

427

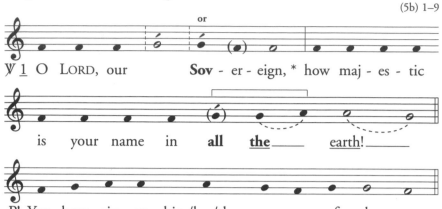

℣ 1 O LORD, our **Sov** - er - eign, * how maj - es - tic

is　your　name　in　**all**　**the** earth!

℟ You have giv - en　him/her/them　a　crown of　glo - ry.

2　　You have set your **gló**ry *
　　　above the **héav**ens.

3　　Out of the mouths of babes and infants ’
　　　you have founded a bulwark because of your **fóes,** *
　　　to silence the enemy and the a**vén**ger.

4　　When I look at your heavens, the work of your **fín**gers, *
　　　the moon and the stars that you have es**táb**lished;

5　　what are human beings that you are mindful of **thém,** *
　　　mortals that you **cáre fór** them?

6　　Yet you have made them a little lower than **Gód,** *
　　　and crowned them with glory and **hón**or.

7　　You have given them dominion over the works of **yóur** hands; *
　　　you have put all things under **théir** feet,

8　　all sheep and **óx**en, *
　　　and also the beasts of **thé** field,

9　　the birds of the air, and the fish of the **séa,** *
　　　whatever passes along the paths of **thé** seas.

10　O LORD, our **Sóv**ereign, *
　　　how majestic is your name in **áll the** earth!

Responsorial Psalm II E 4　　　　　　**Psalm 33 (32V)**
(1b), 1a, 12–14, 18–22

428

℣ 1 Re - joice in　the　LORD, O　you　**right** - eous. *

℟ True hearts are made for praise.

℣2 Hap-py is the na-tion whose God is **the** LORD, *

the peo-ple whom he has cho-sen as his **her**-it-age.

℟ True hearts are made for praise.

3   The LORD looks down from **hèav**en; *
     he sees all **hù**mankind.

4   From where he **sìts** enthroned *
     he watches all the inhabitants of **thè** earth—

5   Truly the eye of the LORD is on those who **fèar** him, *
     on those who hope in his **stèad**fast love,

6   to deliver their **sòul** from death, *
     and to keep them alive in **fàm**ine.

7   Our soul waits for **thè** LORD; *
     he is our **hèlp** and shield.

8   Our heart is **glàd** in him, *
     because we trust in his **hòl**y name.

9   Let your steadfast love, O LORD, be up**òn** us, *
     even as we **hòpe** in you.

Alleluia   Psalm 68 (67V)

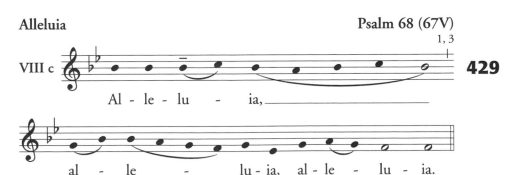

VIII c

Al - le - lu - ia, ___ al - le - lu - ia, al - le - lu - ia.

429

261

All repeat: Alleluia, alleluia, alleluia.

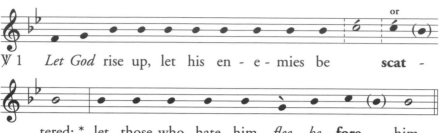

℣ 1 *Let God* rise up, let his en - e - mies be **scat** -

tered; * let those who hate him *flee be-* **fore** him.

All: Alleluia, alleluia, alleluia.

2   *But let* the righteous be joyful; let them exult before **Gód;** *
let them be ju*bìlant* **with** joy.

All: Alleluia, alleluia, alleluia.

or **Alleluia Psalm I D 1 b**   **Psalm 68 (67V)**
                                      1, 3–6, 11, 19–20, 24, 35

430

℣ 1 Let God rise up, let his en - e - mies be

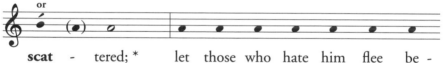

scat - tered; * let those who hate him flee be -

fore him.   ℟ Al - le - lu - ia, ___ al - le - lu - ia.

2   But let the righteous be **jóy**ful; *
let them exult before God; let them be jubilant **wìth** joy.

3   Sing to God, sing praises to his name; '
    lift up a song to him who rides upon the **clóuds—** *
his name is the LORD—be exultant be**fòre** him.

4   Father of orphans and protector of **wíd**ows *
is God in his holy habi**tà**tion.

5   God gives the desolate a home to **lí**ve in; *
he leads out the prisoners to pros**pèr**ity,

6   The Lord gives the com**mánd;** *
great is the company of those who bore the **tì**dings:

7   Blessed be the Lord, who daily **béars** us up; *
God is our salv**à**tion.

<u>8</u>   Our God is a God of salv**á**tion, *
and to GOD, the Lord, belongs esc**à**pe from death.

9   Your solemn processions are seen, O **Gód,** *
the processions of my God, my King, into the sanctu**à**ry—

<u>10</u>   Awesome is God in his sanctuary, the God of Israel; '
he gives power and strength to his **péo**ple *
Blessed **bè** God!

Alleluia Psalm II C I
Psalm 124 (123V)
1–8 (See Performance Notes)

℣ 1 If it had not been the LORD who was on **our** side— * let Is - ra - *el* **now** say—

℟ Al - le - lu - ia, al - le - lu - ia.

2   if it had not been the LORD who was on **óur** side, *
when our enemies *àt***tacked** us,

3   then they would have swallowed us up al**íve,** *
when their anger was kindled *à***gainst** us;

4   then the flood would have swept us a**wáy,** *
the torrent would have *gòne* **o**ver us;

5   then over us would have **góne** *
the rag*ìng* **wa**ters.

6   Blessed be the LORD, who has not **gív**en us *
as prey *tò* **their** teeth.

7   We have escaped like a bird from the snare of the **fówl**ers; *
the snare is broken, and *wè* **have** escaped.

8   Our help is in the name of the **LÓRD,** *
who made heav*èn* **and** earth.

Preparation of the Gifts Antiphon I

Cf. Revelation 7:14

432 VIII G

Hap - py * are⎯ they who wash their⎯ robes⎯ in the blood⎯ of the Lamb.

Psalm 79 (78V)

1–3, 13a (See Performance Notes)

433

℣ 1   O God, the na-tions have come in-to your in-her-i-tance; † they have de-filed your ho-ly **tem** - ple; * they have laid Je-ru-sa-*lem in* **ru** - ins.

2   *They have* given the bodies of your servants to the birds of the air for **fóod,** *
the flesh of your faithful to the wild ani*màls of* **the** earth.

3   *They have* poured out their blood like water all around Jerúsalem, *
and there was no *òne to* **bur**y them.

4   *[But] we* your people, the flock of your **pás**ture, *
will give thanks to *yòu for*ever.

Preparation of the Gifts Antiphon II

Psalm 140:13

434 I g

The just⎯ shall praise⎯ your⎯ name,⎯ O Lord; * the up - right will⎯ dwell⎯ in your

† pres - ence. *E.S.* † pres - ence, al - le - lu - ia.

Psalm 119 (118V)

1, 17, 23, 46

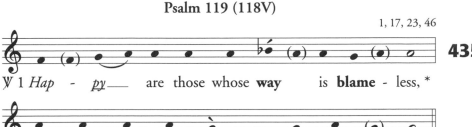

435

℣ 1 *Hap* - *py*___ are those whose **way** is **blame** - less, *

who walk in the *law* *of* **the**___ LORD.

2 *Deal bounti*fully **with** your **ser**vant, *
    so that I may live *ànd ob***serve** your word.

3 *Even though* princes sit **plót**ting a**gainst** me, *
    your servant will meditate *òn your* **stat**utes.

4 *I will* also speak of your de**crées** be**fore** kings, *
    and shall *nòt be* **put** to shame.

Communion Antiphon I

Matthew 16:24

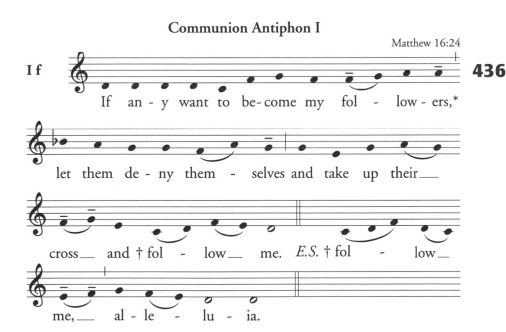

436

If   an - y   want   to   be-come   my   fol - low - ers,*

let   them   de - ny   them - selves   and   take   up   their___

cross___   and † fol - low___ me. *E.S.* † fol - low___

me,___ al - le - lu - ia.

Psalm 34 (33V)

1, 6, 15–20, 22 (See Performance Notes)

437

℣ 1 *I will bless*— the **LORD** at **all** times; * his praise

shall con - tin - ual - *ly be* **in**— my mouth.—

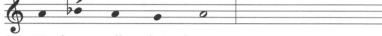

℣ 8 He **keeps** all **their** bones;

2 *This poor* soul cried, and was **héard** by **the** LORD, *
   and was saved from *èvery* **trou**ble.

3 *The eyes* of the LORD are **ón** the **right**eous, *
   and his ears are *òpen* **to** their cry.

4 *The face* of the LORD is against **évil do**ers, *
   to cut off the remembrance *òf them* **from** the earth.

5 *When the right*eous cry for **hélp,** the **LORD** hears, *
   and rescues them from *àll their* **trou**bles.

6 *The LORD* is near to the **bró**ken**heart**ed, *
   and saves the *crùshed in* **spir**it.

7 *Many are* the afflictions **óf** the **right**eous, *
   but the LORD res*cùes them* **from** them all.

8 He **kéeps** all **their** bones; *
   not one of them *wìll be* **bro**ken.

9 *The LORD* redeems the **life** of his **ser**vants; *
   none of those who take refuge in *hìm will* **be** con**demned.**

Communion Antiphon II

Psalm 15 (14V):Cf. 1

438 IV E

Your mar - tyr(s) * shall live in your dwell- ing place, O

Lord,— and find rest— on your ho - ly moun- tain.

Psalm 15 (14V)

1–3, 4bc–5

439

℣1 O LORD, _ who may a- bide *in your* **tent?** * Who

may *dwell on your_* **ho - ly__** hill? *Flex:* their tongue,†

℣6 Those *who do* **these** things * *shall nev - er* **be__** moved.

2   *Those who <u>walk</u>* blamelessly, and do *whàt is* **right,** *
    and *spèak the <u>truth</u>* **from their** heart;

3   *who do <u>not</u>* slander with their tòngue, †
        and do no evil *tò their* **friends,** *
    nor take up a re*pròach <u>against</u>* **their neigh**bors;

4   *but who <u>hon</u>*or those who *fèar the* **LORD;** *
    who stand by their oath *èven <u>to</u>* **their** hurt;

5   *who do <u>not</u>* lend monèy *at* **in**terest, *
    and do not take a *brìbe against the* **inno**cent.

6   Those *whò do* **these** things *
    shàll never **be** moved.

Common of Holy Men

Entrance Antiphon I

Psalm 92 (91V):12

VIII G The just_ man_ * will flour - ish like_ a palm_

tree, and grow_ like a ce- dar of† Leb - a - non.

E.S. † Leb - a - non,___ al - le - lu - ia.

Psalm 92 (91V)

1–5, 13, 15bc

441

℣ 1 *It is* good to give thanks to the **LORD**, *
to sing prais - es to your *name,* O **Most** High;

2 *to de*clare your steadfast love in the **mórn**ing, *
and your faith*fùlness* **by** night,

3 *to the* music of the lute and the **hárp,** *
to the melo*dỳ of* **the** lyre.

4 *For you,* O LORD, have made me glad by your **wórk;** *
at the works of your *hànds I* **sing** for joy.

5 *How great* are your works, O **LÓRD!** *
Your *thòughts are* **ver**y deep!

6 *They are* planted in the house of the **LÓRD;** *
they flourish in the *còurts of* **our** God.

7 *The LORD* is my **róck,** *
and there is no unright*èousness* **in** him.

Entrance Antiphon II

Cf. Psalm 1:3a, 2

442 IV E

By— flow - ing wa-ters * the Lord has plant-ed his

saints; and all— their de-light is in the law of the Lord.

Psalm 1

1–6

443

℣ 1 *Hap - py*— are those who do not fol- low the ad-vice

or

of the **wick** - ed, * or take the path that sin-

-ners tread, or sit *in the seat of* **scof** - fers;

2   *but their* delight is in the law *òf the* **LORD,** *
     and on his law they med*ìtate day* **and** night.

3   *They are like* trees planted by *strèams of* **wa**ter, *
     which yield their *frùit in its* **sea**son,

4   *and their* leaves *dò not* **with**er. *
     In all that *thèy do, they* **pros**per.

5   The *wick*ed *àre not* **so,** *
     but are like chaff *thàt the wind* **drives** **a**way.

6   *Therefore* the wicked will not stand *ìn the* **judg**ment, *
     nor sinners in the congre*gàtion of the* **righ**teous;

7   *for the LORD* watches over the way *òf the* **righ**teous, *
     but the way of the *wicked will* **per**ish.

Responsorial Psalm I E *   **Psalm 112 (111V)**

(1c) 1bc 9 (See Performance Notes)

℣1 Hap - py   are   those who *fear   the*   **LORD,** *

℟ They great - ly de-light___ in your com-mand-ments.

or

℣2 Their des-cen-dants will be migh-ty in the **land;** *

the gen - er - a - tion of the up-right will *be*___ **blessed.**

℟ They great - ly de-light___ in your com-mand-ments.

3   Wealth and riches are in their **hóus**es, *
     and their righteousness endures *fòrev*er.

4   They rise in the darkness as a light for the **úp**right; *
they are gracious, merciful, *ànd* **right**eous.

5   It is well with those who deal generously and **lénd,** *
who conduct their affairs *with* **jus**tice.

6   For the righteous will never be **móved;** *
they will be remembered *fore*ver.

7   They are not afraid of evil **tí**dings; *
their hearts are firm, secure in *thè* **LORD.**

8   Their hearts are steady, they will not be a**fráid;** *
in the end they will look in triumph on *thèir* **foes.**

9   They have distributed freely, they have given to the **póor;** *
their righteousness endures forever; their horn is exalted *in* **hon**or.

Responsorial Psalm II E 1   **Psalm 132 (131V)**
(9b) 9a, 1–2, 10–13, 16–17

445

℣1 Let your priests be clothed *with*___ **right-eous**-ness.

℟ Let your faith-ful___ ones cry out for joy.___

℣2 O LORD, re-mem-ber in Da-vid's **fa** - vor *

all the *hard-ships* **he** en-dured; ℟ Let your faith-

ful___ ones cry out for joy.___

3   how he swore **to thé** LORD *
and vowed to the Mighty *Óne of* **Ja**cob,

4   For your servant **Dá**vid's sake *
do not turn away the face of *yóur a***noint**ed one.

5   The LORD swore to David a sure oath from which he will **nót**
    turn back: *
    "One of the sons of your body I will *sét* **on your** throne.

6   If your sons keep my covenant and my decrees that I shall **téach**
    them, *
    their sons also, forevermore, shall *sít* **on your** throne."

7   For the LORD has chosen **Zí**on; *
    he has desired it for his *hábi*tation:

8   "Its priests I will clothe with sal**vá**tion, *
    and its faithful will *shóut* **for** joy.

9   There I will cause a horn to sprout up for **Dá**vid; *
    I have prepared a lamp for *mý a*nointed one."

For Doctors of the Church

Responsorial Psalm III C 2 g   Psalm 22 (21V)
                                             (22b) 22a, 23–27, 29c–30a

℣ 1 I will tell of your name to my broth-ers and **sis** - ters.

℟ In the Church of God I will praise you, Lord.

℣ 2 You who fear the LORD, praise him! 'All you off-spring of

Ja-cob, glo-ri-fy **him;** * stand in awe of

him, all you off-spring of **Is** - **ra** - el!

℟ In the Church of God I will praise you, Lord.

446

3   For he did not despise or abhor the affliction of the afflícted; *
     he did not hide his face from me, but heard when I críed **to** him.

4   From you comes my praise in the great congregátion; *
     my vows I will pay before those who **féar** him.

5   The poor shall eat and be satisfied; '
        those who seek him shall praise the **LÓRD**. *
     May your hearts live foréver!

6   All the ends of the earth shall remember and turn to the **LÓRD;** *
     and all the families of the nations shall worship befóre him.

7   I shall live for **hím.** *
     Posterity will **sérve** him.

Alleluia   Psalm 37 (36V)
                                    30–31 (See Performance Notes)

447 VIII G

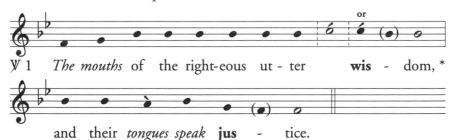

Al - le - lu - ia,__ al - le - lu - ia, al - le - lu - ia.

All repeat: Alleluia, alleluia, alleluia.

℣ 1 *The mouths* of the right-eous ut - ter **wis** - dom, *

and their *tongues speak* **jus** - tice.

All: Alleluia, alleluia, alleluia.

2   *The law* of their God is in their **héarts;** *
     their *stèps do* **not** slip.

All: Alleluia, alleluia, alleluia.

or **Alleluia Psalm I D 1 b**   Psalm 37 (36V)
                            1, 3, 7, 11, 16, 18, 29–31, 37 (See Performance Notes)

448

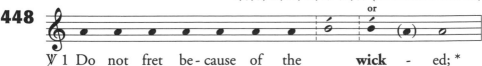

℣ 1 Do not fret be - cause of the **wick** - ed; *

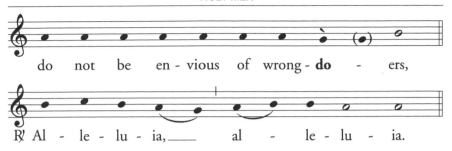

do not be en - vious of wrong - **do** - ers,

℟ Al - le - lu - ia,___ al - le - lu - ia.

2   Trust in the LORD, and do **gó**od; *
    so you will live in the land, and enjoy secùrity.

3   Be still before the LORD, and wait patiently for him; '
    do not fret over those who prosper in **théir** way, *
    over those who carry out evil devìces.

4   But the meek shall inherit the **lánd,** *
    and delight themselves in abundant prospèrity.

5   Better is a little that the righteous **pér**son has *
    than the abundance of many **wìck**ed.

6   The LORD knows the days of the **blá**meless, *
    and their heritage will abide forèver;

7   The righteous shall inherit the **lánd,** *
    and live in it forèver.

8   The mouths of the righteous utter **wís**dom, *
    and their tongues speak jùstice.

9   The law of their God is in their **héarts;** *
    their steps do **nòt** slip.

10 Mark the blameless, and behold the **úp**right, *
    for there is posterity for the **pèace**able.

Alleluia Psalm II C 1   **Psalm 89 (88V)**
                                        1, 3–7, 19–21, 24 (See Performance Notes)

449

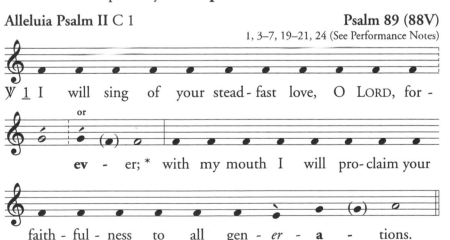

℣ _1_ I will sing of your stead - fast love, O LORD, for -

or

ev - er; * with my mouth I will pro - claim your

faith - ful - ness to all gen - _er_ - **a** - tions.

℟ Al - le - lu - ia, al - le - lu - ia.

2   You said, "I have made a covenant with my **chó**sen one, *
     I have sworn to my ser*vànt* **Da**vid:

3   'I will establish your descendants for**é**ver, *
     and build your throne for all gen*è*rations.' "

4   Let the heavens praise your wonders, O **LÓRD,** *
     your faithfulness in the assembly of *thè* **ho**ly ones.

5   For who in the skies can be compared to the **LÓRD?** *
     Who among the heavenly beings *is* **like** the LORD,

6   a God feared in the council of the **hó**ly ones, *
     great and awesome above all that are *à***round** him?

7   Then you[, God,] spoke in a vision to your faithful one, and said: '
        "I have set the crown on one who is **mígh**ty, *
     I have exalted one chosen from *thè* **peo**ple.

8   I have found my servant **Dá**vid; *
     with my holy oil I have *à***noint**ed him;

9   my hand shall always re**máin** with him; *
     my arm also *shàll* **strength**en him.

10   My faithfulness and steadfast love shall be with **hím;** *
     and in my name his horn shall be *è***xalt**ed."

Preparation of the Gifts Antiphon I

Psalm 21 (20V):3

450 IV A

Lord, you have set __ on his head * a gold - en __ crown.

Psalm 21 (20V)

1–2, 4–5

451

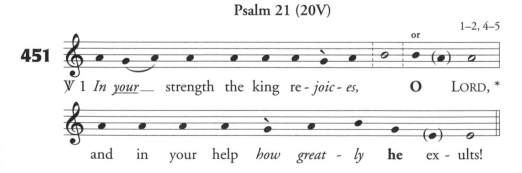

℣ 1 *In your* __ strength the king re - *joic* - *es,* **O** LORD, *

and in your help *how* *great* - *ly* **he** ex - ults!

2   *You* __have__ given him his *hèart's de*sire, *
    and have not withheld the *rèquest of* **his** lips.

3   *He* __asked__ *yòu for* **life;** *
    you gave it to him—length of days for*èver and* **ev**er.

4   *His* __glo__ry is great *thròugh your* **help;** *
    splendor and majes*tỳ you be***stow** on him.

Preparation of the Gifts Antiphon II
(outside of the Lenten Season)

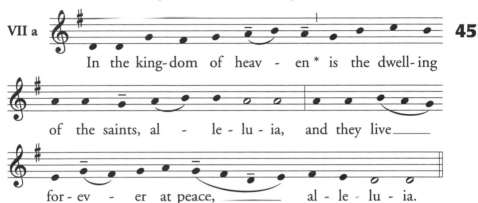

VII a

In the king-dom of heav - en * is the dwell-ing
of the saints, al - le - lu - ia, and they live____
for - ev - er at peace, _____ al - le - lu - ia.

452

Psalm 21 (20V)

1, 3, 6, 13

453

℣ 1   *In___ your__* strength the king re-**joic** - es, **O** LORD,*
      and in your help how **great** - ly **he** ex - __ults!_____

2   *For you* meet **hím** with rich **bless**ings; *
    you set a crown of fine **góld** on **his** __head.__

3   *You* __be__stow on him **bléss**ings forever; *
    you make him glad with the **jóy** of **your** presence.

4   *Be* __ex__alted, O **LÓRD,** in **your** strength! *
    We will **síng** and **praise** your power.

Communion Antiphon I

Cf. Matthew 24:45–47

454 III a

The Lord has put his faith-ful ser - vant * in __ charge __

of his __ † house-hold. *E.S.* † house-hold, __ al - le - lu - ia.

Psalm 34 (33V)

1–10 (See Performance Notes)

455

℣ 1   *I will bless* __ the **LORD**   at   **all** __ times; * his praise

shall con - tin - ual - ly   be   *in*   **my**   mouth. __

2   *My soul* makes its **bóast** in **the** LORD; *
    let the humble hear *ànd* **be** glad.

3   *O magnifý* the LORD **with** me, *
    and let us exalt his name *tò*geth__er.

4   *I sought* the **LÓRD,** and he **answered** me, *
    and delivered me *fròm* **all** my fears.

5   *Look* to **hím,** and be **ra**diant; *
    so your faces shall nev*èr* **be** a__shamed.

6   *This poor* soul cried, and was **héard** by **the** LORD, *
    and was saved from eve*rỳ* **trou**ble.

7   *The an*gel of the LORD encamps around **thóse** who **fear** him, *
    and *dè*livers them.

8   *O taste* and **sée** that the **LORD is** good; *
    happy are those who take re*fùge* **in** him.

9   *O fear* the **LÓRD,** you his **holy** ones, *
    for those who fear him *hàve* **no** want.

10 *The young* lions suffer **wánt** and **hun**ger, *
    but those who seek the LORD *làck* **no** good thing.

276

Communion Antiphon II

John 12:26

456

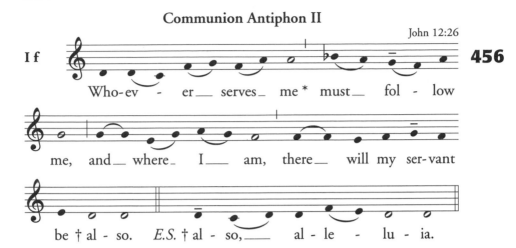

If Who-ev - er__ serves__ me * must__ fol - low
me, and__ where__ I__ am, there__ will my ser-vant
be † al - so. *E.S.* † al - so,__ al - le - lu - ia.

Psalm 34 (33V)

1, 11–13, 17–20, 22 (See Performance Notes)

457

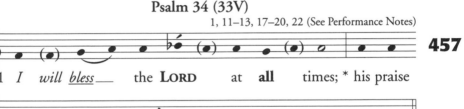

℣ 1 *I will bless*__ the **LORD** at **all** times; * his praise
shall con - tin - ual - *ly* *be* **in**__ my mouth. __

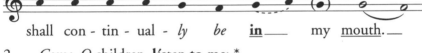

2 *Come, O* children, **lís**ten **to** me; *
   I will teach you the *fèar of* **the** LORD.

3 *Which* of **yóu** de**sires** life, *
   and covets many days *tò en***joy** good?

4 *Keep* your **tón**gue from evil, *
   and your lips from *spèaking* **de**ceit.

5 *When the* **right**eous cry for **hélp,** the LORD hears, *
   and rescues them from *àll their* **trou**bles.

6 *The* LORD is near to the **bró**kenheart**ed,** *
   and saves the *crùshed in* **spir**it.

7 *Many* **are** the afflictions **óf** the **right**eous, *
   but the LORD res*cùes them* **from** them **all.**

8 He **kéeps** all **their** bones; *
   not one of them *wìll be* **bro**ken.

9 *The* LORD redeems the **life** of his **ser**vants; *
   none of those who take refuge in *hìm will* **be** con**demned.**

Common of Holy Women

Entrance Antiphon I

458 VIII G

Psalm 45 (44V):7

Jus-tice you love * and wick-ed-ness you hate: There-fore

God_ has a-noint-ed you_ with the † oil of glad-ness.

E.S. † oil of glad - ness,_____ al - le - lu - ia.

Psalm 45 (44V)

459

1, 9–15

℣ 1 *My heart* ov-er-flows with a good-ly theme; †

I ad-dress my vers-es to the **king;** *

my tongue is like the pen *of a* **read**-y scribe.

2 *Daughters* of kings are among your ladies of **hón**or; *
at your right hand stands the queen in *gòld of* **O**phir.

3 *Hear, O* daughter, consider and in**clíne** your ear; *
forget your people *ànd your* **fa**ther's house,

4 *and the* king will desire your **béau**ty. *
Since he is *yòur lord,* **bow** to him.

5 *The peo*ple of Tyre will seek your favor with **gífts,** *
the richest of the people *with all* **kinds** of wealth.

6 *In many*-colored robes she is led to the **kíng;** *
behind her the virgins, her com**pàn**ions, **fol**low.

7 *With joy* and gladness they are led a**lóng** *
as they enter the *pàlace* **of** the king.

Entrance Antiphon II

Cf. 2 Corinthians 11:2 and James 1:12

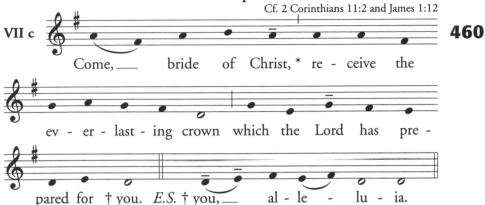

VII c

Come,—— bride of Christ, * re - ceive the
ev - er - last - ing crown which the Lord has pre -
pared for † you. *E.S.* † you,—— al - le - lu - ia.

Psalm 24 (23V)

1–6

℣ 1 *The—— earth——* is the Lord's and **all** that **is** in
it, * the world, and **those** who **live** in it;——

2 *for he* has **fóund**ed it **on** the seas, *
and est**áb**lished it **on** the rivers.

3 *Who shall* ascend the **híll** of **the** LORD? *
And who shall **stánd** in his **ho**ly place?

4 *Those who* have **cléan** hands and **pure** hearts, *
who do not lift up their souls to what is false, and do not **swéar**
de**ceit**fully.

5 *They will* receive **bléss**ing **from** the LORD, *
and vindication from the God of **théir** sal**va**tion.

6 *Such is* the company of **thóse** who **seek** him, *
who seek the **fáce** of the **God** of Jacob.

The Responsorial Psalm is taken from the solemnity of the Immaculate Conception, **395.**

Alleluia Psalm 119 (118V)

1, 10

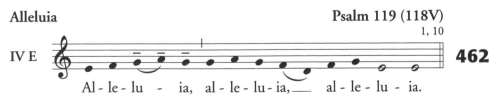

IV E

Al - le - lu - ia, al - le - lu - ia,—— al - le - lu - ia.

All repeat: Alleluia, alleluia, alleluia.

℣ 1 Hap - py___ are those whose *way* *is* **blame** -

less, * who walk *in* *the* *law*___ **of** **the**___ LORD.

All: Alleluia, alleluia, alleluia.

2   *With my whole hèart I* **seek** *you;* *
    do not let me *strày from your com***mand**ments.

All: Alleluia, alleluia, alleluia.

or **Alleluia Psalm I E 2 d**   **Psalm 119 (118V)**
                                          1, 10–11, 30–32, 40, 44–45, 47

463

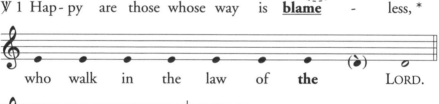

℣ 1 Hap- py   are those whose way   is   **blame**   - less, *

who   walk   in   the   law   of   **the**   LORD.

℟ Al - le - lu - ia,   al - le - lu   -   ia.

2   With my whole heart I **séek** you; *
    do not let me stray from your com**mand**mènts.

3   I treasure your word **in mý** heart, *
    so that I may not sin a**gainst** yòu.

4   I have chosen the way of **fáith**fulness; *
    I set your ordinances be**fore** mè.

5   I cling to your de**crées,** O LORD; *
    let me not be **put** tò shame.

6   I run the way of your com**mánd**ments, *
    for you enlarge my under**stand**ìng.

7   See, I have longed for your **pré**cepts; *
    in your righteousness **give** mè life.

8   I will keep your law con**tín**ually, *
      forever and **ev**èr.

9   I shall walk at **líb**erty, *
      for I have sought your **prec**èpts.

10   I find my delight in your com**mánd**ments, *
      because I **love** thèm.

Alleluia Psalm II D 1 b   **Psalm 119 (118V)**

                                           1, 52, 57, 95–96, 105, 121, 133, 161–162

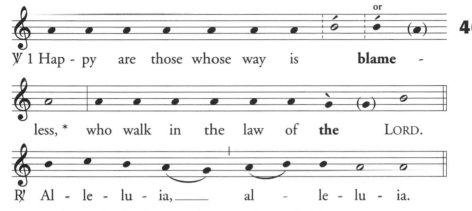

464

℣ 1 Hap-py are those whose way is **blame**-less, * who walk in the law of **the** LORD.

℟ Al-le-lu-ia,___ al-le-lu-ia.

2   When I think of your ordinances from of **óld,** *
      I take comfort, **Ò** LORD.

3   The LORD is my **pór**tion; *
      I promise to **kèep** your words.

4   The wicked lie in wait to de**stróy** me, *
      but I consider **yòur** decrees.

5   I have seen a limit to all per**féc**tion, *
      but your commandment is exceeding**lỳ** broad.

6   Your word is a lamp to my **féet** *
      and a light to **mỳ** path.

7   I have done what is just and **ríght;** *
      do not leave me to my op**prè**ssors.

8   Keep my steps steady according to your **próm**ise, *
      and never let iniquity have dominion **ò**ver me.

9   Princes persecute me without **cáuse,** *
      but my heart stands in awe of **yòur** words.

10   I rejoice at your **wórd** *
      like one who finds **grèat** spoil.

Preparation of the Gifts Antiphon I

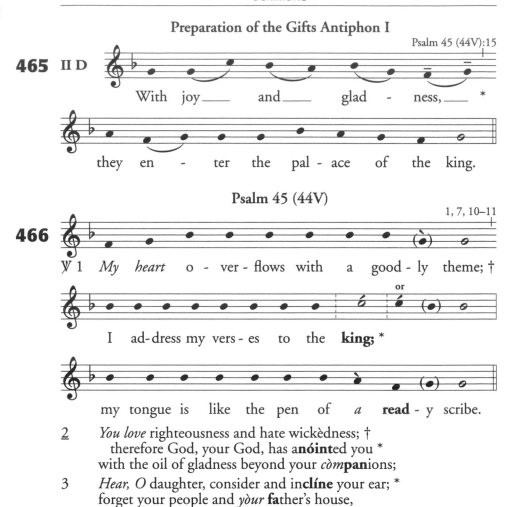

465 II D

Psalm 45 (44V):15

With joy___ and___ glad - ness,___ *

they en - ter the pal - ace of the king.

Psalm 45 (44V)

466

1, 7, 10–11

℣ 1 *My heart* o - ver - flows with a good - ly theme; †

I ad-dress my vers - es to the **king;** *

my tongue is like the pen of *a* **read** - y scribe.

2   *You love* righteousness and hate wickèdness; †
      therefore God, your God, has **anóint**ed you *
   with the oil of gladness beyond your *còm***pan**ions;

3   *Hear, O* daughter, consider and in**clíne** your ear; *
   forget your people and *yòur* **fa**ther's house,

4   *and the* king will desire your **béau**ty. *
   Since he is your *lòrd,* **bow** to him.

Preparation of the Gifts Antiphon II

467 I g 4

Psalm 45 (44V):2bc

Grace is poured * up - on your lips; there-fore God

has___ † blessed you for - ev - er.   *E.S.* † blessed you

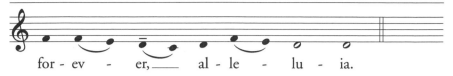

for - ev - er,— al - le - lu - ia.

Psalm 45 (44V)

1, 7, 10–11

468

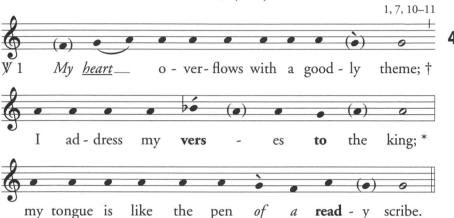

℣ 1 *My heart*— o - ver-flows with a good - ly theme; †

I ad - dress my **vers** - es **to** the king; *

my tongue is like the pen *of a* **read** - y scribe.

2   *You love* righteousness and hate wickèdness; †
      therefore God, your **Gód,** has **anoint**ed you *
    with the oil of gladness beyond *yòur com***pan**ions;

3   *Hear,* O daughter, consider **ánd** in**cline** your ear; *
    forget your people *ànd your* **fa**ther's house,

4   *and the* king will de**síre** your **beau**ty. *
    Since he is *yòur lord,* **bow** to him.

Communion Antiphon I

Matthew 25:6

469

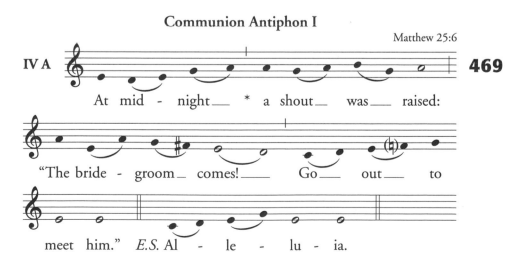

IV A

At mid - night— * a shout— was— raised:

"The bride - groom— comes!— Go— out— to

meet him." *E.S.* Al - le - lu - ia.

Communion Antiphon II

Matthew 12:50

470 IV A

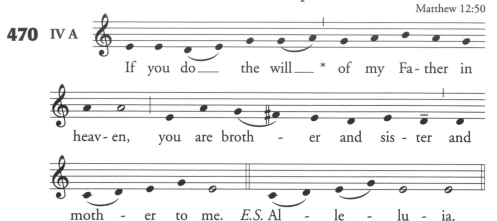

If you do___ the will___ * of my Fa‑ther in

heav‑en, you are broth ‑ er and sis‑ter and

moth ‑ er to me. E.S. Al ‑ le ‑ lu ‑ ia.

Psalm 119 (118V)

1–4, 7, 12–15 (See Performance Notes)

471

℣ 1 *Hap* ‑ *py*___ are those whose *way* *is*

or

blame ‑ less, * who walk in *the law of* **the** Lᴏʀᴅ.

2   *Happy* are those who keep *hìs de***crees,** *
     who seek *hìm with their* **whole** heart,

3   who also *dò no* **wrong,** *
     bùt walk in **his** ways.

4   *You* <u>have</u> command*èd your* **pre**cepts *
     tò be kept **dil**igently.

5   *I will* <u>praise</u> you *wìth an* **up**right heart, *
     when I learn *yòur righteous* **ord**inances.

6   Blessed are *yòu, O* **Lᴏʀᴅ;** *
     tèach me your **stat**utes.

7   With my lips *Ì de***clare** *
     all the ordin*ànces of* **your** mouth.

8   *I* <u>delight</u> in the way of *yòur de***crees** *
     as much *às in all* **rich**es.

9   *I will* <u>med</u>itate *òn your* **pre**cepts, *
     and fix *mỳ eyes on* **your** ways.

I. Ritual Masses

Wedding Mass

Entrance Antiphon

John 2:1

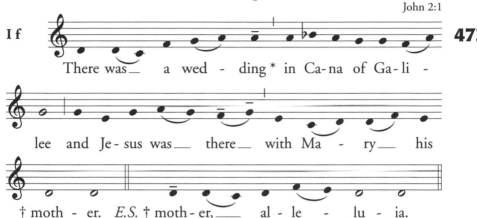

I f **472**

There was a wed - ding * in Ca-na of Ga-li - lee and Je-sus was there with Ma - ry his † moth - er. *E.S.* † moth-er, al - le - lu - ia.

Psalm 37 (36V)

1, 3–6, 11, 16, 18, 23, 25 (See Performance Notes)

473

℣ 1 *Do not* fret be-**cause** of the **wick** - ed; * do not be en-*vious of* **wrong** - do - ers, *Flex:* and now am old, †

2 *Trust* in the **LÓRD,** and **do** good; *
so you will live in the land, and en*jòy se***cur**ity.

3 *Take* de**líght** in the **LORD,** *
and he will give you the de*sìres of* **your** heart.

4 *Commit* your **wáy** to the **LORD;** *
trust in *hìm, and* **he** will a̱c̱t̲.

5 *He will* make your vindication **shíne** like **the** light, *
and the justice of your cause *lìke the* **noon**day.

6 *Better is* a little that the **rígh**teous **per**son has *
than the abundance of *màny* **wick**ed.

7 *The LORD* knows the **dáys** of the **blame**less, *
and their heritage will a*bìde fo***rev**er;

285

8   *Our steps* are made **firm** by **the** LORD, *
     when he de*lights in* **our** way;

9   *though we* stumble, we shall **nót** fall **head**long, *
     for the LORD *hòlds us* **by** the hand.

10   *I have* been young, and now àm old, †
         yet I have not seen the **right**eous for**sak**en *
     or their *chìldren* **beg**ging bread.

Responsorial Psalm E *   Psalm 112 (111V)

(1c) 1bc–9 (See Performance Notes)

474

℣1 Hap - py   are   those who   *fear   the*   LORD, *

℟ They great - ly de-light___ in   your com-mand-ments.

or

℣2 Their des-cen-dants will be migh-ty in the **land;** *

     the gen-er-a-tion of the up-right will *be*___   **blessed.**

℟ They great - ly de-light___ in   your com-mand-ments.

3   Wealth and riches are in their **hóus**es, *
     and their righteousness endures *fore*ver.

4   They rise in the darkness as a light for the **úp**right; *
     they are gracious, merciful, *ànd* **right**eous.

5   It is well with those who deal generously and **lénd,** *
     who conduct their affairs *wìth* **jus**tice.

6   For the righteous will never be **móved;** *
     they will be remembered *fore*ver.

7   They are not afraid of evil **tí**dings; *
     their hearts are firm, secure in *thè* LORD.

8   Their hearts are steady, they will not be a**fráid;** *
     in the end they will look in triumph on *thèir* **foes.**

9   They have distributed freely, they have given to the **póor;** *
     their righteousness endures forever; their horn is exalted *in* **hon**or.

Alleluia   **Psalm 20 (19V)**
                                                        1, 4

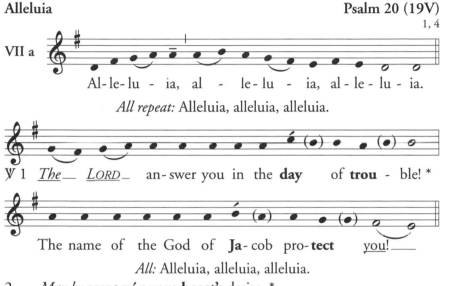

VII a

Al-le-lu - ia, al - le-lu - ia, al - le - lu - ia.

All repeat: Alleluia, alleluia, alleluia.

℣ 1 *The__ LORD__* an-swer you in the **day**   of **trou** - ble! *

The name of the God of **Ja**-cob pro-**tect**   you!__

All: Alleluia, alleluia, alleluia.

2   *May he* grant **yóu** your **heart's** desire, *
     and ful**fíll** all **your** plans.

          All: Alleluia, alleluia, alleluia.

or **Alleluia Psalm** D 1 b   **Psalm 20 (19V)**

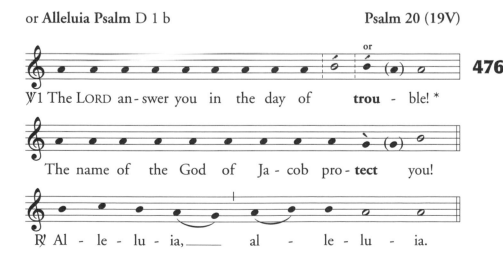

℣ 1 The LORD an-swer you in   the day of   **trou** - ble! *

The name of   the God of   Ja - cob pro - **tect**   you!

℟ Al - le - lu - ia,___   al - le - lu - ia.

287

2   May he send you help from the **sánc**tuary, *
       and give you support from **Zì**on.

3   May he remember all your **óff**erings, *
       and regard with favor your burnt sacrifìces.

4   May he grant you your **héart's** desire, *
       and fulfill all **yòur** plans.

<u>5</u>   May we shout for joy over your victory, '
       and in the name of our God set up our **bán**ners. *
    May the LORD fulfill all your petìtions.

6   Now I know that the LORD will help his anointed; '
       he will answer him from his holy **héa**ven *
    with mighty victories by his **rìght** hand.

Preparation of the Gifts Antiphon

Psalm 37 (36V):9

477 I f

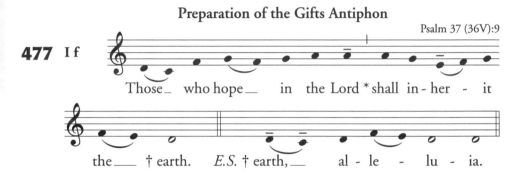

Those who hope in the Lord * shall in-her - it the † earth. *E.S.* † earth, al - le - lu - ia.

Psalm 37 (36V)

27–28b, 29, 40 (See Performance Notes)

478

℣ 1 *De-part* from e - vil, and **do** good; * so you shall a-bide for- **ev** - er. *Flex:* and res-cues them; †

2   For the **LÓRD** loves **jus**tice; *
       he will not for*sàke his* **faith**ful <u>ones</u>.

3   *The* <u>*right*</u>*eous* shall in**hér**it the **land,** *
       and live in *ìt for***ev**<u>er</u>.

4   *The* <u>*LORD*</u> helps them and res**cùes** them; †
       he rescues **thém** from the **wick**ed, *
    and saves them, because they take *rèfuge* **in** <u>him</u>.

288

Communion Antiphon

Psalm 128 (127V):Cf. 1

IV E  **479**

See _____ * what bless - ings will__ come to __

those__ who fear the † Lord. *E.S.* † Lord,__ al - le - lu - ia.

Psalm 128 (127V)

1–6 (See Performance Notes)
or

 **480**

℣ 1 *Hap - py__* is eve-ry-one who *fears the* **LORD,** *

who walks__ **in his__** ways. ℣4 who *fears__* **the__** LORD.

2   *You shall eat* the fruit of the labor *òf your* **hands;** *
    you shall be happy, and it *shàll go well* **with** you.

3   *Your wife* will be like a fruitful vine with*ìn your* **house;** *
    your children will be like olive shoots *àround your* **ta**ble.

4   *Thus shall* the *màn be* **blessed** *
    who *féars* **the** LORD.

5   *The LORD* bless *yòu from* **Zi**on. *
    May you see the prosperity of Jerusalem *àll the days of* **your** life.

6   *May you see* your *chìldren's* **chil**dren. *
    Peace *bè upon* **Isra**el!

For Religious Profession

The Entrance Song is *My eyes are always on the Lord,* **71**.

The Responsorial Psalm is *As a deer longs,* **140**, or *How lovely is your dwelling place,* **31**.

The Alleluia Psalm is *Happy are those* I or II, **463** or **464**.

The Preparation Song is *Those who hope in you,* **6**.

The Communion Song is *O help me, Lord,* **273**, or, if outside the Lenten season, *Seek first God's kingdom,* **246**.

During the Easter season, end the procession song antiphons with the *alleluias* found on p. 378.

II. Masses for Various Needs and Occasions

The Anniversary of the Pope or the Bishop

The Entrance Song is *Sing a new song,* **167**, but outside of the Easter season it is sung thus:

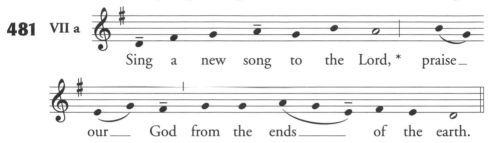

481 VII a

Sing a new song to the Lord, * praise our God from the ends of the earth.

The Responsorial Psalm is *Let your priests,* **445**.

The Alleluia Psalm is *I was glad,* **406**.

The Preparation Song is *The Lord's right hand,* **145**.

The Communion Song for the Anniversary of the Pope is *You are Peter,* **344**; if during the Easter season, end the antiphon with the *alleluia* found on p. 378.

The Communion Song for the Anniversary of the Bishop is *The Lord has put his servant,* **454**.

For Vocations
to the Sacrament of Orders and to the Religious Life

Entrance Antiphon I

Psalm 16 (15V):5

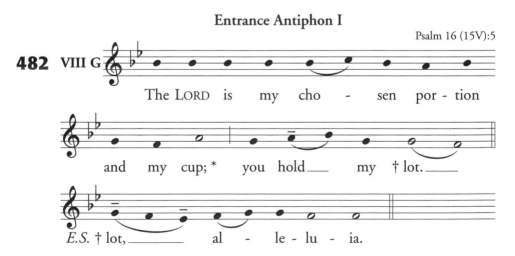

482 VIII G

The LORD is my cho - sen por - tion and my cup; * you hold my † lot.

E.S. † lot, al - le - lu - ia.

Entrance Antiphon II

John 15:16

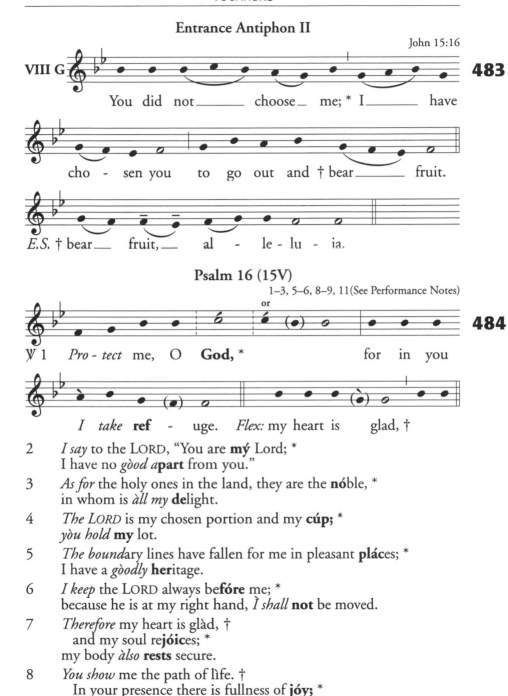

483

VIII G

You did not_____ choose_ me; * I_____ have

cho - sen you   to   go   out   and † bear_____ fruit.

E.S. † bear__ fruit,__ al - le - lu - ia.

Psalm 16 (15V)

1–3, 5–6, 8–9, 11(See Performance Notes)

or

484

℣ 1   *Pro - tect* me,   O   **God,** *   for   in   you

I take **ref** - uge.   *Flex:* my heart is   glad, †

2   *I say* to the LORD, "You are **my** Lord; *
    I have no *gòod a***part** from you."

3   *As for* the holy ones in the land, they are the **nó**ble, *
    in whom is *àll my* **de**light.

4   *The LORD* is my chosen portion and my **cúp;** *
    yòu hold **my** lot.

5   *The bound*ary lines have fallen for me in pleasant **plác**es; *
    I have a *gòodly* **her**itage.

6   *I keep* the LORD always be**fóre** me; *
    because he is at my right hand, *Ì shall* **not** be moved.

7   *Therefore* my heart is glàd, †
    and my soul re**jóic**es; *
    my body *àlso* **rests** secure.

8   *You show* me the path of lìfe. †
    In your presence there is fullness of **jóy;** *
    in your right hand are pleas*ùres* **fore**vermore.

The Responsorial Psalm is *I rejoiced,* **12,** or *How lovely,* **31.**

The Alleluia Psalm is *The Lord is my light,* **33.**

The Preparation Song is *God is my helper,* **244**; if during the Easter season, end the antiphon with the *alleluia* found on p. 378.

The Communion Song is *I will go to the altar,* **89,** or *Whoever serves me,* **256**; if during the Easter season, end either antiphon with the *alleluia* found on p. 378.

For the Unity of Christians

The Entrance Song is *I am the good shepherd,* **158,** but during the Lenten season it is sung thus:

485 III a

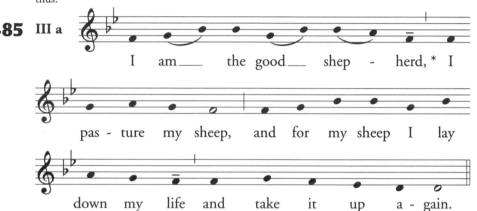

I am___ the good___ shep - herd, * I pas - ture my sheep, and for my sheep I lay down my life and take it up a - gain.

The Responsorial Psalm is *I was glad,* **12.**

The Alleluia Psalm is *When the Lord restored,* **341.**

The Preparation of the Gifts Antiphon is *Those who hope in you,* **6.**

The Communion Antiphon is *The Lord is my light,* **79.**

During the Easter season, end the Preparation and Communion antiphons with the *alleluias* found on p. 378.

For Peace and Justice

The Entrance Song is *Give peace, O Lord,* **269.**

The Responsorial Psalm is *To you, O Lord,* **214.**

The Alleluia Psalm is *In you, O Lord,* **243.**

The Preparation Song is *Do not abandon me,* **253.**

The Communion Song is *O Give us, Lord,* **59.**

During the Easter season, end the processional antiphons with the *alleluias* found on p. 378.

In Any Need

Entrance Antiphon

Psalm 102 (101V):1

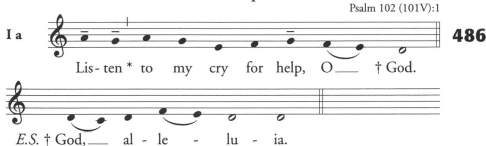

I a   **486**

Lis-ten * to my cry for help, O — † God.

E.S. † God, — al - le - lu - ia.

Psalm 102 (101V)

2, 13, 15–17, 19–21 (See Performance Notes)

487

℣ 1 *Do* *not* — **hide** your **face** from me * in

the *day of* **my** dis - tress. *Flex:* on Zi - on, †

2   In**clíne** your **ear** to me; *
   answer me speedily in the *dày when* **I** call.

3   *You will <u>rise</u>* up and have compassion on Ziòn, †
       for it is **tíme** to **fa**vor it; *
   the ap**pòint**ed **time** has come.

4   *The <u>na</u>*tions will fear the **náme** of **the** LORD, *
   and all the kings of the *èarth your* **glo**ry.

5   *For the <u>LORD</u>* will **búild** up **Zi**on; *
   he will appear *ìn his* **glo**ry.

6   *He <u>will</u>* regard the **práyer** of the **des**titute, *
   and will *nòt de***spise** their prayer.

7   *The <u>LORD</u>* looked **dówn** from his **ho**ly height, *
   from heaven he *lòoked at* **the** earth,

8   *to <u>hear</u>* the **gróans** of the **pris**oners, *
   to set free those *whò were* **doomed** to die;

9   *so <u>that</u>* the name of the LORD may be de**clá**red in **Zi**on, *
   and his praise *ìn Jeru*salem.

Outside of the Lenten and Easter seasons:
The Responsorial Psalm, *Help us, O God,* is taken from Ash Wednesday, **53;** the *Alleluia* is taken from Ordinary Time III, **242;** or the Alleluia Psalm, *I love you, O Lord,* found below.

During the Lenten season:
The Responsorial Psalm or Tract is taken from the Fourth Sunday of Lent, **84** or **86.**

During the Easter season:
Alleluia Psalm I, *In you, O Lord,* is taken from Ordinary Time III, **243.**

Alleluia Psalm II E 2 d   Psalm 18 (17V)
                                                                1–3, 6, 19–20, 27–28

488

℣1   I love you, O LORD, my strength. ' The LORD is   my

rock, my **for** - tress, * and my de - **liv** - er - er,

℟   Al - le - lu - ia,   al - le - lu - ia.

2   my God, my rock in whom I take **réf**uge, *
     my shield, and the horn of my salvation, my **strong**hòld.

3   I call upon the LORD, who is worthy **to bé** praised, *
     so I shall be saved from my **en**èmies.

4   In my distress I called up**on thé** LORD; *
     to my God I **cried** fòr help.

5   From his temple he **héard** my voice, *
     and my cry to him reached **his** èars.

6   He brought me out into a **bróad** place; *
     he delivered me, because he delighted **in** mè.

7   The LORD rewarded me according to my **right**eousness; *
     according to the cleanness of my hands he recom**pensed** mè.

8   For you deliver a humble **péo**ple, *
     but the haughty eyes you **bring** dòwn.

9   It is you who **líght** my lamp; *
     the LORD, my God, lights up my **dark**nèss.

Or the *Alleluia* from Easter Season I, **162.**

Preparation of the Gifts Antiphon

Psalm 109 (108V):30a

489

VII a

I will thank__ the Lord__ * with all__ my__ † heart. *E.S.* † heart,__ al - le - lu - ia.

Psalm 109 (108V)

21c–22, 26, 30–31

490

℣ 1 *De - liv* - er me, for I am **poor** and **need** - y; *

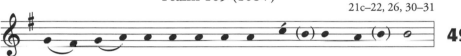

and my heart is **pierced** with - **in** me.__

℣ 2 **Help** me, O **LORD** my God!

2 **Hélp** me, O **LORD** my God! *
Save me according **tó** your **stead**fast <u>love</u>.

3 <u>*With*</u> <u>*my*</u> mouth I will give great **thánks** to the LORD; *
I will praise him in the **mídst** of **the** <u>throng</u>.

4 <u>*For*</u> <u>*he*</u> stands at the right hand **óf** the **need**y, *
to save them from those who would con**démn** them **to** <u>death</u>.

Communion Antiphon

Matthew 7:7

491

VIII G

Ask__ * and you will re - ceive;__ seek__ and you will__ find; knock__ and the door will be

† o-pened. *E.S.* † o - pened,__ al - le - lu - ia.

Psalm 78 (77V)

1–3, 23–29

492

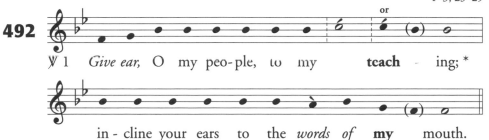

℣ 1 *Give ear,* O my peo-ple, to my **teach** - ing; *

in - cline your ears to the *words of* **my** mouth.

2   *I will* open my mouth in a **pár**able; *
      I will utter dark *sàyings* **from** of old,

3   *things that* we have **héard** and known, *
      that our ances*tòrs have* **told** us.

4   *God com*manded the **skíes** above, *
      and opened the *dòors of* **heav**en;

5   *he rained* down on them manna to **éat,** *
      and gave them the *gràin of* **heav**en.

6   *Mortals* ate of the bread of **án**gels; *
      he sent them food *in a***bun**dance.

7   *He caused* the east wind to blow in the **héav**ens, *
      and by his power he led *òut the* **south** wind;

8   *he rained* flesh upon them like **dúst,** *
      winged birds like the *sànd of* **the** seas;

9   *he let* them fall within their **cámp,** *
      all a*ròund their* **dwell**ings.

10   *And they* ate and were well **fílled,** *
      for he *gàve them* **what** they craved.

III. Votive Masses

For votive Masses, use the chants from the following list of respective solemnities or feasts.

During the Easter season, end the processional antiphons with the *alleluias* found on p. 378.

For a **Votive Mass of the Holy Trinity,** use the chants from the solemnity, beginning on p. 132.

For a **Votive Mass of the Holy Cross,** use the chants from the feast, beginning on p. 228.

For a **Votive Mass of the Holy Eucharist,** use the chants from the solemnity, beginning on p. 137.

For a **Votive Mass of the Sacred Heart,** use the chants from the solemnity, beginning on p. 143.

Votive Mass of the Holy Spirit

Entrance Antiphon

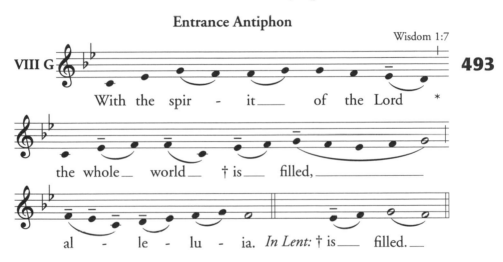

493

With the spir - it___ of the Lord *
the whole___ world___ † is___ filled,_____
al - le - lu - ia. *In Lent:* † is___ filled. ___

Wisdom 1:7

Psalm 104 (103V)

494

1ab, 30–31, 33–35

℣ 1 *Bless the* LORD, O my **soul.** *   O LORD my God,
you are **ver** - y great. *Flex:* from the earth, †

2   *When you* send forth your spirit, they are creáted; *
and you renew the *face of* **the** ground.

3 *May the* glory of the LORD endure for**é**ver; *
   may the LORD rej**ò**ice in **his** works.

4 *I will* sing to the LORD as long as I **lí**ve; *
   I will sing praise to my God while *I have* **be**ing.

5 *May my* meditation be pleasing to **hím,** *
   for I rej**ò**ice in **the** LORD.

6 *Let sin*ners be consumed from the **è**arth, †
      and let the wicked be no **móre.** *
   Bless the L**Ò**RD, O **my** soul.

The Responsorial Psalm is *Rejoice in the Lord,* **428.**

The Alleluia Psalm is *The mighty one, God the Lord,* **187.**

The Sequence is omitted.

The Preparation Song is *Confirm, O God,* **189.** During the Lenten season, end the antiphon thus:

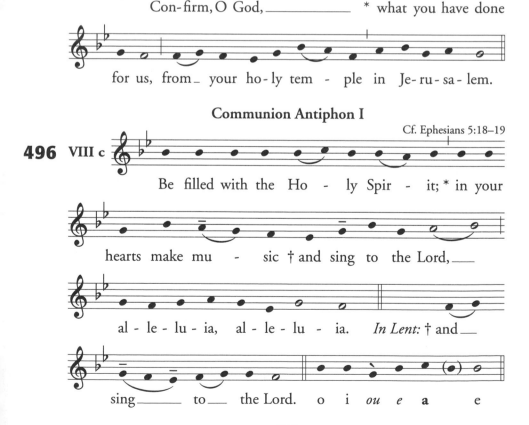

495 VIII c

Con-firm, O God, _____ * what you have done

for us, from_ your ho-ly tem - ple in Je-ru-sa-lem.

Communion Antiphon I

Cf. Ephesians 5:18–19

496 VIII c

Be filled with the Ho - ly Spir - it; * in your

hearts make mu - sic † and sing to the Lord, ___

al - le - lu - ia, al - le - lu - ia. *In Lent:* † and ___

sing ___ to ___ the Lord.   o i *ou* *e* **a**   e

Communion Antiphon II

Acts 2:17

VIII c   **497**

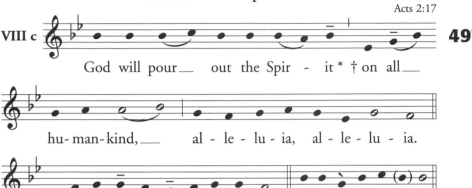

God will pour— out the Spir - it * † on all—

hu - man-kind, — al - le - lu - ia, al - le - lu - ia.

In Lent: † on — all— hu - man-kind. o i *ou e* **a** e

Communion Antiphon III

John 3:34

VIII c   **498**

With-out meas - ure— * † is God's gift of the

Spir-it, al - le - lu - ia, al - le - lu - ia. *In Lent:* † is God's

gift— of the Spir - it. o i *ou e* **a** e

The Communion Psalm is Psalm 78 (77V), *Give ear, O my people,* **192**, sung to Tone VIIIc, indicated by the vowels of "world without end. Amen."

Liturgy for the Dead

I. Mass for the Dead

Entrance Antiphon I

2 (4V) Esdras 2:34–35

499 VI F

Lord, — grant — that they — may —
have * e - ter - nal rest — for —
ev - er in the ra - diance of your light. —

Psalm 65 (64V)

1–4

500

℣ 1 *Praise is due* — to you, O God, *in* **Zi** - on; *
and to you *shall* vows — **be** per - formed,

2   *O you* who ans*wèr* **prayer!** *
    To you *àll flesh* **shall** come.

3   *When deeds* of iniquity ov*èr***whelm** us, *
    you forgive *òur trans*gres*sions.

4   *Happy* are those whom you choose and *brìng* **near** *
    tò live **in** your courts. *

5   *We shall* be satisfied with the goodness of *yòur* **house,** *
    yòur holy **tem**ple.

Entrance Antiphon II

Psalm 118 (117V):19

501 IV E

Lord, grant that they have e - ter - nal rest, — *

300

for ev - er in the ra - diance of your light.

Psalm 6

1–5, 7–9

℣ 1 O LORD, _ do not re-buke me *in your* an - ger, *

or dis - ci - *pline me in____* **your____** wrath.

2 *Be gra*cious to me, O LORD, for *Ì am* **lan**guishing; *
O LORD, heal me, for my bones *àre shaking with* **ter**ror.

3 *My soul* also is *strùck with* **ter**ror, *
while *yòu, O LORD*—**how** long?

4 *Turn, Q LORD, sàve my* **life;** *
deliver me for the sake *òf your stead***fast** love.

5 *For in death* there is no remem*bràance of* **you;** *
in Sheol *whò can give* **you** praise?

7 *My eyes* waste away be*càuse of* **grief;** *
they grow weak be*càuse of all* **my** foes.

8 *Depart* from me, all you work*èrs of* evil, *
for the LORD has heard *thè sound of my* **weep**ing.

9 *The LORD* has heard my *sùpplica*tion; *
the *LÒRD accepts* **my** prayer.

Entrance Antiphon III

Psalm 118 (117V):19

VIII G

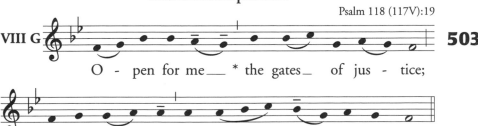

O - pen for me___ * the gates_ of jus - tice;

I shall en - ter and give_____ thanks_ to the Lord.

Psalm 118 (117V)

1, 5–6, 8–9, 13–14, 15c–17, 20–21 (See Performance Notes)

504

℣ 1   O   *give* thanks to   the LORD,   for   he   is   **good;** *

his stead-fast love en-*dures for-* **ev** - er!

Flex: does   val - iant - ly; †

2   *Out of* my distress I called on the **LÓRD;** *
the LORD answered me and set me *ìn a* **broad** place.

3   *With the* LORD on my side I do **nót** fear. *
What can *mòrtals* **do** to me?

4   *It is* better to take refuge in the **LÓRD** *
than to put confi*dènce in* **mor**tals.

5   *It is* better to take refuge in the **LÓRD** *
than to put confi*dènce in* **princ**es.

6   *I was* pushed hard, so that I was **fáll**ing, *
but *thè LORD* **helped** me.

7   *The LORD* is my strength and my **míght;** *
he has become *mỳ sal***va**tion.

8   *"The right* hand of the LORD does val*ìantly;* †
   the right hand of the LORD is ex**ált**ed; *
the right hand of the *LÒRD does* **val**iantly."

9   *I shall* not die, but I shall **líve,** *
and recount the *dèeds of* **the** LORD.

10   *This is* the gate of the **LÓRD;** *
the righteous shall *ènter* **through** it.

11   *I thank* you that you have **án**swered me *
and have become *mỳ sal***va**tion.

Responsorial Psalm I C 2 g   **Psalm 42 (41V)**

(1b) 1–6a

505

℣ 1   As   a   deer longs   for   flow - ing **streams,** *

302

so my soul longs for **you,** O God. _____

℟ My soul___ is long-ing for you,___ O___ God. ___

2   My soul thirsts for God, for the **lí**ving God. *
    When shall I come and behold the **fáce of** God?

3   My tears have been my food day and **níght,** *
    while people say to me continually, "Where is **yóur** God?"

4   These things I remember, as I pour out my **sóul:** *
    how I went with the throng, and led them in procession to
        the **hóuse of** God,

5   with glad shouts and songs of thanks**gív**ing, *
    a multitude keeping **fésti**val.

6   Why are you cast down, O my **sóul,** *
    and why are you disquieted with**ín** me?

7   Hope in God; for I shall again **práise** him, *
    my help and **mý** God.

Responsorial Psalm II E 3   Psalm 89 (88V)
                                                (1a) 1–2, 5–8, 14–17

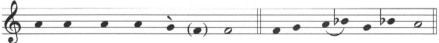

506

℣ 1 Of your stead-fast **love,** O Lᴏʀᴅ, ℟ I will sing_ for ev - er.

℣2 with my mouth I will pro - claim your **faith** - ful - ness *

to all gen - er - **a** - tions. ℟ I will sing_ for ev - er.

3   I declare that your steadfast love is established forevèr; *
    your faithfulness is as firm as the **hèav**ens.

4   Let the heavens praise your wonders, **O Lòʀᴅ,** *
    your faithfulness in the assembly of the **hò**ly ones.

303

5 For who in the skies can be compared to **the** LÒRD? *
Who among the heavenly beings is **like** the LORD,

6 a God feared in the council of the **holy** ones, *
great and awesome above all that are **aròund** him?

7 O LORD God of hosts, who is as mighty as you, **O** LÒRD? *
Your faithfulness surròunds you.

8 Righteousness and justice are the foundation of **your** thròne; *
steadfast love and faithfulness go befòre you.

9 Happy are the people who know the **fest**àl shout, *
who walk, O LORD, in the light of your còuntenance;

10 they exult in your name **all** dày long, *
and extol your **right**eousness.

11 For you are the glory of **their** strèngth; *
by your favor our horn is exàlted.

Responsorial Psalm III D 1 e   **Psalm 122 (121V)**
(1b) 1–9 (See Performance Notes)

507

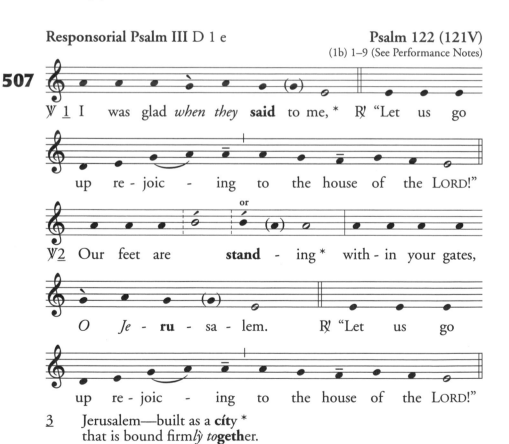

℣ 1 I was glad *when they* **said** to me, * ℟ "Let us go

up re - joic - ing to the house of the LORD!"

or

℣2 Our feet are **stand** - ing * with - in your gates,

O Je - **ru** - sa - lem. ℟ "Let us go

up re - joic - ing to the house of the LORD!"

3 Jerusalem—built as a **cíty** *
that is bound firm*ly* *to***geth**er.

4   To it the tribes go up, the tribes of the **LÓRD,** *
    as was decreed for Israel, to give thanks to the *nàme of the* LORD.

5   For there the thrones for judgment were set **úp,** *
    the thrones of the *hòuse of* **Da**vid.

6   Pray for the peace of Jerúsalem: *
    "May they pros*pèr who* **love** you.

7   Peace be within your **wálls,** *
    and security with*ìn your* **tow**ers."

8   For the sake of my relatives and **fríends** *
    I will say, "Peace *bè with*in you."

9   For the sake of the house of the LORD our **Gód,** *
    Ì *will* **seek** your good.

Alleluia   Psalm 130 (129V)
                                                 1–2

508

Al - le - lu - ia, al - le - lu - ia, al - le - lu - ia.

All repeat: Alleluia, alleluia, alleluia.

℣1 Out   of   the   depths   I   cry   to   *you,*   O   **LORD.** *

or

Lord, *hear*___   **my**___   voice!

All: Alleluia, alleluia, alleluia.

2   Let your ears *bè at***ten**tive *
    to the voice *òf my suppli***ca**tions!
                 All: Alleluia, alleluia, alleluia.

or **Alleluia Psalm I E** *   Psalm 114 (113a V)
                                                 1–8

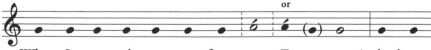

509

When Is - ra - el went out from   E - gypt, * the house

305

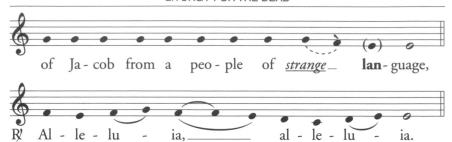

of Ja - cob from a peo - ple of *strange* lan - guage,

R̶ Al - le - lu - ia, _____ al - le - lu - ia.

2   Judah became God's **sánc**tuary, *
Israel *his dò***min**ion.

3   The sea looked and **fléd;** *
Jordan *tùrned* **back.**

4   The mountains skipped like **ráms,** *
the hills, *lìke* **lambs.**

5   Why is it, O sea, that you **flée?** *
O Jordan, that you *tùrn* **back?**

6   O mountains, that you **skíp** like rams? *
O hills, *lìke* **lambs?**

7   Tremble, O earth, at the presence of the **LÓRD,** *
at the presence of the *God òf* **Ja**cob,

8   who turns the rock into a pool of **wá**ter, *
the flint into a *spring òf* **wa**ter.

Alleluia Psalm II D 1 b   **Psalm 63 (62V)**
1–8

510

V̶ 1 O God, you are my God, I   **seek**   you, * my soul

thirsts for you; R̶ Al - le - lu - ia, _ al - le - lu - ia.

2   my flesh **fáints** for you, *
as in a dry and weary land where there is no **wà**ter.

3   So I have looked upon you in the **sánc**tuary, *
beholding your power and **glò**ry.

4   Because your steadfast love is better than **lífe,** *
my lips will **pràise** you.

5   So I will bless you as long as I **líve;** *
I will lift up my hands and call on **yòur** name.

6   My soul is satisfied as with a **rích** feast, *
and my mouth praises you with **jòy**ful lips

7   when I think of you on my **béd**, *
and meditate on you in the watches of **thè** night;

8   for you have been my **hélp**, *
and in the shadow of your wings I **sìng** for joy.

9   My soul **clíngs** to you; *
your right hand up**hòlds** me.

Alleluia Psalm III E 1   **Psalm 130 (129V)**
1–8 (See Performance Notes)

℣1 Out of the depths I cry to **you**, ⟶ O LORD. * Lord,

hear ⟶ **my** ⟶ voice! ℟ Al - le - lu - ia, ⟶ al - le - lu - ia.

                               511

2   Let your ears be at**tén**tive *
to the voice of my *súppli***ca**tions!

3   If you, O LORD, should mark in**í**quities, *
Lord, *whó* **could** stand?

4   But there is forgiveness **wíth** you, *
so that *yóu may* **be re**vered.

5   I wait for the LORD, my **sóul** waits, *
and in his *wórd* **I** hope;

6   my soul waits for the Lord ’
more than those who watch for the **mórn**ing, *
more than those who watch *fór the* **morn**ing.

7   O Israel, hope in the LORD! ’
For with the LORD there is **stéad**fast love, *
and with him is great *pówer* **to re**deem.

8   It is he who will redeem **Í**srael *
from all its in**í**quities.

Tract   **Psalm 123 (122V)**
1–4 (See Performance Notes)

℣1 *To*   *you* ⟶   I   lift   up   **my**   eyes, *

                                 512

O you who are en-throned in *the* **heav** - ens!

2   *As the <u>eyes</u>* of servants look to the hand of their master, '
     as the eyes of a maid to the hand of her **mìs**tress, *
   so our eyes look to the LORD our God, until he has mercy *ù***pon** us.

3   *Have <u>mer</u>*cy upon us, O LORD, have mercy up**òn** us, *
   for we have had more than enough of *còn***tempt**.

4   *Our <u>soul</u>* has had more than its fill of the scorn of those who are **àt**
     ease, *
   of the contempt of *thè* **proud**.

Preparation of the Gifts Antiphon I(A)

Job 19:25

513   **II D**

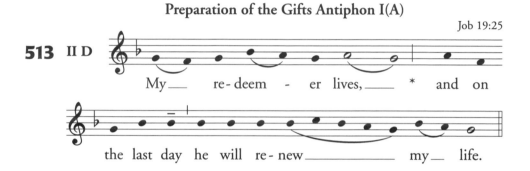

My — re-deem - er lives, — * and on

the last day he will re-new —————— my — life.

Preparation of the Gifts Antiphon I(B)

Psalm 18 (17V):19

514   **II D**

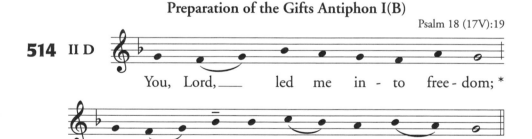

You, Lord, — led me in - to free-dom; *

you saved — me be - cause — you loved — me.

Psalm 18 (17V)

1–2a, 4, 6

515

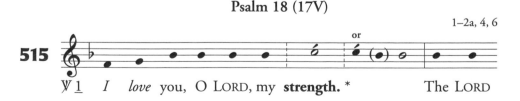

℣1   *I love* you, O LORD, my **strength**. *   The LORD

is my rock, my for-tress, and my *de* - **liv** - er - er.

2 *The cords* of death en**cóm**passed me; *
the torrents of perdition *às***sailed** me;

3 *In my* distress I called upon the **LÓRD;** *
to my God *ì* **cried** for help.

4 *From his* temple he **héard** my voice, *
and my cry to *hìm* **reached** his ears.

Preparation of the Gifts Antiphon II(A)

Psalm 15 (14V):Cf. 1

IV E

516

He/She/They will live___ * in your___ dwell-ing place,

and rest_____ on your ho - ly moun - tain.

Preparation of the Gifts Antiphon II(B)

Preface of Christian Death I

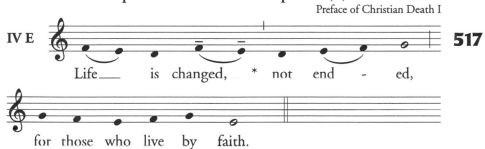

IV E

517

Life___ is changed, * not end - ed,

for those who live by faith.

Psalm 15 (14V)

1–3, 5c

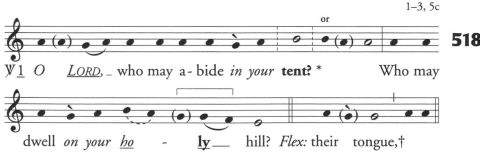

518

℣1 O LORD, _ who may a-bide *in your* **tent?** * Who may

dwell *on your ho* - **ly**___ hill? *Flex:* their tongue,†

℣4 Those who *do these* **things** * shall *nev-er* **be** moved.

2 *Those who walk* blamelessly, and do *whàt is* **right,** *
and *spèak the truth from* **their** heart;

3 *who do not* slander with their tòngue, †
and do no evil *tò their* **friends,** *
nor take up a re*pròach against their* **neigh**bors;

4 Those who *dò these* **things** *
shall *néver* **be** moved.

Preparation of the Gifts Antiphon III

Psalm 138 (137V):1c

519 V a

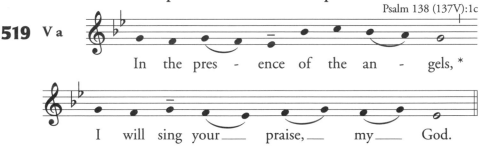

In the pres - ence of the an - gels, *

I will sing your praise, my God.

Psalm 138 (137V)

1, 3, 7a and c, 8
or

520

℣ 1 *I give* you thanks, O LORD, with my **whole** heart; *

for you have heard the **words** of **my** mouth;

Flex: pur - pose for me; †

2 *On the* day I called, you **án**swered me, *
you in**créased** my **strength** of soul.

3 *Though I* walk in the midst of trouble, you pre**sérve** me; *
and your **ríght** hand de**liv**ers me.

310

4   *The* L<small>ORD</small> *will fulfill his purpose for* mè; †
       your steadfast love, O L<small>ORD</small>, endures foré́ver. *
    Do not forsake the **work** of **your** hands.

Communion Antiphon I

2 (4V) Esdras 2:35

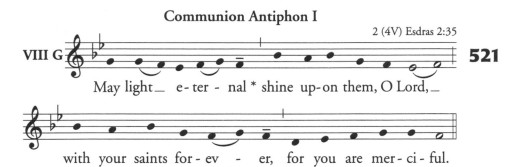

May light___ e-ter - nal * shine up-on them, O Lord,___ with your saints for - ev - er, for you are mer - ci - ful.

Psalm 130 (129V)

1–8 (See Performance Notes)
or

℣1 *Out* *of* the depths I cry to you, O **LORD.** *

   Lord, hear **my** voice! *Flex:* for the LORD,†

2   *Let your* ears be atté́ntive *
    to the voice of my *sùpplic*ations!

3   *If you,* O L<small>ORD</small>, should mark iní́quities, *
    Lòrd, who **could** stand?

4   *But there* is forgiveness with **yóu,** *
    so that *yòu may* **be** revered.

5   *I wait* for the L<small>ORD</small>, my soul **wáits,** *
    and *in his* **word** I hope;

6   *my soul* waits for the Lòrd †
       more than those who watch for the **mórn**ing, *
    more than those who watch *fòr the* **morn**ing.

7   *O Is*rael, hope in the L<small>ÒRD</small>! †
       For with the L<small>ORD</small> there is **stéad**fast love, *
    and with him is great *pòwer* **to** redeem.

8   *It is* he who will redeem Í́srael *
    from all *its ini*quities.

Communion Antiphon II

Revelation 14:13

523 II D

I heard a voice * from heav - en say - ing:

Hap - py are those who___ die in the Lord.___

Psalm 121 (120V)

1–8 (See Performance Notes)
or

524

℣ 1 *I lift* up my eyes to the **hills—** *

from where will *my* **help** come?

2 *My help* comes from the **LÓRD,** *
   who made heav*èn* **and** earth.

3 *He will* not let your foot be **móved;** *
   he who keeps you will *nòt* **slum**ber.

4 *He who* keeps **Ís**rael *
   will neither slum*bèr* **nor** sleep.

5 *The LORD* is your **kéep**er; *
   the LORD is your shade at *yòur* **right** hand.

6 *The sun* shall not strike you by **dáy,** *
   nor *thè* **moon** by night.

7 *The LORD* will keep you from all **évil;** *
   he *wìll* **keep** your life.

8 *The LORD* will keep your going out and your **cóm**ing in *
   from this time on and *fòre*vermore.

Communion Antiphon III

Psalm 142 (143V):Cf. 5b

525 VIII c

Lord,___ give___ me a place * in the

land of the liv - ing.

Psalm 142 (143V)

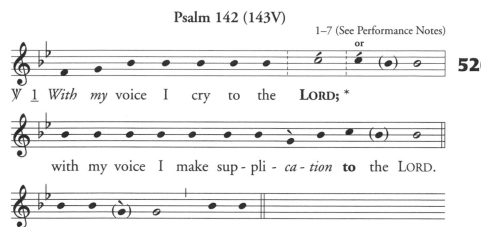

1–7 (See Performance Notes)

526

℣ 1 *With my* voice I cry to the **LORD;** *

with my voice I make sup - pli - *ca - tion* **to** the LORD.

Flex: to you, O LORD; †

2 *I pour* out my complaint be**fóre** him; *
I tell my trou*blè be***fore** him.

3 *When my* spirit is **fáint,** *
yòu know **my** way.

4 *In the* path where I **wálk** *
they have hid*dèn a* **trap** for me.

5 *Look on* my right hand and **sée—** *
there is no one who takes *nòtice* **of** me;

6 *no re*fuge re**máins** to me; *
nò one **cares** for me.

7 *I cry* to you, Ò LORD; †
I say, "You are my **réfuge,** *
my portion in the land *òf the* **liv**ing."

8 *Give heed* to my **crý,** *
for I *àm brought* **ver**y low.

9 *Save me* from my perse**cútors,** *
for they *àre too* **strong** for me.

10 *Bring me* out of **prís**on, *
so that I may give *thànks to* **your** name.

11 The righteous will sur**róund** me, *
for you will deal boun*tìfully* **with** me.

313

II. The Order of Christian Funerals

At the Vigil

At the time when the body is being placed on the bier, the following antiphons with psalms may be sung:

Antiphon I

Psalm 130 (129V):Cf. 4 and 8

527 IV A

For with the LORD_ * there is stead - fast love,

and_ with_ him_ is great pow - er to re-deem.

Psalm 130 (129V)

1–8 (See Performance Notes)

528

℣ 1 *Out____* of the depths I cry to *you,* O

or

LORD. * *Lord, hear* **my** voice!

Flex: hope in the LORD! †

2   *Let your ears bè at*tentive *
    to the voice of *mỳ suppli*cations!

3   *If you,* O LORD, should *màrk in*iquities, *
    Lord, whó **could** stand?

4   *But there is* forgivenèss *with* **you,** *
    so *thàt you may* **be** revered.

5   *I wait* for the LORD, *mỳ soul* **wáits,** *
    ànd in his **word** I hope;

6   *my soul waits* for the Lord more than those who
        watch *fòr the* **morn**ing, *
    more than those who *wàtch for the* **morn**ing.

7   *O Is*rael, hope in the LÒRD! †
        For with the LORD *thère is* **stead**fast love, *
    and with him is *grèat power* **to** redeem.

314

8   *It is <u>he</u>* who will *rèdeem* **Í**srael *
    from *àll its in***iq**uities.

Antiphon II

Cf. Luke 23:42

Re- mem - ber me, * O Lord___ my God,

when you___ come_____ in - to your___ king - dom.

Psalm 23 (22V)

1–6

℣ 1   *The* L**ORD** is my **shep** - herd, * I shall

not want. *Flex:* green pas - tures; †

2   *He makes* me lie down in green pastùres; †
      he leads me beside still **wá**ters; *
    *hè re***stores** my soul.

3   *He leads* me in **ríght** paths *
    fòr his **name's** sake.

4   *Even though* I walk through the darkest vàlley, †
      I fear no evil; for you are **wíth** me; *
    your rod and your *stàff—they* **com**fort me.

5   *You prepare* a table be**fóre** me *
    in the presence *òf my* **en**emies;

6   *you anoint* my head with **óil;** *
    mỳ cup **o**verflows.

7   *Surely good*ness and mercy shall **fól**low me *
    all the *dàys of* **my** life,

8   *and I* shall dwell in the house of the **LÓRD** *
    mỳ **whole** life long.

   Antiphon III: *He/she/they will live in your dwelling place,* **516,** with Psalm 15 (14V) *O*
L**ORD**, *who may abide in your tent,* **517.**

First Station: At the Home of the Deceased

According to the time available, one or more of the following Responsorial Psalms may be sung:

Psalm 130 (129V) *Out of the depths,* with the Response *Lord, listen to my voice,* **84.**

Psalm 23 (22V) *The Lord is my shepherd,* with the Response *In green pastures the Lord will give me rest,* **120.**

Psalm 89 (88V) *Of your steadfast love, O Lord,* with the Response *I will sing for ever,* **506.**

Or another appropriate psalm, with a corresponding response.

The Procession to the Church

If the deceased is to be taken to the church in procession, the following Responsorial Psalms or Antiphons with Psalms may be sung:

I. Psalm 122 (121V) *I was glad,* with the Response *Let us go up rejoicing to the house of the Lord,* **507,** or, if it seems fitting, with the Response *Alleluia,* **406.**

II. Psalm 126 (125V)

(1b) 1–6 (See Performance Notes)

531

℣ 1 When the LORD re - stored the for - tunes of **Zi** -

on, * we were like those **who** dream. ℟ Those who

sow in tears shall sing for joy when they reap.

2   Then our mouth was filled with **làugh**ter, *
and our tongue with **shòuts** of joy;

3   then it was said among the **nà**tions, *
"The LORD has done great **thìngs** for them."

4   The LORD has done great **thìngs** for us, *
and we **rè**joiced.

5   Restore our fortones, **Ò** LORD, *
like the watercourses in the **Nè**geb.

6   May those who **sòw** in tears *
reap with **shòuts** of joy.

7   Those who go out **wèep**ing, *
bearing the seed for **sòw**ing,

8   shall come home with **shòuts** of joy, *
      carrying **thèir** sheaves.

Or with the Response *Alleluia,* **341.**

III. Antiphon

I will please the LORD * in the land of the liv - ing.

Psalm 114V:9

532

Psalm 116 (114V)

1–8 (See Performance Notes)

℣ 1 I *love* the LORD, be-**cause** he **has**

533

heard * my voice and my sup - *pli* - **ca** - tions.

Flex: and an - guish. †

2   *Because* he in**clíned** his **ear to** me, *
      therefore I will call on him as long *às* I live.

3   *The snares* of **déath** en**compassed** me; *
      the pangs of Sheol *làid* **hold** on me;

4   I *suf*fered distress and angùish. †
          Then I **cálled** on the **name** of **the** LORD: *
      "O LORD, I *prày,* **save** my life!"

5   *Gracious* is the **LÓRD,** and **right**eous; *
      our God *is* **mer**ciful.

6   *The LORD* pro**técts** the **sim**ple; *
      when I was brought low, *hè* **saved** me.

7   *Return,* O my **sóul,** to **your** rest, *
      for the LORD has dealt bounti*fully* **with** you.

8   *For you* have delivered my soul from **death,** my **eyes from** tears, *
     my feet *fròm* **stumb**ling.

IV. **Psalm 116 (115V)** *I kept my faith,* **125,** with the Antiphon *My redeemer lives,* **513.**

V. Antiphon

Psalm 51 (50V):8b (See Performance Notes)

534 I f

Let   me   hear   joy____   and   glad - ness; *

let   the   bones   that   you   have   crushed   re - joice.

Psalm 51 (50V)

1–7

535

℣ 1 *Have* *mer* - cy **on** me, **O** God, *

ac - cord - ing *to your* **stead** - fast love;____

2   *accord*ing to your **abún**dant **mer**cy *
     blot out *mỳ trans***gres**sions.

3   *Wash* me thoroughly from **mý** in**iqu**ity, *
     and cleanse *mè from* **my** sin.

4   For I **knów** my transgres**sions,** *
     and my sin is ev*èr be***fore** me.

5   *Against* you, you **alóne,** have **I** sinned, *
     and done what is ev*ìl in* **your** sight,

6   so *that* you are justi**fíed** in your **sen**tence *
     and blameless when *yòu pass* **judg**ment.

7   Indeed, **Í** was born **guilt**y, *
     a sinner when my moth*èr con***ceived** me.

8   *You desire* truth in the **ín**ward **be**ing; *
     therefore teach me wisdom *ìn my* **se**cret heart.

9   *Purge* me with hyssop, and **Í** shall **be** clean; *
     wash me, and I shall be *whìter* **than** snow.

318

VI. Psalm 121 (120V) *I lift up my eyes,* **524,** with the Antiphon *I heard a voice from heaven,* **523.**

VII. Psalm 123 (122V) *To you I lift up my eyes,* **276,** with the Antiphon *Lord God in heaven,* **275.**

Second Station: In the Church

The Mass for the Dead, as above, p. 300.

Final Commendation and Farewell

Antiphon I

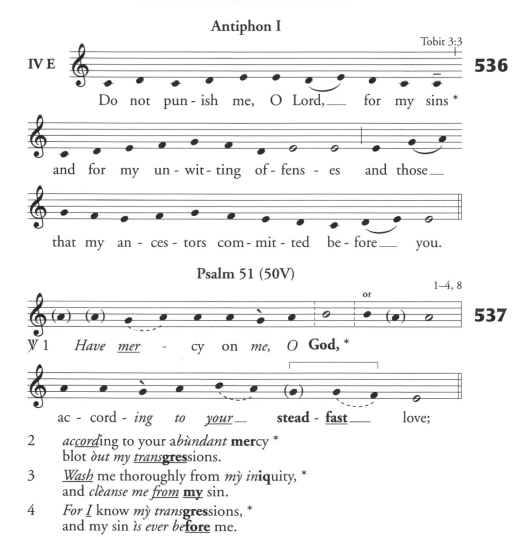

Tobit 3:3

IV E

536

Do not pun-ish me, O Lord,— for my sins *

and for my un-wit-ting of-fens-es and those—

that my an-ces-tors com-mit-ted be-fore— you.

Psalm 51 (50V)

1–4, 8

537

℣ 1 *Have* <u>*mer*</u> - cy on *me,* O **God,** *

ac - cord - ing to *your*— **stead - fast**— love;

2 *accord*ing to your a*bùn*dant **mer**cy *
blot *òut my* <u>*trans*</u>**gres**sions.

3 <u>*Wash*</u> me thoroughly from *mỳ in*iquity, *
and *clèanse me* <u>*from*</u> **my** sin.

4 *For* <u>*I*</u> know *mỳ trans***gres**sions, *
and my sin *is ever be***fore** me.

5   *Let* me hear *jòy and* **glad**ness; *
     let the bones that *yòu have <u>crushed</u>* **re**joice.

Antiphon II

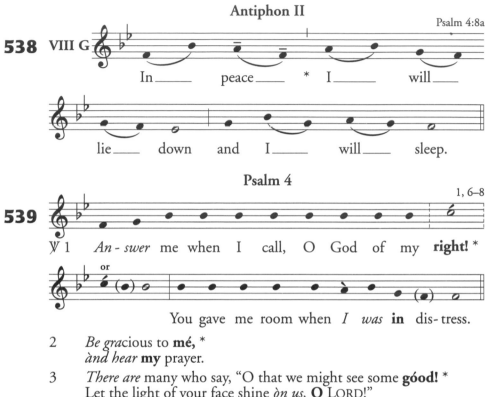

538   VIII G

In_____ peace_____ * I_____ will_____
lie_____ down and I_____ will_____ sleep.

Psalm 4:8a

Psalm 4

539

℣ 1   *An - swer* me when I call, O God of my **right!** *
      You gave me room when *I was* **in** dis- tress.

1, 6–8

2   *Be gra*cious to **mé,** *
     ànd hear **my** prayer.

3   *There are* many who say, "O that we might see some **góod!** *
     Let the light of your face shine *òn us,* **O** LORD!"

4   *You have* put gladness in my **heart** *
     more than when their *gràin and* **wine** abound.

5   *I will* both lie down and sleep in **péace;** *
     for you alone, O LORD, make me lie *dòwn in* **safe**ty.

Antiphon III

Psalm 27 (26V):13

540   IV E

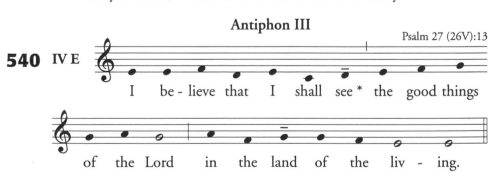

I be - lieve that I shall see * the good things
of the Lord in the land of the liv - ing.

Psalm 27 (26V)

1, 9 (See Performance Notes)

541

℣ 1 *The* LORD__ is my light and *my* *sal* -

or

va - tion; * *whom shall__* I__ fear?

2 *The* LORD is the stronghold *òf my* **life;** *
of whom *shàll I be* **a**fraid?

3 Do not *hìde your* **face** from me. *
Do not turn your servant away in anger, you *whò have been* **my** help.

4 Do not *càst me* **off,** *
do not forsake me, O *Gòd of my sal***va**tion!

While the body is being carried from the Church, the following may be sung:

Antiphon I

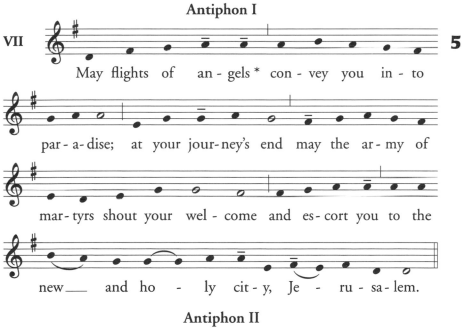

542

VII

May flights of an - gels * con - vey you in - to

par - a - dise; at your jour - ney's end may the ar - my of

mar - tyrs shout your wel - come and es - cort you to the

new__ and ho - ly cit - y, Je - ru - sa - lem.

Antiphon II

543

VIII

May choirs__ of an - gels wel - come you *

321

with their songs— of greet - ing   as you take— your

place with once- poor Laz - a - rus   to en - joy with him

and all— the ho - ly ones ev - er - last - ing rest.

Antiphon III

John 11:25–26

544 II D

I am— the res - ur - rec - tion * and the—

life.— Those who be - lieve in— me, e- ven though

they die, will— live,— and eve - ry - one who lives

and be- lieves— in me will— nev - er die.—

Psalm 114 (133A V)

1–8

545

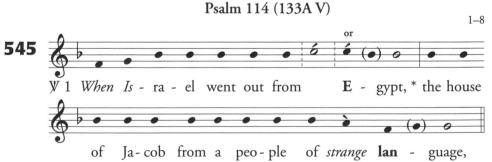

℣ 1 *When Is* - ra - el went out from   E - gypt, * the house

of Ja - cob from a peo- ple of *strange* **lan** - guage,

2 *Judah* became God's **sánc**tuary, *
Israel his *dò***min**ion.

322

3 *The sea* looked and **fléd;** *
   Jor*dàn* **turned** back.

4 *The moun*tains skipped like **ráms,** *
   the *hìlls* **like** lambs.

5 *Why is* it, O sea, that you **flée?** *
   O Jordan, that *yòu* **turn** back?

6 *O moun*tains, that you **skíp** like rams? *
   O *hìlls,* **like** lambs?

7 *Tremble, O* earth, at the presence of the **LÓRD,** *
   at the presence of the God *òf* **Ja**cob,

8 *who turns* the rock into a pool of **wá**ter, *
   the flint into a spring *òf* **wa**ter.

Antiphon IV

(See Performance Notes)

You knew_ me, Lord,_ be-fore_ I was born._ *
You_ shaped_ me in-to your_ im - age and like -
ness._ I breathe_ forth_ my spir - it_ to
you,_ my_ Cre-a-tor. ℣ Mer-ci-ful Lord, I trem -
ble be-fore_ you: I am a-shamed_ of the
things_ I have_ done;_ when you_ come in

546

323

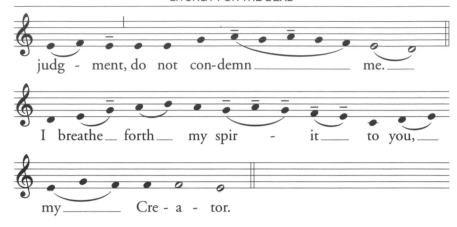

judg - ment, do not con-demn ___ me. ___

I breathe ___ forth ___ my spir - it ___ to you, ___

my ___ Cre - a - tor.

The Procession to the Cemetery

As the body is carried to the cemetery, the following may be sung:

Psalm 118 (117V) *O give thanks to the Lord,* **504,** with the Antiphon, *Open to me,* **503,** or:

Antiphon I

Psalm 118 (117V):20

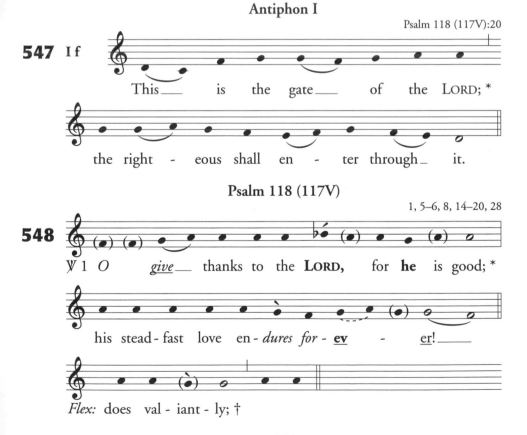

547 I f

This ___ is the gate ___ of the LORD; *

the right - eous shall en - ter through ___ it.

Psalm 118 (117V)

1, 5–6, 8, 14–20, 28

548

℣ 1 O *give* ___ thanks to the **LORD,** for **he** is good; *

his stead-fast love en-*dures for-* **ev** - er!

Flex: does val - iant - ly; †

2 *Out of my* distress I **cálled** on **the** LORD; *
   the LORD answered me and set me *ìn a* **broad** place.

3 *With the LORD* on my **síde** I do **not** fear. *
   What can *mòrtals* **do** to me?

4 *It is bet*ter to take **réf**uge **in** the LORD *
   than to put confi*dènce in* **mor**tals.

5 *The LORD* is my **stréngth** and **my** might; *
   he has become *mỳ sal*vation.

6 *There are* glad **sóngs** of **vic**tory *
   in the tents *òf the* **right**eous:

7 *"The right* hand of the LORD does val*ì*antly; †
      the right hand of the **LÓRD** is ex**al**ted; *
   the right hand of the LÒRD *does* **val**iant*ly.*"

8 *I shall* not **díe,** but I **shall** live, *
   and recount the *dèeds of* **the** LORD.

9 *The LORD* has punished **mé** se**ve**rely, *
   but he did not *gìve me* **over** to death.

10 *Open* to me the **gátes** of **right**eousness, *
   that I may enter through them *ànd give* **thanks to** the LORD.

11 *I thank* you that **yóu** have **an**swered me *
   and have become *mỳ sal*vation.

12 *You are* my God, and **Í** will give **thanks** to you; *
   you are my God, I *wìll* ex**tol** you.

Antiphon II

Psalm 42 (41V):2

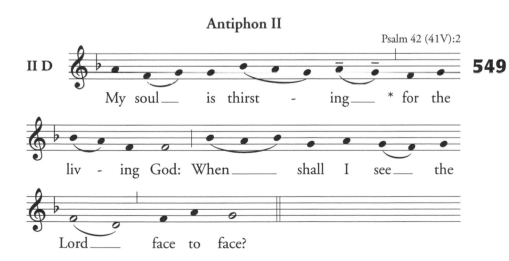

II D

549

My soul— is thirst - ing— * for the liv - ing God: When——— shall I see— the Lord——— face to face?

Psalm 42 (41V)

1–6a, 8

550

℣ 1 *As a* deer longs for **flow**-ing streams, * so my soul

longs *for* **you,** O God. *Flex:* with the throng, †

2 *My soul* thirsts for God, for the **lív**ing God. *
When shall I come and behold *thè* **face** of God?

3 *I went* with the thròng, †
    and led them in procession to the **hóuse** of God, *
    with glad shouts and songs of thanksgiving, a multitude
       keep*ìng* **fes**tival.

4 *O send* out your light and your **trúth;** *
    let *thèm* **lead** me;

5 *let them* bring me to your holy **híll** *
    and to *yòur* **dwell**ing.

6 *Then I* will go to the altar of **Gód,** *
    to God my *èx***ceed**ing joy;

7 *and I* will praise you with the **hárp,** *
    O *Gòd,* **my** God.

8 *By day* the LORD commands his steadfast love, †
    and at night his song is **wíth** me, *
    a prayer to the God *òf* **my** life.

Antiphon III

Psalm 25 (24V):7a

551 VIII G

Do not re-mem-ber * the sins of my youth____

or my trans-gres - sions,____ O____ LORD.____

Psalm 25 (24V)

1–2ab, 4–6, 7b–8, 10–11, 15–16, 18

or

552

℣ 1 *To you,* O LORD, I lift up my **soul.** *

O my God, in you I trust; do not let *me be*

put to shame. *Flex:* and teach me, †

2 *Make me* to know your **wáys,** O LORD; *
   tèach me **your** paths.

3 *Lead me* in your truth, and teach mè, †
      for you are the God of my salvátion; *
   for you *Ì wait* **all** day long.

4 *Be mind*ful of your mercy, O LORD, and of your **stéad**fast love, *
   for they *hàve been* **from** of old.

5 *Accord*ing to your steadfast love re**mém**ber me, *
   for your *gòodness'* **sake,** O LORD!

6 *Good and* upright is the **LÓRD;** *
   therefore he instructs sin*nèrs in* **the** way.

7 *All the* paths of the LORD are steadfast love and **fáith**fulness, *
   for those who keep his cove*nànt and* **his** decrees.

8 *My eyes* are ever toward the **LÓRD,** *
   for he will pluck my *fèet out* **of** the net.

9 *Turn to* me and be gracious to **mé,** *
   for I am lonely *ànd af***flict**ed.

10 *Consid*er my affliction and my **tróu**ble, *
   and for*gìve all* **my** sins.

Antiphon IV

Psalm 16 (15V):9b

VII c

553

My_ bod - y * will rest_ in_ hope.

Psalm 16 (15V)

1–2, 5–9a, 10–11

554

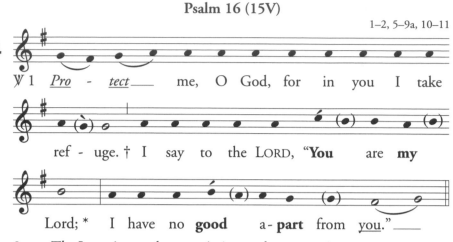

℣ 1 *Pro* - *tect* me, O God, for in you I take ref - uge. † I say to the LORD, "**You** are **my** Lord; * I have no **good** a- **part** from you."

2   *The LORD* is my chosen **pór**tion and **my** cup; *
    yóu hold **my** lot.

3   *The bound*ary lines have fallen for me in **pléas**ant **plac**es; *
    I have a **góod**ly **heri**tage.

4   *I bless* the LORD who **gíves** me **coun**sel; *
    in the night also my **héart** in**structs** me.

5   *I keep* the LORD **ál**ways be**fore** me; *
    because he is at my right hand, **Í** shall **not** be moved.

6   *Therefore* my heart is glad, and my **sóul** re**joic**es; *
    my body **ál**so **rests** se**cure**.

7   *For you* do not give me **úp** to **She**ol, *
    or let your **fáith**ful one **see** the Pit.

8   *You show* me the path òf life. †
    In your presence there is **fúll**ness **of** joy; *
    in your right hand are **pléas**ures fo/ever**more**.

Third Station: At the Cemetery

At the graveside the cantor(s) and the assembly may sing the customary songs used by the local community, they may repeat songs already sung at the vigil or at the funeral, or they may sing songs from these rites which were not yet sung.

CHANTS FOR THE ORDER OF THE MASS

I. Introductory Rites

The Sign of the Cross

555

In nó - mi - ne Pa - tris, et Fí - li - i,
In the name of the Fa - ther, and of the Son,

et Spí - ri - tus San - cti. ℟ A - men.
and of the Ho - ly Spir - it. ℟ A - men.

The Greeting

A.

556

Grá - ti - a Dó - mi - ni no - stri Ie - su Chri - sti,
The grace of our Lord Je - sus Christ

et cá - ri - tas De - i, et com - mu - ni - cá - ti - o San-
and the love of God and the fel - low-ship of the Ho-

cti Spí - ri - tus sit cum ó - mni - bus vo - bis.
ly Spir - it be with you all.

℟ Et cum spí - ri - tu tu - o.
℟ And al - so with you.

B.

557

Grá - ti - a vo - bis et pax a De - o Pa - tre no - stro et
The grace and peace of God our Fa - ther and

329

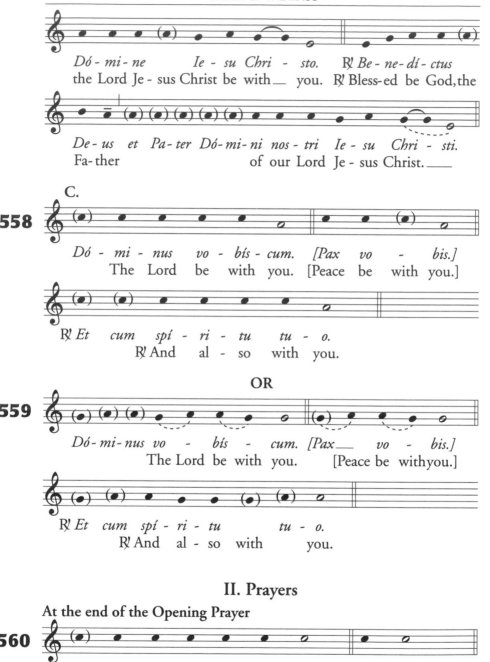

Dó - mi - ne   Ie - su Chri - sto.   R̷ Be - ne - dí - ctus
the Lord Je - sus Christ be with ___ you.   R̷ Bless-ed be God, the

De - us   et   Pa - ter   Dó - mi - ni   nos - tri   Ie - su   Chri - sti.
Fa - ther   of   our   Lord   Je - sus   Christ. ___

C.

558

Dó - mi - nus   vo - bís - cum.   [Pax   vo - bis.]
The   Lord   be   with   you.   [Peace   be   with   you.]

R̷ Et   cum   spí - ri - tu   tu - o.
R̷ And   al - so   with   you.

OR

559

Dó - mi - nus vo - bís - cum.   [Pax ___ vo - bis.]
The Lord be with you.   [Peace be with you.]

R̷ Et   cum   spí - ri - tu   tu - o.
R̷ And   al - so   with   you.

II. Prayers

At the end of the Opening Prayer

560

. . . sae - cu - la   sae - cu - lo - rum.   R̷ A - men.
. . . for   ev - er   and   ev - er.   R̷ A - men.

At the end of the other Prayers

Per Chri-stum Dó - mi - num no - strum. ℟ *A - men.*
Grant this through Christ our Lord. ℟ A - men.

561

OR

At the end of the Opening Prayer

... sae - cu - la sae - cu - lo - rum. ℟ *A - men.___*
... for ev - er and ev - er. ℟ A - men.___

562

At the end of the other Prayers

Per Chri-stum Dó - mi - num no - strum. ℟ *A - men.___*
Grant this through Christ our___ Lord. ℟ A - men.___

563

This tone is more suitable for the Prayer over the Gifts when the Preface Dialogue is also sung because it leads well from the one to the other.

III. Liturgy of the Word

After the First Reading

Jubilate Deo

Ver - bum Dó - mi - ni. ℟ *De - o grá - ti - as.*
The word of the Lord. ℟ Thanks be to God.

564

After the Second Reading
or if there is only one reading before the Gospel

Jubilate Deo

Ver - bum Dó - mi - ni. ℟ *De - o grá - ti - as.*
The word of the Lord. ℟ Thanks be to God.

565

The Gospel

Before the Gospel

Jubilate Deo

566

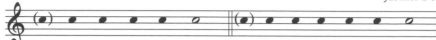

Dó - mi - nus vo - bís - cum. R̹ Et cum spí - ri - tu   tu - o.
The Lord be with you.   R̹ And al - so with you.

Lé - cti - o san - cti E - van - gé - li - i   se - cún - dum N . . .
A read-ing from the gos-pel ac- cord-ing   to   N . . .

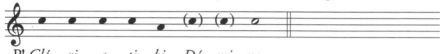

R̹ *Gló - ri - a   ti - bi, Dó - mi - ne.*
R̹ Glo - ry   to you, [O]   Lord.

After the Gospel

Jubilate Deo

567

Ver - bum   Dó -   mi - ni.   R̹ Laus ti - bi,
The gos - pel   of the Lord.   R̹ Praise to   you, Lord Je -

Chri - ste. _____
sus Christ. _____

OR

Before the Gospel

568

The Lord be with you. R̹ And   al - so with you.

A read-ing from the gos - pel ac- cord-ing to   N.

332

R̶⁷ Glo - ry   to you, [O] Lord.

After the Gospel

569

Ver - bum   Dó - mi - ni.   R̶⁷ Laus ti - bi,
The gos - pel   of the Lord. R̶⁷ Praise to you, Lord Je -

Chris - te. _____
sus Christ. _____

OR

Before the Gospel

570

The Lord be ___ with ___ you. R̶⁷ And al - so with you.

A read-ing from the gos - pel ac- cord-ing to   N.

R̶⁷ Glo - ry   to you, [O] Lord.

After the Gospel

571

Ver - bum   Dó   -   mi - ni.
The   gos - pel   of   the   Lord.

R̶⁷ Laus _____   ti - bi, ___   Chri - ste.
R̶⁷ Praise ___   to you, Lord Je - sus   Christ.

IV. Liturgy of the Eucharist

The Preface Dialogue (Latin)

Jubilate Deo

572 ℣ Dó-mi-nus vo - bís - cum. ℟ Et cum Spí-ri-tu tu - o.

℣ Sur - sum cor - da.____

℟ Ha-bé - mus ad Dó - mi-num.____

℣ Grá-ti - as__ a-gá - mus Dó-mi-no__ De - o no - stro.

℟ Di - gnum et iu - stum est.____

The Preface Dialogue (English)

573 ℣ The Lord____ be with you. ℟ And al - so with you.

℣ Lift____ up____ your hearts.____

℟ We lift__ them up to the Lord.____

℣ Let us give thanks to the Lord__ our God.

334

℟ It is right to give him thanks and praise.

Memorial Acclamation (Latin)

Jubilate Deo

574

℣ My-sté - ri - um fí - de - i.

575

Or: My-sté - ri - um fí - de - i.

576

℟ Mor-tem tu - am an-nun-ti - á-mus, Dó - mi-

ne, et tu - am re - sur - re - cti - ó - nem

con - fi - té - mur, do - nec vé - ni - as.

Memorial Acclamations (English)

577

The mys - ter - y of faith.

A.

578

℟ Christ has died, Christ is ris - en,

Christ will come a - gain.

335

B.

579 R Dy - ing you de - stroyed____ our death and ris - ing you re - stored our life. Lord Je - sus, come__ in glo - ry.

C.

580 R When we eat__ this bread and drink____ this cup, we pro - claim your death, Lord Je - sus, un - til you come. in glo - ry.

D.

581 R Lord, by your cross and res - ur - rec - tion you have set us free. You are the Sav - ior of the world.

The Great Amen

Jubilate Deo

...per ó - mni - a sáe - cu - la sae - cu - ló - rum.
...for ev - er and ev - er.

582 R A - men.____

583 or:
R A - men.__ A - men.__ A - men.__

V. Communion Rite

The Lord's Prayer (Latin)

Jubilate Deo

584

Prae - cép - tis sa - lu - tá - ri - bus mó - ni - ti,

et di - ví - na in - sti - tu - ti - ó - ne for - má -

ti, au - dé - mus dí - ce - re:

Pa - ter no - ster, qui es in cae - lis: san - cti - fi - cé -

tur __ no - men tu - um; ad - vé - ni - at re - gnum

tu - um; fi - at vo - lún - tas tu - a, sic - ut in cae -

lo, __ et __ in ter - ra. Pa - nem no - strum

co - ti - di - á - num da no - bis hó - di - e; et di -

mít - te no - bis dé - bi - ta no - stra, sic - ut

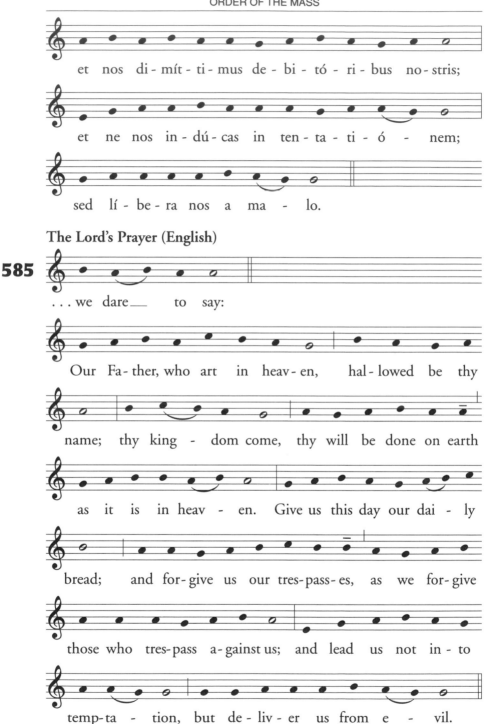

et nos di - mít - ti - mus de - bi - tó - ri - bus no - stris;

et ne nos in - dú - cas in ten - ta - ti - ó - nem;

sed lí - be - ra nos a ma - lo.

The Lord's Prayer (English)

585

...we dare___ to say:

Our Fa- ther, who art in heav- en, hal- lowed be thy

name; thy king - dom come, thy will be done on earth

as it is in heav - en. Give us this day our dai - ly

bread; and for- give us our tres- pass- es, as we for- give

those who tres- pass a- gainst us; and lead us not in- to

temp- ta - tion, but de - liv- er us from e - vil.

Doxology

Jubilate Deo

... et ad-vén-tum Sal-va-tó-ris no-stri Ie-su Chri - sti.
... at the com-ing of our Sav-ior, Je-sus Christ.

586

R̷ Qui - a___ tu - um est re-gnum, et po - tés -
R̷ For the king-dom, the pow - er and the glo - ry

tas, _____ et gló-ri - a in sáe-cu - la.
are yours, now and for ev - er.

The Sign of Peace

Jubilate Deo

587

... in sáe-cu - la sáe-cu - ló - rum. R̷ A - men.___
Or: ... for ev - er and ev - er.

Pax Dó - mi - ni sit sem-per vo - bís - cum.
The peace of the Lord be with you al - ways.

588

R̷ Et cum spí - ri - tu tu - o.
R̷ And al - so with you.

VI. Concluding Rite

The Simple Blessing

589

Dó-mi - nus vo - bís-cum. R̷ Et cum spí - ri - tu tu - o.
The Lord be with you. R̷ And al - so with you.

Be - ne - dí - cat vos o - mní - po - tens De - us,   Pa - ter,
May al-might-y God bless you,   the   Fa - ther,

et Fí - li - us, et Spí - ri - tus San - ctus. ℟ A - men.
and   the Son, and the Ho - ly Spir - it.

OR

590

Dó- mi- nus vo - bís - cum. ℟ Et cum spí - ri - tu tu - o.
The   Lord be__ with__ you.   ℟ And al - so with   you.

Be - ne - dí - cat vos o - mní - po - tens De - us,   Pa - ter,
May   al- might- y God bless you,   the Fa - ter,

et Fí - li - us,   et Spí - ri - tus San - ctus. ℟ A- men.__
and the   Son, and the Ho - ly Spir - it.

In Solemn Blessings answer each invocation of the Prayer over the People with the Amen which responds to the foregoing blessing.

The Blessing of the Bishop

591

Dó - mi - nus vo - bís - cum. ℟ Et cum spí - ri - tu tu - o.
The Lord be with you.   ℟ And al - so with you.

℣ Sit no - men Dó - mi - ni be - ne - dí - ctum.
℣ Bless - ed   be   the name of   the Lord.

℟ *Ex hoc nunc et us - que in sáe - cu - lum.*
℟ Now and for ev - er.

℣ *Ad - iu - tó - ri - um no - strum in nó - mi - ne Dó - mi - ni.*
℣ Our help is in the name of the Lord.

℟ *Qui fe - cit cae - lum et ter - ram.*
℟ Who made heav - en and earth.

Be - ne - dí - cat vos o - mní - po - tens De - us,   Pa - ter,
May al - might - y God bless you,   the Fa - ther,

et Fí - li - us,   et Spí - ri - tus San - ctus. ℟ *A - men.*
and   the Son, and the Ho - ly Spir - it.

OR

592

Dó - mi - nus vo - bís - cum. ℟ *Et cum spí - ri - tu tu - o.*
The Lord be _ with _ you.   ℟ And al - so with   you.

℣ *Sit no - men Dó - mi - ni be - ne - dí - ctum.*
℣ Bless - ed be the name of the Lord.

℟ *Ex hoc nunc et us - que in sáe - cu - lum.*
℟ Now and for ev - er.

℣ Ad - iu - tó - ri - um no-strum in nó - mi - ne Dó - mi - ni.
℣ Our help is in the name of the Lord.

℟ Qui fe - cit cae - lum et ter - ram.
℟ Who made heav - en and earth.

Be - ne - dí - cat vos o - mní - po-tens De - us, Pa - ter,
May al-might-y God bless you, the Fa- ther,

et Fí - li - us, et Spí - ri - tus San - ctus. ℟ A- men. __
and the Son, and the Ho - ly Spir - it.

The Dismissal (Latin)

593

I - te, __ mis - sa est. ℟ De - o __ grá - ti - as.

The Dismissal (English)

ICEL

594

Go in peace to love and serve the Lord. ___
Go in the peace of Christ. ___
The Mass is end - ed, go in peace. ___

℟ Thanks __ be to God. ___

For the Dismissal during the Easter Season see **147.**

342

CHANTS FOR THE ORDINARY OF THE MASS

I

Jubilate Deo (Kyrie XVI)

III · **595**

Ký-ri - e,— e-lé-i-son. Ký-ri - e,— e-lé-i-son.

Chri-ste,— e-lé-i-son. Chri-ste,— e-lé-i-son. Ký-ri - e,—

e-le-i-son. Ký-ri - e,— e-le - i-son.

Jubilate Deo (Gloria VIII)

V · **596**

Gló-ri - a in ex-cél-sis De - o. Et in

ter-ra pax ho-mí-ni-bus bo-nae vo-lun-tá - tis.

Lau-dá - mus te. Be-ne-dí-ci-mus— te.—

Ad-o-rá - mus— te. Glo-ri-fi-cá-mus te.

Grá-ti-as á-gi-mus— ti-bi pro-pter ma-gnam

gló-ri-am tu-am. Dó-mi-ne De-us, Rex cae-lés-tis,

De- us___ Pa - ter___ o - mní - po - tens.

Dó- mi - ne Fi - li u - ni - gé - ni - te, Ie - su___

Chri - ste. Dó- mi - ne De- us,___ A - gnus De - i,

Fí - li - us___ Pa - tris. Qui tol - lis pec-

cá- ta mun - di,___ mi - se - ré - re___

no - bis. Qui tol - lis pec - cá - ta mun - di, sús - ci -

pe de - pre - ca - ti - ó - nem___ no - stram.___

Qui se - des ad déx - te - ram Pa - tris, mi - se - ré - re

no - bis. Quó - ni - am tu so - lus San - ctus. Tu so - lus___

Dó - mi - nus. Tu so- lus Al - tís - si - mus,___

Ie - su — Chri - ste. Cum San - cto — Spí - ri - tu,

in gló - ri - a De - i Pa - tris. —

A - men. —

(Gloria XV)

IV

597

Gló - ri - a — in ex - cél - sis De - o. Et in

ter - ra pax ho - mí - ni - bus bo - nae vo - lun - tá - tis.

Lau - dá - mus te. Be - ne - dí - ci - mus te. Ad - o -

rá - mus te. Glo - ri - fi - cá - mus te. Grá - ti - as á - gi -

mus ti - bi pro - pter ma - gnam gló - ri - am tu - am.

Dó - mi - ne De - us, Rex cae - lés - tis, De - us Pa - ter

o - mní - po - tens. Dó - mi - ne Fi - li u - ni - gé - ni - te,

Ie - su Chri - ste. Dó - mi - ne De - us, A - gnus De - i,

Fí - li - us Pa - tris. Qui tol - lis pec - cá - ta mun - di,

mi - se - ré - re no - bis. Qui tol - lis pec - cá - ta mun - di,

sús - ci - pe de - pre - ca - ti - ó - nem no - stram.

Qui se - des ad déx - te - ram Pa - tris, mi - se - ré - re

no - bis. Quó - ni - am tu so - lus San - ctus. Tu so - lus

Dó - mi - nus. Tu so - lus Al - tís - si - mus, Ie - su

Chri - ste. Cum San - cto Spí - ri - tu, in gló - ri - a

De - i Pa - tris. A - men.

(based on Gloria XV)

598 IV

Glo - ry to God in the high-est, and peace to

his peo-ple on earth. Lord God, heav-en - ly King,

al-might-y God and Fa-ther, we wor-ship you,

we give__ you thanks, we praise you for your glo-ry.

Lord__ Je-sus Christ, on-ly Son of the Fa - ther,

Lord__ God, Lamb__ of God, you take a-way the sin of

the world: have mer-cy on us; you are seat-ed at the

right hand of the Fa-ther, re-ceive__ our prayer. For you

a-lone are the Ho-ly One, you a-lone are the Lord,

you a-lone are the Most High, Je-sus Christ,____

with the Ho-ly Spir-it, in the glo-ry of God the

Fa - ther. A - men.__

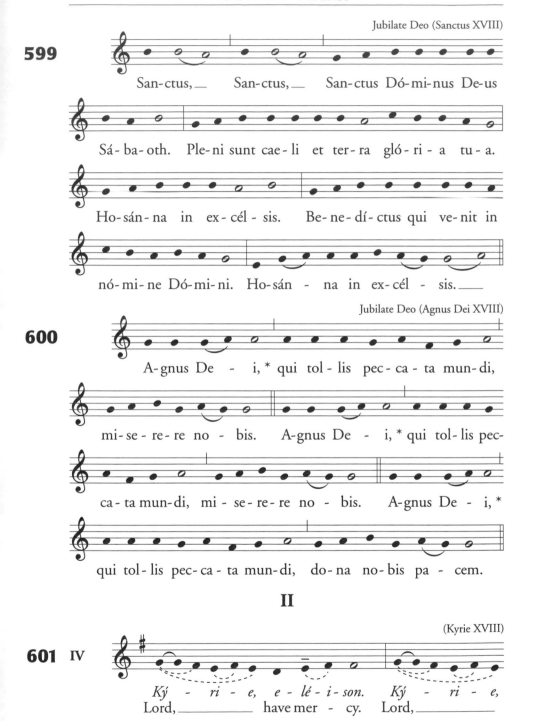

Jubilate Deo (Sanctus XVIII)

599

San-ctus, — San-ctus, — San-ctus Dó-mi-nus De-us

Sá-ba-oth. Ple-ni sunt cae-li et ter-ra gló-ri-a tu-a.

Ho-sán-na in ex-cél-sis. Be-ne-dí-ctus qui ve-nit in

nó-mi-ne Dó-mi-ni. Ho-sán - na in ex-cél - sis. —

Jubilate Deo (Agnus Dei XVIII)

600

A-gnus De - i, * qui tol-lis pec-ca-ta mun-di,

mi-se-re-re no - bis. A-gnus De - i, * qui tol-lis pec-

ca-ta mun-di, mi-se-re-re no - bis. A-gnus De - i, *

qui tol-lis pec-ca-ta mun-di, do-na no-bis pa - cem.

II

(Kyrie XVIII)

601 IV

Ký - ri - e, e - lé - i - son. Ký - ri - e,
Lord, _____ have mer - cy. Lord, _____

e - lé - i - son. Chri-ste, ___ e - lé - i - son. Chri-ste, ___
have mer - cy. Christ, ___ have ___ mer - cy. Christ, ___

e - lé - i - son. Ký - ri - e, e - lé - i - son.
have ___ mer - cy. Lord, ___ have mer - cy.

Ký - ri - e, ___ e - lé - i - son.
Lord, ___ have ___ mer - cy.

(from the Litany of the Saints)

602

Ký - ri - e, e - lé - i - son. Ký - ri - e, e - lé - i - son.
Lord, have mer - cy. Lord, have mer - cy.

Chri-ste, e - lé - i - son. Chri-ste, e - lé - i - son.
Christ, have mer - cy. Christ, have mer - cy.

Ký - ri - e, e - lé - i - son. Ký - ri - e, ___ e - lé - i - son. ___
Lord, have mer - cy. Lord, ___ have ___ mer - cy. ___

(in the Mozarabic style)

603

Glo - ry to God in the high - est, and peace

to his peo-ple on ___ earth. Lord God, heav-en - ly ___

349

King, al-might-y God and Fa - ther, we wor - ship you,

we give you — thanks, we praise you for your glo - ry.

Lord Je - sus Christ, on - ly Son of the Fa - ther,

Lord God, Lamb of God, — you take a - way the sin of

the — world: have mer - cy on us; you are seat-ed at the

right hand of the Fa - ther, re - ceive our — prayer.

For you a - lone are the Ho - ly — One, you a -

lone are the Lord, you a - lone are the Most — High,

Je - sus Christ, — with the

Ho - ly Spir - it, in the glo - ry of God —

the ___ Fa - ther. ___ A - men.

(based on Sanctus XVI)

II **604**

Ho- ly, ___ * ho- ly, ___ ho- ly Lord, ___ God ___ of

pow- er and might, heav- en and earth ___ are full of your

glo - ry. Ho-san-na ___ in the high - est. ___

[O how] bless - ed is he ___ who comes ___ in the

name ___ of the Lord. Ho- san - na ___ in the

high - est. ___

(based on Agnus Dei XVI)

I Cantor(s), Schola, or Choir   All   **605**

O ___ Lamb ___ of ___ God, ___ * you take ___ a-

way ___ the sins ___ of the world, have mer - cy on us. ___

351

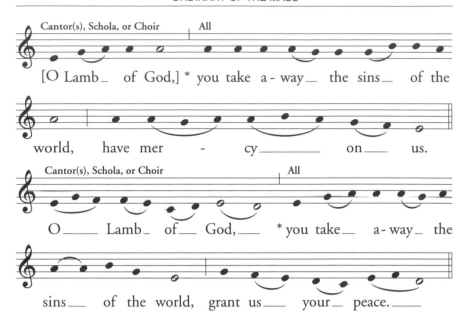

[O Lamb of God,] * you take a-way the sins of the world, have mer - cy on us.

O Lamb of God, * you take a-way the sins of the world, grant us your peace.

This setting of the Litany for the Breaking of the Bread is performed thus:

The first petition is sung; the second is sung as many times and with as many invocations of Christ as are necessary to accompany the breaking and pouring of the elements; the last petition is reserved for the very end of the Fraction Rite. To the tune within the brackets of the second petition, the following invocations may be sung:

O Bread of Life	O Pledge of Life
O Prince of peace	O Lord of lords
O risen Lord	O Lasting Light
O Word of Life	O Font of love
O Word made flesh	O Saving God
O King of Kings	O Son of God

III

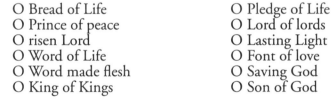

606

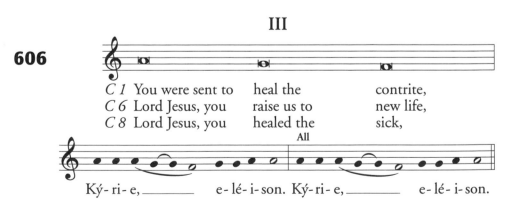

C 1 You were sent to heal the contrite,
C 6 Lord Jesus, you raise us to new life,
C 8 Lord Jesus, you healed the sick,

Ký- ri- e, e- lé- i-son. Ký-ri- e, e- lé- i-son.

C 1 You came to call sinners,
C 6 Lord Jesus, you for - give us our sins,
C 8 Lord Jesus, you for - gave sinners,

All

Chri - ste, _____ e - lé - i - son. Chri - ste, _____ e - lé - i - son.

C 1 You plead for us at the right hand of the Father,
C 6 Lord Jesus, you feed us with your body and [your] blood,
C 8 Lord Jesus, you give us yourself to heal us and bring us strength,

All

Ký - ri - e, _____ e - lé - i - son. Ký - ri - e, e - lé - i - son.

All

I   607

Ký - ri - e, e - lé - i - son. Ký - ri - e, e - lé - i - son.
Lord, _____ have _ mer - cy. Lord, _____ have _ mer - cy.

All

Chri - ste, e - lé - i - son. Chri - ste, e - lé - i - son.
Christ, _____ have _ mer - cy. Christ, _____ have _ mer - cy.

All

Ký - ri - e, e - lé - i - son. Ký - ri - e, e - lé - i - son.
Lord, _____ have _ mer - cy. Lord, _____ have _ mer - cy.

(in the Ambrosian style)

608

Glo - ry to God in the high - est, and peace to his

353

peo-ple on earth. Lord God, heav-en - ly King, al-might - y

God and Fa - ther, we wor-ship you,

we give you thanks, we praise you for your glo - ry.

Lord Je - sus Christ, on - ly Son_____ of the

Fa - ther, Lord God, Lamb of God,

you take a - way the sin of the world: have mer -

cy _ on us; you are seat-ed at the right hand of the Fa -

ther, re-ceive our prayer. For you a-lone are the Ho-ly One,

you a-lone are the Lord, you a-lone are the Most High,

Je - sus Christ,_____

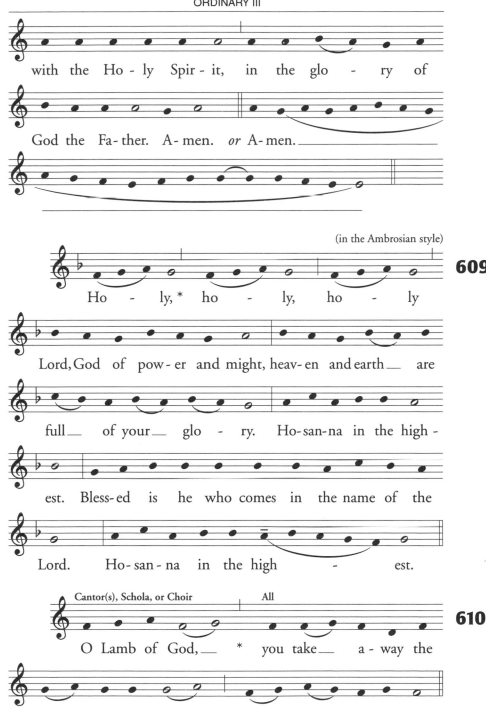

with the Ho-ly Spir-it, in the glo-ry of

God the Fa-ther. A-men. *or* A-men.

(in the Ambrosian style)

609

Ho - ly,* ho - ly, ho - ly

Lord, God of pow-er and might, heav-en and earth are

full of your glo-ry. Ho-san-na in the high-

est. Bless-ed is he who comes in the name of the

Lord. Ho-san-na in the high - est.

Cantor(s), Schola, or Choir   All

610

O Lamb of God,__ * you take__ a-way the

sins__ of the world,__ have__ mer-cy on us.

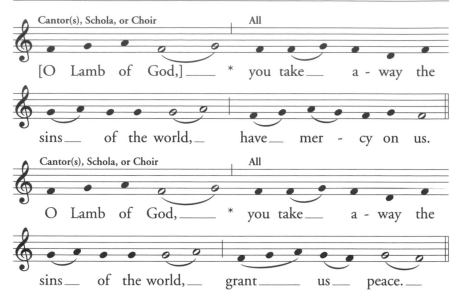

Cantor(s), Schola, or Choir — All

[O Lamb of God,]__ * you take__ a - way the sins__ of the world,__ have__ mer - cy on us.

Cantor(s), Schola, or Choir — All

O Lamb of God,__ * you take__ a - way the sins__ of the world,__ grant__ us__ peace.__

This setting of the Litany for the Breaking of the Bread is performed thus:

The first petition is sung; the second is sung as many times and with as many invocations of Christ as are necessary to accompany the breaking and pouring of the elements; the last petition is reserved for the very end of the Fraction Rite. To the tune within the brackets of the second petition, the following invocations may be sung:

O Bread of Life	O Pledge of Life
O Prince of peace	O Lord of lords
O risen Lord	O Lasting Light
O Word of Life	O Font of love
O Word made flesh	O Saving God
O King of Kings	O Son of God

IV

(based on Kyrie XII)

611 VIII

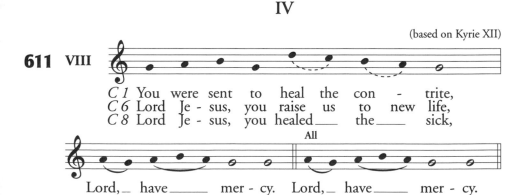

C 1 You were sent to heal the con - trite,
C 6 Lord Je - sus, you raise us to new life,
C 8 Lord Je - sus, you healed__ the__ sick,

All

Lord,_ have__ mer - cy. Lord,_ have__ mer - cy.

C 1 You came to call sin - ners,
C 6 Lord Je - sus, you for - give us our sins,
C 8 Lord Je - sus, you for - gave sin - ners,

All
Christ, have mer - cy. Christ, have mer - cy.

C 1 You plead for us at the right hand of the Fa - ther,
C 6 Lord Je - sus, you feed us with your bod - y and [your] blood,
C 8 (See next system.)

C 8 Lord Je - sus, you give us your-self to heal us and bring us strength,

All
Lord,_____ have mer - cy. Lord,_____ have mer - cy.

(based on Kyrie XII)

VIII

612

C 2 Lord Je - sus, you came to gather the nations into the
C 3 Lord Je - sus, you are might - y
C 4 Lord Je - sus, you came to reconcile us to one an -
C 7 Lord Je - sus, you have shown us the

peace of God's king - dom: Lord,__ have__
God and Prince of Peace:
other and to the Fa - ther:
way to the Fa - ther:

All
mer - cy. Lord,__ have__ mer - cy.

357

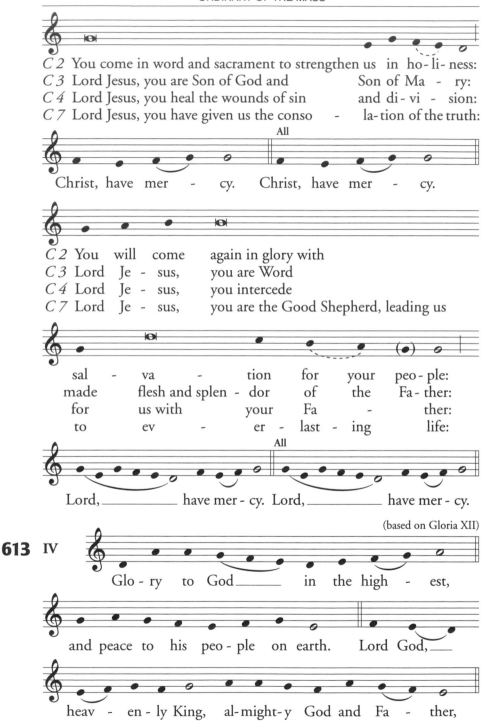

C 2 You come in word and sacrament to strengthen us in ho-li-ness:
C 3 Lord Jesus, you are Son of God and Son of Ma - ry:
C 4 Lord Jesus, you heal the wounds of sin and di - vi - sion:
C 7 Lord Jesus, you have given us the conso - la-tion of the truth:

All

Christ, have mer - cy. Christ, have mer - cy.

C 2 You will come again in glory with
C 3 Lord Je - sus, you are Word
C 4 Lord Je - sus, you intercede
C 7 Lord Je - sus, you are the Good Shepherd, leading us

sal - va - tion for your peo - ple:
made flesh and splen - dor of the Fa - ther:
for us with your Fa - ther:
to ev - er - last - ing life:

All

Lord, _____ have mer - cy. Lord, _____ have mer - cy.

(based on Gloria XII)

613 IV

Glo - ry to God _____ in the high - est,

and peace to his peo - ple on earth. Lord God, _____

heav - en - ly King, al-might-y God and Fa - ther,

614 VIII

(based on Sanctus XIII)

Ho - ly, * ho - ly, ho - ly Lord, God of pow-er and might, _ heav-en and earth _ are full of your glo - ry. Ho-san - na in the high - est. Bless-ed is he who comes _ in the name _____ of the Lord. Ho-san - na _____ in the high - est.

615 VI

(based on Agnus Dei, ad lib. II)

Cantor(s), Schola, or Choir   All

O Lamb _ of God, * you take a - way the sins of the world, have mer - cy on us. _____

Cantor(s), Schola, or Choir   All

[O Lamb _ of God,] * you take a - way the sins of the world, have mer - cy on us. _____

Cantor(s), Schola, or Choir   All

O Lamb _ of God, * you take a - way the

sins of the world, grant us peace.

Cantor(s), Schola, or Choir | **All**

616

Lamb of God, _____ * you take a - way the

sins of the world, have mer - cy on us.

Cantor(s), Schola, or Choir | **All**

[Lamb of God,] _____ * you take a - way the

sins of the world, have mer - cy on us.

Cantor(s), Schola, or Choir | **All**

Lamb of God, _____ * you take a - way the

sins of the world, grant us [your] peace.

These settings of the Litany for the Breaking of the Bread are performed thus:

The first petition is sung; the second is sung as many times and with as many invocations of Christ as are necessary to accompany the breaking and pouring of the elements; the last petition is reserved for the very end of the Fraction Rite. To the tune within the brackets of the second petition, the following invocations may be sung:

[O] Bread of Life	[O] Pledge of Life
[O] Prince of peace	[O] Lord of lords
[O] Risen Lord	[O] Lasting Light
[O] Word of Life	[O] Font of love
[O] Word made flesh	[O] Saving God
[O] King of Kings	[O] Son of God

V

617

Ký - ri - e, e - lé - i - son. Ký - ri - e, e - lé - i - son.
Lord, _____ have mer - cy. Lord, _____ have mer - cy.

Chri - ste, e - lé - i - son. Chri - ste, e - lé - i - son.
Christ, _____ have mer - cy. Christ, _____ have mer - cy.

Ký - ri - e, e - lé - i - son. Ký - ri - e, e - lé - i - son.
Lord, _____ have mer - cy. Lord, _____ have mer - cy.

618 I

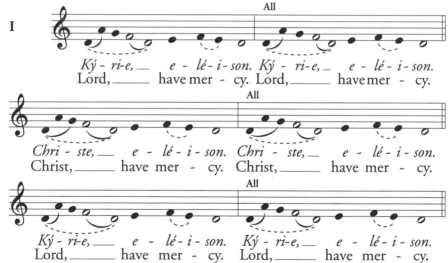

Ký - ri - e, ___ e - lé - i - son. Ký - ri - e, ___ e - lé - i - son.
Lord, _____ have mer - cy. Lord, _____ have mer - cy.

Chri - ste, ___ e - lé - i - son. Chri - ste, ___ e - lé - i - son.
Christ, _____ have mer - cy. Christ, _____ have mer - cy.

Ký - ri - e, ___ e - lé - i - son. Ký - ri - e, ___ e - lé - i - son.
Lord, _____ have mer - cy. Lord, _____ have mer - cy.

(based on Gloria X)

619 VIII

Glo - ry to God in the high - est,

and peace to his peo - ple on earth.

Lord God, heav - en - ly King,

al - might - y God and Fa - ther,

we wor-ship you, we give you thanks, we praise you

for your glo - ry.

Lord Je - sus Christ, on - ly Son of the Fa - ther,

Lord God, Lamb of God,

you take a - way the sin of the world:

have mer - cy on us;

you are seat - ed at the right hand of the

Fa - ther, re - ceive our prayer.

For you a-lone are the Ho - ly One,

you a - lone are the Lord,

you a-lone are the Most High, Je-sus Christ,

with the Ho - ly Spir - it, in the

glo - ry of God the Fa - ther.

A - men.

620 IV

(based on Sanctus X)

Ho - ly, * ho - ly, ho - ly

Lord, God of pow-er and might, heav - en and earth

are full of your glo - ry. Ho-san - na in the high -

364

- est. Bless- ed is he — who comes — in the

name — of the Lord. Ho-san - na in the high - est.

(based on Agnus Dei X)

IV **621**

Cantor(s), Schola, or Choir   All

O Lamb — of God, — * you take a - way the

sins — of the world, have mer - cy on us.

Cantor(s), Schola, or Choir   All

[O Lamb of God,] * you take a - way the sins — of the

world, have — mer - cy — on — us.

Cantor(s), Schola, or Choir   All

O Lamb — of God, — * you take a - way the

sins — of the world, grant — us — peace.

Cantor(s), Schola, or Choir   All **622**

Lamb of God, — * you take a - way the sins

Cantor(s), Schola, or Choir

of the world, have mer - cy on us. [Lamb of God,] — *

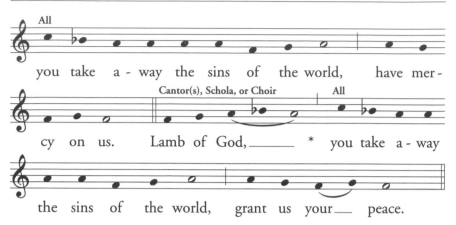

you take a - way the sins of the world, have mer -

Cantor(s), Schola, or Choir   All

cy on us. Lamb of God, _____ * you take a - way

the sins of the world, grant us your __ peace.

These settings of the Litany for the Breaking of the Bread are performed thus:

The first petition is sung; the second is sung as many times and with as many invocations of Christ as are necessary to accompany the breaking and pouring of the elements; the last petition is reserved for the very end of the Fraction Rite. To the tune within the brackets of the second petition, the following invocations may be sung:

[O] Bread of Life   [O] Pledge of Life
[O] Prince of peace   [O] Lord of lords
[O] Risen Lord   [O] Lasting Light
[O] Word of Life   [O] Font of love
[O] Word made flesh   [O] Saving God
[O] King of Kings   [O] Son of God

Nicene Creed (Latin)

Jubilate Deo (Credo III)

623 V

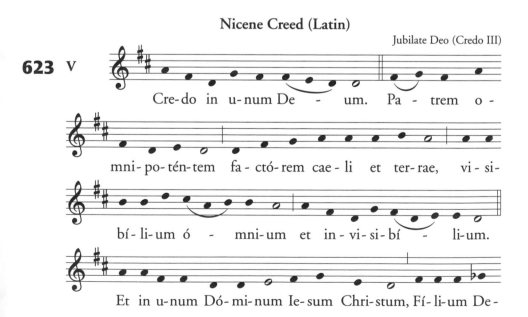

Cre-do in u-num De - um. Pa - trem o -

mni- po-tén-tem fa - ctó-rem cae - li et ter-rae, vi- si-

bí- li-um ó - mni-um et in - vi- si- bí - li-um.

Et in u-num Dó- mi-num Ie- sum Chri-stum, Fí- li-um De -

- i u - ni - gé - ni - tum. Et ex Pa - tre na - tum an - te

ó - mni - a sae - cu - la. De - um de De - o, lu - men de

lú - mi - ne, De - um ve - rum de De - o ve - ro. Gé - ni -

tum, non fa - ctum, con - sub - stan - ti - á - lem Pa - tri:

per quem ó - mni - a fa - cta sunt. Qui pro - pter nos hó - mi - nes

et prop - ter no - stram sa - lú - tem de - scén - dit de _ cae - lis.

Et in - car - ná - tus est de Spí - ri - tu San - cto

ex Ma - rí - a Vír - gi - ne, et ho - mo fa - ctus est.

Cru - ci - fí - xus é - ti - am pro no - bis

sub Pón - ti - o Pi - lá - to; pas - sus et se - púl - tus est.

Et re-sur-ré-xit tér-ti-a di-e, se-cún-dum Scrip-tú-
ras. Et a-scén - dit in cae - lum, se-det ad
déx-te-ram Pa - tris. Et í-te-rum ven-tú-rus est cum
gló-ri-a, ju-di-cá-re vi-vos et mór-tu-os, cu-ius re-
gni non e-rit fi-nis. Et in Spí-ri-tum San-ctum, Dó-mi-
num et vi-vi-fi-cán-tem: qui ex Pa-tre Fi - li - ó-que
pro - cé-dit. Qui cum Pa-tre et Fí-li-o si-mul a-do-rá-
tur et con-glo-ri-fi-cá-tur: qui lo-cú-tus est per
pro - phé-tas. Et u-nam, san-ctam, ca-thó-li-cam et a-pos-
tó-li-cam Ec-clé-si-am. Con-fí-te-or u-num bap - tís-

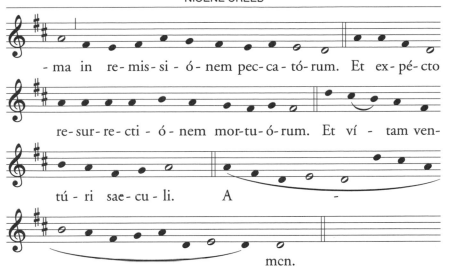

-ma in re-mis-si-ó-nem pec-ca-tó-rum. Et ex-pé-cto

re-sur-re-cti-ó-nem mor-tu-ó-rum. Et ví-tam ven-

tú-ri sae-cu-li. A-

men.

Nicene Creed

(based on Credo I)

624

IV

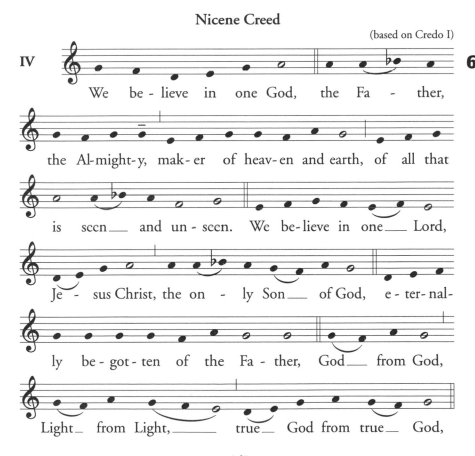

We be-lieve in one God, the Fa-ther,

the Al-might-y, mak-er of heav-en and earth, of all that

is seen and un-seen. We be-lieve in one Lord,

Je-sus Christ, the on-ly Son of God, e-ter-nal-

ly be-got-ten of the Fa-ther, God from God,

Light from Light, true God from true God,

be-got-ten, not__ made, one in Be-ing with the Fa-ther.

Through__ him all__ things__ were made. For us men and for

our sal-va-tion he came down from heav - en: by the

pow-er of the Ho - ly__ Spir-it he was born

of the Vir - gin Ma - ry and be-came_____ man.

For our sake he was cru-ci-fied un - der Pon -

tius Pi-late; he suf - fered, died, and was bur-ied.

On the third day he rose a-gain in ful-fill - ment

of the Scrip-tures; he as-cend-ed in-to heav-en and__ is

seat-ed at the right hand of the Fa-ther. He will come a-

-gain in glo - ry_____ to judge the liv - ing

and_ the dead, and his king-dom will have no end.

We be-lieve in the Ho-ly Spir - it,_____ the Lord,_ the

giv - er of life, who pro-ceeds from the Fa - ther and the

Son. With the Fa-ther and the Son he is wor-shipped and

glor - i - fied. He_ has spo-ken through the Proph - ets.

We be-lieve in one ho - ly cath - o - lic_____

and_ ap - os - tol - ic Church. We ac-know-ledge one bap-

tism for the for - give-ness of sins. We look for the

res - ur - rec - tion of the dead, and the life of the

world— to come. A - men.——

Apostles' Creed

(in the Ambrosian style)

625

I [We] be-lieve in God, the Fa-ther al-might-y,

cre-a-tor of heav-en and earth. I [We] be-lieve in Je-sus Christ,

his on-ly Son, our Lord. He was con-ceived by the pow-er of

the Ho-ly Spir-it and born of the Vir-gin Ma-ry. He suf-fered

un-der Pon-tius Pi-late, was cru-ci-fied, died, and was bur-ied.

He des-cend-ed to the dead. On the third day he rose a-

gain. He as-cend-ed in-to heav-en, and is seat-ed

at the right hand of the Fath-er. He will come a-gain

to judge the liv-ing and the dead. I [We] be-lieve in

the Ho - ly Spir- it,   the ho - ly cath-o - lic Church, the com-

mun-ion of saints, the for- give-ness of sins,   the res- ur- rec-

tion of the bod- y,   and the life ev - er - last - ing.

A - men.

Apostles' Creed in Question Form

(in the Ambrosian style)

626

Priest

Do you be- lieve in God?

People

We be-lieve in God, the Fa-ther al-might- y,   cre - a - tor

of heav- en and earth.

Priest

Do you be- lieve in Je - sus Christ?

People

We be- lieve in Je - sus Christ, his on - ly Son, our Lord.

He was con-ceived by the pow- er of the Ho - ly Spir- it

and born of the Vir-gin Ma-ry. He suf-fered un-der Pon-tius

Pi-late, was cru-ci-fied, died, and was bur-ied. He des-cend-ed

to the dead. On the third day he rose a-gain. He as-cend-ed

in-to heav-en, and is seat-ed at the right hand of the

Fath-er. He will come a-gain to judge the liv-ing and the dead.

Priest

Do you be-lieve in the Ho-ly Spir-it?

People

We be-lieve in the Ho-ly Spir-it, the ho-ly cath-

o-lic Church, the com-mun-ion of saints, the for-give-ness

of sins, the res-ur-rec-tion of the bod-y, and the

life ev-er-last-ing. A - men.

COMMON TONES

I. Doxologies
for the Processional Chants in the Eight Modes

I — **627**

Give glo - ry to the Fa-ther, and to the Son, and to

the **Ho** - ly **Spir** - it: * *as* *it* was in the

I a

be-**gin** - ning, **is** now, * and will be for *ev-er.* **A** - men.

I a 2 — **I g**

be for *ev-er.* **A** - men.___ be for *ev-er.* **A** - men.

I g 2 — **I g 4**

be for *ev-er.* **A** - men.___ be for *ev-er.* **A** - men.

I f — **I D 2**

be for *ev-er.* **A** - men.___ be for *ev-er.* **A** - men.

II — **628**

Glo - ry to the Fa-ther, and to the Son, and to

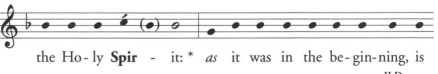

the Ho - ly **Spir** - it: * *as* it was in the be-gin-ning, is

II D

now, * and will be for ev - er. **A** - men.

631

V

Glo - ry to the Fa- ther, and to the Son, and to the Ho- ly **Spir** - it: * *as* it was in the be - gin-ning, **is** now, * and will be for **ev** - er. **A** - men.

632

VI

Give *glo* - ry to the Fa- ther, and to the Son, and to the Ho- *ly* **Spir** - it: * *as* *it* was in the be- gin-ning, *is* **now,** * and will be *for* *ev - er.* **A** - men.

633

VII

Glo - *ry* to the Fa- ther, and to the Son, and to the **Ho** - ly **Spir** - it: * *as* *it* was in the be- **gin** - ning, **is** now, * and will be for **ev** - er. **A** - men. for **ev** - er. **A** - men.

634 VIII

Glo - ry to the Fa - ther, and to the Son, and to the Ho - ly **Spir** - it: * *as* it was in the be - gin-ning, is **now,** * and will be for *ev - er.* **A** - men.

be for *ev - er.* **A** - men.

II. Alleluias at the End of Processional Antiphons
for the Easter Season (unless otherwise given)

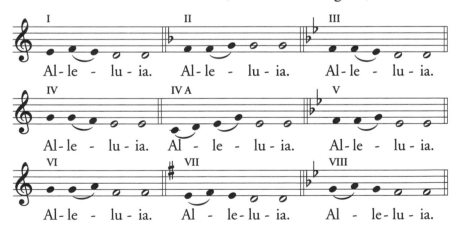

Appendix

I. The Rite of Sprinkling

Outside the Easter Season

Psalm 51 (50V):7

VII · 635

Lord, — cleanse me from my sin, * and I — will be pur-er — than — gush - ing wa-ter; Lord, — scour and purge — me and — I shall — be bright - er — than snow.

Psalm 51 (50V):1–3, 8

℣ 1 *Have* — *mer* - cy on me, O God, ac-cord-ing **to** your **stead**-fast love; * ac-cord-ing to your a-bun-dant mer-cy blot out **my** trans-**gres** - sions. —

According to the time available, repeat the antiphon after each of the following verses.

2 *Wash* me thoroughly **fróm** my in**iquity**, *
and **cléanse** me **from** my sin.

3 *For I* **knów** my trans**gres**sions, *
and my sin is **éver** be**fore** me.

4 *Let me* hear **jóy** and **glad**ness; *
let the bones that **yóu** have **crushed** rejoice.

During the Easter Season

Cf. Daniel 3:78–79

636 I a 3

Springs of wa - ter, *and all that move___ in the wa - ter,

sing a hymn of praise _ to God, ___ al - le - lu - ia.

Psalm 118 (117V):1, 6, 21, 28

℣ 1 O *give*___ thanks to the **Lord,** for **he** is good; *

his stead-fast love en - *dures for* - **ev** - er! ___

According to the time available, repeat the antiphon after each of the following verses.

2 *With the LORD* on my **síde** I do **not** fear. *
What can *mòrtals* **do** to me?

3 *I thank* you that **yóu** have **an**swered me *
and have become *mỳ salva*tion.

4 *You* are my God, and **Í** will give **thanks** to you; *
you are my God, I *wìll extol* you.

II. The Universal Prayer

637 A

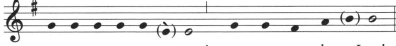

† we pray to the Lord:

℟ Hear our prayer, Lord, hear our prayer.

638 B

† to the Lord_ we pray:

℟ Hear our prayer, Lord, ____ hear our prayer.

C **639**
† to the Lord ___ we ___ pray: ___

℟ Christ, hear ____ us, Christ, ___ hear ___ us.

D **640**
† to the Lord ___ we pray: ___

℟ Lord, _____ have mer - cy.

E **641**
† to the Lord we pray: ___

℟ Hear _____ us, O Christ. ___

F **642**
† to the Lord we pray: ___

℟ Ký - ri - e, e - lé - i - son.

643 G

† we pray— to the Lord:

℟ Ký - ri - e, e - lé - i - son.

644 H

† we pray— to the Lord:

℟ Grant this, e - ter - nal and al – might - y God.

III. Communion Chants

Psalm 34 (33V) may substituted at any Mass in place of the communion antiphon and its psalm, as either a responsorial psalm with a threefold alleluia as its antiphon (see Tone I below) or as a responsorial psalm with its own antiphon (see Tone 2 below). Other suitable communion chants are listed after Tone 2.

Tone 1

Mozarabic (Old Spanish)

645

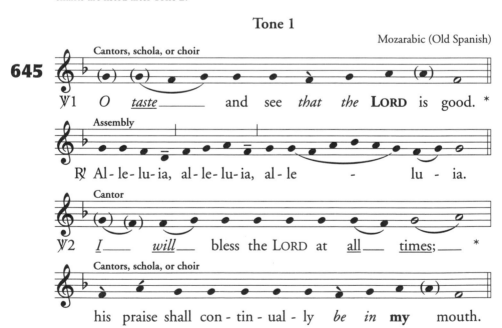

Cantors, schola, or choir

℣1 O taste____ and see *that* *the* **LORD** is good. *

Assembly

℟ Al - le - lu - ia, al - le - lu - ia, al - le – lu - ia.

Cantor

℣2 I____ *will*____ bless the LORD at all___ times;___ *

Cantors, schola, or choir

his praise shall con - tin - ual - ly *be* *in* **my** mouth.

℟ Al- le- lu- ia, al- le- lu- ia, al- le - lu - ia.

3   *My soul* makes its boast in the LORD; *
    lèt thé humble *hèar and* **be** glad.

4   *O mag*nify the LORD with me, *
    ànd lét us exalt his *nàme togeth*er.

5   *I sought* the LORD, and he answered me, *
    ànd délivered me *fròm all* **my** fears.

6   *Look* to him, and be radiant; *
    sò yóur faces shall *nèver* **be** ashamed.

7   *This poor* soul cried, and was heard by the LORD, *
    ànd wás saved from *èvery* **trou**ble.

8   *The an*gel of the LORD encamps around those who fear him, *
    ànd de*liv*ers them.

9   *O taste* and see that the LORD is good; *
    hàppý are those who take *rèfuge* **in** him.

10 *O fear* the LORD, you his holy ones, *
    fòr thóse who fear *hìm have* **no** want.

11 *The young* lions suffer want and hunger, *
    bùt thóse who seek the LORD *làck no* **good** thing.

12 *Come,* O children, listen to me; *
    Ì wíll teach you the *fèar of* **the** LORD.

13 *Which* of you desires life, *
    ànd cóvets many days *tò en***joy** good?

14 *Keep your* tongue from evil, *
    ànd yóur lips from *spèaking* **de**ceit.

15 *Depart* from evil, and do good; *
    sèek péace, *ànd pur***sue** it.

16 *The eyes* of the LORD are on the righteous, *
    ànd hís ears are o*pèn to* **their** cry.

17 *The face* of the LORD is against evildoers, *
    tò cút off the remembrance of *thèm from* **the** earth.

18 *When the* righteous cry for help, the LORD hears, *
    ànd réscues them from *àll their* **trou**bles.

19 *The LORD* is near to the brokenhearted, *
    ànd sáves the *crùshed in* **spir**it.

20 *Many* are the afflictions of the righteous, *
    bùt thé LORD rescues *thèm from* **them** all.

21 *He keeps* all their bones; *
    nòt óne of them *will be* **bro**ken.

22 *Evil* brings death to the wicked, *
    ànd thóse who hate the rightèous *will* **be** condemned.

23 *The LORD* redeems the life of his servants; *
    nòne óf those who take refuge in *hìm will* **be** condemned.

The following doxology may be added at will and is sung by the cantors, schola, or choir:

Glo - ry to the Fa-ther, and to the Son, and to the

Ho - ly Spir - it:_____ * as it was in the be-

gin-ning, is now, * and will be for ev - er. A - men.

All sing the threefold Alleluia for the last time.

Tone II

This tone may be used, especially during Lent, with the response *Taste and See*, as indicated.

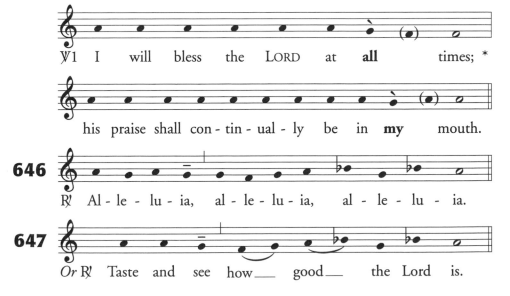

℣1 I will bless the LORD at **all** times; *

his praise shall con - tin - ual - ly be in **my** mouth.

646 ℟ Al - le - lu - ia, al - le - lu - ia, al - le - lu - ia.

647 *Or* ℟ Taste and see how___ good___ the Lord is.

2   My soul makes its boast in **thè** LORD; *
     let the humble hear and **bè** glad.

3   O magnify the LORD **wìth** me, *
     and let us exalt his name to**gèth**er.

4   I sought the LORD, and he **àn**swered me, *
     and delivered me from **àll** my fears.

5   Look to him, and be **rà**diant; *
     so your faces shall never **bè** ashamed.

6   This poor soul cried, and was heard by **thè** LORD, *
     and was saved from every **tròu**ble.

7   The angel of the LORD encamps around those who **fèar** him, *
     and de**lì**vers them.

8   O taste and see that the **LÒRD** is good; *
     happy are those who take refuge **ìn** him.

9   O fear the LORD, you his **hò**ly ones, *
     for those who fear him have **nò** want.

10   The young lions suffer want and **hùn**ger, *
     but those who seek the LORD lack **nò** good thing.

11   Come, O children, listen **tò** me; *
     I will teach you the fear of **thè** LORD.

12   Which of you de**sìre**s life, *
     and covets many days to en**jòy** good?

13   Keep your tongue from **èvil**, *
     and your lips from speaking **dè**ceit.

14   Depart from evil, and **dò** good; *
     seek peace, and pur**sùe** it.

15   The eyes of the LORD are on the **rìght**eous, *
     and his ears are open to **thèir** cry.

16   The face of the LORD is against evil**dòe**rs, *
     to cut off the remembrance of them from **thè** earth.

17   When the righteous cry for help, the **LÒRD** hears, *
     and rescues them from all their **tròu**bles.

18   The LORD is near to the broken**hèart**ed, *
     and saves the crushed in **spìr**it.

19   Many are the afflictions of the **rìght**eous, *
     but the LORD rescues them **fròm** them all.

20   He keeps **àll** their bones; *
     not one of them will be **brò**ken.

21   Evil brings death to the **wìck**ed, *
     and those who hate the righteous will **bè** condemned.

22   The LORD redeems the life of his **sèr**vants; *
      none of those who take refuge in him will **bè** condemned.

The following doxology may be added as desired:

Glory to the Father, and to the Son, and to the Holy **Spìr**it: *
as it was in the beginning, **ìs** now, and will be for ever. **À**men.

Other Chants for Communion

Psalm 23 (22V)
211, with the antiphon *I am the living bread*, **210**.

The Canticle of Mary
414, with the Antiphon *My soul glorifies his holy name*, **413**.

Where We Live as Friends in Loving Kindness
123, with its proper antiphon.

IV. Miscellaneous Chants

1. FOR BENEDICTION OF THE BLESSED SACRAMENT

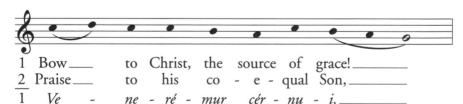

III

648

1 Come, a - dore this___ won-drous pres - ence;
2 Glo - ry be to___ God the Fa - ther,

649

1 *Tan - tum er - go___ sa - cra - mén - tum*
2 *Ge - ni - tó - ri___ ge - ni - tó - que*

1 Bow___ to Christ, the source of grace!___
2 Praise___ to his co - e - qual Son,___
1 *Ve - ne - ré - mur cér - nu - i,___*
2 *Laus___ et iu - bi - lá - ti - o,___*

386

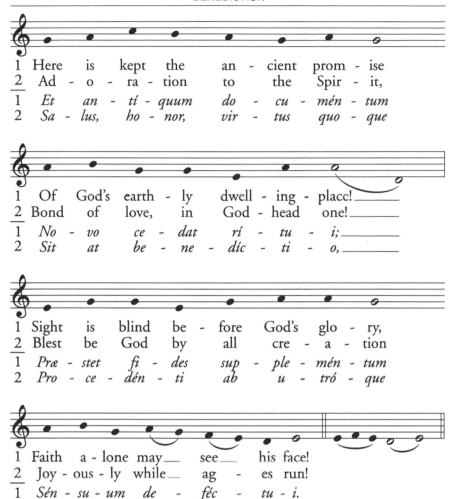

1 Here is kept the an - cient prom - ise
2 Ad - o - ra - tion to the Spir - it,
1 Et an - tí - quum do - cu - mén - tum
2 Sa - lus, ho - nor, vir - tus quo - que

1 Of God's earth - ly dwell - ing - placc!
2 Bond of love, in God - head one!
1 No - vo ce - dat rí - tu - i;
2 Sit at be - ne - díc - ti - o,

1 Sight is blind be - fore God's glo - ry,
2 Blest be God by all cre - a - tion
1 Præ - stet fi - des sup - ple - mén - tum
2 Pro - ce - dén - ti ab u - tró - que

1 Faith a - lone may see his face!
2 Joy - ous - ly while ag - es run!
1 Sén - su - um de - féc - tu - i.
2 Com - par sit lau - dá - ti - o. A - men.

2. FOR INVOKING THE HOLY SPIRIT

Veni Creator Spiritus

650 VIII

1 Ve - ni, cre - á - tor— Spí - ri - tus, men - tes tu - ó-
2 Qui dí - ce - ris Pa - rá - cli - tus, al - tís - si - mi
3 Tu sep - ti - fór - mis— mú - ne - re, dígi - tus pa - tér-
4 Ac - cén - de— lu - men— sén - si - bus, in - fún - de a - mó-
5 Hos tem re - pél - las— lón - gi - us pa - cém - que do-
6 Per te sci - á - mus— da Pa - trem nos - cá - mus at-

1 rum— ví - si - ta, im - ple— su - pér - na— grá - ti-
2 do - num De - i, fons vi - vus,— i - gnis,— cá - ri-
3 nae— déx - te - rae, tu ri - te— pro - mís - sum Pa-
4 rem— cór - di - bus, in - fír - ma— nó - stri cór - po-
5 nes— pró - ti - nus; duc - tó - re— sic— te— práe - vi-
6 que— Fí - li - um, te - que u - tri - ús - que— Spí - ri-

1 a, quae— tu cre - ás - ti,——— péc - to - ra.
2 tas, et— spi - ri - tá - lis——— únc - ti - o.
3 tris ser - mó - ne— di - tans——— gút - tu - ra.
4 ris, vir - tú - te— fir - mans——— pér - pe - ti.
5 o, vi - té - mus— o - mne——— nó - xi - um.
6 tum cre - dá - mus— o - mni——— tém - po - re. A - men. —

℣. Emítte Spíritum tuum et creabúntur.

℟. Et renovábis faciem terrae.

Orémus.

Deus, qui corda fidélium Sancti Spíritus illustratióne docuísti, † da nobis in eodem Spíritu recta sápere, * et de eius semper consolatióne gaudére. Per Christum Dóminum nostrum. ℟. Amen.

Come, O Spirit Creator

VIII   651

1 Come, O Spir-it cre-a-tor, come to us.
2 Come, O you who are called the Par-a-clete.
3 Sev-en heav-en-ly gifts are yours to give;
4 Kin-dle dis-cern-ing light in all our minds;
5 Keep our en-e-mies far from hurt-ing us.
6 Spir-it, give us to know our Fa-ther God.

1 Vis-it us with your trans-form-ing love.
2 Come, O most high Gift of God Most High,
3 yours, the touch of God's ca-ress-ing hand.
4 Pour the pow'r to love in all our hearts;
5 Nev-er cease to bring peace near to us.
6 Spir-it, help us rec-og-nize the Son.

1 Re-fash-ion all of those you made with so much care.
2 O Font of liv-ing wa-ter, Fire, and Char-i-ty,
3 You are the ver-y gift the Fa-ther prom-ised us:
4 And strength-en all our bod-ies, lest dis-ease and sin
5 With you as guide be-fore us, light-en-ing our way,
6 And may you al-ways show your-self in ways that speak

1 Fill and re-fresh us with grace___ that o-ver-flows.
2 Oil which a-noints us as proph-ets and roy-al priests.
3 Lend___ our lyr-ics the lan-guag-es of your love.
4 Steal from your tem-ples the signs that you dwell with-in.
5 We shall be safe from all harms___ that might be-fall.
6 To our faith that you are the Love of Both of Them.

℣. Come, Holy Spirit, fill the hearts of your faithful.
℟. And kindle in them the fire of your love.

℣. Send forth your Spirit and they shall be created.

℟. And you will renew the face of the earth.

Let us pray.

Lord, by the light of the Holy Spirit you have taught the hearts of your faithful. In the same Spirit help us to relish what is right and always rejoice in your consolation. We ask this through Christ our Lord.

3. SONGS OF PRAISE AND THANKSGIVING

Te Deum Laudamus

Jubilate Deo

652 III

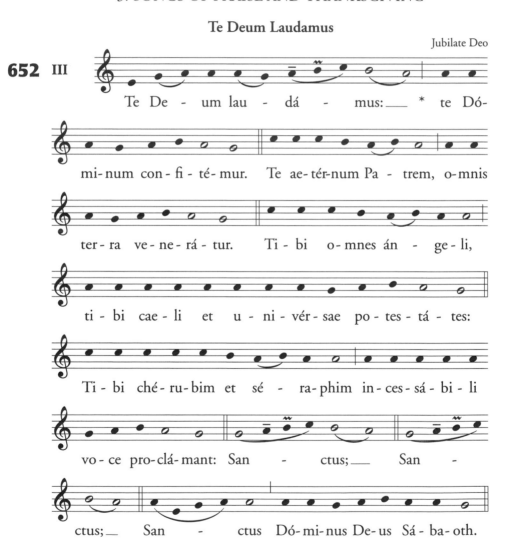

Te De - um lau - dá - mus: ___ * te Dó-
mi-num con - fi - té- mur. Te ae-tér-num Pa - trem, o-mnis
ter- ra ve-ne-rá - tur. Ti - bi o- mnes án - ge- li,
ti - bi cae - li et u - ni - vér- sae po- tes - tá - tes:
Ti - bi ché - ru- bim et sé - ra- phim in-ces-sá - bi - li
vo- ce pro-clá- mant: San - ctus; ___ San -
ctus; ___ San - ctus Dó-mi-nus De- us Sá - ba- oth.

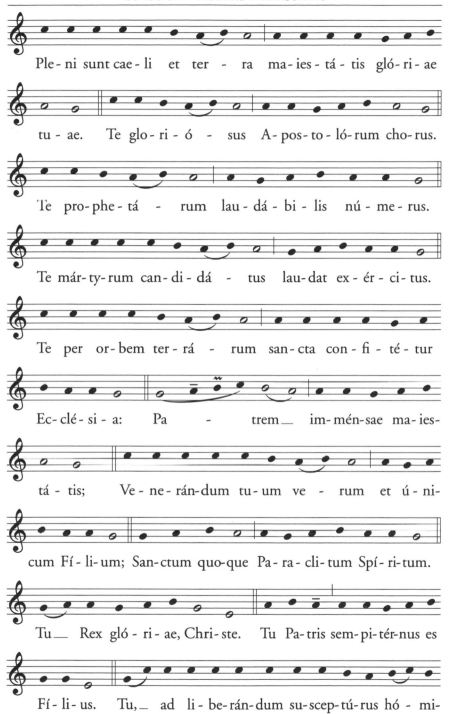

Ple-ni sunt cae-li et ter - ra ma-ies-tá-tis gló-ri-ae
tu - ae. Te glo-ri-ó - sus A-pos-to-ló-rum cho-rus.
Te pro-phe-tá - rum lau-dá-bi-lis nú-me-rus.
Te már-ty-rum can-di-dá - tus lau-dat ex-ér-ci-tus.
Te per or-bem ter-rá - rum san-cta con-fi-té-tur
Ec-clé-si-a: Pa - trem im-mén-sae ma-ies-
tá - tis; Ve-ne-rán-dum tu-um ve - rum et ú-ni-
cum Fí-li-um; San-ctum quo-que Pa-ra-cli-tum Spí-ri-tum.
Tu Rex gló-ri-ae, Chri-ste. Tu Pa-tris sem-pi-tér-nus es
Fí-li-us. Tu, ad li-be-rán-dum su-scep-tú-rus hó-mi-

-nem, non hor-ru - í - sti Vír-gi-nis ú - te-rum. Tu,__ de-ví-cto

mor-tis a - cú - le - o, a - pe-ru - í - sti cre-dén-ti-bus

re-gna cae-ló-rum. Tu__ ad déx-te-ram De-i se - des__

in gló-ri - a Pa-tris. Iu-dex cré-de-ris es-se ven-tú - rus.

Te__ er-go quáe-su-mus, tu - is fá-mu-lis súb - ve-ni,

quos pre-ti - ó - so sán-gui-ne re-de-mís - ti. Ae-tér -

na__ fac__ cum san-ctis tu - is in gló-ri - a

nu - me-rá - ri.

The concluding part of the hymn may be omitted:

653 III

Sal-vum__ fac pó-pu-lum tu-um, Dó-mi-ne,__

et bé - ne-dic he-re - di-tá-ti__ tu - ae.

Et re - ge é - os,___ et ex - tól - le il - los

us-que in ae-tér - num. Per sín-gu-los di - es,___

be-ne-dí - ci-mus te: Et lau-dá-mus no-men tu-um in

sáe - cu-lum, et in sáe-cu-lum sáe-cu - li. Dig-ná-re,

Dó-mi-ne, di - e i - sto___ si- ne pec-cá-to nos cu-sto-

dí - re. Mi-se-ré-re no-stri, Dó - mi-ne, mi-se-ré-re no-stri.

Fi - at mi-se - ri-cór-di - a tu-a, Dó-mi-ne, su - per nos

quem-ád-mo-dum spe-rá - vi-mus in te. In te,___ Dó -

mi-ne, spe - rá - vi:___ non con - fún -

dar___ in æ - tér - num.

℣. Benedicámus Patrem et Fílium cum Sancto Spíritu.

℞. Laudémus et superexaltémus eum in sáecula.

℣. Benedíctus es, Dómine, in firmaménto caeli.

℞. Et laudábilis, et gloriósus, et superexaltátus in sáecula.

℣. Dómine, exáudi oratiónem meam.

℞. Et clamor meus ad te véniat.

Orémus.

Deus, cuius misericórdiae non est númerus et bónitas infinítus est thesáurus, † piísimae maiestáti tuae pro collátis donis grátias ágimus, tuam semper cleméntiam exortántes, * ut qui peténtibus postuláta concédis, eósdem non déserens, ad práemia futúra dispónas. Per Christum Dóminum nostrum. ℞. Amen.

You Are God: We Praise You

654 III

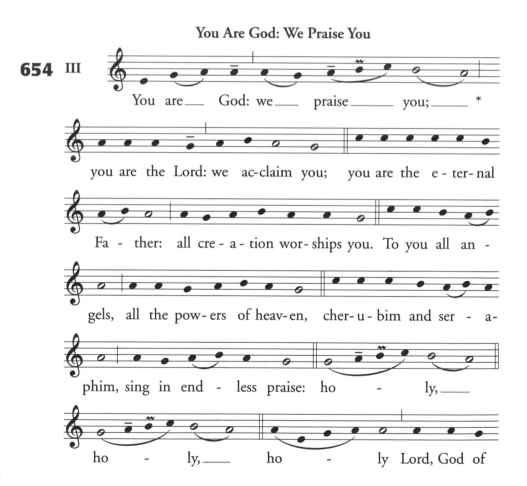

You are God: we praise you; *
you are the Lord: we ac-claim you; you are the e - ter-nal
Fa - ther: all cre - a - tion wor-ships you. To you all an -
gels, all the pow-ers of heav-en, cher-u-bim and ser - a-
phim, sing in end - less praise: ho - ly, __
ho - ly, __ ho - ly Lord, God of

pow-er and might, heav-en and earth_ are full of your glo-ry.

The glor-ious com - pan-y of a-pos-tles praise you.

The no-ble fel - low-ship of proph-ets praise you.

The white-robed ar - my of mar-tyrs praise you.

Through-out the world_ the ho-ly Church ac-claims you:

Fa - ther,_ of maj-es-ty un-bound-ed,

your true and on - ly Son, wor-thy of all wor-ship,

and the Ho-ly Spir-it, ad-vo-cate and guide. You,_

Christ, are the king of glo-ry, the e-ter-nal Son of the

Fa-ther. When_ you be-came man to set_ us free

you did not spurn the Vir-gin's womb. You__ o-ver-came the

sting__ of death, and o-pened the king-dom of heav-en to

all be-liev-ers. You__ are seat-ed at God's__ right hand in

glo-ry. We be-lieve that you will come and be our judge.

Come__ then, Lord, and help your peo - ple,__ bought with

the price of your own blood, and__ bring__ us__

with your saints to glo-ry ev-er-last - ing.

The concluding part of the hymn may be omitted:

655

Save your__ peo-ple, O Lord,__ and bless__ your__

in - her - i-tance. Gov-ern and up-hold__ them

now__ and al - ways. Day by day we bless__ you.__

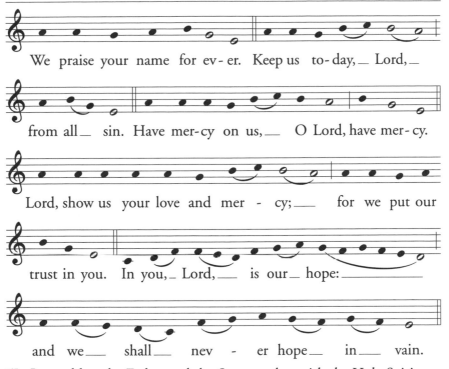

We praise your name for ev-er. Keep us to-day,— Lord,—

from all— sin. Have mer-cy on us,— O Lord, have mer-cy.

Lord, show us your love and mer - cy;—— for we put our

trust in you. In you,— Lord,—— is our— hope:——

and we— shall— nev - er hope— in — vain.

℣. Let us bless the Father and the Son together with the Holy Spirit.

℟. Let us praise and exalt Him for ever.

℣. Blessed are you, Lord, in the firmament of heaven.

℟. And praiseworthy and glorious and exalted for ever.

℣. Lord, hear my prayer.

℟. And let my cry come to you.

Let us pray.

O God whose mercies are without number and whose treasure of goodness is limitless, we thank your gracious majesty for the gifts we have received. We continually appeal to your mercy to grant petitioners what they ask for. Never abandon them but prepare them for your future rewards through Christ our Lord. ℟. Amen.

To You Belongs Our Praise

656

I

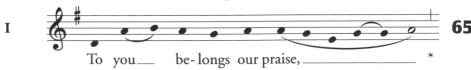
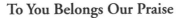

To you— be-longs our praise,———— *

to you we sing hymns, to you we give glo-ry, God the Fa-ther and God the Son and God the Ho-ly Spir-it, for ev - er and ev - er. A - men.

We Give You Praise

(in the Ambrosian style)

657 VII

We give you praise,*al-might-y Lord, who sit a-bove the cher-u-bim and the ser-a-phim; all the an-gels and arch-an-gels bless you; the pro-phets and a-pos-tles give you praise. We give you praise, Lord, rev-'rent-ly pray -

- ing to you— who came to free the world from sin.

We in-voke you as our great Re-deem -

- er, whom the Fa-ther sent as shep-herd of the sheep.

You are the Sav-ior con-ceived by the Spir -

- it, and born of the Bless-ed Vir-gin Ma-ry.

Use this final phrase after Communion only

Of this most ho-ly chal-ice we have all___

par-tak - en; from ev-'ry sin and fail-ing free us al-ways.

4. MARIAN ANTIPHONS

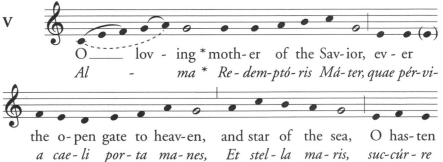

658

O___ lov - ing *moth-er of the Sav-ior, ev - er
*Al - ma * Re-demp-tó-ris Má-ter, quae pér-vi-*

the o-pen gate to heav-en, and star of the sea, O has-ten
a cae-li por-ta ma-nes, Et stel-la ma-ris, suc-cúr-re

to aid us, who, though fall-ing strive to rise a-gain.
ca-dén-ti súr-ge-re qui cu-rat pó-pu-lo:

Bear-ing, as a vir-gin, while na-ture stood in awe, your own
Tu quae gen-u-í-sti, na-tú-ra mi-rán-te, tu-um

Mak-er, your own ho-ly Lord,___ ev-er vir-gin, af-ter
san-ctum Gen-i-tó-rem:___ Vir-go pri-us ac po-

as be-fore, when the mouth of Gab-ri-el ut-tered that
sté-ri-us, Ga-bri-é-lis ab o-re su-mens il-

great "A-ve," O take pit-y___ on us sin-ners.
lud A-ve, pec-ca-tó-rum___ mi-se-ré-re.

659 VI

We greet you, Ma-ry, heav-en's queen and la-dy of
*A-ve Re-gí-na cae-ló-rum, * A-ve Dó-mi-*

the choirs of an-gels, root of Jes-se, gate of morn-
na An-ge-ló-rum: Sal-ve ra-dix, sal-ve por-

ing through whom the world's true light has dawned.
ta, Ex qua mun-do lux est or-ta:

400

Re-joice, O vir-gin most re-nowned, beau-ti - ful be-yond
Gau - de Vir - go glo - ri - ó - sa, Su - per o - mnes spe -

all oth - ers. Hail to you, queen o most love - ly,
ci - ó - sa: Va - le, o val - de de - có - ra,

pray for us and with us to Christ our sav - ior.
Et pro no - bis Chri-stum ex - ó - ra.

V **660**

Hail, Ma- ry, moth-er * and queen of ten-der mer - cy,
*Sal - ve, Re - gí - na, * ma - ter mi - se - ri - cór-di-ae:*

our life, our com - fort, and our hope, we hail__ you.
Vi - ta dul - cé - do, et spes no - stra, sal - ve.

From this for-eign land Eve's sons and daugh-ters cry to you.
Ad te cla - má-mus, éx - su - les, fí - li - i He-vae.

So lost, so full of fear, we mourn, we grieve, we sigh from
Ad te su - spi - rá-mus, ge - mén - tes et flen-tes in

this tear-ful vale of ex - ile. Ah, then, our help, our
hac la - cri - má-rum val - le. E - ia er - go, Ad-

401

ad - vo-cate and guide, turn now to us the gaze of your all-
- vo - cá - ta no - stra, il - los tu - os mi - se - ri - cór - des

lov - ing eyes, so full of mer - cy. And Je - sus— your
ó - cu - los ad nos con - vér - te. Et Je - sum,— be-

Son, and Lord, your womb's most bless- ed fruit—show him to
ne - dí - ctum fruc - tum ven - tris tu - i, no - bis post

us when we com-plete our so - journ. O
hoc ex - sí - li - um o - stén - de. O

gen - tle, O lov - ing,
cle - mens, O pi - a,

O be-lov - ed, O Vir - gin Ma - ry.
O dul - cis Vir - go Ma - rí - a.

661 VII

As our place of pro-tec-tion we fly to you, *
*Sub tu - um prae-sí - di - um con-fú - gi-mus, **

God's own ho-ly Moth - er. Hear the prayers we put be-
san - cta De - i Gé - ni-trix; no-stras de - pre-ca-ti-

-fore __ you; in our need do not __ re-ject our sup-pli-
-ó - nes ne de-spí-ci-as __ in __ ne-ces-si-

ca - tions; but from all dan-gers that threat-en us free us
tá-ti-bus; sed a pe-rí-cu-lis cun - ctis lí-be-

now and al - ways, _____ Vir-gin ev-er
ra nos sem - per, _____ Vir-go glo-ri-

glor - ious __ and __ ev - er __ bless - ed.
ó - sa __ et __ be - ne - díc - ta.

During the Easter Season:

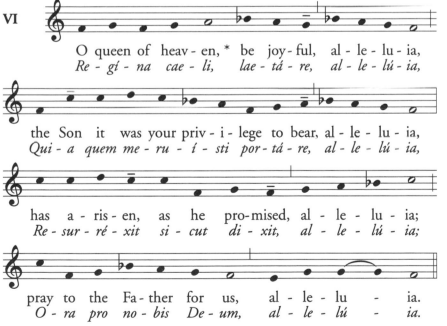

VI **662**

O queen of heav-en, * be joy-ful, al - le - lu - ia,
Re - gí - na cae - li, lae - tá - re, al - le - lú - ia,

the Son it was your priv - i - lege to bear, al - le - lu - ia,
Qui - a quem me - ru - í - sti por - tá - re, al - le - lú - ia,

has a - ris - en, as he pro-mised, al - le - lu - ia;
Re - sur - ré - xit si - cut di - xit, al - le - lú - ia;

pray to the Fa - ther for us, al - le - lu - ia.
O - ra pro no - bis De - um, al - le - lú - ia.

V. The Litany of the Saints for Solemn Occasions

I. Prayer to God

A

663

Cantor(s)

Lord, have mer - cy.
Christ, have mer - cy.
Lord, have mer - cy.

Assembly

Lord, have mer - cy.
Christ, have mer - cy.
Lord, have mer - cy.

or

664

Cantor(s)

Ký - ri - e, e - le - i - son.

Assembly

Ký - ri - e, e - le - i - son.

Cantor(s)

Chri - ste, e - le - i - son.

Assembly

Chri - ste, e - le - i - son.

Cantor(s)

Ký - ri - e, e - le - i - son.

Assembly

Ký - ri - e, e - le - i - son.

Or: B

665

God our Father in heav - en, ℟ have mer - cy on us.

or: ℟ mi - se - re - re no - bis.

God the Son, our redéemèr,   have mercy on us.
God the Holy Spírìt,   have mercy on us.
Holy Trinity, one Gód,   have mercy on us.

II. Invocation of the Saints

666

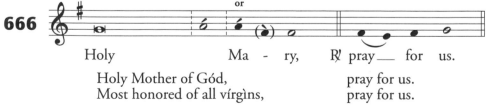

Holy Ma - ry, ℟ pray — for us.

Holy Mother of Gód,   pray for us.
Most honored of all vírgìns,   pray for us.

Saints Michael, Gabriel, and Ráphàel, pray for us.
All holy angels of Gód, pray for us.

PROPHETS AND ANCESTORS OF OUR FAITH

Holy Abraham, Moses, and Elíjàh, pray for us.
(Saint Zachary and Saint Elízàbeth, pray for us.)
Saint John the Báptìst, pray for us.
(Saint Joachim and Saint Ánn, pray for us.)
Saint Jósèph, pray for us.
All holy ancestors and próphèts, pray for us.

APOSTLES AND FOLLOWERS OF CHRIST

Saint Peter and Saint Pául, pray for us.
Saint Ándrèw, pray for us.
Saint John and Saint Jámes, pray for us.
Saint Thómàs, pray for us.
Saint Mátthèw, pray for us.
All holy apóstlès, pray for us.
Saint Lúke, pray for us.
Saint Márk, pray for us.
Saint Bárnàbas, pray for us.
Saint Mary Mágdàlene, pray for us.
(Saints Mary, Martha, and Lázàrus, pray for us.)
All holy disciples of the Lórd, pray for us.

MARTYRS

Saint Stéphèn, pray for us.
Saint Ignátìus [of Ántìoch], pray for us.
Saint Pólỳcarp, pray for us.
Saint Jústìn, pray for us.
Saint Láwrènce, pray for us.
Saint Cýprìan, pray for us.
Saint Bónìface, pray for us.
Saint Stánìslaus, pray for us.
Saint Thómàs [Béckèt], pray for us.
Saint John [Fisher]
    and Saint Thómàs [Móre], pray for us.
Saint Pául [Míkì], pray for us.
Saint Isaac [Jogues]
    and Saint Jóhn [de Brebéuf], pray for us.
Saint Pétèr [Chanél], pray for us.
Saint Chárlès [Lwángà], pray for us.
Saint Perpetua and Saint Felícìty, pray for us.
Saint Ágnès, pray for us.

Saint María [Goréttì],	pray for us.
All holy martyrs for Chríst,	pray for us.

BISHOPS AND DOCTORS

Saint Leo and Saint Grégòry,	pray for us.
Saint Ámbròse,	pray for us.
Saint Jeróme,	pray for us.
Saint Augústìne,	pray for us.
Saint Athanásìus,	pray for us.
Saint Basil and Saint Grégòry [Naziánzèn],	pray for us.
Saint Jóhn [Chrýsostòm],	pray for us.
Saint Mártìn,	pray for us.
Saint Pátrìck,	pray for us.
Saint Cyril and Saint Methódìus,	pray for us.
Saint Chárlès [Borroméò],	pray for us.
Saint Fráncìs [de Sáles],	pray for us.
Saint Pìus [the Ténth],	pray for us.
(St. Jóhn [Néumànn],	pray for us.)

PRIESTS AND RELIGIOUS

Saint Ánthòny,	pray for us.
Saint Bénèdict,	pray for us.
Saint Bérnàrd,	pray for us.
Saint Francis and Saint Dómìnic,	pray for us.
Saint Thómàs [Aquínàs],	pray for us.
Saint Ignátìus [Loyólà],	pray for us.
Saint Fráncìs [Xávìer],	pray for us.
Saint Víncènt [de Pául],	pray for us.
Saint John Márỳ [Viánnèy],	pray for us.
Saint Jóhn [Bóscò],	pray for us.
Saint Cáthèrine [of Siénà],	pray for us.
Saint Terésà [of Ávìla],	pray for us.
Saint Róse [of Límà],	pray for us.
(Saint Elizabeth Ánn [Sétòn],	pray for us.)
(Saint Frances Xávìer [Cabrínì],	pray for us.)

LAITY

Saint Lóuìs,	pray for us.
Saint Mónìca,	pray for us.
Saint Elízàbeth [of Húngàry],	pray for us.
(Saint Isidore and Saint María,	pray for us.)
All holy men and wómèn,	pray for us.

III. Invocations of Christ

A

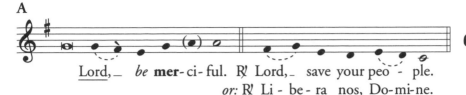

667

Lord,__ *be* mer-ci-ful. ℟ Lord,__ save your peo - ple.

or: ℟ Li - be - ra nos, Do-mi-ne.

Fròm *all* **ev**il,	Lord, save your people.
Fròm *every* sin,	Lord, save your people.
From an*gèr and* **ha**tred,	Lord, save your people.
From every *evìl inten*tion,	Lord, save your people.
From *èver*lasting death,	Lord, save your people.
By your *ìncar*nation,	Lord, save your people.
By your **birth**,	Lord, save your people.
By your bap*tìsm and* **fast**ing,	Lord, save your people.
By your *suffèrings* **and** cross,	Lord, save your people.
By your *dèath and* **bur**ial,	Lord, save your people.
By your risìng *to* **new** life,	Lord, save your people.
By your return in glory	
tò the **Fa**ther,	Lord, save your people.
By your gift of the *Hòly* **Spir**it,	Lord, save your people.
By your coming a*gàin in* **glo**ry,	Lord, save your people.

Or: B

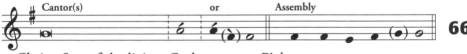

668

Christ, Son of the living God, ℟ have mer-cy on us.

or: ℟ mi - ser - re - re no-bis.

You came into this wórld,	have mercy on us.
You suffered for us on the cróss,	have mercy on us.
You died to sáve ùs,	have mercy on us.
You lay in the tómb,	have mercy on us.
You rose from the déad,	have mercy on us.
You returned in glory to the Fáthèr,	have mercy on us.
You sent the Holy Spirit	
upon the Apóstlès,	have mercy on us.
You are seated at the right hand	
of the Fáthèr,	have mercy on us.
You will come again to judge	
the living and the déad,	have mercy on us.

IV. Prayers for Various Needs

A

669

Lord, be merci-*ful* **to** us. ℟ Hear our prayer, Lord, hear our prayer.

or: ℟ Te ro - ga - mus, au - di nos.

Give us true *rè***pent**ance:	Hear our prayer, Lord...
Strengthen us in *yòur* **ser**vice:	Hear our prayer, Lord...
Reward with eternal life	
all who *dò* **good** to us:	Hear our prayer, Lord...
Bless the fruits of the earth	
and of *òur* **la**bor:	Hear our prayer, Lord...
(Bring rain to wa*tèr* **the** earth:	Hear our prayer, Lord...)

670 Or: **B**

Lord, show us *yòur* **kind**ness:	Hear our prayer, Lord...
Raise our thoughts and *dè***sires** to you:	Hear our prayer, Lord...
Save us from final *dàm***na**tion:	Hear our prayer, Lord...
Save our friends	
and all who *hàve* **helped** us:	Hear our prayer, Lord...
Grant eternal rest	
to all who have died *ìn* **the** faith:	Hear our prayer, Lord...
Spare us from disease, hun*gèr,* **and** war:	Hear our prayer, Lord...
(From the scourge *òf* **earth**quake:	Hear our prayer, Lord...)
(Bring rain to wa*tèr* **the** earth:	Hear our prayer, Lord...)
Bring all peoples together	
ìn **trust** and peace:	Hear our prayer, Lord...

671 **C** (always used)

Guide and protect *yòur* **ho**ly Church:	Hear our prayer, Lord...
Keep the pope and all the clergy	
in faithful service *tò* **your** Church:	Hear our prayer, Lord...
Bring all Christians together *ìn* **u**nity:	Hear our prayer, Lord...
Lead all peoples	
to the light of *thè* **Gos**pel:	Hear our prayer, Lord...

V. Conclusion

A (Simple Ending)

672

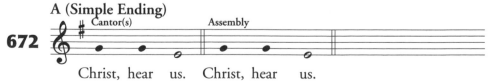

Christ, hear us. Christ, hear us.

or

673

Or: B (Solemn Ending)

674

675

or

Cantor(s)

A-gnus De - i, qui tol-lis pec-cá-ta mun-di,

Assembly

℟ mi-se-ré-re no - bis. *(three times)*

Cantor(s)   Assembly

Chri-ste, ___ au - di nos. Chri-ste, ___ au - di nos.

Cantor(s)   Assembly

Chri-ste, ex - áu - di nos. Chri-ste, ex - áu - di nos.

Cantor(s)   Assembly

Ký - ri - e, e - lé - i - son. Chri-ste, e - lé - i - son.

All

Ký - ri - e, ___ e - lé - i - son. ___

Let us pray.

God of love, our strength and our protection, hear the prayers of your Church. Grant that when we come to you in faith, our prayers may be answered. Through Christ our Lord. ℟. Amen.

or:

Lord God, you know our weakness. In your mercy grant that the example of your Saints may bring us back to love and serve you. Through Christ our Lord. ℟. Amen.

VI. The Tones for Sung Readings

The First Reading

Isaiah 63:16b–17, 64:8

676

A read-ing from the book of the proph-et I - **sa** - iah.

You, O LORD, are our **fa** - ther; our Re-deem-

er from of old is **your** name. Why, O LORD,

do you make us stray from **your** ways and hard-en

our heart, so that we do *not fear you?* . . .

Yet, O LORD, you are our Fa-ther; we are **the** clay,

and you are our pot-ter; we are all the work of

your hand. *Ver - bum Dó - mi - ni.*
The word of the Lord.

R̹ *De - o grá - ti - as.*
R̹ Thanks be to God.

411

The Second Reading
(or the First Reading, if there is only one reading before the gospel)

Hebrews 1:1a, 2b, 4, 5b

677

A read-ing from the Let-ter **to**_____ the **He** - brews.

God . . . has spo-ken to us by a Son, who . . . sat down

at the right hand of *the* **Maj** - es - **ty** on high,

hav - ing be - come as much su - per - i - or to an -

gels as the name he has in - her - i - ted is more

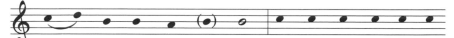

ex - cel-lent **than** theirs. For to which of the an -

gels did God ev - er say, "You are my Son; to - day

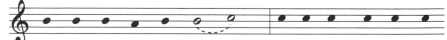

I have be - *got - ten you*"?__ . . . And a-gain, when he brings

the first-born in - to the world, he says, "Let all God's

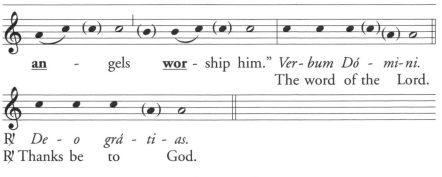

an - gels **wor** - ship him." *Ver- bum Dó - mi - ni.*
The word of the Lord.

℟ *De - o grá - ti - as.*
℟ Thanks be to God.

The Gospel

Matthew 5:13, 16

A

The Lord be with you. ℟ And al - so with you.

A read-ing from the gos- pel ac- cord-ing to Matt-hew.

℟ Glo - ry to you, [O] Lord.

At that time, Je - sus said to his dis - ci - ples: "You are the salt

of the earth; but if salt has lost its taste, how can its salt - i -

ness *be re - stored?* It is no long - er good for an -

y - thing, but is thrown out and tram - pled un - der foot.

678

413

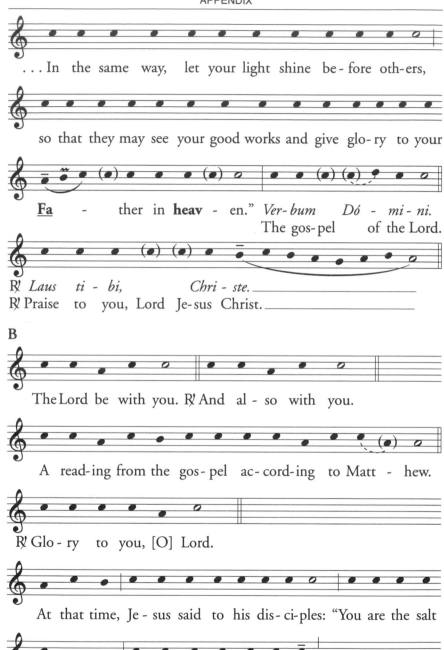

...In the same way, let your light shine be-fore oth-ers,

so that they may see your good works and give glo-ry to your

Fa - ther in **heav** - en." *Ver- bum Dó - mi - ni.*
The gos-pel of the Lord.

℟ *Laus ti - bi, Chri - ste.* _____
℟ Praise to you, Lord Je-sus Christ. _____

B

679

The Lord be with you. ℟ And al - so with you.

A read-ing from the gos- pel ac- cord-ing to Matt - hew.

℟ Glo - ry to you, [O] Lord.

At that time, Je - sus said to his dis- ci- ples: "You are the salt

of the earth; but if salt has lost its taste, how can its salt- i-

414

-ness *be re-stored?* It is no long-*er* **good** for **an**-y-thing,

but is thrown out and tram - pled **un-der** foot. . . . In the

same way, let *your* **light** shine be-fore **oth** - ers, so that they may

see your good works and give glo-ry to your **Fa** - ther

in **heav** - en." *Ver-bum Dó - mi - ni.* The gos-pel of the Lord.

℟ *Laus ti - bi, Chri - ste.*
℟ Praise to you, Lord Je-sus Christ.

C

680

The Lord be with you. ℟ And al - so with you.

A read-ing from the gos - pel ac-cord-ing to Matt-hew.

℟ Glo-ry to you, [O] Lord.

415

At that time, Je-sus said to his dis-ci-ples: "You are the salt

of the **earth;** but if salt has lost its taste, how can its salt-i-

ness *be re-stored?* It is no long-*er* **good** for **an** - y-thing,

but is thrown out and tram-pled un-der **foot.** ... In the

same way, let *your* **light** shine be-fore **oth** - ers, so that they may

see your good works and give glo-ry to your **Fa** - ther

in **heav** - en." *Ver-bum Dó - mi - ni.*
The gos-pel of the Lord.

℟ *Laus* *ti - bi,* *Chri - ste.*
℟ Praise to you, Lord Je - sus Christ.

Performance Notes

Roman eucharistic liturgy has two official song books, called "graduals": the Roman Gradual and the Simple Gradual. The eucharistic musical traditions of the other western liturgical churches have many of their roots in the Roman Gradual.

The following notes give general remarks about the seasons and feasts, followed by specific remarks for the performance of individual songs. The general remarks briefly describe the season or feast, suggest uses by applying the principles of the Simple Gradual, and summarize the connections between the Roman Gradual and the Simple Gradual so that the church musician can see the care with which the Simple Gradual tries to preserve the best of the musical and textual tradition of the Roman Rite.

Abbreviations: "Choir" refers at a minimum to another cantor joining the cantor or alternating with the cantor; "choir one" and "choir two" can refer at a minimum to other cantors alternating with each other, e.g., women and men or children and adults. "Schola" refers to the two or more psalmists needed to sing any verse of a chant between the readings meant to be sung by a group (indicated by the underlined verse number). "RG" refers to the Roman Gradual, 1974 edition. "SG" and "typical edition" refers to the authoritative, second edition (1988) of the *Graduale Simplex*. "Hanson" refers to Richard Hanson, *The Psalms in Modern Speech* (Philadelphia: Fortress, 1968).

Advent (pp. 1–11)

"Advent has a twofold character: as a season to prepare for Christmas when Christ's first coming to us is remembered; as a season when that remembrance directs the mind and heart to await Christ's second coming at the end of time. Advent is thus a period for devout and joyful expectation" (*General Norms for the Liturgical Year and Calendar,* 39). In the SG, there are two suites of chants for the Advent season, Advent Season I and Advent Season II.

The first, Advent Season I, "directs the mind and heart to await Christ's second coming at the end of time" by using the two traditional psalms of trust of the First Sunday of Advent (RG), Psalm 25, "To you, O Lord, I lift up my soul," and Psalm 85, "Lord, you were favorable." Advent Season I also includes Psalm 80, "Give ear, O Shepherd of Israel," which figures prominently on the Second Sunday of Advent (RG). This suite's entrance, alleluia, preparation, and communion songs are the same as those for the First Sunday of Advent (RG).

Advent Season II prepares us "for Christmas when Christ's first coming to us is remembered" by adding to the three psalms already mentioned the two other traditional psalms of later Advent: Psalm 19, "The heavens are telling" and Psalm 122, "I was glad." This suite's entrance and preparation songs are the same as those for the Fourth Sunday of Advent (RG).

The "not yet" and "already" of Christ's advent comes to a bright focus in the use by both suites of Psalm 85 for the communion psalm, with this important distinction which the antiphons underscore: In early Advent we sing, "The Lord *will* give us what is good"; in late Advent we sing, "The Lord *has* blessed our land."

Advent Season I, Alleluia Psalm (**5**), verse 4: Pronounce "toward" as a mono-syllable. Communion Psalm (**9**): Only verses 8–12 and verse 14 are in the typical edition and are the focus of thematic attention on this Sunday; verses 1–7 and 13 are provided for longer communion processions (if you expect a shorter communion procession, begin with verse 8). Verse 10: Pronounce "toward" as a monosyllable.

Advent Season II, Responsorial Psalm (**12**): Hanson suggests that today's psalm is best performed by two choirs alternating on the verses (e.g., choir one sings verse 1, choir two sings verse 2, etc.), in imitation of the way the crowds of pilgrims sang this song as they entered Jerusalem to the encouragement of its residents. Communion Psalm (**18**): Only verses 8–14 are in the typical edition and are the focus of thematic attention on this Sunday; verses 1–7 are provided for longer communion processions (if you expect a shorter communion procession, begin with verse 8).

Christmas (pp. 12–28)

Christmas Day, Entrance Psalm (**20**), verse 4: Pronounce "iron" as a mono-syllable. Communion Psalm (**27**): The entire text of Psalm 98 is provided for longer communion processions (if you expect a shorter communion procession, omit verses 2 through 5 because they are not included in the typical edition).

Holy Family, Entrance Psalm (**30**): This psalm is best performed by two scholas: Schola one (preferably women) sings verses 1 and 2, schola two (preferably men) sings verse 3, 4, and the first part of verse 5, with both scholas joining to sing, "Peace be upon Israel!" Responsorial Psalm (**31**): The schola joins the psalmist in singing the last half of verse 9: "O LORD of hosts, . . . " Alleluia Psalm (**33**): Schola one sings verses 6 and 7, schola two sings verses 8 and 9; both sing verse 10.

Epiphany, Alleluia Psalm (**42**): Hanson suggests that today's alleluia psalm is best performed by two alternating scholas: Schola one sings verses 1, 2, 5 and 6; schola two sings verse 3, 4, and 7. Communion Psalm (**46**): Verses 9b and 10 are added to what is given in the typical edition in order to provide more verses for a longer communion procession.

Lent (pp. 29–59)

Two features unique to the Lenten section of the SG are the Tract and the Accla-mation Antiphon. The Tract represents the direct singing of a psalm by the assembly, choir, schola, or psalmist mentioned as the "other chant" in GIRM 37 and LMI 20. The Tract may be sung every day during Lent. The Acclamation Antiphons are provided for the Sundays of Lent as a very solemn form of greeting the gospel.

Ash Wednesday, Alternate Entrance canticle (**51**): The text from Wisdom is also provided because it has been sung as the entrance song for Ash Wednesday since the sixth century. It may be sung by a solo voice, by a schola, or by the choir (if it needs to be abbreviated, delete verse 5 and verse 2).

First Sunday of Lent, Psalm 91 (used in **62** and **63**) has been traditionally the psalm of the First Sunday of Lent, so much so that in the RG all the antiphons of the day are taken from it only, especially the unequaled Tract *Qui habitat,* the longest chant in the entire RG.

Two official documents, the *Ceremonial of Bishops* (§261) and *Preparing and Celebrating the Paschal Feasts* (§23) recommend the use of the Litany of the Saints for Solemn Occasions (see **663–675**) as the song for the Entrance Rite at the parish mass from which the catechumens and the candidates are sent to the Rite of Election and the stational mass at which the Rite of Election takes place. The most solemn form of this procession is when the cantors, assembly, the presider, and other ministers can sing the litany as they process from another place into the church; when the litany concludes, the presider leads all in the opening prayer of the Mass. The Liturgy of the Word follows. It is appropriate to enter the names of the patron saints of the catechumens and candidates and also to insert particular prayers for urgent church, world, and local needs in the appropriate places in the litany.

Entrance Psalm (**62**): The pronoun "You" was added at the beginning of verse 2 to clarify for the assembly who is the subject of the verb "will say." Responsorial Psalm I (**63**): Hanson suggests that, in order to depict God's promise of help in every kind of temptation, the best way to sing this psalm is for one psalmist to sing verses 1–5 and for another psalmist—speaking as God—to sing verses 6–8. Acclamation Antiphon (**65**): In light of the gospel readings for Years A and C, it would be better to sing the acclamation antiphon (**75**) on these two Sundays.

Third Sunday of Lent, Responsorial Psalm II (**73**): Hanson suggests that this psalm is best performed by two scholas: Schola one sings verses 1 and 2 and schola two sings verses 3 and 4. Tract (**76**): Hanson suggests that this psalm is best performed by two scholas alternating on the verses (e.g., schola one sings verse 1, schola two sings verse 2, etc.) but coming together to sing, "Peace be upon Israel!" in verse 5. Communion Psalm (**80**): Only verses 1–5 and 13–14 are in the typical edition and are the focus of thematic attention on this Sunday; verses 6–12 are provided for longer communion processions (if you expect a shorter communion procession, omit verses 6–12).

Fourth Sunday of Lent, Entrance Psalm (**82**): In verse 1, 2, 6, 7, and 8, the cantor sings up to the asterisk and the choir completes the verse. Responsorial Psalm II (**84**) and Tract (**86**): Hanson suggests that Psalm 130 is best performed by two scholas: Schola one sings verses 1–4 and 6 and schola two sings verses 5 and 7; both scholas would sing verse 8 together. Communion Psalm (**90**): The typical edition provides only the five verses of Psalm 43; the first five verses of Psalm 42 (the companion of Psalm 43) are provided for longer communion processions (if you expect a shorter communion procession, omit verses 6–10).

Fifth Sunday of Lent, Responsorial Psalm I (**93**): When singing Psalm 22, a psalm of confidence in great distress, and if there is time for only five verses, always include verse 10 because it ends the psalm on a note of confidence. Responsorial Psalm II (**94**): Hanson suggests that the psalmist sing verse 1, schola one sing verse 2, and schola two sing verses 3–7. Tract (**96**): Note that there are no intonations after verse 1; Hanson suggests that the psalmist sing verse 1, schola one sing verses 2 and 3, and schola two sing verses 4–6.

Holy Week (pp. 60–71)

Passion Sunday (Palm Sunday), Gathering (**101–102**): In verse 1 the cantor sings up to the asterisk and the choir responds, "his steadfast love endures forever!"; in verse 5 the cantor sings up to the asterisk and the choir responds, "The LORD is God, and he has given us light." Procession Psalm II (**107**): in verse 9 the cantor sings up to the asterisk and the choir responds, "For the shields of the earth belong to God; he is highly exalted." Procession Psalm III (**110**): in verse 5 the cantor sings up to the asterisk and the choir responds, "his steadfast love endures forever!"

Chrism Mass, Entrance Psalm (**112**): Verse 5 is not intoned. Responsorial Psalm I (**113**): In verses 2–5 God is speaking.

The Triduum (pp. 72–94)

Evening Mass of the Lord's Supper, Entrance Psalm (**119**): Hanson suggests that the cantor sings the first party of verse 6, up to the asterisk; the choir concludes: "God, our God, has blessed us." Responsorial Psalm I (**120**) and the psalm for the Washing of the Feet (**122**) may be sung by the psalmist, the schola, or by the choir. Washing of the Feet (**122**): Verse 7 is not intoned.

Easter Vigil, Responsorial Psalm II (**133**): Hanson suggests that this psalm should be sung by an individual. Responsorial Psalm III (**134**): Verse 8 marks the beginning of the Canticle of Miriam and deserves to be sung by the women of the schola or choir. Alleluia Psalm (**142**): In verses 2–4, the psalmist or cantor sings up to the asterisk and a schola or the choir responds: "His steadfast love endures forever"; an ideal way to perform this rite is for the psalmist and schola either to sing this psalm from the ambo (if it is large enough) or near the ambo or even to form part of the gospel procession. Antiphon for the Sprinkling of Water after the Renewal of Baptismal Promises (**144**): If more verses of the Canticle of Daniel are needed, see **199** for verses 2, 3, and 4 (verse 5, a doxology, would not be appropriate); note that Psalm Tone I a 3 has two notes (g and a) over the penultimate syllable in the final cadence.

Easter (pp. 95–131)

Easter Sunday, Entrance Hymn (**148**): In order to illustrate the dialogic character of the text, a female cantor may sing verses 3, 8, and 9; another cantor, representing the angel of the resurrection, may sing verses 4, 5, and 6; and a schola or the choir may sing verses 1, 2, and 7. Responsorial Psalm (**149**): Hanson suggests that the schola sing the first part of verse 5, up to the asterisk; the psalmist concludes verse 5 and sings the first party of verse 6, up to the asterisk; the schola concludes: "The LORD is God, and he has given us light." No Alleluia is provided by the typical edition in order to encourage the use of the Alleluia Psalms on this solemnity. Note that the melody of Alleluia Psalm I (**149**) is the same for Easter, Ascension, and Pentecost in order to link the one mystery which is celebrated in these three solemnities.

Easter Season I, Entrance Psalm (**159**): Verses 3 and 6 are not intoned.

Easter Season II, Entrance Psalm (**168**): Hanson suggests that the choir conclude verse 10 by joining the cantor after the flex (†) and singing: "He will judge the world with righteousness, * and the peoples with equity."

Ascension: No Alleluia is provided by the typical edition in order to encourage the use of the Alleluia Psalms on this solemnity. Alleluia Psalm I (**178**): In verse 10, "shields" refers metonymically to rulers. Note that the melody of Alleluia Psalm I is the same for Easter, Ascension, and Pentecost in order to link the one mystery which is celebrated in these three solemnities.

Pentecost: Entrance Psalm (**185**): Hanson suggests that in verse six, the cantor sings up the asterisk and the choir concludes, "Bless the LORD, O my soul." No Alleluia is provided by the typical edition in order to encourage the use of the Alleluia Psalms on this solemnity. Note that the melody of Alleluia Psalm I (**186**) is the same for Easter, Ascension, and Pentecost in order to link the one mystery which is celebrated in these three solemnities.

Ordinary Time (pp. 132–190)

The nine suites of antiphons and psalms for Ordinary Time are thematic in character; but only the ninth has a designated use, "the Last Weeks in Ordinary Time," weeks thirty-two through thirty-four and, by extension, any time when the lectionary readings focus on the end times. Ordinary Time I was designed for the first edition of the SG as the Epiphany Season suite; it is especially effective on Sundays and weekdays in the time after the Christmas season and before Lent, and in the ninth and twenty-second weeks when the Matthean and Lukan versions of the beginnings of Jesus' ministry are proclaimed in the gospels. Similarly, Ordinary Time VIII was designed for the first edition as the suite for the old feast of the Holy Name of Jesus; it is especially effective on Sundays and days when readings underscore the ways in which God is true to God's name, "I will be with you." The themes of the other suites are: Ordinary Time II—trust and hope in God; Ordinary Time III—petitioning God for assistance; Ordinary Time IV—thanksgiving to God, especially in God's house; Ordinary Time V—God's justice; Ordinary Time VI—God's peace and loving kindness; and Ordinary Time VII—reverence and love for God.

Holy Trinity, Alleluia (**196**): Hanson suggests that this segment of Psalm 150 is best performed thus: The psalmist sings verse 1; in verse 2 schola one sings up to the asterisk and schola two completes the verse. Alleluia Psalm (**197**): Hanson suggests that Psalm 150 is best performed thus: The psalmist sings verses 1 and 2; in verses 3–5 schola one sings up to the asterisk and schola two completes each verse; finally, the psalmist sings verse 6 up to the asterisk and both scholas respond with the last "Praise the LORD!" Communion Psalm (**201**): The typical edition provides only the first six verses of the Canticle of David; five other verses are provided for longer communion processions (if you expect a shorter communion procession, omit verses 7–11); in verse 11 pronounce "toward" as a monosyllable.

Sacred Heart, Entrance Psalm (**213**): Verses 3, 4, 7 and 10 are not intoned.

Ordinary Time I, Communion Psalm (**229**): Verse 3 is not intoned.

Ordinary Time II, Communion Psalm (**238**): If the procession is lengthy, consider adding verses from Psalm 121 (120V), at **524**.

Ordinary Time III, Communion Psalm (**247**): In verse 1, pronounce "envious" as two syllables rather than "en-vi-ous."

Ordinary Time IV, Entrance Psalm (**249**): If you expect a shorter entrance procession or gathering rite, delete verses 4 and 5. Alleluia (**251**): Verse 2 is not intoned.

Ordinary Time V, Alleluia (**263**): Verse 2 is not intoned. Preparation Psalm (**266**): In verse 4, pronounce "bountifully" as three syllables, "boun-ti-f'ly."

Ordinary Time VI, Entrance Psalm (**270**): Hanson suggests that today's entrance psalm is best performed by two choirs alternating on the verses (e.g., choir one sings verse 1, choir two sings verse 2, etc.), in imitation of the way the crowds of pilgrims sang this song as they entered Jerusalem. If you expect a shorter entrance procession or gathering rite, delete verses 4 and 5. Preparation Psalm (**272**): Hanson suggests that this psalm is best performed by two choirs: Choir one (preferably men) sings verses 1 and 3, choir two (preferably women) sings verse 2 and the first part of verse 4, with both choirs joining to sing, "Peace be upon Israel!"

Ordinary Time VII, Entrance Psalm (**276**): Hanson suggests that this psalm is best performed by two choirs: Choir one sings verses 1, 2 and 3 and choir two sings verses 4 and 5. Preparation Psalm (**278**): Hanson suggests that this psalm is best performed by two choirs: Choir one (preferably women) sings verses 2 and 4, choir two (preferably men) sings verse 5 and the first part of verse 6, with both choirs joining to sing, "Peace be upon Israel!"

Last Weeks of Ordinary Time, Communion Psalm (**295**): If there are two male cantors, the first male cantor, representing St. John, should sing verses 3 through 6 and verses 11 through 12; the second male cantor, representing Christ, should sing verses 9 through 10 and the first part of verse 13 up to the asterisk; the whole choir concludes, "Amen. Come, Lord Jesus!"

Christ the King, Communion Psalm (**301**): The typical edition provides only the first six verses of the Canticle of David; five other verses are provided for longer communion processions (if you expect a shorter communion procession, omit verses 7–11); in verse 11 pronounce "toward" as a monosyllable.

Proper of the Saints (pp. 191–247)

Peter and Paul, Entrance Psalm (**338**): Verse 2 is not intoned. Alleluia Psalm (**341**): Hanson suggests that Psalm 126 is best performed by two scholas: Schola one sings verses 1–3 and 6 and schola two sings verses 4–5 and 7–8.

Transfiguration of the Lord, Preparation Psalm (**352**): Hanson suggests that Psalm 133 is best performed by two choirs: Choir one sings verses 1 and 3 and choir two sings verses 2 and 4. Communion Psalm (**354**): In verse 5 the word order of the NRSV translation, "of the king's enemies" was changed for the sake of mediant cadence.

Assumption, Entrance Psalm (**356**): Hanson suggests that the choir conclude verse 10 by joining the cantor after the flex (†) and singing: "He will judge the world with righteousness, * and the peoples with equity." Responsorial Psalm (**357**): To best convey the sense of these extracts from the Song of Songs, a schola or choir of women should sing verses 2, 4, 6, and 10, a female psalmist should sing verse 5, and a male psalmist should sing verses 1, 3, 7, 8, and 9.

Triumph of the Cross, Preparation Psalm (**372**): In verse 1 the initial word "How" was added to the NRSV text to facilitate intonation. Communion Psalm (**374**): Hanson suggests that choir one sing verses 1–3 and choir two sing verses 4–5; in verse eight, choir one sings up the asterisk and choir two sings, "Happy are all who take refuge in him."

St. Michael, St. Gabriel, and St. Raphael, Alleluia Psalm (**379**): Hanson suggests that, in verse ten, the psalmist sings up the asterisk and the schola sings, "Bless the LORD, O my soul."

All Saints, Responsorial Psalm (**386**): Hanson suggests that Psalm 150 is best performed thus: The psalmist sings verses 1 and 2; in verses 3–5 schola one sings up to the asterisk and schola two completes each verse; the psalmist sings verse 6 up to the asterisk and both scholas respond with the last "Praise the LORD!" Communion Psalm (**392**): Hanson suggests that Psalm 126 is best performed by two choirs: Choir one sings verses 1–3 and 6 and choir two sings verses 4–5 and 7–8. Verse 6 is not intoned.

Immaculate Conception, Alleluia (**396**): Ideally one male cantor sings the two verses from the Song of Songs. Alleluia Psalm (**397**): Ideally one male psalmist sings verses 1 and 5 through 10; one female psalmist sings verses 2 through 4.

Commons (pp. 248–284)

There are two general rules for making selections from the Commons: (1) choose the antiphons and psalms most in harmony with the readings and the occasion; and (2) in Easter time, favor the alleluia psalms and the antiphons which end with an "alleluia." With respect to the second rule, however, "alleluia" can be added to any antiphon by consulting the mode number printed in the space before the clef sign and matching it to the chart on p. 378.

Common of the Dedication of a Church: Hanson suggests that today's Alleluia (**405**) and Alleluia Psalm (**406**), Psalm 122, is best performed by two scholas alternating on the verses (e.g., schola one sings verse 1, schola two sings verse 2, etc.), in imitation of the way the crowds of pilgrims sang this song as they entered Jerusalem. Communion Psalm (**410**): Verses 5 and 6 and not intoned.

Common of Martyrs, Alleluia Psalm II (**431**): If you have time to sing only the minimum five verses and you wish to preserve the meaning of the psalm, sing verses 6,

7, and 8 with any combination of verse 1 (or verse 2) and verse 3 or verse 4 or verse 5 (e.g., 1, 5, 6, 7, 8). Preparation Psalm I (**433**): In verse 4 the initial word "But" was added to the NRSV text to facilitate understanding and intonation. Communion Psalm I (**437**): In each verse the cantor sings up to the asterisk and the choir completes the verse.

Common of Holy Men, Responsorial Psalm I (**446**), Alleluia (**447**), and Alleluia Psalm I (**448**): These wisdom psalms may be sung either by the psalmist, by the schola, or by the choir. Alleluia Psalm II (**449**): In verse 8 "God" is supplied in brackets to make it clearer that God is speaking. Communion Psalms I (**455**) and II (**457**): In each verse the cantor sings up to the asterisk and the choir completes the verse. Communion Psalm II (**457**): Verse 8 is not intoned.

Common of Holy Women, Communion Psalm (**471**), in verses 5 and 7 pronounce "ord'-nanc-es" as three syllables; verses 3, 6 and 7 are not intoned.

Ritual Masses, Masses for Various Needs, Votive Masses (pp. 285–299)

Wedding Mass, Entrance Psalm (**473**) and Preparation Psalm (**478**): This wisdom psalm may be sung either by the cantor or by the choir. Preparation Psalm (**478**): Verse 2 is not intoned. Communion: Hanson suggests that this psalm is best performed by two choirs: Choir one (preferably women) sings verses 1, 2, and 4, choir two (preferably men) sings verse 3, 5, and the first part of verse 6, with both choirs joining to sing, "Peace be upon Israel!"

For Vocations, if you choose to use Entrance Antiphon II (**483**), you may omit verse 4 of the psalm (**484**).

In Any Need, Entrance Psalm (**487**): Verse 2 is not intoned.

Liturgy for the Dead (pp. 300–374)

Mass for the Dead, Entrance Psalm III (**500**): The cantor sings up to the asterisk and the choir responds, "his steadfast love endures forever!" Responsorial Psalm III (**507**): Hanson suggests that Psalm 122 is best performed by two scholas alternating on the verses (e.g., schola one sings verse 1, schola two sings verse 2, etc.), in imitation of the way the crowds of pilgrims sang this song as they entered Jerusalem. Tract (**512**): Hanson suggests that this psalm is best performed by two scholas. Schola one sings verses 1 and 2 and schola two sings verses 3 and 4. Alleluia Psalm III (**511**) and Communion Psalm I (**522**): Hanson suggests that Psalm 130 is best performed by two choirs: Choir one sings verses 1–4 and 6 and choir two sings verses 5 and 7; both choirs would sing verse 8 together. Communion Psalm II (**524**): Hanson suggests that Psalm 121 is best performed by two choirs alternating on the verses (e.g., choir one sings verse 1, choir two sings verse 2, etc.), in imitation of the way the crowds of pilgrims sang this song as they entered Jerusalem. Communion Psalm III (**526**): in verse 11 sing "bountifully" as a three-syllable word, thus: "boun-ti-f'ly."

Order of Funerals, **Vigil** Procession Psalm III (**533**): In verse 7 sing "bountifully" as a three-syllable word, thus: "boun-ti-f'ly." Vigil Procession Psalm V (**535**): Verses 4 and 7 are not intoned.

Order of Funerals, **Final Commendation and Farewell:** Psalm III (**541**): Verses 3 and 4 are not intoned. Antiphon IV (**546**): This ancient funeral antiphon may sung entirely by a cantor; but, ideally, the assembly sings the sentence, "I breathe forth my spirit to you, my Creator," both times it is assigned to be sung; the sentence marked with the ℣ may be sung by the most skilled cantor or the schola.

Common Tones (pp. 375–378)

Doxologies for the Processional Chants in the Eight Modes are provided for optional use by the cantor(s), schola, choir, or even the assembly at the end of the processions at the Entrance, Preparation of the Gifts, and Communion. Among Roman Catholics it is not the custom to sing the doxology at the end of the procession during Preparation of the Gifts and the typical edition does not mention it specifically. Other communions always sing the doxology at this time. Singing the doxology would also depend on the level of solemnity.

About the entrance and communion songs the *General Instruction of the Roman Missal* tells us:

> The purpose of [the entrance] song is to open the celebration, intensify the unity of the gathered people, lead their thoughts to the mystery of the season or feast, and accompany the procession of priest and ministers (GIRM 26).

> The function [of the communion song] is to express outward the communicants' union in spirit by means of the unity of their voices, to give evidence of joy of heart, and to make the procession to receive Christ's body [and blood] more fully an act of the community (GIRM 56i).

As was said above (p. xxix), every minister knows instinctively when unity and prayerfulness are evident in the assembly; every liturgist knows that there is more to gathering and communing than the mere cessation of ritual movement. Here presider and cantor have a special need to communicate well with each other so that, when unity and prayerfulness are evident, the one may indicate to the other that is is time to sing the last verse of the psalm or to begin the doxology. During the doxology the entire liturgical assembly may bow from the waist for the words, *[Give g]lory to the Father, and to the Son, and to the Holy Spirit.*

Alleluias at the End of Antiphons for the Easter Season are provided for use at the conclusion of the antiphons sung during the processions at the Entrance, Preparation of the Gifts, and Communion when these antiphons do not have alleluias already indicated. These are used on the occasion of celebrating local solemnities and feasts which fall during the Easter season, such as the feast of the saint(s) or mystery for which the parish, school, or community is named. These are also used for ritual masses and votive masses which are celebrated during the Easter season. The antiphons themselves may thus be taken from any solemn, festal, common, ritual, or votive mass.

Appendix (pp. 379–416)

II. The Universal Prayer (Prayer of the Faithful) provides eight settings for the tones to which the deacon, reader, psalmist or cantor sings the intentions marked according to the pattern indicated. Each tone ends in a formula which invites the acclamation of the assembly. Ideally the petitions are so worded as to invite the assembly to exercise their baptismal priesthood by praying silently (or even in a subdued voice) on behalf of the universal Church, the world, those in special need, and the local community. In which case, the singer of the intentions pauses for the prayer of the assembly between the intention and the closing formula.

III. At Communion. In the performance of Psalm 34 in either Tone 1 (**645**) or Tone 2 (**646, 647**), a single cantor sings up to the asterisk, after which (an)other cantor(s), a schola, or even the entire choir joins in. The last verse ("The LORD redeems the life of his servants; none of those who take refuge in him will be condemned") is sung by the cantors, schola, or the choir. The doxology is optional. The assembly sings the response after every verse.

Tone I is a Mozarabic or Old Spanish chant in which both halves of the psalm verses are intoned to a flexible system of word accents. Performance Note: the second half of verse eight is not intoned.

IV. Miscellaneous Chants
3. Songs of Praise and Thanksgiving after Communion are provided both for great occasions and for the liturgical seasons. Roman liturgy prefers this form to a closing song: All stand and sing this song together after communion and before the post-communion prayer. Other Christian churches may prefer to sing this song at the close of the worship service.

In the *Te Deum Laudamus* (**652, 653**) and its English version (**654, 655**), the cantors may intone up to the asterisk and the assembly sing the rest to the end, or all may begin together. Or the schola or choir may begin and sing up to the first double-bar; the assembly may sing the next sentence up to the next double-bar; and thus schola/choir and assembly alternate all the way to the end, when they sing together the last petition *(Æterna fac . . . /In te, Domine . . . ; and bring us . . . /In you, Lord . . .)*. The *We Give You Praise* (**657**) may be sung similarly.

In the *To You Belongs Our Praise* (**656**), the cantors may intone up to the asterisk and the assembly sing the rest to the end, or all may begin together.

4. Antiphons of the Blessed Virgin Mary are provided for celebrations of Marian solemnities and feasts and for the Saturday celebrations in the *Collection of Masses of the Blessed Virgin Mary*, according to the liturgical seasons. If used after communion and before the post-communion prayer, all stand and sing this song together.

5. The Litany of the Saints for Solemn Occasions (Please note that this litany is not to be confused with the litany for the final rites of initiation during the Easter Vigil, nor for the dedication of a church, or ordinations, or religious professions—all of which rites have their own proper litanies.)

Worshipping communities are encouraged to restore the ancient practice of singing the Litany of the Saints for Solemn Occasions for the entrance procession at the principal Mass for the First Sunday of Lent.[1] St. Mark's Day (April 25), the three days before the Ascension, St. Isidore and St. Mary's Day (May 15) are also days when litanies to implore God's protection against calamity and God's blessing on the crops are traditionally sung. This litany can be especially effective on All Saints Day as the Entrance Song or the General Intercessions.

The Litany of the Saints for Solemn Occasions may also be used during the principal celebration of the six special periods of prayer mentioned in the *General Instruction of the Roman Missal*, §331, and elaborated upon in the *Appendix of the U.S. Bishops* (the precise dates can be found in the particular calendar which applies to each community):

> Week of Prayer for Christian Unity
> Week/Day of Prayer for General Needs of Humankind[2]
> Weekdays of Preparation for the Coming of the Holy Spirit[3]
> Week/Day of Prayer for Human Rights and Equality[4]
> Week/Day of Prayer for Harvest and Fruits of the Earth[5]
> Week/Day of Prayer for World Justice and Peace.[6]

In those sections which contain several sets of invocations marked by A and B, one or the other may be chosen as desired as indicated by the "Or" on the left. It is also possible to sing the more familiar sections of the litany in Greek and Latin, also indicated by the "or." The names of other saints may be added in the appropriate place in the litany (for example, patrons, titular saints of churches, founders, and the like). Petitions adapted to the place and the occasion may be added to the petitions for

---

[1] See the *Circular Letter Concerning the Preparation and Celebration of the Easter Feasts*, dated January 16, 1988, of the Congregation for Divine Worship, §23, and the *Ceremonial of Bishops*, §261. The Litany takes the place of the Entrance Song and all the Introductory Rites up to the Opening Prayer. In the solemn form of the procession, the people assemble in a suitable place other than the church. The presider is dressed in alb, stole, and cope. After a suitable gathering song, the presider greets the people and he (or another priest or a deacon) gives a brief introduction. The presider then says an opening prayer (several alternatives are suggested in the *Ceremonial*) and then puts incense in the censer. The deacon announces, Let us go forth in peace, and the procession moves to the church. When it reaches the church, all go to their places; the presider reverences and incenses the altar; then the presider goes to the chair and exchanges the cope for a chasuble. At the end of the Litany, the presider sings or says the Opening Prayer of the Mass.

[2] Frequently assigned to the Fourth Week of Lent or to Ash Wednesday in the U.S.

[3] Observed on the weekdays after Ascension and before Pentecost (see the *General Norms for the Liturgical Year and Calendar*, §26).

[4] Frequently assigned to the first full week of resumed Ordinary Time or to Independence Day in the U.S.

[5] Frequently assigned to the third week of the month of September or to Thanksgiving Day in the U.S.

[6] Frequently assigned to the first week of Advent or to New Year's Day in the U.S.

various needs. Such additional names and petitions need to be set in a different kind of type or enclosed in parentheses (as in the litany which follows).

If the litany is to be printed in its entirety, the surnames and cognomens (e.g., Becket, Chrysostom) should be enclosed brackets and not sung; this is the tradition when the litany is sung in Latin. However, St. John the Baptist and St. Mary Magdalene are always invoked with their cognomens; and St. John Mary Vianney is always invoked by his first and middle names. The Blessed Virgin Mary may be invoked in the litany under several titles, but restraint is advised. If the litany is not to be printed for the assembly, sing the surnames and cognomens in brackets.

6. The Tones for the Sung Readings. Singing the readings may be done when the solemnity or feast warrants it, if it enhances the intelligibility of the readings and the overall impact of the Liturgy of the Word, and if it accords with the way each worshipping community observes the various levels of solemnity (see "How to Use This Book"). Liturgists will want to see that such singing does not overload the Liturgy of the Word.

The reading to be sung before any other is generally the gospel. It is always appropriate to sing the gospel on the feast of one of the evangelists and it is often appropriate to sung the gospel on solemnities. Singing the New Testament reading is appropriate when an epistle writer's feast is celebrated; liturgy planners might also want to enhance the second reading when it carries a special theme through a season (as in Easter Season of Year C). Singing the Old Testament reading can be very useful to highlight a change of season, such as the first Sunday of Advent or the First Sunday of Lent.

The formulas are adapted for English from the *Ordo Cantus Missæ* (1973) and also provide for the Latin dialogue at the close of the reading as set out in *Jubilate Deo*. The reader preparing to sing a reading should note that each formula has an announcement tone, a text tone, an interrogative tone (indicated by italics), and a conclusion tone (in addition, the gospel tones have a formula for the beginning of the text, called the incipit). The reader should note where each tone applies in the reading to be sung, paying special attention to every full stop in the text (period, exclamation point, and question mark).

Information and Instructions
for Assembly Editions

Except for the one-time use of assembly parts and for the regular use of assembly parts in worship aids, no one may reprint the words or the music *intended to be sung by the cantor(s), the schola, and/or the choir* without the written permission of The Liturgical Press, Collegeville, MN 56321. Please contact: Reprint Permission, 1-800-858-5450 or 1-800-445-5899 (FAX).

One-time Use of Assembly Parts

The Liturgical Press is pleased to grant permission to reprint any words and music *intended to be sung by the assembly* (e.g., antiphon, acclamation, ritual chant, sequence, hymn, marian antiphon, or part of the order or ordinary of the Mass) at no charge for one-time special events such as an anniversary, baptism, confirmation, funeral, jubilee, ordination, or wedding. If not given as a souvenir, copies must be destroyed after use. Reprints must include (1) the general notice of copyright (listed below) in the credits section of the worship aid as well as the copyright notice specific to each piece (listed below), and (2) the following reference printed immediately below each piece: "From *By Flowing Waters*; see copyright information on page [insert the page number of the credit section of your worship aid]."

Regular Use of Assembly Parts

The Liturgical Press is pleased to grant permission to the owner of this volume to reproduce the following words and music *for the assembly* in worship aids which are not intended for sale:

- the words and music of the antiphons of all processional and ritual chants,
- the words and music of the hymns and marian antiphons,
- the words and music of the initial verse(s) of the responsorial and alleluia psalms and the words and music of the responses themselves,
- the words and music of the alleluias and the other gospel acclamations,
- the words and music of the assembly's responses in the Order of the Mass, and
- the words and music of the assembly's parts in the Ordinary of the Mass,

provided that the following is included: (1) the general notice of copyright (listed below) in the *credits section* of the worship aid as well as the copyright notice specific to each piece (listed below), and (2) the following reference printed *immediately below* each piece: "From *By Flowing Waters*; see copyright information on page [insert the page number of the credit section of your worship aid]."

General Notice of Copyright

The following is the general notice of copyright which must be printed in full in the credits section of the worship aid:

From *By Flowing Waters: Chant for the Liturgy*, Copyright © 1999 by Paul F. Ford. All rights reserved. Published and Administered by The Liturgical Press, Collegeville, Minnesota 56321. Used with Permission.

SPECIFIC NOTICES OF COPYRIGHT

The following are the specific notices of copyright which must also be printed in the credits section of the worship aid.

• All **antiphons in the Antiphonary** section of this book (except for **8, 108, 113, 115, 123, 126, 131, 132, 133, 135, 136, 138, 139, 151, 175, 188, 198, 207, 217, 259, 281, 288, 292, 294, 302, 306, 312, 348, 436, 444, 456, 482, 527, 529, 532, 534, 536, 538, 542, 543, 544, 547, 551,** and **553**) must carry the following specific notice of copyright:

> Textual and musical adaptation copyright © 1999 by Paul F. Ford. All rights reserved. Used with Permission. English translation of the response is from *The Simple Gradual* © 1968 ICEL. All rights reserved. Used with Permission.

• All **Responsorial Psalms** must carry the following specific notice of copyright:

> Textual and musical adaptation copyright © 1999 by Paul F. Ford. All rights reserved. Used with Permission. English translation of the response is from *The Simple Gradual* © 1968 ICEL. All rights reserved. Used with Permission. English Translation of the psalm is from *New Revised Standard Version* © 1989 Division of Christian Education of the National Council of Churches. All rights reserved. Used with Permission.

• All **Alleluia Psalms** must carry the following specific notice of copyright:

> Musical adaptation copyright © 1999 by Paul F. Ford. All rights reserved. Used with Permission. English Translation of the psalm is from *New Revised Standard Version* © 1989 Division of Christian Education of the National Council of Churches. All rights reserved. Used with Permission.

• All **Alleluias** (gospel acclamations) must carry the following specific notice of copyright:

> Musical adaptation copyright © 1999 by Paul F. Ford. All rights reserved.

• Numbers **108, 113, 175, 281, 302, 306, 529, 532, 538, 542, 543, 553, 635, 636, 637, 638, 639, 640, 641, 641, 642, 651, 656, 657, 658, 659, 660, 661,** and **662** must carry the following specific notice of copyright:

> English translation and musical adaptation copyright © 1999 by Paul F. Ford. All rights reserved.

• Numbers **8, 198, 217, 259, 312, 348, 436, 444, 456, 482, 527, 534, 536, 544, 547,** and **551** must carry the following specific notice of copyright:

> Musical adaptation copyright © 1999 by Paul F. Ford. All rights reserved. Used with Permission. English Translation from *New Revised Standard Version* © 1989 Division of Christian Education of the National Council of Churches. All rights reserved. Used with Permission.

- Number **115** must carry the following specific notice of copyright:

  English translation from *The Sacramentary* (Revised Edition) © 1998, ICEL. All rights reserved. Used with Permission.

- Number **123** must carry the following specific notice of copyright:

  English translation copyright © 1969 by Paul F. Ford and Robert C. Trupia. All rights reserved.

- Numbers **126** and **648** must carry the following specific notice of copyright:

  English translation copyright © 1969 James Quinn, S.J., administered by Selah Publications and Geoffrey Chapman, an imprint of Cassell, London, United Kingdom. All rights reserved. Used with Permission.

- Numbers **131, 132, 133, 135, 136, 138, 139, 288, 292,** and **294** must carry the following specific notice of copyright:

  Music copyright © 1999 by Paul F. Ford. All rights reserved. English Translation from *New Revised Standard Version* © 1989 Division of Christian Education of the National Council of Churches. All rights reserved. Used with Permission.

- Number **151** must carry the following specific notice of copyright:

  English translation copyright © 1983 Peter J. Scagnelli. All rights reserved. Used with Permission.

- Number **188** must carry the following specific notice of copyright:

  The text of the sequence for Pentecost is by Roger Nachtwey and Dennis Fitzpatrick, © 1964 Dennis Fitzpatrick. All rights reserved. Used with Permission.

- Number **207** must carry the following specific notice of copyright:

  The text of this sequence is taken from the Roman Missal approved by the National Conference of Bishops of the United States, ©1964 by the National Catholic Welfare Conference, Inc. All rights reserved. Used with Permission.

- All **chants for the Order of the Mass** must carry the following specific notice of copyright:

  Musical adaptation copyright © 1999 by Paul F. Ford. All rights reserved. Used with Permission. English translation of *The Roman Missal* © 1973, ICEL All rights reserved. Used with Permission.

- All **chants for the Ordinary of the Mass** (except for **595, 596, 597, 599,** and **600,** which are in the public domain), **654–655** and **663–675** must carry the following specific notice of copyright:

  Musical adaptation copyright © 1999 by Paul F. Ford. All rights reserved. Used with Permission. English translation prepared by the International Consultation on English Texts.

For your convenience, then, the following pieces have specific copyright notices which must be printed immediately following the piece (as spelled out above): **8, 108,**

431

113, 115, 123, 126, 131, 132, 133, 135, 136, 138, 139, 151, 175, 188, 198, 207, 217, 259, 281, 288, 292, 294, 302, 306, 312, 348, 436, 444, 456, 482, 527, 529, 532, 534, 536, 538, 542, 543, 544, 547, 551, 553, 635, 636, 637, 638, 639, 640, 641, 641, 642, 648, 651, 654, 655, 656, 657, 658, 659, 660, 661, 662, and **663–675**.

The publisher thus gratefully acknowledges the copyright owners who have given permission to include their material in this collection. Every effort has been made to determine copyright ownership of texts and music used in this edition and to get permission for their use. The publisher regrets any oversight that may have occurred and will gladly make proper acknowledgments in future printings.

I. Biblical Index

II. Index of Chants

1. Entrance Antiphons (63)

2. Responsorial Psalms (57)

3. Alleluia Psalms (46)

4. Alleluias (31)

5. Acclamation Antiphons (4)

6. Tracts (6)

7. Preparation Antiphons (56)

8. Communion Antiphons (62)

9. Other Ritual Chants (45)

10. Sequences, Hymns, and Marian Antiphons (25)

11. Chants for the Order of the Mass (27)

12. Chants for the Ordinary of the Mass (32)

III. Index of Modes

Unclassified Tones

IV. Alphabetical Index of Antiphons